Enslaving Connections

Enslaving Connections

Changing Cultures of Africa and Brazil during the Era of Slavery

edited by
José C. Curto and Paul E. Lovejoy

Humanity Books

an imprint of Prometheus Books

Published 2004 by Humanity Books, an imprint of Prometheus Books

Enslaving Connections: Changing Cultures of Africa and Brazil during the Era of Slavery. Copyright © 2004 by José C. Curto and Paul E. Lovejoy. All rights reserved. No part of this publication may be reproduced, stored in a retrieval system, or transmitted in any form or by any means, digital, electronic, mechanical, photocopying, recording, or otherwise or conveyed via the Internet or a Web site without prior written permission of the publisher, except in the case of brief quotations embodied in critical articles and reviews.

Inquiries should be addressed to
Humanity Books
4501 Forbes Boulevard, Suite 200,
Lanham, Maryland 20706
www.rowman.com
Distributed by NATIONAL BOOK NETWORK
800-462-6420

Library of Congress Cataloging-in-Publication Data

Enslaving connections : changing cultures of Africa and Brazil during the era of slavery / edited by José C. Curto and Paul E. Lovejoy.

    p. cm.

Includes bibliographical references and index (p.).

ISBN 978-1-59102-153-7 (cloth)

1. Slavery—Brazil—Congresses. 2. Brazil—Civilization—African influences—Congresses. 3. Africa, West—Civilization—Brazilian influences—Congresses. 4. Slave-trade—Africa, West—Congresses. 5. Slave-trade—Brazil—Congresses. 6. Blacks—Brazil—History—Congresses. 7. Brazilians—Africa, West—History—Congresses. I. Curto, José C. II. Lovejoy, Paul E.

HT1126.E57 2003

306.3'62'0981—dc21   2003014778

To Alberto da Costa e Silva,
a tireless proponent of things African in Brazil

Contents

Preface   9

Introduction. Enslaving Connections and the Changing Cultures
    of Africa and Brazil during the Era of Slavery
    José C. Curto and Paul E. Lovejoy   11

SECTION I: THE LUSO-BRAZILIAN SLAVE TRADE

1. Africa-Brazil-Africa during the Era of the Slave Trade
    Alberto da Costa e Silva   21

2. "Slaves Are a Very Risky Business . . .":
   Supply and Demand in the Early Atlantic Slave Trade
    Ivana Elbl   29

3. Slave Trading and Slave Traders in Rio de Janeiro, 1790–1830
    Manolo G. Florentino   57

4. Retention, Reinvention, and Remembering: Restoring Identities through
   Enslavement in Africa and under Slavery in Brazil
    Joseph C. Miller   81

SECTION II: WESTERN AFRICANS IN BRAZIL— THE FLUIDITY AND EVOLUTION OF IDENTITIES

5. *Muitas Línguas*: The Linguistic Impact of Africans in Colonial Brazil
   Gregory R. Guy   125

6. "Not a Thing for White Men to See":
   Central African Divination in Seventeenth-Century Brazil
   James H. Sweet   139

7. Ethnicity and Family Formation among Slaves on Tobacco Farms in the Bahian Recôncavo, 1698–1820
   Linda Wimmer   149

8. Guiné, Mina, Angola, and Benguela: African and Crioulo Nations in Central Brazil, 1780–1835
   Mary C. Karasch   163

SECTION III: THE IMPACT OF BRAZIL AND AFRO-BRAZILIANS UPON WESTERN AFRICA

9. Francisco Felix de Souza in West Africa, 1820–1849
   Robin Law   187

10. "Afro-Brazilians" of the Western Slave Coast in the Nineteenth Century
    Silke Strickrodt   213

11. The Saga of Kakonda and Kilengues:
    Relations between Benguela and Its Interior, 1791–1796
    Rosa Cruz e Silva   245

12. Brazil and the Commercialization of Kongo, 1840–1870
    Susan J. Herlin   261

Glossary   285

Bibliography   291

Contributors   311

Index   315

Preface

This volume contains a collection of essays, most of which were presented at a conference held at York University, October 12–15, 2000. The conference was organized by a committee consisting of José C. Curto, who served as chair; Professor Ivana Elbl, Department of History, Trent University; Professor Gregory Guy, at the time a member of the Department of Languages, Literatures, and Linguistics at York University and now in the Department of Linguistics at New York University; Ibrahim Hamza, a Ph.D. student in the Department of History at York University; Professor Paul E. Lovejoy, Canada Research Chair in African Diaspora History; David V. Trotman, a member of the Department of History and the Division of Humanities at York University; and Dr. Renée Soulodre-La France, at the time Coordinator of Research for the York/UNESCO Nigerian Hinterland Project and now Assistant Professor at King's College, University of Western Ontario. The conference was made possible by grants from the Social Sciences and Humanities Research Council of Canada; Serviçio da Cooperação para o Desenvolvimento, Fundação Calouste Gulbenkian, Portugal; Programa Lusitânia, Instituto Camões e Fundação para a Ciência e Tecnologia, Portugal; Departamento da Cultura, Ministério das Relações Exteriores, Brasil; and Consulado Geral de Portugal, Toronto. At York University, we wish to thank the Department of History, the York/UNESCO Nigerian Hinterland Project, the Office of the Academic Vice-President, the Office of the Dean of Arts, Founders College, and the African Studies Programme for their support. Finally, our thanks to Eugene Onutan, Webmaster of the Harriet Tubman Resource Centre on the African Diaspora, York University, for his work on the maps.

José C. Curto
Paul E. Lovejoy
Toronto, 6 April 2003

Introduction

Enslaving Connections and the Changing Cultures of Africa and Brazil during the Era of Slavery

José C. Curto and Paul E. Lovejoy

The forced shipment of millions of Africans to the Americas, where their enslavement became the basis of intense exploitation, profoundly influenced the development of the American societies that used slaves, the African societies from which the victims originated, and the European nations centrally involved in colonizing the Americas. The interactions between Africa and the Americas that developed through the Atlantic slave trade thereby have shaped the ideological parameters and social history of the modern world. Transatlantic slavery and the forces that produced its formal abolition in the nineteenth and twentieth centuries were clearly vital in helping to define the identities of both black and white people and in setting the stage for European colonialism and imperialism in a new, global world. These factors have left legacies of racism and division with important social consequences throughout the Atlantic world. Indeed, the slave trade, slavery, and abolition continue to raise fundamental issues informing discussions of community and identity for people in Europe, Africa, and the Americas. This explains why African slavery and the black diaspora remain subjects of research in the social sciences and the humanities in the attempt to explain interactions across the Atlantic to a wider, transatlantic public concerned with human rights, economic self-sufficiency, and social identity.

The focus of this volume is on the transatlantic linkages between western Africa and Brazil during the era of the slave trade. Between 1600 and 1850, approximately 4.5 million enslaved Africans went to Brazil, ten times as many as went to North America and indeed more than the total number of Africans who went to all of the Caribbean and North America combined.[1] The great majority of the enslaved Africans sent to Brazil came from Angola and other parts of West Central Africa; they included speakers of Kimbundu, Kikongo, and Umbundu, as well as other enslaved individuals from further inland who tended to learn one of these closely related Bantu languages. Often referred to as Kongo or Angola in the Americas, these people constituted perhaps the greatest concentrations of individuals of similar ethnic and linguistic background in the Americas, and nowhere was this concentration more noticeable than in Brazil.

Enslaved Africans arriving in Brazil also came from the Bight of Benin, the notorious "Slave Coast" of European accounts, and included especially speakers of the various Gbe languages (Ewe, Fon, Allada) as well as Yoruba and an identifiable Muslim population from the far interior. These people were variously known in Brazil as Gege or Mina, in the case of the Gbe group of languages, and the Brazilian term for the Yoruba was "Nagô," while Muslims from the Central Sudan of West Africa were known as Malês. Finally, Mozambique also provided a significant number of Africans for the Brazilian market, especially in the last decades of the eighteenth century and the first few decades of the nineteenth. Thus, despite the preponderance of individuals from West Central Africa, the size of the Brazilian population was on such a scale that slaves from the Bight of Benin and Mozambique also formed significant concentrations of population in Brazil.

In focusing on the connections between western Africa and Brazil, this book examines the central role of Portuguese, and later, Brazilian, merchants and seamen in linking the transatlantic worlds of Africa and Brazil, forming a "black Atlantic" in the Southern Hemisphere that to a considerable extent bypassed direct European mediation in the maintenance of a transatlantic system, unlike the "black Atlantic" of the Anglophone world of North America and the Caribbean.[2] This Brazilian-centered world was complex ethnically and racially, with many of the merchants and seamen involved in the transatlantic connections actually being *mulatto*, *pardo*, or otherwise racially mixed and referred to as *pardo* (f. *parda*) or *mulatto* (f. *mulatta*). The ambiguity in the use of these terms is clear in several chapters in this volume, which reflects the contemporary confusion over racial and status categories. In many contexts, *pardo/parda* appears to have been a generic term for anyone of apparent mixed background, involving some European ancestry and varying degrees of African ancestry. By contrast, *mulatto/mulatta* seems to refer to individuals whose fathers were Portuguese, whether or not the mother was African or *parda*.[3] In Angola, as well, *pardo/parda* appears to have been a convenience to refer to anyone of mixed ancestry, while *mulatto/mulatta* had a more restrictive meaning in terms of the European ancestry of fathers. In both Angola and Brazil, these terms were categories of classification that are not entirely racial in meaning, and to assume that they are is anachronistic, arising from a false comparison, often, with the United States. The terms in fact reveal a more complex social and economic landscape that evolved from the transatlantic linkages highlighted in this book. Until recently, however, these multiple connections between western Africa and Brazil during the era of slavery have been considered in a compartmentalized and isolated fashion.[4] Scholars of the African impact upon Brazil have rarely interacted with those studying Brazilian influence on Africa. As these chapters demonstrate, a wealth of new data makes it possible to consider this hitherto neglected theme in slave studies in more detail.

The forced migrants who went to Brazil helped to shape the demographic, linguistic, cultural, economic, political, and religious formation of both colonial and postindependence Brazil. In return, the impact of Brazil on western Africa was no less profound. Brazilians, whether of African or of European background and often mixed, also affected the demographic, economic, political, religious, and cultural composition of the coastal ports of the Bight of Benin[5] and the towns and commercial centers of Angola.[6]

There are three interrelated sections to *Enslaving Connections*.

In the first, Alberto da Costa e Silva provides an introduction to the problem of the interaction between Brazil and Africa during the slave trade era. Da Costa e Silva does an excellent job situating the volume in the gaping hole in Brazilian historiography that has hitherto concentrated on relations with Portugal rather than on the direct interaction with Africa. This chapter is particularly compelling in explaining the process of community formation and sets the tone for the fluidity of identities that the editors want to emphasize. As the history of Casa da Mina demonstrates, the interactions across the Atlantic were profound. The Casa was Dahomean in origin, an interesting connection that requires further elaboration. Ivana Elbl studies the Luso-Brazilian slave trade, focusing specifically on supply and demand in the early Portuguese slave trade. Elbl offers an important correction to the literature by carefully incorporating the "supply," that is, the African, side of the transatlantic slave trade into her analysis. In addition, the author complicates the sometimes simplistic depiction of fluctuations in certain characteristics of the trade by exploring a host of economic, political, and cultural events in all regions of the Atlantic. Most centrally, Elbl's argument that Europeans were "only an addition" to a "well-established West African slave system" resonates especially well with the known history of western Africa.

By the end of the eighteenth century, as Manolo Florentino establishes, the transatlantic trade was organized far differently. By this time, merchants in Brazil dominated the trade, as Florentino demonstrates in establishing the role of slave traders in Rio de Janeiro in the late eighteenth and early nineteenth centuries. The transatlantic interaction involved Portugal and many other parts of the world, but these connections were subordinate to a direct trade between Brazil and Angola, as well as with Mozambique and the Bight of Benin.

Likewise, Joseph Miller's chapter, "Retention, Reinvention, and Remembering: Restoring Identities through Enslavement in Africa and under Slavery in Brazil," provides a nice bridge between the preceding articles on the slave trade and the subsequent chapters on culture and identities. Miller's caveat that the chapter is "methodologically challenging" and "dangerously conjectural" is important, but he presents a persuasive case for the speculation in which he engages. In particular, Miller's attempt to break out of models that emphasize the "survival" of African cultural traits or the rapid adaptation of enslaved Africans to new cultures in the Americas is especially compelling. As Miller suggests, Sidney Mintz, Richard Price, and Philip Morgan have emphasized the importance of agency in the reaction of the enslaved population to their situation,[7] while scholars such as Gwendolyn Hall and Douglas Chambers have emphasized the continuity of the African past to these adjustments.[8] How these forces actually interacted is a subject of debate that might well benefit from further comparison with other groups who are forced to live together, whether as inmates, refugees, or immigrants. This idea fits well with the main argument of Miller's chapter and deserves more attention.

The second section of this volume examines the impact of western Africa and Africans in the making of colonial and postindependence Brazil, which is revealed especially through the fluidity and evolution of identities. Gregory Guy covers the linguistic influences of Africans in "Muitas Linguas: The Linguistic Impact of Africans in Colonial Brazil," identifying the specific ways in which Africans not only had an impact on but also became part of Brazilian society. James Sweet focuses on divination rituals from West Central Africa, establishing the "spiritual potency" of Africans, "not a thing for white men to see."

Linda Wimmer's chapter, "Ethnicity and Family Formation among Slaves on Tobacco Farms in the Bahian Reconcavo, 1698–1820," is an important contribution to the corpus of scholarship on slave families and kinship. As her study demonstrates, African ethnicities acquire more explanatory power if the exogamous nature of many African marriages is taken as a starting point. Wimmer suggests that the characteristic of marriages between Africans of different ethnicities was the principal mechanism behind the emergence of pluralized social identities.

Likewise, Mary Karasch offers a refreshingly honest depiction of the methodological problems inherent in researching "nationhood." She identifies several African and creole (born in the Americas) nations in "Guiné, Mina, Angola, and Benguela: African and Crioulo Nations in Central Brazil, 1780–1835," thereby reinforcing the central theme of this volume. As she concludes, the ways in which the preservation of Afro-Brazilian cultural traditions have developed are a powerful indication of the need for elaboration.

The final section explores the impact of Brazil and Afro-Brazilians on western Africa. Robin Law investigates the career of the notorious Brazilian slave trader Francisco Felix de Sousa between 1800 and his death in 1849. De

Sousa's activities at Ouidah ranged from political intrigue in supporting the overthrow of the Dahomey king in 1818 to slave trading. Silke Strickrodt dissects the Afro-Brazilian community on the western "Slave Coast" in the mid-nineteenth century, which included an assortment of individuals from the Americas, who moved to the port towns of the Bight of Benin and formed a recognizable community by the middle part of the nineteenth century that was variously known as Aguda, Afro-Brazilian, or simply Brazilian, even though those so identified comprised a much more heterogeneous population that included former slaves from Brazil, Cuba, Trinidad, Sierra Leone, and probably elsewhere. This population included "whites," Africans, and *mulatto* or *pardo*, in the sense used in Brazil and its Atlantic diaspora in the nineteenth century. Marriage preferences, social interaction, and business blurred racial categories; references to origins were as much to do with relative wealth and freeborn status as with racial distinctions. The essays here problematize the meanings of *mulatto* and *pardo*, as well as creole and, by implication, European and Portuguese. Similarly, Rosa da Cruz e Silva examines the reverberations of the Brazilian trade on the interior of Benguela, specifically on Kakonda and Kilengues in the 1790s. She demonstrates the crucial role of Brazilian merchants, many of whom were *mulatto* or *pardo*, in the slave trade of the interior at the end of the eighteenth century. Finally, Susan Herlin concentrates on Brazilian commercial penetration of Kongo in the mid-nineteenth century. The chapters in this section offer the often overlooked perspective that the economic and cultural processes in the Atlantic world did not flow only from Africa to the Americas.

Enslaving Connections thus represents a tightly organized volume on the transatlantic linkages between western Africa and Brazil during the era of the slave trade. *Enslaving Connections* is addressed to a wide public that is increasingly fascinated with the interactions resulting from African slavery and the black diaspora and interested in understanding how identities have been shaped over the course of the past several centuries. This volume presents cutting-edge research and analysis as a contribution to our understanding of the history of slavery and the development of African cultures in the Atlantic world. Most significantly, the collection pushes the boundaries of scholarship beyond the now overstudied "transfer" of "survivals" of African cultures under New World enslavement. Presenting the interconnectedness of Brazil and western Africa, the volume is a collective attempt to demonstrate how these connections, cultures, and identities were fluid and always subject to the influences of the major groups involved in Atlantic slavery. At once exacting specificity in reference to cultural processes and connecting those specific issues to the broader picture of the Atlantic world, the collection is both a refreshing statement on the state of scholarship in the field and a road map for future inquiries.

As a collection, this set of essays offers a model for studying the Atlantic world that promotes an integrated view of how identities were shaped, especially those deriving from cultures and societies of western Africa. The volume takes as a starting point the expanding literature on the relationship between Brazil and Africa, of which the pioneering study of Joseph Miller and the excellent collection of essays edited by Linda Heywood are prominent.[9] This volume supersedes these earlier studies in two important respects. Whereas the earlier work focuses only on Angola, this volume studies the Bight of Benin as well as West Central Africa, recognizing the importance of the Bight of Benin in the settlement of Brazil. Moreover, earlier studies viewed the interconnections between Angola and Brazil as unidirectional, from Africa to Brazil, while the essays here consider the interaction across the Atlantic as complex and fluid. This volume is structured around the concept of interconnections, following the pioneering lead of Pierre Verger in his study of the relationship between the Bight of Benin and Bahia.[10] The emphasis is on the complexity of the ethnic background of the enslaved population, rather than a view of a sort of homogenous central African identity. In fact, all of the chapters establish that there were significant differences among the enslaved population that are best addressed through biographical study, as in the case of Mahommah Gardo Baquaqua.[11]

NOTES

1. David Eltis, Stephen Behrendt, David Richardson, and Herbert Klein, *The Transatlantic Slave Trade: A Database on CD-ROM* (New York: Cambridge University Press, 1999).

2. For a discussion of the "black Atlantic," see Paul Gilroy, *The Black Atlantic: Modernity and Double Consciousness* (Cambridge: Harvard University Press, 1993). Also see Paul E. Lovejoy, "The Black Atlantic in the Development of the 'Western' World: Alternative Approaches to the 'Europeanization' of the Americas," in *Diversity in History: Transcultural Interactions from the Early Modern Mediterranean World to the Twentieth-Century Postcolonial World*, ed. Dirk Hoerder (New York: Berghahn Books, 2003), pp. 109–33.

3. With respect to Brazil, see for example Mariza de Carvalho Soares, "Descobrindo a Guiné no Brasil Colonial," *Revista do Instituto Histórico e Geográfico Brasiliero* 161: 407 (2000): 71–94; and *Devotos da cor: Identidade étnica, religiosidade e escravidão no Rio de Janiero (século XVIII)* (Rio de Janiero: Civilização Brasiliera, 2000). With respect to Angola, see José C. Curto, "'As If from a Free Womb': Baptismal Manumissions in the Conceição Parish, Luanda, 1778–1807," *Portuguese Studies Review* 10 (2002): 26–57; and José C. Curto and Raymond R. Gervais, "The Population History of Luanda during the Late Atlantic Slave Trade, 1781–1844," *African Economic History* 29 (2001): 1–59.

4. Some notable exceptions include: José H. Rodrigues,"The Influence of Africa on Brazil and of Brazil on Africa," *Journal of African History* 3 (1962): 49–67; and Pierre Verger, *Trade Relations between the Bight of Benin and Bahia from the 17th to the 19th Century* (Ibadan: University of Ibadan Press, 1976).

5. Aside from the work by Verger cited above, see: Lorenzo D. Turner, "Some Contacts of Brazilian Ex-Slaves with Nigeria, West Africa," *Journal of Negro History* 27 (1942): 55–67; Pierre Verger, "Influence du Brésil au Golfe du Bénin," *Les Afro-Americains, Memoires de l'IFAN* 27 (1953): 11–101; Pierre Verger, "Retour des 'Bresiliens' au Golfe du Benin au XIXème Siècle," *Études Dahoméennes* 8 (1966): 5–28; J. F. de Almeida Prado, "Les Relations de Bahia (Brésil) avec le Dahomey," *Revue d'Histoire des Colonies* 16 (1954): 167–226; Norberto Francisco de Souza, "Contribution a l'histoire de la famille de Souza," *Études Dahoméennes* 15 (1955): 17–21; Anthony B. Laotan, "Brazilian Influence on Lagos," *Nigeria* 69 (1964): 156–65; David A. Ross, "The Career of Domingo Martinez in the Bight of Benin 1833–64," *Journal of African History* 6 (1965): 79–90; David A. Ross, "The First Chacha of Whydah: Francisco Felix da Souza," *Odu* New Series 2 (1969) 19–28; D. E. K. Amenumey, "Geraldo da Lima: A Reappraisal," *Transactions of the Historical Society of Ghana* 9 (1968): 65–78; Richard D. Ralston, "The Return of Brazilian Freedmen to West Africa in the 18th and 19th Centuries," *Canadian Journal of African Studies* 3 (1969): 577–92; Júlio Santanna Braga, "Notas Sobre o 'Quartier Bresil' no Daomé," *Afro-Ásia* 6–7 (1968): 56–62; Jerry Michael Turner, "Les Brésiliens: The Impact of Former Brazilian Slaves upon Dahomey" (Ph.D. diss., Boston University, 1974); Jerry Michael Turner, "Cultura afro-brasileira na África Ocidental,"*Estudos Afro-Asiáticos* 1 (1978): 19–25; Jerry Michael Turner, "Africans, Afro-Brazilians, and Europeans: 19th Century Politics on the Benin Gulf," *África* (Universidade de São Paulo) 4 (1981): 3–31; Jerry Michael Turner, "Identidade étnica na África Ocidental: o caso especial dos afro-brasileiros no Benin, na Nigéria, no Togo e em Ghana nos séculos XIX e XX," *Estudos Afro-Asiáticos* 28 (1995) 85–99; Manuela Carneiro da Cunha, "Religião, Comércio e Etnicidade: Uma Interpretação Preliminar do Catolicismo Brasileiro em Lagos, no Século XIX," *Religião e Sociedade* 1 (1977): 51–60; Manuela Carneiro da Cunha, *Negros, Estrangeiros: Os Escravos Libertos e Sua Volta à África* (São Paulo: Brasilience, 1985); Marianno Carneiro da Cunha, *Da Senzala ao Sobrado: A Arquitectura Brasileira na África Ocidental* (São Paulo: Nobel, 1985); S. Y. Boadi-Siaw, "Brazilian Returnees of West Africa," in *Global Dimensions of the African Diaspora*, 2d ed., ed. Joseph E. Harris (Washington, D.C.: Howard University Press, 1993), pp. 421–39; Lisa A. Lindsay, "'To Return to the Bosom of their Fatherland': Brazilian Immigrants in Nineteenth-Century Lagos," *Slavery and Abolition* 15 (1994): 22–50; Bellarmin C. Codo, "Les Afro-brésiliens de retour," in *La Chaine et le lien: une vision de la traite negrière*, ed. Doudou Diene (Paris: UNESCO, 1998), pp. 95–105; Milton Guran, *Agudás: Os 'brasileiros' do Benim* (Rio de Janeiro: Editora Gama Filho, 1999); Robin Law and Kristin Mann, "West Africa in the Atlantic Community: The Case of the Slave Coast," *William and Mary Quarterly* 46 (1999): 306–34; J. Lorand Matory, "The English Professors of Brazil: On the Diasporic Roots of the Yorùbá Nation," *Comparative Studies in Society and History* 41 (1999): 72–113; Robin Law, "The Evolution of the Brazilian Community in Ouidah," *Slavery and Abolition* 22 (2001); the relevant essays in Kristin Mann and Edna G. Bay, eds., *Rethinking the African Diaspora: The Making of a Black Atlantic World in the Bight of Benin and Brazil*. (London: Frank Cass, 2001). See also the pertinent chapters in José C. Curto and Renée Soulodre–La France, eds., *Africa and the Americas: Interconnections during the Slave Trade* (New Brunswick, N.J.: Africa World Press, forthcoming).

6. Corcino M. dos Santos, "Relações de Angola com o Rio de Janeiro (1736–1808)," *Estudos Históricos* 12 (1973): 7–68; Manuel dos Anjos da Silva Rebelo, *Relações entre Angola e Brasil (1808–1830)* (Lisbon: Agência Geral do Ultramar, 1970); Joseph C. Miller, *Way of Death. Merchant Capitalism and the Angolan Slave Trade, 1730–1830* (Madison: University of Wisconsin Press, 1988); José C. Curto, *Alcoól e Escravos: O comércio luso-brasileiro do alcoól em Mpinda, Luanda e Benguela durante o tráfico atlântico de escravos (c. 1480–1830) e o seu impacto nas sociedades da África Central Ocidental* (Lisbon: Editora Vulgata, Colecção "Tempos e Espaços Africanos," 2002); José C. Curto, "Luso-Brazilian Alcohol and the Legal Slave Trade at Benguela and its Hinterland, c. 1617–1830," in *Négoce Blanc en Afrique Noire: L'évolution du commerce à longue distance en Afrique noire du 18e au 20e siècles*, ed. Hubert Bonin and Michel Cahen (Paris: Publications de la Société Française d'histoire d'outre-mer, 2001), pp. 351–69; "The Anatomy of a Demographic Explosion: Luanda, 1844–1850," *International Journal of African Historical Studies* 32 (1999): 381–405; "Vinho verso Cachaça: A Luta Luso-Brasileira pelo Comércio do Álcoól e de Escravos em Luanda, 1648-1703," in *Angola e Brasil nas Rotas do Atlântico Sul*, ed. Selma Pantoja and José F. S. Saraiva (Rio de Janeiro: Bertrand Brasil, 1999), pp. 69–97; José C. Curto and Raymond R. Gervais, "The Population History of Luanda during the Late Atlantic Slave Trade, 1781–1844," *African Economic History* 29 (2001): 1–59; Linda M. Heywood, "The Angolan-Afro-Brazilian Cultural Connections," *Slavery and Abolition* 20 (1999): 9–23; and the pertinent essays in Linda M. Heywood, ed., *Central Africans and Cultural Transformations in the American Diaspora* (New York: Cambridge University Press, 2002).

7. Sidney Mintz and Richard Price, *The Birth of African-American Culture: An Anthropological Perspective* (Boston: Beacon Press, 1992); and Philip D. Morgan, *Slave Counterpoint: Black Culture in the Eighteenth-Century Chesapeake and Lowcountry* (Chapel Hill: University of North Carolina Press, 1997).

8. See, for example, Gwendolyn Midlo Hall, "African Ethnicities and the Meanings of Mina," in *Trans-Atlantic Dimensions of Ethnicity*, ed. Paul E. Lovejoy and David V. Trotman (London: Continuum, 2003); and Douglas Chambers, "'My Own Nation': Igbo Exiles in the Diaspora," *Slavery and Abolition* 18, no. 1 (1997): 72–97.

9. Miller, *Way of Death*; and Heywood, *Central Africans and Cultural Transformations*.

10. Verger, *Trade Relations between the Bight of Benin and Bahia*.

11. See Robin Law and Paul E. Lovejoy, eds., *The Biography of Mahommah Gardo Baquaqua: His Passage from Slavery to Freedom in Africa and America* (Princeton: Markus Wiener, 2001).

Section I

The Luso-Brazilian Slave Trade

1
Africa-Brazil-Africa during the Era of the Slave Trade

Alberto da Costa e Silva

In 1641, when the Dutch fleet left Recife to conquer Luanda, the capital of the Portuguese colony of Angola and expanding slave exporting town, it took on board three companies of Brazilian soldiers:[1] two hundred Amerindians,[2] and probably a small number of *mamelucos*, or free mestizos of European and Amerindian ancestry. In the three expeditions that left Brazil between 1645 and 1648 to regain Angola for the Portuguese, there were also Amerindian troops; also present in at least one of these expeditions was a group of black soldiers from the troops of the black military chief Henrique Dias,[3] probably with a predominance of creoles (blacks born in the Americas). One of these creoles, Sergeant Major Paulo Pereira, became famous during the fight against the Dutch in Angola.[4] Although we know very little, or almost nothing, about his companions, one may nevertheless conclude that many of them died in the struggle, some returned to Brazil, and others remained forever in Africa. The same happened to the Amerindians. They were very good auxiliary troops, as the Portuguese governor of Angola, Francisco de Sotomaior, acknowledged. He applauded their ability to build stockades and horse stalls, and their readiness in "helping as they could the soldiers and the people from the sea."[5] It is possible that even before these expeditions a small number of *mamelucos* from Brazil already lived in Luanda and in some of the Portuguese factories along the Kwanza River, for we know that at the end of the sixteenth century there were about five hundred of them in the neighboring kingdom of Kongo.[6]

In Brazil at about the same time, cities such as Salvador, Recife, and Rio de Janeiro had among their inhabitants a small number of free Africans. By then, they had most likely already distinguished themselves from the slaves because they did not walk barefoot. Some of them were Ndongo (Angola) dignitaries, political troublemakers who had been sent to Brazil by the Portuguese, or expelled by the Dutch together with their Portuguese allies. When the Portuguese organized their military expeditions to regain Angola, they considered the possibiliy of including in their troops some of these Ndongo dignitaries. On at least one occasion, they effectively did so.

Some of the Ndongo aristocrats that the Portuguese sent to Brazil as political exiles were enslaved as soon as they landed in Rio de Janeiro or Salvador. Thereafter, they were taken to plantations owned in Brazil by high colonial officials in Luanda, something which the latter's enemies did not tire of making public. Many of these Africans, however, like those that the Portuguese Crown wished to send back as fighters to Angola, never lost their freedom. A few obtained land in Brazil to cultivate and thereby sustain themselves,[7] however, the majority were placed in the army. Of these, some were eventually taken back to Africa. A number of the twenty-six chiefs sent to Brazil in 1622 following the defeat of the *Mani Kasanze* at the hands of the Portuguese, for example, returned to Angola before 1640. One of these, holding the title of *Panji* [king] *a Ndona*, recreated the kingdom of Kasanze and its *nsaka*, or capital, between the lower Dande and Bengo.[8]

Sometimes these African dignitaries traveled in government ships. In other cases, whether they were political exiles, ambassadors, or businessmen, they traveled as passengers aboard slave ships. This was, after all, the usual way for European traders and their mulatto agents to travel to and from Africa. On the way to Africa there would be few passengers aboard. But on the journey from Africa to Brazil, free passengers, some indifferent to the human suffering around them and others heartbroken by it, had to confine themselves to a small corner of a ship ruled by violence and crowded with scared, tired, hungry, and thirsty slaves.

As soon as a slave arrived in Brazil, he or she might meet earlier arrivals from the same kingdom, the same village, or perhaps a neighboring small town. The slave might even meet members of his or her own extended family or lineage, and transmit news about what was happening on the other side of the Atlantic. Similarly, when the predominately ex-slave crews of Brazilian ships landed in Africa, these sailors carried news and even messages from the people who lived as slaves in Brazil, especially those for whom slavery was synonymous with political exile and who still had family and supporters in their country of origin. The slave ship, consequently, functioned both as a newspaper and as a courier. This is the only way to explain how King Kpengla of Dahomey (1774–1789) could have known so precisely the whereabouts of his childhood friend Prince Fruku, sold as a slave by Tegbesu, the previous ruler of Dahomey. As soon as he became king of Dahomey, Kpengla had no difficulty in bringing Fruku back from Bahia to Abomey.[9]

Topics such as these have not yet received the attention that they deserve in the historiography of Brazil. When compared to broader issues, such as the Atlantic slave trade, the buying in Africa of great numbers of people who would become the ancestors of Brazilians today, or the functioning of the Brazilian slave system (the longest and deepest process in our history), they seem to have little importance. Yet these same topics shed a great deal of light on how intense and complex were the contacts between the Atlantic shores. A fairly extensive literature already exists, although it has not been adequately studied. For example, in the case of relations between Bahia and the Bight of Benin and the former slaves who returned from Brazil to western Africa, we have various books, dissertations, and articles.[10] Included are, of course, the magnificent works of Pierre Verger,[11] as well as others like Gilberto Freyre's on the Afro-Christian funerary monuments (probably influenced from Brazil) in the cemetery built in Moçamedes (Namibe) by nineteenth-century refugees from Pernambuco,[12] Luiz da Câmara Cascudo's *Made in Africa*,[13] or José Honório Rodrigues' *Brasil e África: outro horizonte*.[14] Yet, until recently, historians (not to mention anthropologists and sociologists) of Brazil have been studying the slave only from the moment that he or she landed in Brazil, without making any attempt to link capture and enslavement to events within Africa, or to see the slave as having a history of his or her own.

Nina Rodrigues was the first great exception to this rule, with *Os africanos no Brasil*,[15] which he completed in 1905. His example was not followed by historians who wrote about slavery. It was, however, followed by one of his disciples, the anthropologist Arthur Ramos, in several books written about Brazilian blacks or black Brazilians (in his works the word "Negro" is used more as an adjective than as a noun) and in the eight long chapters on the descendants of Africans in his two-volume *Introdução à Antropologia Brasileira*.[16] By examining the bibliography of this work, extremely up to date for its time, we can see that Ramos was devoting a great amount of his time to the study of Africa and African peoples. Unfortunately, his endeavors were interrupted in 1949 by his untimely death at the age of forty-six. Although he was Yorubacentric, as were so many scholars who studied in Bahia, Ramos made a great effort to identify the different origins of the slaves, to portray the environment in which they lived in Africa, to tell the histories of their nations, to describe their social and political structures, their religion and culture, and to register the particular contributions of at least each large group of African peoples (as they were classified at that time) to the Brazilian way of life.

Finally, the situation is changing. A growing contingent of young historians and anthropologists are now following the path set by Nina Rodrigues.[17] We are beginning to correct, although very slowly, an imperfect vision that impairs the rich Brazilian historiography on slavery. In this historiography, the African side of the story is given scant attention, if mentioned at all: the slaves treated as if they had been born on a slave ship.

As for the Brazilian slave ship, I have never laid my eyes upon a systematic study dedicated to it, at least any study similar to Leif Svalesen's book on one of its Scandinavian counterparts.[18] I am thinking of a study in which one gathers, collects, and analyzes the scattered information we have on the evolution, for more than three hundred years, of the types and sizes of the ships used for the Brazilian slave trade; how and where they were built; the composition of their crews; the handling of their cargo; and the economic returns of their trips. We know very little about some of their routes, for instance, those that linked Santiago de Cabo Verde, Cacheu, and other Upper Guinea ports to Parnaíba and the harbors of Maranhão. We have just began to study the slave trade from Brazil to Buenos Aires; and we still have no comprehensive study on the slave trade from Brazil to the Caribbean islands and to the United States, and vice versa since the direction of the trade alternated from time to time according to the demand in each place.

How can we understand the associations organized by the slaves in Brazil to buy their own freedom without studying the *esusu*, or traditional lending association, of the Yorubas? How can we analyze and interpret the little we know about Palmares without trying to identify its African roots? Was this *kilombo*, or maroon settlement, a reproduction of Mbundu (Angola) political structures, or was it an amalgamation of different groups, with different political traditions, under a strong Mbundu leadership? What was the Amerindians' role in it? Why have the excavations at Palmares not brought out a single African piece of pottery, but a lot of pottery in Amerindian Tupinambá style instead?[19] Could it be that Amerindians, especially women, had a larger influence upon Palmares than we have been led to believe? Or could the Tupinambá pottery be explained by the absence of African ceramists in Palmares? Good potters might seldom be sold to slave traders because African chiefs probably preferred to keep them for themselves. The people of Palmares may have learned and adopted the local styles because they did not have an African potter to teach them. It has already been suggested that the world of Palmares was not confined to the interior area of the *Serra da Barriga*. Archaeological findings show that this *kilombo* had connections with the Brazilian coast, and through it, with Europe and Africa.[20] What kind of connections, though probably not direct and certainly sporadic, did the state we know as Palmares, which was called by its people Angola Janga, the "Little Angola," have with the Mbundu nation and the *ngola a kiluanje*, the honorific title of Mbundu monarchs? Why, as Manoel Querino informed us,[21] did the Malinke not join the Malês' revolution in 1835 in Bahia? Before making a detailed investigation in the Sokoto archives in Nigeria, how are we to choose between the different interpretations of the Malês' rebellion presented by Nina Rodrigues and João José Reis?

I could go on and on asking questions to reiterate what for me seems obvious. The history of Brazil, including almost four hundred years of slavery, cannot be written without considering what was happening on the other side of the Atlantic, in each of the regions from which Brazil was receiving slaves to develop and settle its vast territory. In 1843 Bernardo Pereira de Vasconcelos, one of the great politicians of the Brazilian Empire, stated in Parliament that "Africa civilized America." But "Africa" is a vague word. Like the word "Africans," it conceals cultural and political diversity. And we need to know precisely from what regions of an immense, varied, and differentiated continent were brought the peoples who helped to create Brazil. We need to know from which specific areas and nations, according to the period, came those who changed the face of a great part of our continent. Finally, we need to know why they and not other groups were enslaved and brought to the different regions of Brazil.

Although Italian and German immigrants are both Europeans, no one confuses them. We know that an Italian immigrant who arrived in Brazil in the middle of the nineteenth century behaved differently and played a different role in society than one who arrived at the beginning of the twentieth century. Besides, the immigrant's situation would be different according to where he or she was going to live: whether in a colony of Italian immigrants or in areas where people from varied origins coexisted. Even here, however, we are able to differentiate Italian cultural influences from others. It is our Italian heritage, not a vague European heritage, that we are studying. In the same way, we should also be able to differentiate what we owe to the Ijesha from what we owe to the Kongo or to the Hausa.

We are well aware that the slave who arrived in Brazil alone among strangers had a different kind of fear, insecurity, and perception of destiny from one who came in a ship surrounded by people he or she knew well. The slave experience was also different according to whether one was to work on a plantation or in an urban setting where a group of slaves of the same origin or language could be found. Therefore, it may not have been too difficult for some groups of slaves of the same nation to remake and reorganize their life in Brazil according to some of their traditional values. This was the case of a small group of enslaved Fon from Dahomey who, in the second quarter of the nineteenth century, arrived on the same ship at São Luís do Maranhão, a town where there was already a considerable number of Fon. Since they had brought with them, according to traditional accounts, the sacred objects necessary to continue their religious cults in the land of exile, they were able to found, as soon as some of them became free, the Querebetam of Zomadonu, or Casa da Mina.[22] And so, they continued the royal cult of Abomey in Brazil.

As for a Pepel or Bijago slave woman from the Upper Guinea coast, who was attracted to this Dahomean sanctuary in São Luís do Maranhão because her owner lived in the neighborhood, she went through a double transformation. She not only had to surrender, like the Fon did, to the rules of behavior the white master imposed upon her. She also had to give up a substantial and even essential part of her inner truth as she converted to the Fon religion. In the process, it is true, she also acquired new spiritual, family, and affective values, those of the Fon, and thereby adopted the traditions of the Fon as her own. She became culturally Fon, or "Mina": yet not a Mina from the coast of Togo, but a Mina from Maranhão!

The history of the Casa da Mina, however, did not start in Brazil. Rather, it began in the old kingdom of Dahomey. It is also on that side of the Atlantic that many other histories began, the histories with which we write the history of the Brazilian people. This history did not start in a mythic Africa, but in each of the nations that existed and continue to exist in that continent. Only by knowing the history of these nations during the nearly four centuries of the transatlantic slave trade can we begin to answer the following fundamental questions. First, why and how did men and women from some nations and not others come in such great numbers to different regions of Brazil? Second, why and how did they create new ethnic identities in Maranhão, Pernambuco, Bahia, Minas Gerais, or Rio de Janeiro such as Angola, Benguela, Cabinda, Mina, Jeje, Nagô, and Mozambique? And finally, why and how did they become intermingled in such a way that today it is almost impossible to disentangle them?

NOTES

1. Ralph Delgado, *História de Angola* (Lisbon: Banco de Angola, n.d.), vol. 2, p. 217.
2. António da Silva Rego, *A dupla restauração de Angola, 1641–1648* (Lisbon: Agência Geral das Colônias, 1948), p. 31.
3. "Consulta do Conselho Ultramarino," 28 April 1645, and "Carta do Governador do Brasil," 16 February 1645, *Arquivos de Angola*, 2d series, vol. 5 (1948): 19–21 and 22–23, respectively; note by José Matias Delgado in Antonio de Oliveira Cadornega, *História geral das guerras angolanas*, ed. José Matias Delgado (Lisbon: Agência Geral das Colônias, 1940), vol. 1, p. 324.
4. "Relação da vaigem g. fizerão o capitão mór Antonio Teixeira de Mendonça e o sargento mór Domingos Lopes de Siqueira" and "Patente do Sargento-mor Reformado Paulo Pereira," *Arquivos de Angola*, 2d series, vol. 1 (1943–44): 136–37 and 193–94, respectively.
5. Letter by Francisco de Soutomaior to King D. João VI, quoted by Delgado, *História de Angola*, vol. 2, p. 308.
6. According to the report by the judge of the Court of Appeals Domingo de Abreu e Brito, quoted by Delgado, *História de Angola*, vol 1, p. 358.
7. According to the report of Manoel Severim de Faria, concerning the period of March 1621 to February 1622, transcribed in Cadornega, *Historia Geral das Guerras Angolanas*, vol. 1, p. 103.
8. Joseph C. Miller, "A Note on Kasanze and the Portuguese," *Canadian Journal of African Studies* 6, no. 1 (1972): 53.
9. Archibald Dalzel, *The History of Dahomey, an Inland Kingdom of Africa* (1793; reprint, London: Frank Cass, 1967), p. 223; A. Akinjogbin, *Dahomey and Its Neighbors, 1784–1863* (Cambridge: Cambridge University Press, 1967), pp. 116, 171, 178.
10. One of the earliest of which is the pioneering essay, written in 1949, by J. F. de Almeida Prado, "Bahia e as suas relações com o Daomé," in *O Brasil e o colonialismo europeu* (São Paulo: Companhia Editora Nacional [Brasiliana], 1956).

11. *Flux et reflux de la traite des nègres entre le golf du Bénin et Bahia de Todos os Santos, du dix-septième au dix-neuvième siècle* (Paris: Mouton, 1968); English rev. and enl. ed., *Trade Relations between the Bight of Benin and Bahia, 17th–19th Century*, trans. Evelyn Crawford (Ibadan: Ibadan University Press, 1976); Portuguese edition, *Fluxo e Refluxo do Tráfico de Escravos entre o Golfo de Benin e a Bahia de Todos os Santos, dos Séculos XVII ao XIX*, trans. Tasso Gadzanis (São Paulo: Corrupio, 1987).

12. *Em torno de alguns túmulos afro-cristãos de uma área contagiada pela cultura brasileira* (Salvador: Universidade da Bahia/Livraria Progresso Editora, n.d. [1959]).

13. Luiz da Camara Cascudo, *Made in Africa: Pesquisas e Notas* (Rio de Janeiro: Civilização Brasileira, 1965).

14. José Honório Rodrigues, *Brasil e África: Outro horizonte* (Rio de Janeiro: Civilização Brasileira, 1961).

15. Nina Rodrigues, *Os Africanos do Brasil* (São Paulo: Companhia Editora Nacional [Brasiliana], 1936). The book was published only after his death.

16. Arthur Ramos, *Introdução à Antropologia Brasileira* (Rio de Janeiro: Casa do Estudante do Brasil, vol. 1, 1943; vol 2, 1947).

17. Some examples: João José Reis, *Rebelião Escrava no Brasil* (São Paulo: Brasiliense, 1986), in English, *Slave Rebellion in Brazil*, trans. Arthur Brakel (Baltimore: John Hopkins University Press, 1993); Manolo Florentino, *Em costas negras: Uma história do tráfico de escravos entre a África e o Rio de Janeiro Cséculos XVIII e XIX* (Rio de Janeiro: Arquivo Nacional, 1995); Selma Pantoja and José Flávio Sombra Saraiva, eds., *Angola e Brasil nas rotas do Atlântico Sul* (Rio de Janeiro: Bertrand do Brasil, 1998); Robert Slenes, *Na senzala, uma flor* (Rio de Janeiro: Nova Fronteira, 1999); Luis Felipe de Alencastro, *Trato dos viventes: Formação do Brasil no Atlântico Sul* (São Paulo: Companhia das Letras, 2000); and Roquinaldo A. Ferreira, "Dos Sertões ao Atlântico: Trafico ilegal de escravos e comérccolícito em Angola, 1830–1860" (Dissertação de Mestrado, Universidade Federal do Rio de Janeiro, 1997).

18. Leif Svalensen, *The Slave Ship Fredensborg* (Indianapolis: Indiana University Press, 2000).

19. Pedro Paulo A. Funari, "Archeology Theory in Brazil: Ethnicity and Politics at Stake," *Historical Archaeology in Latin América* 12 (1996): 1–13, and "Novas perspectivas abertas pela Arqueologia da Serra da Barriga," conference on May 25, 1996, in a series of studies on Afro-Brazilian culture coordinated by Lilia M. Schwarcz; and "A Arqueologia de Palmares-Sua contribuição para o conhecimento da história da cultura afro-americana," in *Liberdade por um fio*, ed. Juão José Reis and Flávio dos Santos Gomes (São Paulo: Companhia das Letras, 1996), pp. 34–35.

20. Funari, "Novas perspectivas," p. 6.

21. Manoel Querino, *Costumes Africanos no Brasil* (Recife: Massangana, 1988), pp. 66, 72–73.

22. Nunes Pereira, *A Casa das Minas* (1947; reprint, Petropolis: Vozes, 1979), pp. 24, 38; Pierre Verger, "Le culte des vodoun d'Abomey aurait-il été apporté à Saint-Louis de Maranhon par la mère du Roi Ghézo?" in *Les Afro-Américains* (Dakar: Mémoires de l'Institut Français d'Afrique Noire, 1953); Sergio Ferretti, *Querebetam de Zomadanu* (Natal, 1983, mimeographed), pp. 43, 171; *Querebetã de Zomadônu: etnografia da Casa das Minas do Maranhão* (São Luís: Editora da Universidade Federal do Maranhão, 1996).

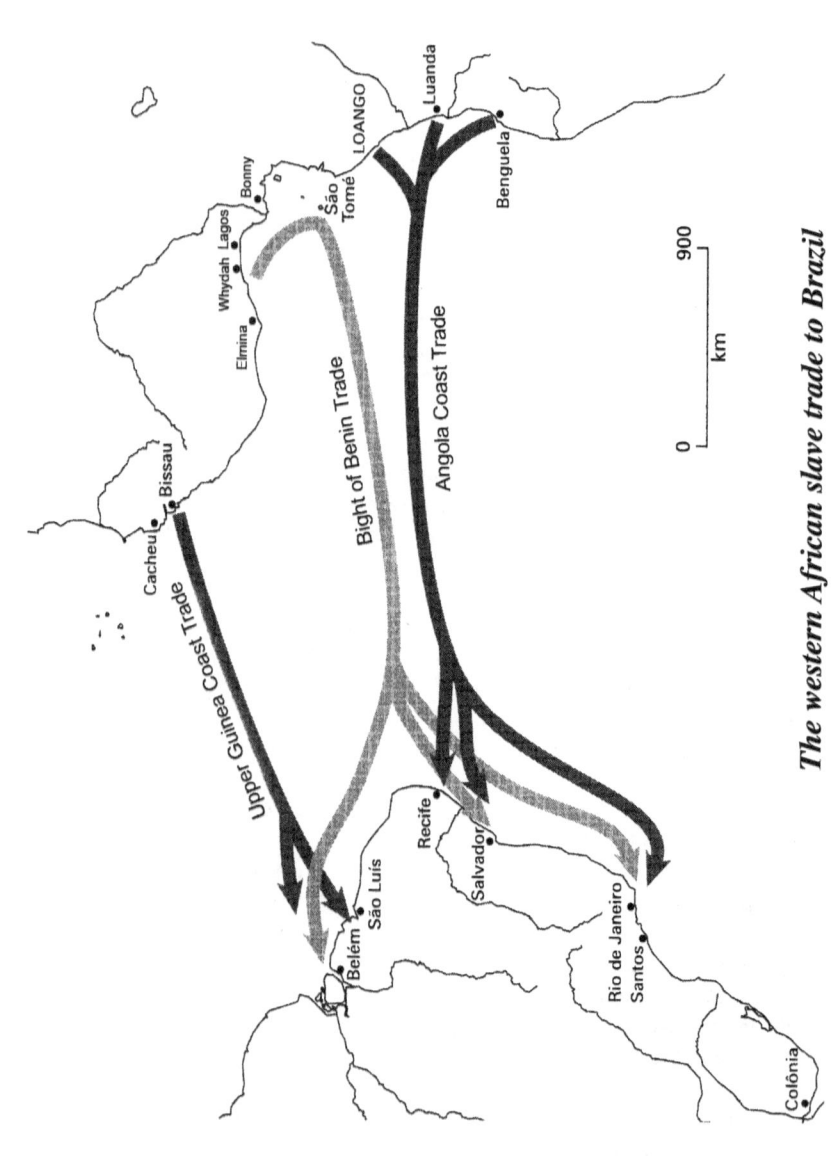

The western African slave trade to Brazil

2
"Slaves Are a Very Risky Business..."
Supply and Demand in the Early Atlantic Slave Trade

Ivana Elbl

Although slaves were not necessarily the most sought-after commodity in the early Atlantic slave trade, they were the most commonly offered one. As I have argued in an earlier article, the volume of the early Atlantic slave trade was, from the very beginning in the mid-1400s, substantially higher than previously estimated and was subject to rapid growth.[1] By the end of the fifteenth century, the annual volume of the trade tripled, from under 900 slaves in 1450–1465 to 2,200 slaves in 1480–1499. In the course of the first two decades of the sixteenth century it nearly doubled again, from 2,650 slaves in 1500–1509 to 3,500 slave in 1510–1515 and 4,500 slaves in 1516–1521. The lower volume in the opening period was due not to lack of supply but to the fact that it took the Portuguese several decades to explore the West African coast and organize their own trade infrastructures.[2]

This finding poses an interesting challenge to the long-debated issue of the impact of the Atlantic market on slavery and slave trading in West Africa. Earlier scholars have argued that the presumably very slow buildup of slave supply to the transoceanic trade suggests that Europeans were responsible for a transformation of slavery from a marginal institution into a key social institution in many areas, particularly in Upper Guinea, the main supplier of slaves in the opening period of the Atlantic slave trade. This argument relied largely on two claims: (a) that the slave trade volume in the opening period was quite low, and in some areas nonexistent; and (b) that the fifteenth-century European sources were silent or ambiguous on the subject of domestic slavery and internal slave trade in coastal West African societies. Since then, John Thornton has demonstrated persuasively that the early Atlantic slave trade merely tapped into preexisting patterns of reliance on slaves as a source of wealth and power, and that selling slaves to European traders simply meant another possible utilization of slaves as a resource, as opposed to domestic exploitation.[3]

The rapid establishment of commercial contacts between Europeans and Africans in newly explored regions, and the equally rapid growth in the volume of the early slave trade, both lend support to Thornton's conclusions. A ready supply of slaves was the key advantage from which the early Atlantic slave trade benefitted. Slaves were the most common commodity offered for sale to the Europeans. The richest West African source of slaves was Upper Guinea: after the settlement of the Cape Verde Islands in the mid-1460s it accounted for at least 60 percent of the slaves bought by the Portuguese, except in the late 1510s and early 1520s. The Mauritanian Coast was the main supplier in the opening period, 1450–1465. Following the period 1480–1499, the share of the Gulf of Guinea lingered around 20 percent of the total. After 1515, West Central Africa assumed a leading role, delivering approximately 50 percent of the slaves. Sierra Leone and the Grain Coast sold a limited number of slaves, but their main assets were, respectively, gold and malagueta (spice: *Aframomum melegueta* and *Aframomum granum paradisi*). The Ivory Coast did not trade during the period 1440–1525, and the Gold Coast was a net importer of slaves. In most regions of West Africa, however, supply was unflagging: slaves formed between 60 and 95 percent of all Atlantic exports.[4]

However, despite the availability of slaves, the Atlantic trade faced a number of constraints on both the supply and the demand sides. As Thornton pointed out, the Europeans had to compete with a domestic and interregional demand for slaves, which could effectively limit and in some cases choke off the supply.[5] The progressive increase of slave prices in most West African regions within a few decades of the opening of the trade and the relative decline of trade volumes in some slave supplying regions most probably attest to a competing domestic demand for slaves, especially in ongoing power struggles, as well as to the availability of other market outlets. The early Atlantic slave trade was far from a buyer's market. Except perhaps in Kongo where the Portuguese leverage may have been higher than in West Africa,[6] the Africans were in control. In order to obtain slaves on a sustained basis, the Europeans had to offer attractive merchandise and good prices, in other words, provide incentives and demonstrate effective demand.

In the opening period of the Atlantic slave trade (1440–1525), however, the effectiveness of European demand was subject to several significant constraints. These included the restrictive and often erratic trade policies of the Portuguese Crown, poor management of the royal enterprise, daunting logistics, and a high level of risk. Where such constraints were reduced, the establishment and consolidation of the Portuguese trading infrastructure was almost always followed by rapid increases in the volume of trade. The best example is the trade with Upper Guinea, which expanded dramatically after the settlement of the Cape Verde Islands had provided a permanent offshore base, removing some of the logistic limitations faced by expeditions sailing directly from Portugal.

The policies of the Portuguese Crown certainly constituted one of the key constraints. The Crown was a dominant player in the slave trade not necessarily because of its share in the enterprise, but because of the paramount political and legislative power it wielded. The bull *Romanus Pontifex* (January 8, 1455) granted the Portuguese Crown *dominium* over Christian contact with Africa as a divine reward for its efforts in fighting the infidel. Any profits and advantages that the Portuguese Crown might derive from its new territories represented a just reward for its service to God, and reparation for losses and damages suffered in the process.[7] All subsequent royal decrees forcefully stressed the Crown's right to legislate the modalities of contact with Africa, to benefit from it on a preferential basis, and to decide how the trade was to be conducted. They also proclaimed severe penalties, both secular and spiritual, for those who disobeyed.

With its rights to the African trade soundly established, the Crown had a number of options to choose from. It could attempt full monopolization, imperfect regional monopoly, or imperfect commodity monopoly; or simply choose to compete as one of the participants, although one of superior rank, owing to its resources, network positioning, and legislative powers. It could also elect to concentrate on taxation as the best way to obtain revenues from its West African enterprises. This might involve the removal of legal barriers to entry in order to attract large numbers of participants, or attempts to rely on longer-run contracts with a few large oligopolistic players to secure a more risk-free and predictable net income. Through the initial period of the expansion, the Crown found itself forced continually to reassess and recombine these basic options.

Indirect exploitation of the overseas enterprise, through customs, taxation, licensing, fixed payments for regional or commodity contracts, and tax farms, provided a less laborious and less costly mode of revenue generation. However, the various indirect exploitation options ranked second best to direct involvement well into the first half of the sixteenth century. The Crown resorted to indirect exploitation either in the very early stages of a regional enterprise or in the case of ventures and commodities perceived as marginal or too uncertain. This affected the process by which much of western Africa (Senegal, Gambia, the Guinea Rivers trade zone south of the Casamance River, and Sierra Leone) emerged as specific *tratos*, or lease regions.

However, as soon as the relative profitability of various regions and commodities emerged more clearly, the Crown tended to opt for various monopolistic versions of direct involvement, or for contracts with major partners only. In 1469, Dom Afonso V leased exclusive rights to the West African trade to Fernão

Gomes, a wealthy Lisbon merchant, except for trade in specific reserved commodities, such as malagueta spice (grains of paradise), for which Gomes had to contract separately.[8] This arrangement violated both the privileges granted to the Cape Verde settlers in 1466 and the licence system reaffirmed in 1470,[9] which de facto contradicted the Gomes contract.

This confusion was rectified only in 1474 when Crown Prince Dom João assumed direct control over the African enterprise. The decree of August 31, 1474, provided the foundation on which the subsequent laws, issued until the end of Dom Manuel's reign in 1521, were based. It restated, in very forceful terms, that the right to profit from contacts with Atlantic Africa was a reward for the services the Portuguese kings rendered to God and Christianity, and that, therefore, they could regulate them as they wished. The decree specified unequivocally that all traffic south of Cape Bojador was prohibited, except at the Crown's order or with a valid licence.[10] The provisions were confirmed in 1481,[11] and again reaffirmed in principle in 1514.[12]

The Crown returned time and again to the idea that taking over a promising segment of trade directly would secure about four times the normal revenue, and in acting on this assumption it repeatedly dealt severe blows both to the trade with West Africa and, ironically, to its own revenues. Although the assumption that a full monopoly would be the most rewarding alternative underlay most of the Crown's pronouncements on the early overseas ventures, the Crown attempted to impose such an option only briefly, in 1518–1520.[13] Until then, it relied largely on regional and commodity monopolies, or on exclusive renewable contracts with private entrepreneurs. The penal code of June 1514, later incorporated into the *Ordenações Manuelinas* (law compendium of King Manuel I), proclaimed that all private trading had to be limited to merchandise and areas specified in the respective licence or contract,[14] although civet cats were the only commodity that required a special additional licence.[15] Yet many of these restrictions were blunted by exemptions in the form of special permissions, or through nonenforcement or later cancellation of the ordinances.[16]

The Crown also sought to derive additional advantage from using its legislative power to function as a compulsory middleman. The São Tomé charters of 1485 and 1493 demanded that the settlers purchase all their manillas (heavy brass or copper bracelets), one of the most important European exports to West Africa, from the royal factor either in São Jorge da Mina (Elmina on the Gold Coast) or in Lisbon, and that all malagueta spice, "tailed" pepper, and slaves be sold to Crown agencies for a fixed and disadvantageous price.[17] These requirements significantly delayed the progress of the São Tomé settlement and, although they were softened in 1500, continued to have a negative impact on the supply of slaves to São Jorge da Mina.[18]

In the late 1510s, the Crown attempted to displace the Cape Verde Islanders in the flourishing slave trade with Upper Guinea by forbidding them to trade in imported commodities and, a year later, to buy slaves for export.[19] The Crown claimed that the Cape Verde settlers caused major damage to its *proveito e serviço* (profit and service) by competing vigorously, and to that section of the trade in general because they offered the Africans better terms than the Crown expeditions. This measure, combined with the 1518 law reserving the Guinea trade for the Crown alone, led to an almost complete collapse of the slave trade in Upper Guinea, lowering the volume from approximately 2,000 to 80, and had to be revoked shortly after 1520.[20]

The Crown faced serious difficulties in directly exploiting the African trade in all branches of its activity but particularly in the management of its Arguim Island factory, off the coast of Mauritania, which handled most of the royal slave trade. Supply ships came only three or four times a year.[21] Little effort was undertaken to make fresh, attractive merchandise available during the first half of the year, when much of the trading took place.[22] The supply of victuals was a particularly nagging problem. Each year, the summer brought a period of shortfall and hunger to the Arguim fort.[23] The factors faced chronic difficulties in organizing transport to Portugal for the slaves they bought. One of the complications was simply a lack of casks to supply the slaves with water. In 1509 many slaves starved at Arguim while awaiting embarkation and, subsequently, en route to Portugal.[24]

Coordinating supply and responding to demand was made more complex by the perceived need to keep tight control over Crown employees and agents.[25] All Crown agencies labored in an atmosphere of persistent suspicion and distrust.[26] The Crown devised tortuously elaborate security and policy measures to prevent theft, embezzlement, and private-account trading. The security measures involved ship and personal searches, complicated locking and unlocking of money chests, and an accounting system that was almost entirely geared toward inventory control, ending with a full audit of each ranking employee at the end of his spell of duty.[27] The policy measures included equally elaborate sets of instructions (*regimentos*) and officially established price lists (*taixas*), from which Crown agents could not deviate without great risk to their careers.[28]

This system not only bred mediocrity and systematic avoidance of responsibility, but also punished unauthorized initiative. Francisco de Almada, the zealous and devoted factor of Arguim from 1508 to 1511,[29] substantially increased the volume of the Arguim slave trade through actively advertising the factory on the mainland. His legitimate concerns about feeding the slaves, and his unauthorized food appropriations, which were nonetheless direly necessary and clearly safeguarded the investment the Crown had in the slaves, prompted a special audit of his management of grain supplies.[30] He was not able to obtain a letter of quittance (audit clearance) until eight years after the end of his tour of duty.[31]

The twists and turns of the royal policies and the inefficiencies of the Crown enterprises were only one of the constraints affecting the early Atlantic slave trade. The second major constraint was the inherent risk involved in slave trading. Compared to low-bulk, high-value, inanimate merchandise, such as gold, slaves represented both a substantial business risk and a logistical challenge. Keeping, transporting, and marketing slaves was expensive and often took many weeks or even months to complete. The merchants of Santiago, the most important of the Cape Verde Islands, wrote in a 1512 letter to the king that, as His Highness surely knew, "slaves are a very risky commodity and many of them die."[32] The king was certainly aware of this: mortality was a problem for the Crown as well as for other participants and it increased with the length of the sea voyage. P. D. Curtin suggested that the mortality in the West African slave trade normally varied between 5 and 25 percent,[33] and this is consistent with the available data on the early Portuguese trade.

The mortality during a sea voyage from Arguim to Portugal seems to have been lower. It fluctuated between 1.0 and 4.9 percent in most cases, though on several occasions it was as high as 12 to 15 percent.[34] On the other hand, at least one case is known when the mortality was nil.[35] Mortality between the mainland of Africa and Santiago Island was low because of the short distance involved. A number of slaves died nonetheless, because the Santiago settlers did not hesitate to invest in sick slaves or in very young children.[36] Bound for Portugal, the ship *Santiago*, which bought a contingent of slaves on the Cacheu River in 1526, lost 12 percent of her cargo on the return voyage that lasted two and a half months, including a prolonged stay in the Cape Verde Islands and a short stop in the Azores.[37] The Santiago traders, however, typically considered double-digit mortality exceptional and disastrous.[38]

Mortality on the sea route between the Niger Delta or Kongo and the island of São Tomé should not have been too high because of the similarities between the two regions. P. D. Curtin suggested a mortality rate of 5 percent.[39] The ship *São Miguel* lost two slaves, or 3.2 percent of her cargo, during two months of trading in Benin and a month-long return voyage to the island. It also carried the slaves belonging to the *Santa Maria de Conceição*, which had been trading on the Forcados River and become disabled. Of these slaves, three died aboard the *São Miguel*. This represents 2.5 percent mortality among the *Conceição*'s slave cargo.[40] In addition, the *Conceição* lost 6.8 percent of its cargo before the slaves were transferred to the *São Miguel*, for an overall mortality of 9.3 percent. Most of the losses had occurred while the *Conceição* was still trading along the coast.[41] It is possible that a less prolonged and troubled voyage than the voyages of these two ships would have resulted in even lower mortality.

On the São Tomé–Mina route mortality tended to be low. According to J. L. Vogt, only one or two slaves in each shipment were expected to be lost at sea.[42] There were exceptions, however, and some ships, like the *São Cristôvão* in 1535, lost up to 20 percent of their cargo.[43] The heavy losses coincided with delays and adverse conditions at sea—hunger, thirst, and exposure to the elements—rather than disease.[44]

Mortality on the route from São Tomé to Lisbon was by contrast usually high. According to A. Saunders, losses of 9 percent were considered small.[45] Documents from 1525 to 1530 attest to mortality rates ranging from 16 percent in 1527 to over 30 percent in 1526 and 1532. The rate was higher on ships carrying over one hundred slaves than on ships carrying thirty to sixty slaves.[46]

The Portuguese Crown tried to counter the losses in transport by instructing its employees to buy only prime slaves whenever possible.[47] A prime slave was usually a healthy man or woman between twenty and thirty years of age who would sell in Portugal for at least 8,000 *réis*.* The price of a prime slave was the same for both sexes. However, more men between thirty and forty counted as prime slaves than women of the same age. An older woman could also fetch a high price if she was thought to have special skills. More women in the age group fifteen to nineteen, or even some ten- to fourteen-year-old girls, were considered prime slaves than males of the same age. Few men between fifteen and nineteen years of age were sold to the Portuguese, but boys aged ten to fourteen were almost always sold at a discount.[48] In the Crown's Arguim factory the entire pricing structure was geared toward prime slaves. The bundle of goods paid for a prime slave was calculated to correspond to 15 *dobra*, gold coins and money-of-account commonly used in late medieval Portugal (6,575 *réis*). The factor paid a lower price only if he bought a child or an old or disabled person, which occurred relatively seldom.[49]

The quality of slaves from the Upper Guinea Coast deviated quite often from the "prime slave" construct, because the Cape Verde Islands traders had an incentive to take risks; they did not need to conform to royal instructions, bought slaves at low cost, and made relatively short voyages from the mainland to the Islands, where slaves could be taxed at a low rate and seasoned for resale at a much higher rate. The resulting stiff competition urged them to buy as much as they could. A large percentage of slaves imported to the Cape Verde Islands were children and adolescents of both sexes. This matches the findings of V. Cortes on the imports of black slaves to Valencia, Spain, in the late fifteenth and early sixteenth centuries. According to Cortes, children and young teenagers constituted 30 to 35 percent of the slave cargoes. P. E. H. Hair suggested that a high ratio of children is further supported by the low average price of the bulk shipments of Wolof slaves

---

*Editor's note: During the time period addressed by this chapter, *réis* (the Portuguese monetary unity which existed only as money of account) was not written with the $ symbol. This became standard practice only in the 1700s. Consequently the *réis* monetary unit is written here without the $ symbol. In the remaining chapters, all of which deal with the post-1700 period, *réis* is written with the $ symbol between hundreds and thousands (i.e., 6$000 as opposed to 6,000).

to Valencia in the same period.[50] Yet while children and adolescents were likely to be purchased more often in Upper Guinea than, for example, at Arguim, it should also be kept in mind that children were bound to be particularly noted in the customs valuations, because officials had to justify the discount. Moreover, the low average valuations of bulk shipments do sometimes represent a wholesale discount, but they are sometimes misleading, for purely arithmetical reasons.

In the Cape Verde Islands prime and high-quality slaves (valued at between 4,000 and 7,500 *réis*) accounted for 56.3 percent of the total, according to available data. Most men in this category were twenty to thirty-five years of age, and women fifteen to thirty, though older women could sometimes fetch a high price. Middle-quality slaves (3,000–3,750 *réis*) represented 19.4 percent, and low-quality slaves (0–2,900 *réis*) made up 24.3 percent. Children seldom cost more than 3,000 *réis*. Their usual price lay in the low-quality category, between 1,500 and 2,500 *réis*. Some children cost as little as 600 to 1,000 *réis*. They shared the low-quality category with old people and the sick. Despite the high percentage of prime slaves in this particular set of data, the low-quality slaves pushed the average price under 4,000 *réis*.[51]

In the Niger Delta, the sex and age structure of slave cargoes generally resembled the rest of West Africa, although the gender ratio might have been slightly in favor of women. The cargo of the São Tomé ship *Santa Maria de Conceição*, which traded on the Forcados River in 1522, consisted of 46 percent men and 64 percent women. Most men were between twenty and thirty years old, and women between sixteen and twenty-five years. The ship bought only one child, but adolescents constituted 20 percent of the males in the cargo and 18.7 percent of the females.[52] In Benin, the slaves' gender came to be used as a negotiating tool by the *oba* (king). Both male and female slaves were originally available. As late as 1506–1507 the royal factor easily acquired 117 slaves of both sexes.[53] The Portuguese royal policy of fixed prices, however, clashed with the *oba*'s interests. In retaliation, the ruler limited the sales of male slaves to the Portuguese.[54] Throughout the 1510s this was an object of frequent negotiations between Benin and the representatives of the Portuguese Crown, the more so during this period as the *oba* did not hesitate to sell slaves of both sexes to private São Tomé merchants.[55] As the relations between the Portuguese Crown and Benin continued to fluctuate during the 1520s, the royal trade was almost exclusively limited to female slaves, mostly adolescents and young girls between fifteen and nineteen years of age. In 1522, only two men were bought, as salary for two members of the trading ship's company.[56]

The obvious unpredictability and logistical problems involved in trading slaves ought to explain why slaves were not necessarily perceived as the most preferred goods. Yet a widespread and deeply ingrained feeling prevails among historians and social scientists that the early Atlantic slave trade brought superprofits to the European merchants. Speculations to this effect have been fueled by a few references in the narrative sources. Thus Alvise Cà da Mosto (Cadamosto) was told that in Guinea he would turn every *soldo*, a Venetian money-of-account, he invested into seven or even ten.[57] Taking at face value this "sales pitch" directed at a young Venetian merchant new to the West Africa trade, J. W. Blake spoke confidently of "huge" profits of 500 to 800 percent made in trading gold and slaves. The peak, according to Blake, was precisely Cadamosto's period, the 1450s, when the profits ranged between 500 and 700 percent.[58] Walter Rodney acknowledged that "the actual dimensions [of the profits] are not easy to fix," but felt so certain "the profits were fabulous" that he accused those who would suggest otherwise of distorting the evidence.[59] By contrast, E. Ashtor has shown that in the well-established late medieval Italian trade with the Levant, trading profits seldom exceeded 40 percent and usually fluctuated between 5 and 20 percent, even though it is possible to find scattered examples of exceptionally high-yielding ventures.[60] Careful analysis of the data has shown that even at the peak of the later Atlantic slave trade, much more developed and better organized than the Portuguese African trade in the later fifteenth and early sixteenth centuries, profits fluctuated around a modest 10 percent mark. R. Anstey's analysis of the Liverpool and London shipping records has demonstrated persuasively that in the second half of the eighteenth century, profits generally stayed under 10 percent and losses on individual expeditions were not uncommon.[61]

Arguim, the Crown outpost most involved in the slave trade, hardly yielded superprofits. In the first eight months of 1508, for which a ledger exists, the factory made purchases in Africa that were valued in Portugal at 935,941 *réis*.[62] The salaries payable to crews and garrison amounted to about 290,000 *réis*. Supplies for the fortress cost some 132,800 *réis*. The trading goods brought from Europe had been worth approximately 230,500 *réis* in Portugal.[63] Transport added at least 75 percent to the price of the merchandise and more in the case of bulky commodities.[64] The total cost thus amounted to at least 826,000 *réis*. The profit was thus only 109,741 *réis*, or 13.2 percent, provided that the cargoes from Arguim both reached Portugal safely and were sold at a profit. In other years, for example 1506 and 1507, the fortress ran at a loss, having acquired very little gold from the hinterland.[65]

The Crown shipboard slave trade also brought relatively small net yields. The royal ship *Santa Maria de Conceição* purchased 118 slaves, 4,025 *cori* beads, and 19 tusks of ivory in 1522. The total value of the exports was 1,074,325 *réis*.[66] The purchasing price of the trading truck had been approximately 463,125 *réis*.[67] At least 100 percent must be added for transport to São Tomé, which makes the cost of the trading goods on arrival in Africa 926,250 *réis*. Part of the merchandise was used to pay for transport services, supplies, and purchases of slaves for the crew. Seven slaves who died and four who escaped meant a loss of 88,000 *réis*.[68] The profit from the expedition was thus a mere 60,075 *réis* or 6.5 percent, on the assumption that the African commodities and slaves sold well. The *São Miguel* expedition to Benin in the same year acquired in Africa goods worth 701,100 *réis*.[69] The primary cost of the trading truck had been 321,874 *réis*, or 643,748 *réis* counting the markup for transport.[70] The expedition lost only three slaves (24,000 *réis*).[71] It returned with a profit of 33,352 *réis*, or 5.2 percent.

Technically, the Crown should have been in an advantageous position because it did not pay customs or taxes, but its static marketing mechanism caused it to sell slaves for 5,000–6,000 *réis*, while a private trader with good connections could count on getting 8,000 *réis*.[72] The private merchants could also economize on transport by teaming together and spreading the costs, or even by employing petty entrepreneurs as sailors in exchange for food and free freight for their goods.[73]

But although private trade was on various counts more competitive than the Crown trade, it was burdened with high customs or with lease and contract payments. The most common taxes were the *quarto* (the 25 percent tax on assessed market value of overseas merchandise) and the *vintena* (the one-twentieth tax on assessed value of overseas goods, minus the cost of the *quarto* or *quinto*), which amounted to 28.4 percent of the estimated value of the imported goods.[74] These two taxes were sometimes replaced by a lower one, the *quinto*, or 20 percent on booty or war prizes.[75] Apart from this, some traders could be charged the *dízima*, the 10 percent foreign trade tax, and other, smaller dues payable in Portugal, such as the *saca*, the export toll, or the *portagem*, the local toll. Still, profits in private trade could be very good, especially in the opening period of the African trade. Cadamosto may have achieved a profit of about 260 percent if he indeed managed to sell trading truck worth three hundred ducats for one hundred slaves and some parrots.[76] But the initial low prices of African merchandise and slaves soon doubled, tripled, even quadrupled. This of course cut into the profits of both the Crown and private merchants. From the 1490s onward, a private trader could not hope for more than about 10 to 30 percent profit, the level current in the Mediterranean.[77]

The well-known ship *Santiago*, dispatched in 1526 by the Guinea Rivers lease holders to Sierra Leone and to the Cacheu River, brought back after a nine-month voyage 101 slaves and 45 *quintais* (2,632.5 kilograms) of ivory, worth some 795,000 *réis*.[78] Its trading goods were too diversified to be estimated exactly but they amounted approximately to 160,000 *réis*, or, allowing for transport, 320,000 *réis*.[79] Supplies were paid from the trading truck. The ship lost fifteen slaves during the nine months, representing a loss of 90,000 *réis*.[80] The records do not include the crew's wages, which probably amounted to at least 140,000 *réis*.[81] This would mean a profit of 44.5 percent. If the venturers managed to sell the slaves for more than 6,000 *réis* per slave, the profit was higher.

Yet the relatively high overall lease, which cost the contract holders 3,434,000 réis in 1525,[82] probably wiped out much of the net profit.

The other misconception is that Africans usually got the worse end of the bargain because they were paid in valueless trifles.[83] The same perception admittedly prevailed among the authors of some of the Portuguese narrative and descriptive sources. Following a pattern common to both Christian and Muslim medieval writers, Pacheco Pereira tells his readers again and again how slaves and gold were bought in Africa for "things of little value."[84] Valentim Fernandes comments that goods not worth more than 3 *dobras* in Portugal sold for 15 *dobras* in Arguim.[85] Yet it is not enough simply to contrast prices at source and at destination—the stark differences remain dramatic only if we disregard operating costs and ignore the divergences in European and African value systems.

Put simply, a bargain is determined not only by the supply price at the source but by the relative scarcity and desirability of the commodity at the destination. A commodity that is scarce but not desired in the importing country will not sell. If it is both scarce and desired, it will fetch a very high price. For example, in an area where slavery and slave holding are commonplace while horses are rare, prestigious, and suffer from high natural mortality, fifteen human beings for one imported horse[86] could be perceived as a bargain. If a commodity is desired but in abundant supply, the price will go down. Thus European goods quickly lost some of their scarcity value but not their appeal, hence eliciting expanding slave supply, but only at rising prices.

In the opening days of the trade most West African regions were willing to pay the Portuguese the price paid for similar goods imported overland. Thus horses in Senegambia would sell for nine to fourteen slaves in the 1450s, the same price that was paid to the Zenaga merchants from Mauritania.[87] As the trade became routine, the price dropped to six to seven slaves per horse.[88] In the Rio Grande estuary, the price of a horse was twelve slaves, then it dropped to ten slaves, and by the beginning of the sixteenth century to six or, at the very best, eight slaves.[89] In terms of manillas, the price of a slave rose from the original six to seven pieces to twenty to twenty-five pieces.[90] On the Grain Coast, an *alqueire* (13 dry litres) of malagueta spice initially cost one brass manilla, and a slave two barber's basins. By the beginning of the sixteenth century, the price of malagueta spice rose to five or six manillas and the price of a slave to four or five basins.[91] In the Niger Delta, the price of slaves rose from the opening level of between eight and fifteen copper manillas per slave to over fifty in the second and third decades of the sixteenth century.[92]

Both horses and metals continued to be desired commodities through the early period. In the opening stage, however, they were relatively scarce and inaccessible for many potential customers. After the first few years the original demand was satisfied but the supply increased. This situation forced the prices down, increased competition among the Portuguese, and opened access to the trade for more customers. Problems occurred when the social or economic use of an import commodity proved limited, as in the case of copper in the Niger Delta, where it had previously been valued as a precious metal and used mostly for decorative purposes, for ritual sculpture, or as a store of wealth. If Latham was right in his suggestion that copper manillas were already used in southeastern Nigeria as currency before the arrival of the Portuguese, the drop in demand could be explained as an anti-inflationary trend.[93] It took some time before the use of copper expanded and the perception of its inherent value changed.

The Portuguese Crown, as already mentioned, attempted to control the prices offered for African commodities in order to maintain control over its employees as well as to keep prices at a certain level. The price lists were drawn up in Lisbon on the basis of information received from West African outposts and elicited from private parties.[94] The pricing policy involved two steps. First, the Crown set the prices of Portuguese commodities in terms of their selling potential in the West African market for which they were intended. In Arguim the prices were set in *dobras*, in Mina either in *dobras* or in marks of gold.[95] These units functioned as money of account, or rather as "prices of account," similar to the later trade ounce on the Gold Coast or iron bars in the Senegambia.[96] The price list determined the assortment of commodities that could be contained in a unit of payment for African staples such as gold or slaves.[97] Second, the Crown determined the maximum that its representatives were permitted to pay for a unit of any African staple. In Arguim, for example, a slave could cost a maximum of 15 *dobras*.[98] In the early sixteenth century a *dobra* of gold corresponded to a *dobra* of account.[99]

In other parts of West Africa, the Crown fixed the *taixas*, the maximum prices of gold and slaves, in terms of the main barter goods, and other African commodities were purchased with reference to the fractions of cost of these leading staples.[100] In the 1520s, faced with falling prices and unable to cope with private competition, the Crown also imposed the *taixas* on private trade, by including them in the *regimento*, the voyage instructions of each trading ship.[101]

Under these conditions, trade negotiations in Africa concentrated on the assortment of goods that made up the payment. As in the case of iron bar prices, the early Portuguese system included, within each fixed unit, goods that were either more costly at the source than others, or more in demand.[102] It would have been in the interest of the Portuguese to sell as much of the cheaper assortments, such as *bordate* (inexpensive cotton) cloth, as possible because it inflated the amount of goods that a trade *dobra* would buy and pushed down the purchasing price of slaves. Their customers, however, usually came with an established idea of what they wanted to buy, and there was little the Portuguese could do to influence the selection in the final count.[103]

The same African export goods could be purchased with items whose primary price differed considerably. Slave prices in horses were considerably higher than those in metalware.[104] Metals and textiles were often sold to local merchants who distributed them further through the African regional networks and could expect additional profit. They could therefore afford to be more generous than the immediate consumer. This did not necessarily mean, however, that it was advantageous to buy slaves for metals rather than horses. Horses often found a more assured market than metals. The actual price depended on the state of supplies in the area and on the qualities of the horse.[105]

In Arguim, in 1508, the majority of slave transactions involved several major items, such as burnouses (large, expensive woolen garments, elaborately dyed and decorated) or saddles, complemented by minor items, such as chamber pots, berets, or pieces of *bordate* cloth. Only in about one-third of the cases did the shopping basket consist entirely of minor items worth less than 1.5 *dobra*.[106] Cattle and gum arabic were purchased with minor items because of the low unit value of these commodities, though there was a noted tendency to obtain at least one object over 1 *dobra* of local value in most transactions.[107]

The outcome of a bargain was a combined function of supply and effective demand. The Africans had a slight advantage here, except for long-distance traders, who in order to trade with the Portuguese had to come from far away and forfeit opportunities elsewhere. Local merchants and buyers operated on their home ground and could eventually obtain goods similar to those sold by the Portuguese through trans-Saharan channels. The Portuguese either had to sell or suffer losses, given the time constraints of any given trading voyage or of the expeditions that resupplied factories and took away slaves. Their urge to sell was therefore somewhat more pressing than that of the African side to sell or buy. Whereas the African side, when discontented with the bargaining, could rather more easily pack and go elsewhere, the Portuguese often had to buy whatever was offered or go empty-handed, shouldering the expenses of long sea journeys, continuing to amortize the cost of trading posts, paying and supplying garrisons, and absorbing opportunity costs. Thus in 1526, when the *Santiago* found that the slaves it expected to buy from the *lançados* (Portuguese males settled on the West African coast and integrated into local societies) of São Domingos were not available, it was forced to buy surplus ivory although it had already obtained the desired quantity in an earlier trading session in Sierra Leone.[108] Fixed installations in principle offered more opportunity to accept only good bargains and otherwise wait for the markets to turn favorable, but they were far from immune to the whims of supply. The Arguim factory usually had to do most of its business in slaves, despite the fact that its primary target was supposed to be gold.[109]

If we concentrate purely on price behavior and exchange mechanisms, the terms of the early trade were certainly favorable to the African side. Both the volume of trade and the prices for African commodities were increasing, and many African traders had reasonably good access to alternative outlets and sources of supply, either domestic sources or those linked to the trans-Saharan system. This does not mean, however, that the Portuguese merchants or Crown agents were in a no-win situation. If the prices rose too high and they could not pass the increase on to the final user, they could remove themselves to another region or diversify into other commodities or services.[110]

Still, the early European slave traders were constrained by the fact that they operated within an already well-established West African trade system, to which they became only an addition. They were far away from the protection of their home country and faced the same problems that any West African trader encountered in a foreign territory. They needed to examine the market, identify suitable ports of call, establish working commercial relations with their African counterparts, and work out an arrangement with local authorities in order to obtain permission to trade and to be guaranteed safety. Without good relations with the local powers and trading partners, the commerce, whether in slaves or in other commodities, would not have been possible.

The Europeans could expect the same treatment as any other foreign traders. They were welcome as long as they were useful, or in other words, as long as they offered attractive merchandise at a price perceived to be acceptable. They were, however, also strangers, and their wealth in trade goods invited attack, theft, or fraud. The Portuguese sources are full of complaints about incidents of this sort.[111] The Bullom of the Sherbro River were especially notorious for quickly and unpredictably switching from peaceful trade to hostility and back again.[112] The protection or at least the good will of local political authorities was essential for the conduct of trade. But even such protection was often not enough. The Serer of Siin had a very belligerent reputation for attacking and mistreating Europeans, despite the fact that their ruler was a good customer of the Portuguese and tried to protect traders.[113]

The Portuguese were aware of the importance of appeasing the local powers. Even if not attacking the Portuguese directly, a hostile ruler could forbid his subjects to trade, or could harass foreign traders coming to meet the Europeans. The *oba* of Benin was prone to close or limit the trading whenever he thought that he was not treated appropriately. Although he received expensive gifts on occasion from the Portuguese Crown,[114] he regulated the volume of merchandise for sale to the Portuguese according to the quantity as well as the value of the gifts that both he and his officials received. In 1516 he allowed as many as four hundred slaves to be sold to an interloping São Tomé expedition that gave him presents worth about fifty slaves.[115] This amounted to about 12 percent of the return cargo. To the agents of the royal contract holder, Antonio Carneiro, the *oba* released only one hundred female slaves and replied to their complaints that if he were given "proper" presents he would immediately open the market in slaves of both sexes, as well as any other merchandise that would be of interest to the Portuguese.[116] In 1522 the captain of the *São Miguel* brought especially for the *oba* twenty *onças* (0.6 kg) of coral, four Indian caps, and one piece of satin. The *oba* obviously did not think much of the gift, because he permitted only female slaves to be sold to the Portuguese.[117]

Other rulers were less demanding. The gifts given al-Mansur, the overlord of the hinterland of Nouakchott Bay ("Amterote"), during the 1508 annual expedition from Arguim, were worth only about 5.4 percent of the merchandise that the expedition purchased. Al-Mansur's selection of presents included a full set of equestrian equipment, some cheap cloth, headgear, and an assortment of metal utensils.[118] The chiefs in the Niger Delta required only relatively modest presents. The *Conceição* expedition gave out only fifty-seven *covados* (some 37.5 metres) of linen cloth, worth about four slaves, to the notables on the Forcados River, while purchasing 135 slaves and other merchandise.[119]

In 1526 the captain of the *Santiago* gave each of the headmen (*capitão*) of the three villages in the Scarcies estuary a present of twenty to thirty manillas and a small cloth. All these together would have bought twenty-five bars of iron, which in turn would have bought less than one slave on the Cacheu River.[120] The Banhun rulers on the Cacheu were equally undemanding. The ruler of the São Domingos village was content with only ten bars of iron and the ruler of Buguendo with six bars.[121] In both cases, however, the local potentates could hope to make additional profit from the *lançados* settled in their area. Both the Niger Delta and the Upper Guinea trade also involved gifts to officials in charge of trade and gifts to members of the ruler's retinue, which were usually smaller than those given to their superiors.[122]

When a Portuguese trading ship arrived at a prospective trading spot, it announced its arrival through interpreters to the local ruler or his representative in order to secure his consent and to work out security measures.[123] In the early days these often involved an exchange of hostages. The ruler was also informed of the composition of the trading truck and invited to inspect it personally. He often proved the best customer, especially in Senegal. At any rate he could expect presents from the Portuguese. In the early days the ruler usually showed up in person, with a large armed following. He was often allowed the first pick of the merchandise, after which trade was opened to all. The negotiation and haggling, conducted through an interpreter, usually took many hours and often days. If the transaction required a prolonged stay, the ruler often felt obligated to provide food and lodging for the traders. The conclusion of the trading session was a festive occasion. First the local ruler hosted the Portuguese, and the next day they played host to him, his family, and his chief followers aboard the ship, which enlivened the occasion.[124]

Once trade became routine, it lost some of its luster. In larger and more frequented locations, the local ruler or chief left the handling of the foreigners to trade officials, a common occurrence in West Africa. On the Gambia and Cacheu Rivers, this official was often the chief of the sea- or riverside village where the ships docked.[125] In Benin matters were handled by the chief of Gwato, the port of Benin, but at the *oba*'s court the person responsible for the Portuguese was the *osodin*, one of the four leading town chiefs. The Portuguese were also assigned an official court interpreter. All of the *oba*'s officials responsible for dealing with the Portuguese were also entitled to presents.[126]

Private Portuguese commerce continued to be a shipboard trade, but its volume quickly increased to the point where the African customers or traders could count on meeting at least one Portuguese ship at a given landing place within a long but reasonable period of waiting. The relatively sustained links made it possible for the Portuguese to target the market in advance, instead of searching for a trading spot while they were already off the coast. Some African buyers acquired a preferred customer standing, for example, "Budomel," the ruler of Kajoor, in the 1450s;[127] or Jelen, the *bumi* (high-ranking official, often second only to the *buurba* or ruler) of Jolof, in the 1480s. The preferred customer status brought with it the possibility of catering to special orders, as well as eligibility for credit. Jelen, for example, both bought and sold on credit. He would pay even for the horses that died at sea, because he considered them to be a preordered delivery to him. His reputation among the Portuguese was so high that even in times of his greatest political and military troubles he was still granted credit.[128]

The need for credit often stemmed from either the undersupply of African goods or the oversupply of the European commodities. Undersupply could result in losses for the Portuguese because of the long waits for payment and depletion among the crews through defection and disease.[129] If the relationship with their African counterparts was fairly well established, the Portuguese might leave their merchandise behind and return the next year, or have another merchant pick up the payment due.[130] If the Africans did not pay, the Portuguese would avoid the spot, which was usually a sufficient incentive for the Africans to meet their obligations. Among Mande traders, at least, an oral contract was always honored.[131] Oversupply, especially of slaves, was disadvantageous to the African parties. It was better for them to sell on credit to a familiar merchant and stipulate the payment in advance. If the Portuguese did not return with payment, the local authorities could seize the disembarked goods and the shore party of the next visiting European ship.

All such matters were greatly facilitated by the establishment of landlord-stranger relationships, but the real breakthrough came when some of the Portuguese, to be known as *lançados*, settled on the mainland permanently, became integrated into local societies, and started to provide services for both sides as intermediaries. In this they were no different from the members of other commercial diasporas. They settled mainly in the Guinea Rivers region, especially in the Banhun states of São Domingos and Buguendo, and in Sierra Leone.[132] This arrangement considerably increased the efficiency of the Cape Verde Islands trading expeditions, to the detriment of the Crown, which tried several times to brand the *lançados* as traitors and outlaws.[133]

Even so, ignoring the political and commercial realities of a trading region could be extremely damaging to the success of both individual expeditions and long-term trading relationships. In Benin lengthy negotiations with the *oba* were necessary before any trading could start, and this typically extended the duration of expeditions to the Niger Delta from Mina or São Tomé, already up to four months long.[134] In 1522 it took the *São Miguel* a month to begin actual sales and purchases and then two months before the cargo was collected.[135] The *Conceição*, trading that same year in the Forcados River, spent almost three troubled months there before assembling its cargo. The reason was the lack of suitable merchandise on the Portuguese side, and the lack of local contacts, rather than a lack of export goods on the African side.[136] The 1516 expedition of the São Tomé interlopers went much more smoothly because it employed local Ijo intermediaries and was wise enough to appease the *oba* and the appropriate officials at his court.[137]

Under the circumstances, a fixed installation—fort or trading post—could arguably perform better, by accumulating over time a fund of local intelligence, developing more stable contacts, and being able to handle trade all year long. This option, however, was reserved mainly for the Crown, for whom shipboard venturing represented only a minor stake, and whose policy was to promote its protected trade and strategic interests at crucial locations by establishing permanent factories. Only permanent trading stations, whether royal factories or official and rogue *lançados*' establishments, could perform a large number of small transactions spread out over time, or act as collecting stations. In Arguim the slaves trickled to the fortress in small groups all year long.[138]

If a Portuguese ship arrived at a station or anchorage unexpectedly or outside of the normal trade season, it either had to leave without cargo or had to stay until suitable merchandise was collected. According to Valentim Fernandes, however, the Senegalese nobles sometimes had a simple recipe in such cases: they attacked the nearest slave village in order to assemble the payment.[139] With sufficient incentives, and under the right circumstances, supply could thus be "forced."

A complex question is whether such "forcing of supply" occurred on a grander scale during the early period of the Atlantic slave trade, in particular in the case of the kingdom of Kongo. Writing around 1506, Duarte Pacheco Pereira complained in his geographical and commercial guide to Atlantic Africa that the kingdom of Kongo was very poor and only few slaves could be obtained there.[140] Yet from 1515 onward, West Central Africa is estimated to have supplied 50 percent of the annual Atlantic slave exports. In March 1517, a Crown inspector,

Bernardo de Segura, wrote to the king of Portugal that as many as 4,072 *peças* slaves were brought to São Tomé from Kongo alone between January 8 and December 18, 1515. Segura estimated that the trade could support a regular shuttle traffic of nine ships, each with a carrying capacity of 250 slaves, making for an annual turnover of 6,750 slaves.[141]

Anne Hinton argued that before 1512 very few slaves were indeed available for sale in Kongo, and that the Portuguese demand induced the sudden marked increase in supply, which had to be generated exclusively through warfare and by expanding the radius of raids.[142] The 1526 letter from Afonso I (Nzinga Mbemba) of Kongo to the king of Portugal, imploring him to stop his subjects from ravaging Afonso's realm by their insatiable demand for slaves, is now a well-established item in the world history undergraduate canon.[143] Hinton's view is consistent with much of the earlier literature, which interpreted the obsequious tone of Afonso I's correspondence with his Portuguese counterpart as evidence of an early colonial relationship between an African state and a European power.

John Thornton, however, has effectively challenged this view, showing that Afonso I skillfully manipulated the Kongo-Portuguese relations for his own purposes, and that the language of the documents is more a result of the style used by the Portuguese scribes whom he employed than of any acknowledgment of inferiority on his part.[144] According to Thornton, Kongo had already been identified as a potentially important source of slaves in 1493, in the second charter to the São Tomé settlers, and functioned as such a source as early as 1502, if we trust, for instance, the evidence of the *Cantino Atlas*.[145] As early as 1509, Portuguese military auxiliaries in Kongo expected to be compensated in slaves.[146] Thornton identified as the main problem of the early period the tension between the importance of slaves for export on the one hand, and centralization and statebuilding on the other. This tension became particularly strong in the mid-1520s, when the conflict with Ndongo temporarily constricted Kongo's access to fresh slaves.[147]

There is little doubt that the emergence of a sustained Portuguese commercial demand for slaves put Kongo and its ruler under considerable pressure, especially in the 1510s and 1520s. Afonso I was caught between the slave-trading activities of São Tomé islanders, led by their captain, Fernão de Melo, and the demands of the Portuguese Crown. He hoped that the Crown would control de Melo and also the Portuguese traders who took up residence in Kongo. The Portuguese Crown shared his wish, but its motive was of course to replace the São Toméans as the main beneficiary of the slave supply.

The Crown's early policy on Kongo was consistent with its approach to trade with the other parts of Atlantic Africa. In the opening period, it left the initial exploration and buildup of the trading infrastructure to the settlers of São Tomé. The letters of Pero Alvares de Caminha, nephew of the first captain, reveal the logistical challenges that the Caminha family and their group had faced.[148]

The next captain, Fernão de Melo, was presented with an easier situation, further facilitated by the generous charter he and the São Tomé settlers had received from the Crown in 1500. It authorized them to trade freely from Rio Real to the "whole land" of the *mani* or king of Kongo.[149]

The Crown was, however, keenly interested in directly profiting from its relations with Kongo and its neighbors. The royal instructions to Simão da Silva, leader of the 1512 Portuguese embassy to Kongo, were very explicit in this respect. The embassy was to find out about the availability of trading commodities (specifically slaves, copper, and ivory) and ascertain the organization of trade in Kongo. The Crown wanted to know if the trade had to be conducted through the king, or if there were private merchants to conduct business with. The ambassadors were also to obtain information about the "provinces" of Kongo, its neighbors and their military and trading potential.[150] The Crown was unequivocal in that it expected trade goods, especially slaves, in exchange for the spiritual, technological, and political aid it was providing to Afonso I. Afonso I was equally explicit in his expectation that the Portuguese Crown would control its subjects operating in his lands. The voluminous correspondence of the late 1510s and 1520s illustrates quite clearly the Crown's inability or unwillingness to fulfill this requirement. In 1519 the king of Portugal declared that only royal ships could carry slaves and other merchandise from Kongo,[151] in effect revoking an important part of the São Tomé charter. It is debatable, however, whether this was done in response to Afonso's complaints or in the hope of monopolizing what the 1517 report of Bernardo da Segura portrayed as a very lucrative enterprise.[152] The order was ineffective and business continued as usual. During the reign of Dom João III, responses to Afonso I's letters became increasingly more sporadic and abrupt, indicating a loss of the Crown's direct interest in Kongo.[153]

In Kongo, the exports of slaves were substantially more sensitive to the European presence than in West Africa. The forceful demands of the Portuguese Crown, Afonso I's political and ideological susceptibilities, and the ability of the São Tomé–based traders to evade both Kongolese and Portuguese central authorities, indeed combined to create considerable pressure on Kongo to supply slaves through warfare. However, Thornton's arguments against overstating this consideration should not be underestimated; after all, most of Afonso I's concerns had to do with injury to his authority and personal interests, rather than with slave trading itself.[154]

In conclusion, the early Atlantic slave trade must be considered in the full range of the complex realities in which it operated, both on the African and on the European sides. It existed in a broad context of political, socioeconomic, and cultural realities from which it cannot be easily dissociated. The mechanism of supply and demand was only one of these factors. The relatively high volume of the slave trade in the opening period supports the argument that the Europeans merely plugged into an already existing and complex nexus between the slave trade and slavery in Africa. However, tapping into or stimulating slave supply was very much contingent on a number of serious constraints: the oscillating policies of the Portuguese Crown, logistics, the real and perceived risks of slave trading, the ability of various European parties to compete for slaves, and other factors influencing the effectiveness of demand. These constraints often seriously restricted the European ability to purchase slaves (and other commodities). The volume of the early Atlantic slave trade thus cannot be taken as an indicator of the full potential of slave supply from Atlantic Africa during this period, because of the inefficiencies and bottlenecks of European demand.

NOTES

1. Ivana Elbl, "The Volume of the Early Atlantic Slave Trade, 1450–1521," *Journal of African History* 38 (1997): 31–76.
2. Ibid., pp. 75–76.
3. John K. Thornton, *Africa and Africans in the Making of the Atlantic World* (Cambridge: Cambridge University Press, 1992, 2d ed. 1998), pp. 72–116; and John K. Thornton, *Warfare in Atlantic Africa, 1500–1800* (London: University College, London, Press, 1999), particularly chapter 6. Thornton also provides an effective summary of the debate about slavery and slave trade in fifteenth-century Atlantic Africa. Much of the debate was based on a prolonged exchange of opinions between Walter Rodney ("African Slavery and Other Forms of Social Oppression on the Upper Guinea Coast in the Context of the Atlantic Slave Trade,"*Journal of African History* 7 [1966]: 431–43; *West Africa and the Atlantic Slave Trade* [Dar-es-Salaam: Historical Association of Tanzania, Paper #3, 1967]; *How Europe Underdeveloped Africa* [Dar-es-Salaam, 1972], chapter 4) and J. D. Fage ("Slavery and Slave Trade in the Context of African History," *Journal of African History* 10 [1969]: 393–404; "Slaves and Society in Western Africa, c.1445–c.1700," *Journal of African History* 21 [1980], 289–310; "African Societies and the Atlantic Slave Trade," *Past and Present* 125 [1989]: 97–115). See also Paul E. Lovejoy, "The Impact of the Atlantic Slave Trade on Africa: A Review of the Literature," *Journal of African History* 30, no. 3 (1989): 365–94.
4. Ivana Elbl, "The Portuguese Trade with West Africa, 1440–1521" (Ph.D. diss., University of Toronto, 1986), pp. 449–57.
5. Thornton, *Africa and Africans*, pp. 110–12.
6. Thornton, *Warfare*, p. 135.
7. J. M. de Silva Marques, ed., *Descobrimentos Portugueses: documentos para a sua história* (Lisbon: Edição do Instituto da Alta Cultura, 1944–1971), vol. 1, p. 505.
8. Ibid., vol. 3, doc. 97; João Barros, *Asia. Primeira Década*, ed. H. Cidade and M. Múris (Lisbon: Agência Geral das Colónias, 1945), p. 72.
9. Silva Marques, *Descobrimentos Portugueses*, vol. 3, doc. 60, p. 86.
10. Ibid., doc. 115, pp. 153–54.

11. Ibid., doc. 152.
12. Antonio Brásio, *Monumenta Missionaria Africana: África Occidetal* (Lisbon: Agência Geral do Ultramar, 1958), 2d series, vol. 2, docs. 26 and 28.
13. Ibid.
14. Ibid., doc. 28, p. 81.
15. Ibid., p. 90.
16. Ibid.
17. Silva Marques, *Descobrimentos Portugueses*, vol 3, doc. 200, p. 207; and doc. 289, pp. 428–29.
18. Ibid., doc. 361.
19. Brásio, *Monumenta Missionaria Africana*, 2d series, vol. 2, docs. 43, 44, 45, and 47.
20. See Elbl, "Volume," pp. 52, 69. For more extensive discussion of the fortunes of the Cape Verde Islands see Luís de Albuquerque and Maria Emilia Madeira Santos, eds., *História Geral de Cabo Verde*, vols. 1–2 (Lisbon and Praia: Instituto de Investigação Científica Tropical, 1991, 1994).
21. Arquivo Nacional de Torre do Tombo (ANTT) Lisbon, Núcleo Antigo, no. 888, fos. 172–77.
22. ANTT, Gaveta 20, maço 2, doc. 67; ibid., maço 5, doc. 42.
23. In the summer, wheat rations decreased significantly for both the garrison and the slaves. ANTT, Núcleo Antigo, no. 888, fos. 55–59. See also ANTT, Gaveta 20, maço 5, doc. 42.
24. ANTT, Gaveta 20, maço 5, doc. 42.
25. For similar problems faced later by chartered companies see Ann M. Carlos, "Bonding and the Agency Problem: Evidence from the Royal African Company, 1672–1691," *Explorations in Economic History* 31 (1994): 313–35; Ann M. Carlos and Stephen Nicholas, "Agency Problems in the Early Chartered Companies: The Case of Hudson's Bay Company," *Journal of Economic History* 50 (1990): 853–75.
26. See for example Brásio, *Monumenta Missionária Africana*, 2d series, vol. 2, doc. 28, p. 89; ANTT, Corpo Cronológico, parte II, maço 50, doc. 22 (the record of the trial of a royal official, António Froes, filled with accusations and counteraccusations).
27. Damião Peres, ed., *Regimento das Casas da India e Mina* (Coimbra: Faculdade de Letras, Universidade de Coimbra, 1947), pp. 6–7, 8–9, 11–15, 23–24, 26–29, 89–90, 95. For documentary evidence pertaining to concrete situations see, for example, ANTT, Corpo Cronológico, parte I, maço 8, doc. 72 (unauthorized trading during the unloading process); ANTT, Corpo Cronológico, parte I, maço 17, doc. 4 (complaints about the transfer of goods between royal pilots and the officials of São Jorge da Mina); Brásio, *Monumenta Missionaria Africana*, 2d series, vol. 2, doc. 28, pp. 86–87.
28. For examples of ships' *regimentos* see A. Teixeira da Mota, "A viagem do navio 'Santiago' a Serra Leoa e Rio de S. Domingos em 1526 (Livro de Armação)," *Boletim Cultural de Guiné Portuguesa* 24 (1969): 562–67; A. F. C. Ryder, "An Early Portuguese Trading Voyage to the Forcados River," *Journal of the Historical Society of Nigeria* (1959): 301–305; A. Teixeira da Mota and R. Mauny, "Livre de l'armement du navire São Miguel de l'île de São Thomé au Benin (1522)," *Bulletin de l'IFAN* 40, series B (1979): 68–71.

29. A. Braacamp Freire, ed., "Cartas de Quitação del-Rei D. Manuel," *Arquivo Histórico Português* (*AHP*) 2 (1904): 354, doc. 237.
30. ANTT, Corpo Cronológico, parte I, maço 12, doc. 8.
31. Freire, "Cartas," AHP 2, 354, doc. 237.
32. Brásio, *Monumenta Missionaria Africana*, 2d series, vol. 2, doc. 19, p. 54.
33. Philip D. Curtin, *The Atlantic Slave Trade: A Census* (Madison: University of Wisconsin Press, 1969), pp. 99–100; Elbl, "The Portuguese Trade with West Africa," p. 499, table 28.
34. ANTT, Corpo Cronólogico, parte II, maço 29, doc. 64; maço 8, doc. 89; Núcleo Antigo, no. 799, fls. 507–508.
35. ANTT, Corpo Cronólogico, parte II, maço 29, doc. 64, April 10, 1514.
36. See Elbl, "The Portuguese Trade with West Africa," p. 496, table 26.
37. ANTT, Núcleo Antigo, no. 197, in A. Teixeira da Mota, "A viagem do navio *Santiago* a Serra Leoa e Rio de S. Domingos em 1526," *Boletim Cultural de Guiné Portuguesa* 24 (1969): 561–78.
38. Brásio, *Monumenta Misionaria Africana*, 2d series, vol. 2, doc. 198, p. 55.
39. Curtin, *The Atlantic Slave Trade*, p. 100.
40. ANTT, Corpo Cronológico, parte II, maço 149, doc. 19, in Teixeira da Mota and Mauny, "Livre de l'armement," pp. 68–85.
41. ANTT, Corpo Cronológico, parte II, maço 102, doc. 20, in A. F. C. Ryder, "An Early Portuguese Trading Voyage to the Forcados River," *Journal of the Historical Society of Nigeria* 1 (1959): 300–21. Published in the original Portuguese by A. Brásio, "Um extraordinário documento quinhentista," *Studia* 15 (1965): 155–74. Also published in French by R. Mauny, "Le livre de bord du navire *Santa Maria da Conceição* (1522)," *Bulletin de l'IFAN* 13, B, (1967): 512–33.
42. J. L. Vogt, "The Early São Thomé-Príncipe Slave Trade with Mina, 1500–1540," *International Journal of African Historical Studies* 5 (1973): 460–61.
43. Ibid., p. 461.
44. Ibid.
45. A. C. de C. M. Saunders, *A Social History of Black Slaves and Freedmen in Portugal, 1441–1555* (Cambridge: Cambridge University Press, 1982), p. 14.
46. Ibid., p. 21, table 2.
47. See the *regimentos* in Teixeira da Mota, "Livre de l'armement," and Ryder, "An Early Portuguese Trading Voyage." Also J. L. Vogt, *The Portuguese Rule on the Gold Coast, 1469–1682* (Athens: University of Georgia Press, 1979), p. 74.
48. Ibid.
49. ANTT, Núcleo Antigo, no. 888, fls. 12–23 (verso), 32–36 v, 45, 46–47 v, 61–62.
50. P. E. H. Hair, "Black African Slaves at Valencia, 1482–1516: An Onomastic Inquiry," *History in Africa* 7 (1980): 127. See also V. Cortes Alonso, "Procedencia de los esclavos nehros en Valencia (1482–1516)," *Revista española de antropologia americana* 7 (1972): 138.
51. Elbl, "The Portuguese Trade with West Africa," p. 499, table 28.
52. Ibid., p. 503, table 29.
53. ANTT, Chancelaria de D. Manuel, livro 7, fl. 24; ANTT, :Livro das Ilhas, fl. 192, in Braacamp Freire, "Cartas," *AHP* 5 (475): doc. 5.

54. A. F. C. Ryder, *Benin and the Europeans* (London: Longmans, 1969), pp. 42–53. Also ANTT, Corpo Cronólogico, parte I, maço 20, doc. 19 and 127.
55. ANTT, Corpo Cronólogico, parte I, maço 20, doc. 19.
56. ANTT, Corpo Cronológico, parte II, maço 149, doc. 149, in Teixeira da Mota and Mauny, "Livre de l'armement," pp. 68–85.
57. Cadamosto, *Viagens de Luís de Cadamosto and Pedro de Sintra* (Lisbon: Academia Portuguesa de História, 1948), p. 7.
58. John W. Blake, *The Quest for God and Gold, 1454–1578* (London: Curzon Press, 1977), pp. 16–17. Blake, however, relied for his data on an article by H. Fitzler, which, as V. Rau, B. W. Diffie, and A. Iria proved, was based on nonexistent archival data. The issue is covered in Virginia Rau and Bailey W. Diffie, "Alleged Fifteenth-Century Portuguese Joint-Stock Companies and the Articles of Dr. Fitzler," *Bulletin of the Institute of Historical Research* 26 (1953): 181–200.
59. Rodney, *How Europe Underdeveloped Africa*, pp. 93–94.
60. E. Ashtor, *Levant Trade in the Later Middle Ages* (Princeton: Princeton University Press, 1983), pp. 428–32.
61. R. Anstey, "The Volume and Profitability of the British Slave Trade, 1761–1807," in *Race and Slavery in the Western Hemisphere: Quantitative Studies*, ed. S. Engerman and E. Genovese (Princeton: Princeton University Press, 1975), pp. 10–21, especially tables 6 and 7.
62. 472,813 *réis* woth of gold and 414,000 *réis* worth of slaves (counting 6,000 *réis* per slave), and 49,128 *réis* worth of gum arabic (c. 300 *réis* per sac). The prices are based on the trade *dobras*, and usually correspond with the price that the commodity was expected to fetch in Portugal.
63. ANTT, Núcleo Antigo, no. 888, fls. 101–34 (fls. 102–106 and 135–38 are missing). This includes 99,010 *réis* of wheat, 24,000 *réis* of wine, and 10,970 *réis* of locally purchased meat. Based on trade *dobras*.
64. According to Oliveira Marques the transport cost 110 to 115 percent of the cargo ("Navigation entre la Prusse et le Portugal au debut du XVe siècle," *Vierteljahrschrift für Sozial- und Wirtschaftgeschichte* 46 [1959]: 489).
65. ANTT, Núcleo Antigo, no. 888, fl. 103.
66. Ryder, "An Early Portuguese Trading Voyage," passim. The slaves were worth 952,000 *réis* (based on 8,000 *réis* as the average price of a slave in São Tomé); the *cori* beads 100,725 *réis* (25 *réis* per *cori*) and ivory c. 21,600 *réis* (15.5 kg per tusk at 73.4 *réis* per kilogram. See Braacamp Freire, "Cartas," p. 434, doc. 258).
67. 290,625 *réis* worth of cowries (a rough estimate, based on their slave purchasing power and relations to manillas), 160,400 *réis* worth of manillas, 1,600 *réis* worth of crystal beads, and 10,500 *réis* worth of textiles (Ryder, "Early Portuguese Trading Voyage," p. 302, notes 3–4).
68. Ibid., pp. 317–18, 320–21; Teixeira da Mota and Mauny, "Livre de l'armement," pp. 84–85.
69. Teixeira da Mota and Mauny, "Livre de l'armement," passim. 251,432 *réis* worth of ivory, 424,000 *réis* worth of slaves, 35,675 *réis* worth of *coris*. For prices see the preceding notes.

70. Ibid. 229,560 *réis* worth of manillas, 24,950 *réis* worth of cloth, 7,729 *réis* worth of beads, and 59,644 *réis* worth of cowries.
71. Ibid., pp. 72–73.
72. Elbl, "The Portuguese Trade with West Africa," vol. 2, pp. 626–31, table 39.
73. Ibid., chap. 6; and also ANTT, Núcleo Antigo, no. 757, fls. 14–119.
74. ANTT, Núcleo Antigo, no. 757, fls. 14–119.
75. Ibid., for example fls. 95–98.
76. Cadamosto, *Viagens*, pp. 34 and 35, counting 8,000 *réis* per slave and 360 *réis* per parrot (p. 45) and deducting 50 percent of the cargo, as per Cadamosto's contract with Dom Henrique (p. 7).
77. See Ivana Elbl, "Portuguese Slave Trade in the Fifteenth Century: Prices and Profits," unpublished paper presented to the 12th Canadian Association of African Studies Conference, Toronto, May 1982.
78. Teixeira da Mota, "A viagem," pp. 560–78, counting 6,000 *réis* per slave, 4,200 *réis* of ivory.
79. Where no prices or indications were available, either one-third of the Arguim *dobra* prices was used (Ivana Elbl, "The Arguim Trade in the Early 1500s," unpublished paper presented to the South/South Congress, Montreal, 15–17 May 1985, note 32; Vogt, *Portuguese Rule*, pp. 90 and 219 [appendix C]), or the approximate price was calculated in terms of iron (80 *réis* per bar, Teixeira da Mota, "A viagem," p. 556).
80. Teixeira da Mota, "A viagem," pp. 574–75.
81. Peres, *Regimento*, pp. 91–92.
82. ANTT, Núcleo Antigo, no. 590, fl. 59v.
83. See for example Blake, *The Quest for God and Gold*, p. xiii.
84. Pacheco Pereira, *Esmeraldo de Situ Orbis*, ed. A. E. da Silva Dias (Lisbon: Edição Commemorative do Primeiro Centenário da Sociedade de Geografía, 1905), pp. 76–82, 85, 101, 115.
85. Valentim Fernandes, *O Manuscrito "Valentim Fernandes,"* ed. António Baião (Lisbon: Academia Portuguesa da História, 1940), p. 45.
86. Cadamosto, *Viagens*, p. 17.
87. Ibid., pp. 17, 47.
88. Diogo Gomes, *As viagens dos descrubrimentos*, ed. J. M. Garcia (Lisbon: Editorial Presença, 1983), p. 46; Pacheco Pereira, *Esmeraldo*, pp. 79, 82, 85, 86.
89. Fernandes, *O Manuscrito*, p. 87; Pacheco Pereira, *Esmeraldo*, p. 91.
90. Fernandes, *O Manuscrito*, p. 87.
91. Pacheco Pereira, *Esmeraldo*, p. 105.
92. Pacheco Pereira, *Esmeraldo*, p. 124; Ryder, *Benin and the Europeans*, p. 40.
93. John Latham, "Currency, Credit, and Capitalism on the Cross River in the Pre-Colonial Era," *Journal of African History* 12 (1971): 599. For other uses of copper see for example Pacheco Pereira's description of the large copper pendants worn by the Ijo of Bonny (Pacheco Pereira, *Esmeraldo*, p. 125).
94. Fernandes, *O Manuscrito*, p. 45. On the Crown's market-information gathering see Peres, *Regimento*, pp. 25–26.
95. Fernandes, *O Manuscrito*, p. 45. A *dobra* was identical with the *mithqal*, which

greatly facilitated trade with Berber and Sudanese merchants. On practices in Mina see Vogt, *The Portuguese Rule*, p. 74.

96. On "iron bars," "bar prices," and "assortment bargaining" see Philip D. Curtin, *Economic Change in Precolonial Africa, Senegambia in the Era of the Slave Trade* (Madison: University of Wisconsin Press, 1975), pp. 240–53; on the "trade ounce" see Marion Johnson, "The Ounce in Eighteenth-Century West African Trade," *Journal of African History* 7, no. 2 (1966): 197–214.

97. See for example the structure of prices paid for slaves in Arguim in 1508 (ANTT, Núcleo Antigo, no. 888, fls. 12–23v).

98. ANTT, Núcleo Antigo, no. 888, fls. 12–23v; Fernandes, *O Manuscrito*, p. 45.

99. ANTT, Núcleo Antigo, no. 888, fls. 32–36v.

100. See for example Teixeira da Mota, "A viagem," pp. 564–65.

101. See the *regimento* issued to the captain of the ship *Santiago* that sailed to Sierra Leone and then the Guinea Rivers in 1526 (ibid.).

102. See for example, ANTT, Núcleo Antigo, no. 888, fls. 12–23v. On "assortment bargaining" see Curtin, *Economic Change*, pp. 240–53.

103. ANTT, Núcleo Antigo, no. 888, fls. 12–23v; also Teixeira da Mota, "A viagem," p. 565.

104. Elbl, "The Portuguese Trade with West Africa," vol. 2, pp. 608–11, table 38.

105. Ivana Elbl, "The Horse in Fifteenth-Century Senegambia," *International Journal of African Historical Studies* 28, no. 1 (1991): 85–109. Reprinted in *European Intruders: The European Impact on Behaviour and Customs in Africa, America, and Asia before 1800*, Ser. An Expanding World: The European Impact on World History, ed. John Russell-Wood (Aldershot, England: Ashgate Press, 1998).

106. ANTT, Núcleo Antigo, no. 888, fls. 12–23v.

107. Ibid., fls. 46–47v, 61–62; ANTT, Núcleo Antigo, no. 599, fls. 87, 88.

108. Teixeira da Mota, "A viagem," pp. 573, 569.

109. Elbl, "The Portuguese Trade with West Africa," chap. 6.

110. See for example, Cadamosto, *Viagens*, p. 34; Gomes, *As Viagens*, p. 46.

111. Pacheco Pereira, *Esmeraldo*, pp. 83, 85, 86, 102. According to Fernandes, "the Wolof men or merchants . . . steal from friends just as from enemies" (*O Manuscrito*, p. 69). The Manding were seen as more honest than the Wolof (p. 78).

112. Pacheco Pereira, *Esmeraldo*, p. 102.

113. Ibid., 86.

114. In 1505, for example, the *Oba* received "a caparisoned horse, a necklace of Indian beads, a piece of printed chintz from Cambay, a *marlota* (Moorish short cape with a hood) of orange taffeta and white satin, six linen shirts, and a shirt of blue Indian satin" (Ryder, *Benin and the Europeans*, p. 41).

115. ANTT, Corpo Cronológico, parte I, maço 20, doc. 19.

116. Ibid.

117. Teixeira da Mota and Mauny, "Livre de l'armement," passim and p. 71.

118. AN/TT, Núcleo Antigo, no. 888, fls. 19–36v, 50–51v.

119. Ryder, "An Early Portuguese Trading Voyage, passim and p. 306.

120. Teixeira da Mota, "A viagem," p. 567; Elbl, "The Portuguese Trade with West Africa," vol. 2, table 38.

121. Teixeira da Mota, "A viagem," p. 572.

122. Ibid.; Ryder, "An Early Portuguese Trading Voyage," p. 306; Teixeira da Mota and Many, "Livre de l'armement," p. 71; ANTT, Núcleo Antigo, no. 888, fl. 51.

123. Cadamosto, *Viagens*, pp. 34, 64–65; Gomes, *As Viagens*, pp. 40, 41–42; Eustache de la Fosse, "Viagem de Eustache de la Fosse á costa ocidental de África," in Brásio, *Monumenta Missionaria Africana*, 2d series, vol. 1 (1958), doc. 73, p. 470.

124. Cadamosto, *Viagens*, pp. 34, 43, 64–65; Gomes, *As Viagens*, pp. 40–42; Vogt, *The Portuguese Rule*, pp. 63, 79–80.

125. Teixeira da Mota, "A viagem," p. 572.

126. Rui de Pina, *Crónica de el-Rey D. João. II*, ed. Alberto Martins de Carvalho (Coimbra: Atlântida, 1950), p. 74; Teixeira da Mota and Mauny, "Livre de l'armement," pp. 71, 77; Ryder, "An Early Portuguese Trading Voyage," pp. 305–306.

127. Cadamosto, *Viagens*, p. 34.

128. Barros, *Asia: Primeira Década*, pp. 99, 100–101.

129. See for example Teixeira da Mota, "A viagem," pp. 564, 574.

130. See for example Jelen's business dealing (Barros, *Asia: Primeira Década*, pp. 99–101).

131. Fernandes, *O Manuscrito*, pp. 52, 78.

132. George Brooks, *Landlords and Strangers* (Boulder: Westview Press, 1993), chap. 7, 8, and 9; Fernandes, *O Manuscrito*, pp. 82, 85; Teixeira da Mota, "A viagem," pp. 571–73.

133. See Brásio, *Monumenta Missionaria Africana*, 2d series, vol. 2, doc. 47, pp. 149–50.

134. ANTT, Corpo Cronológico, parte I, maço 13, doc. 18 and maço 20, doc. 19.

135. Teixeira da Mota and Mauny, "Livre de l'armement," passim.

136. Ryder, "An Early Portuguese Trading Voyage," passim. The ship carried too many manillas, which did not sell, and too small a quantity of the cowries that were in demand (Ryder, pp. 326–27).

137. ANTT, Corpo Cronológico, parte II, maço 20, doc. 19.

138. ANTT, Núcleo Antigo, no. 888, fls. 12–23v.

139. Fernandes, *O Manuscrito*, p. 69.

140. Pacheco Pereira, *Esmeraldo*, p. 134: "nesta terra se Resguatam algus escrauos em pouca candidade"[some slaves are available for purchase in this land but in small quantity].

141. ANTT, Corpo Cronológico, parte I, maço 22, doc. 59, in Brásio, *Monumenta Missionaria Africa*, 2d series, vol. 1, doc. 108, pp. 377–92, in particular p. 378.

142. Anne Hilton, *The Kingdom of Kongo* (New York: Oxford University Press, 1985), pp. 58–59.

143. See for example the section "An African Voice of Protest," in Afread J. Andrea and James H. Overfield, *The Human Record: Sources for Global History*, 2d ed. (Boston, Toronto: Houghton Mifflin Company, 1994), pp. 403–405.

144. John K. Thornton, "Early Kongo-Portuguese Relations: A New Interpretation," *History in Africa* 8 (1981): 183–204.

145. Thornton, *Africa and Africans*, p. 96, note 99.

146. Ibid., pp. 96, 108.

147. Ibid., p. 109.
148. Brásio, *Monumenta Missionaria Africana*, 2d series, vol. 1, pp. 167–68, 174–77.
149. ANTT, Leitura Nova, Livro das Ilhas, fl. 81, in Brásio, *Monumenta Missionaria Africana*, 2d series, vol. 1, doc. 48, p.183.
150. ANTT, Leitura Nova, Leis, livro 2, fl. 25, in Brásio, *Monumenta Missionaria Africana*, 2d series, vol. 1, doc. 65, p. 241. A few years later similar considerations influenced the opening of relations with the *Ngola* of Ndongo (Brásio, *Monumenta Missionaria Africana*, 2d series, vol. 1, doc. 126, p. 429).
151. Brásio, *Monumenta Missionaria Africana*, 2d series, vol. 1, doc. 126, p. 429.
152. Segura, a royal inspector, visited São Tomé in 1516 to examine its trade, evaluate its potential, and scrutinize trading practices and adherence to royal edicts. See his report of 15 March 1517 in Brásio, *Monumenta Missionaria Africana*, 1st series, vol. 1, doc. 108, pp. 377–92.
153. Ivana Elbl, "Cross-Cultural Trade and Diplomacy: Portuguese Negotiations in West Africa, 1440–1521," *Journal of World History* 3, no. 2 (1992): 192–93. For a slightly different interpretation see Thornton, "Early Kongo-Portuguese Relations," pp. 183–204.
154. See for example ANTT, Corpo Cronológico, parte I, maço 21, doc. 109, in Brásio, *Monumenta Missionaria Africana*, 2d series, vol. 1, doc. 111, pp. 404–405.

3

Slave Trading and Slave Traders in Rio de Janeiro, 1790–1830*

Manolo G. Florentino

From 1790 to the end of the legal Atlantic slave trade in 1830, Rio de Janeiro saw nearly 700,000 Africans offloaded at its port. This number represents two-thirds of all imports into Brazil during the same time period, with 80 percent arriving from West Central Africa alone (graph 1).[1] If we accept, for the moment, that this was a business operating with high profits, such a large import volume also denotes the existence of an impressive circuit of capital accumulation. My purpose here is to address the question of whether this accumulation took place outside of Brazil, as some would have it, or if it was part and parcel of a powerful nucleus of endogenous accumulation. By concentrating on the slave trade in the port of Rio de Janeiro, I argue that the profits derived therefrom allowed the merchants of souls to occupy the highest echelons of the Brazilian colonial elite. Such a position enabled them to decisively influence the internal and external destinies of the State, which constituted the precondition for their resistance over four decades (1810–1850) against the powerful pressures of the British to end the traffic.

The viability of the slave trade required many things, including the acquisition or lease of ships, the buildup of stocks of trade goods, the payment of wages to sailors, advances to intermediaries on the African side of the commerce, food and water to keep slaves alive during the Middle Passage, and, lastly, insurance on the captives, the items of exchange, and the equipment involved in crossing the Atlantic. All of this translated, in one word, into credit. Slaving required massive and, after 1700, ever-increasing amounts of financing. Between 1808 and

---

*Translated by José C. Curto

Graph 1

Fluctuations in the Number of Africans Disembarked at Rio de Janeiro, 1790–1830[2]

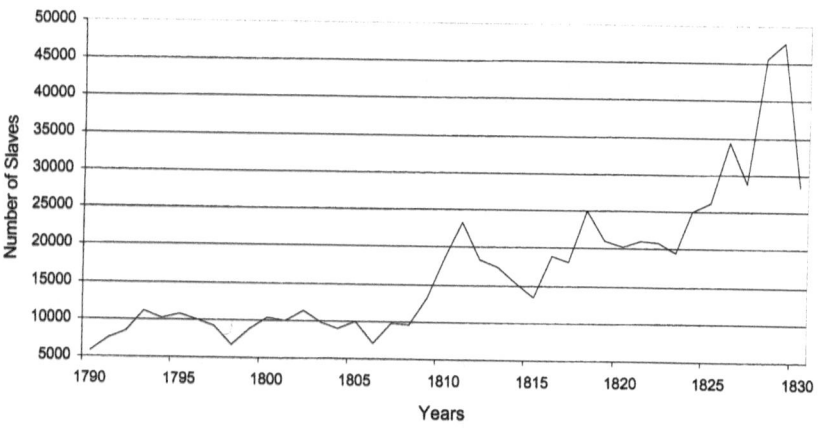

1830, Rio de Janeiro's slave traders were perfectly capable of meeting such financial requirements. Three-quarters of all vessels that connected Brazil's southern emporium to Africa were theirs.[3] Aside from trade goods, the slave traders supplied the dried meats, manioc flour, rice, and cured bacon required by both sailors and slaves, whether during the outbound voyage, the stay along the African coast, or the return trip.[4] Among goods sent to Africa, textiles and cane brandy were present in 86 percent and 94 percent of the cargoes, respectively. Military wares, such as gunpowder, firearms, swords, knives, and bows and arrows, followed closely on 80 percent of ships destined for Africa, while among goods leaving Brazil, sugar accounted for 58 percent, tobacco for 52 percent, and alcohol for 24 percent. A variety of other, less important items, such as iron bars, kitchen and hardwares, glass beads, cotton, and cowrie shells were also regularly found aboard slave vessels outbound from Rio de Janeiro. And in the case of 12 percent of the cargoes, all of which went to Mozambique, the slave ships even transported weights of Spanish silver.[5]

The types of goods used for slaving is of particular interest because they demarcate a specific movement of Rio de Janeiro's trading capital. In the case of textiles, Rio essentially reexported cloths originating in Europe and Goa, which required an initial investment.[6] In the case of textiles, the slave traders had to be connected to the international market, including other areas throughout the Portuguese Empire, to where parts of the profits obtained through the buying and selling of Africans were transferred.

Companies established in Rio de Janeiro insured all the slave vessels, as well as the equipment, the provisions, and the trade goods they transported.[7] The strength and credibility of these local insurance companies is demonstrated by the fact that even British merchants insured their vessels with them, as did Angolan and Mozambican merchants and even Cuban slave traders supplying their market with "Angola/Congo" captives. This thriving, local insurance business drew upon numerous slave traders as accountants and directors of its constituent companies. In 1829, to give but one example, the merchants of souls led 70 percent of these insurance companies.[8] The Rio de Janeiro trading community, as owners of slave vessels, suppliers of stockpiled trade goods, and insurers of slaving ventures, thus itself guaranteed the necessary conditions for the reproduction of its business. It was precisely this privileged role that allowed these merchants to subordinate the African end of the slave trade. The whole process turned around the advancement of trade goods. Traders established along the African coasts received textiles, cane brandy, tobacco, firearms, and gunpowder on consignment from the captains of recently arrived vessels, thereby indebting themselves with Rio's slaving capital. Debts with local authorities, the holders of slave contracts, or even private suppliers were paid through bills of exchange passed and acquitted by merchants in Rio de Janeiro. During the eighteenth century, these bills or notes of debt even came to circulate as specie in Benguela.[9]

Correspondence between slave traders in Brazil and their counterparts in Africa clearly shows that the basic mechanism for the subordination of Angola to Brazil lay in the consignment of trade goods.[10] The current accounts best clarify such subordination.[11] The existence of current accounts is, by itself, sufficient to characterize the market as structurally restricted; not only were relations between economic agents personal, but competition was minimal since individuals were associated with one another. The sources suggest a repetitive pattern, with the Rio slave trader appearing as the holder of significantly high sums destined to finance slaving expeditions, constantly forwarding goods for the acquisition of slaves, and subsequently paying off third parties. On the African side, the slaves were forwarded to Brazil as compensation for the consigned goods. The repetition over time of this pattern entangled merchants in Africa in a web of debt, which, by the first decade of the 1800s, attained considerable proportions. The logical outcome was nearly always the insolvency of the debtor, decreed whenever the creditor desired to do so.

Securing high profits was the illusion that moved slave merchants. Yet, as soon as a slaving venture began to be organized, fear also overtook their dreams. They knew well that more than half of the slaves could die while still on African soil. Joseph Miller has calculated that one out of every twenty slaves who survived the trek from the place of capture inland to the coast either fled or, if extremely sick, was simply abandoned at the port of embarkation.[12] Nothing, however, equaled the risks of the Atlantic crossing. While at sea, slaves could be lost to pirates or shipwrecks.[13] But it was other types of losses that affected more directly the slave merchants of Rio de Janeiro. During the Middle Passage, many slaves died as a result of sickness, the lack of foodstuffs and drinking water, ill treatment, tight-packing, and the dread that debilitated body and soul through fear. Slave mortality at sea varied from vessel to vessel. On some, very few slaves died. But on others, mortality eliminated half of their human merchandise. There are even cases of slave vessels reaching Brazil without a single slave alive.[14]

As graph 2 shows, mortality for slaves embarked along the Indian Ocean was two to three times greater than among captives exported from West Central Africa. Such a large differential is explained by the length of the sea voyage: slavers with cargoes from Angola required thirty-three to forty-three days to reach Rio de Janeiro, while those from Mozambique took up to seventy-six days. Over time, slave mortality rates at sea decreased considerably. Between the end of the eighteenth century and the 1820s, the average time to reach Rio de Janeiro declined by 15 percent from the West Central African coast and by 20 percent for the coast of Mozambique. It is quite possible that increased speed in the crossing reduced mortality, which was related to the increased use of smaller vessels that were usually quicker. Still, some 10 percent of the African slaves destined for Brazil perished while on the high seas.[15] In short, the risk of losing slaves and in many cases the vessels themselves was a constant danger that everyone had to confront. The responses of slave merchants, however, depended upon the ability to absorb significant financial losses. Wealthier individuals, especially those who specialized in the business of slaving, were thus at less risk, even though ruin was always possible.[16]

Between 1811 and 1830, some 279 firms composed of Rio slave merchants were responsible for a total of 1,181 slaving ventures. Only 5 percent of these firms operated throughout the whole period, financing one or more slaving voyages per year. Nevertheless, they were responsible for 43 percent of the ventures. These specialized slave merchants thus constituted an oligopoly. There was also a group of companies, about 9 percent of all firms, which, for a variety of reasons, financed a slaving venture every two or three years. These firms were responsible for about 20 percent of the 1,181 expeditions. There were, finally, other entrepreneurs who participated only sporadically in the Atlantic slave trade. Accounting for 86 percent of the total number of firms, they organized but one slaving venture every four or more years and were responsible for mounting 33 percent of all voyages to Africa. This was an adventurous group of entrepreneurs, nonspecialized economic agents who merely speculated in the slave trade.[17]

The commerce in human beings was highly concentrated. It is obvious that the buying or renting of ships outfitted with specialized crews and equipment, foodstuffs, and, most important, goods for trade turned slaving voyages into

Graph 2

Regional Fluctuations in Slave Mortality on Ships Trading to Rio de Janeiro (Mortality per Thousand), 1795–1830[18]

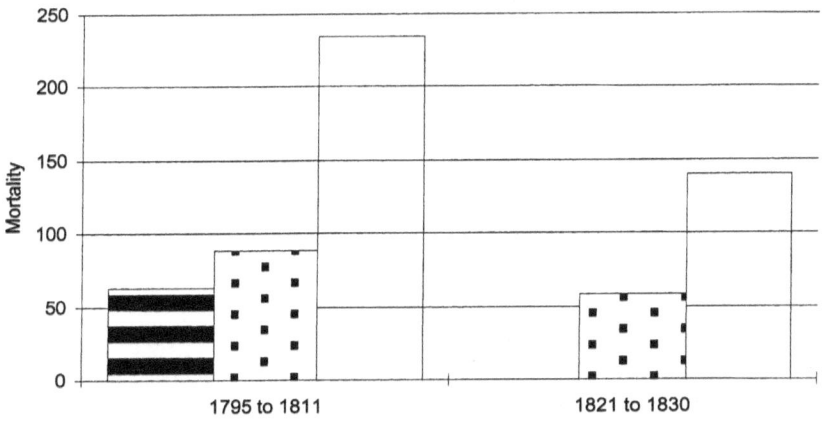

■ West Africa ▨ West Central Africa □ Eastern Africa

extremely expensive affairs. Thus, while a slaving vessel and its equipment could reach a nominal cost of 15,199$820 *réis*, as was the case of the *Voador* in 1814, and the cost of trade goods and foodstuffs alone could reach 26,600$000 *réis*, as was the case with the *Andorinha* in 1812, expenditures to cover commissions, import and export taxes, wages, and general costs increased the overall amount further still.[19] Recognizing how risky it was to buy and sell human beings allows a better understanding of why only a few entrepreneurs possessed sufficient capital to become the wholesale merchants of souls. The fact that they continuously engaged in this trade, organizing on average one or more expeditions per year, further reveals professional specialization on the part of these merchants. Since they tended to centralize their business in a single port on both sides of the Atlantic, they were also geographically specialized.[20] The large-scale merchants possessed profound economic, social, cultural, and especially, political influence in the port communities and with local traders in both Brazil and Africa.

The slave trade, costly as it was and consequently economically selective, was a business where the speculator nevertheless assumed a central role. Even though almost 90 percent of slave traders in Rio de Janeiro engaged in slaving irregularly, these speculators were still responsible for one-third of the ventures destined for Africa. This high involvement clearly points to their importance in supplying Brazil's slave labor requirements. The speculators only periodically engaged in the slave trade, as urban merchants who at given moments sought higher profits through the sale of human beings but otherwise left the trade to others. Not a few had been captains of slaving vessels who, in that crucial role, sustained the links between Brazil and the merchants in Africa, and some acquired the knowledge, experience, and means to mount their own trading ventures and thus turn themselves into slave traders.

The profits secured from this business seem, at first glance, to have depended exclusively on the price differentials of the commodities between points of purchase and of sale. Here, the Brazilian slave traders held a substantial advantage since the slave was a product of pure and simple violence embodied in capture and hence initially had an extremely low value. This explains why slave merchants, even when selling at a low price in Brazil, could nonetheless realize significant profits. Slave traders, as in the case of other merchants, were not driven by a quest for "reasonable" profits but rather hoped to get the highest possible return.

To understand the options available, it should be recognized that even the most impoverished of proprietors in Brazil might well own at least one captive.[21] During the era of the slave trade, poor peasants, urban artisans, fishermen, and even some slaves were owners of human merchandise, which suggests prices generally were not exorbitant. The profitability of slaving expeditions was fundamentally based on the high markup in price of Africans sold in Brazil. Slave traders could force their commercial agents in Africa to buy at low prices because of the credit that they gave. Through their control of credit, the Rio merchants were able to secure high rates of return, and they maximized this advantage by importing the largest number of slaves possible. In short, Brazilian slave traders augmented their returns by pressuring suppliers in Africa to lower prices and thereby increase price differentials between points of purchase and of sale.

After almost two decades of relative stability, the arrival of the Portuguese Court in Brazil in 1808 and the liberalization of commerce between Portuguese colonial port towns greatly stimulated the slave trade to Rio de Janeiro. While an average of 9,200 slaves were imported annually between 1790 and 1808, this number increased to more than 13,000 African slaves in 1809, almost 19,000 in 1810, and 22,500 in 1811. By 1812, the market had become saturated, leading to an appreciable decline until 1815. Recovery set in during the following three years. Slave imports thereafter remained stable until 1825, the only exception being 1823 due to trepidation over the independence of Brazil. As table 1 indicates, the average prices of slaves in Rio de Janeiro and in West Central Africa moved in tandem. As demand rose, pushing prices up in Rio, a similar phenomenon occurred in Luanda, whereas if demand fell, so did prices on both sides of the Atlantic.

During 1810–1812 fewer Africans were brought to Rio, which produced a chain reaction across the south Atlantic. This decline was reflected in prices; the

Table 1
Average Prices of Enslaved Africans in Luanda and Rio de Janeiro, 1810–1820[22]

Year	Slave Imports at Rio de Janeiro	Slave Exports from Luanda to Rio de Janeiro	Average Slave Prices, in *réis*, Rio de Janeiro (A)	Average Slave Prices, in *réis*, Luanda (B)	Difference between (A) and (B)
1808	9,602	8,588	—	67$000	—
1809	13,171	7,331	—	72$000	—
1810	18,677	8,837	119$000	70$000	+49$000
1811	22,520	9,098	—	70$000	—
1812	18,270	6,891	104$000	69$000	+35$000
1813	17,280	6,126	—	75$000	—
1814	15,300	—	—	—	—
1815	13,330	7,370	109$000	70$000	+39$000
1816	18,140	6,115	—	68$000	—
1817	17,670	5,425	132$000	75$000	+57$000
1818	24,500	4,645	—	75$000	—
1819	20,800	4,873	—	75$000	—
1820	21,140	8,215	152$000	75$000	+77$000

average price of slaves imported at Rio fell from 119$000 to 104$000 *réis*, while at Luanda the drop in prices was from 70$000 to 69$000 *réis*. Such a decline resulted in fewer slaves sent to Brazil; the number dropped from 8,000 to 6,891. Imports fell to 13,330 in 1815, their lowest level since the liberalization of commerce between Portuguese colonial ports in 1808. The number of slaves coming from Luanda, paradoxically, actually increased in 1815 because the intermittent slave traders who speculated in the slave trade withdrew, leaving the trade more concentrated in the hands of the big merchants. The slave trade then came to be dominated by the real merchants, here designated as traditional, since they were the ones continuously engaged in trading slaves. Always attentive to the fluctuations of a market they understood well, these traditional merchants were the first to realize that 1815 announced the end of a saturated market. Behind the slave prices of that year, slightly higher than during the previous three years, they could hear the ocean calling. The time was ripe to acquire even more souls in Africa.

Price fluctuations in the demand and the supply sectors, although always moving in the same direction, nonetheless resulted from totally distinct rhythms specific to Brazil and Africa, respectively. Throughout the 1810s, the difference between the highest and lowest nominal slave prices reached 46 percent in Rio de Janeiro and less than 12 percent in Luanda. While the former denotes brisk variation, the latter represents relative stability. It is important to note that in the midst of the export boom at Luanda after 1815, the median cost of slaves there remained constant at 75$000 *réis*.

Such differing rhythms only confirm one of the strategies used by the large-scale slave traders to increase their profits, subordinating their intermediaries in Africa through indebtedness. In their position as creditors, the Rio slave traders had enough power to resist pressures to pay higher prices for slaves. In sum, the strategy of the entrepreneurs of Rio was to control prices, or at least to inhibit rising prices. Once successful in this strategy, the profitability of the slaving venture came to lie more in augmenting the number of slaves to be acquired and less in the difference between prices at the point of purchase and at their eventual sale across the Atlantic. The key to understanding the profitability of the commerce in souls is the initial investment required to obtain the trading goods whose value defined the quantity of slaves to be purchased.

There were other mechanisms that increased the profitability of the slave trade, as demonstrated in table 2, which shows the profit levels secured by fourteen slave-trading ventures at Luanda, Benguela, and Mozambique in 1812, all originating in Rio de Janeiro. During this particular year, we know that the average price of an African slave in the Rio market was 104$000 *réis*; the median cost of these slaves in Luanda was 69$000 *réis*, compared with 50$000 *réis* in Benguela, and 40$000 *réis* in the island of Mozambique. We could argue from these data that profits increased in proportion to declining prices in the areas of slave purchases. The highest profits were obtained by trading at Benguela and Mozambique, where slave prices were far lower than at Luanda. As the third column of table 2 shows, the average cargo at Benguela and Mozambique comprised 410 slaves, much less than the 485 median per cargo of vessels at Luanda. Because of the higher prices at Luanda, it could be argued that traders obtaining slaves at Luanda compensated for higher slave prices by increasing the number of African slaves purchased. Even so, slaves from Benguela and Mozambique usually realized high profit levels, while those purchased at Luanda almost all became losses.

This paradox is explained through an analysis of table 2, which shows an inverse correlation between mortality rates during the Middle Passage and profits obtained from any given slaving venture; that is, higher mortality rates at sea resulted in lower profits and, conversely, lower Middle Passage mortality rates led to higher net profit margins. The importance of the mortality factor is highlighted when it is realized that however elastic the price of slaves, all slaving ventures would have been profitable if no slaves had died in the passage.

A consideration of Middle Passage mortality rates was fundamental to the logic of the slave traders. Such logic was part of a particular economic calculation based on augmenting profits by increasing the number of slaves aboard any given vessel. Given the physical limitations of ships, this was not without risk. Nevertheless, raising the number of slaves transported merely meant investing

Table 2
Estimated Net Profits of Some
Slaving Ventures in 1812[23]

Ship	Port of Purchase in Africa	Number of Slaves Acquired	Total Investment	Percentage of Slaves Dead	Number of Slaves Sold in Rio de Janiero	Earnings from Slave Sales	Net Profit (%)
Mercúrio	Benguela	404	27:270$000	5.0	384	39:936$000	+46.4
Feliz Dia	Mozambique	235	12:690$000	5.1	223	23:192$000	+82.8
S. J. Americano	Benguela	547	36:922$000	5.7	516	53:664$000	+45.3
Carolina do Sul	Benguela	571	38:542$500	6.1	536	55:744$000	+44.6
Providente	Inhambane	247	13:338$000	7.3	229	23:816$000	+78.6
N. S. Conceição	Luanda	478	44:525$700	7.9	440	45:760$000	+2.8
Canoa	Luanda	534	49:742$100	10.9	476	49:504$000	–0.5
M. Dafne	Luanda	572	53:281$800	11.5	506	52:624$000	–1.2
Fiança	Luanda	473	44:059$950	12.5	414	43:056$000	–2.3
Flor do Mar	Luanda	462	43:035$300	12.6	404	42:016$000	–2.4
Feliz Indiana	Luanda	462	43:035$300	12.6	404	42:016$000	–2.4
Guadalupe	Benguela	458	30:915$000	15.9	385	40:040$000	+29.5
Júlia	Luanda	500	46:575$000	16.0	420	43:680$000	–6.2
Protector	Luanda	397	36:980$550	38.0	246	25:584$000	–30.8

more in outfitting vessels with trade goods and covering the small costs associated with sustaining extra captives during the Middle Passage.

There were risks associated with such a strategy during the last leg of the slave trade. We know that Rio slave imports escalated significantly between 1827 and 1830. Since a similar upward trend took place in slave prices, then it may be that the differential between purchase and sale was far higher than during 1822–1826. As table 3 demonstrates, slave vessels returning from ports in the Atlantic and Indian Oceans experienced different mortality rates, which can be compared by region of embarkation in each of these two periods. The data show that Rio slave traders operating in the Atlantic and Indian Oceans sought to increase their profit margins by augmenting the absolute number of slave imports. This is evident in the rise in the average number of slaves purchased in each slaving venture. As is clear, moreover, increased numbers of slaves per voyage hardly affected the rate of slave mortality during the Middle Passage. Estimating the risk of losing slaves was part of the calculation, and increasing the number of slaves per voyage had little impact on losses in transit and hence could raise the profitability of slaving ventures. Risks were not taken blindly. Rather, slave traders sought to increase the total number of slaves purchased without also increasing onboard mortality rates.

The key to understanding the profitability of the slave trade lay in determining the initial investment to outfit slaving vessels with the goods required for

Table 3
Fluctuations in the Mortality Rates (per thousand) of the Slave Trade to Rio de Janeiro, 1822–1830[24]

Region of Origin	1822–1826				1827–1830			
	Number of Outbound Ships	Number of Slaves Exported	Mortality Rates	Average Number of Slaves per Ship	Number of Outbound Ships	Number of Slaves Exported	Mortality rates	Average Number of Slaves per Ship
Congo and Angola	241	90,998	56	378	266	104,655	54	530
Eastern Africa	60	31,823	147	393	67	39,584	140	591

trade (which set the volume of slave purchases) and the amount needed to purchase the consumables to sustain slaves during oceanic transit (which affected mortality rates). Some slave traders were overly frugal in this calculation, subsequently losing many slaves and thereby ruining themselves. Confronted with these requirements, however, slave traders with a tradition of operating in the Atlantic circuit held considerable advantages over intermittent participants. In maintaining a closer relationship with their intermediaries in Africa, they could obtain slaves in better health and at lower prices, for whom they then demanded greater sums in the market of Rio de Janeiro. At the same time, possessing larger financial resources, they were more likely to purchase larger numbers of slaves because they had the resources to sustain them.

In seeking to diminish costs and, simultaneously, the loss of slaves in transit, they instructed their captains to buy slaves as fast as possible so that the Middle Passage could be undertaken with as much speed as possible. It is consequently not a coincidence that the most prominent Rio slave traders achieved the lowest mortality rates of the Atlantic slave trade, operating at 6.5 percent losses, compared to standard losses in maritime transit of 10 percent.

The average net profits of the Brazilian slave traders depended upon the value of the trade goods required to purchase slaves, as well as other items whose cost had to be assumed by slave traders. These costs included the foodstuffs that sustained the slaves onboard and the ship crews, the wear and tear of equipment, the salaries of the sailors, import-export taxes, and other expenses. By estimating the cost of these items and subtracting these overheads from the value of slave sales in Rio, it is possible to determine the median net profit levels in the Luanda-Rio trade. Profits varied significantly in the decade 1810–1820; in 1810, profits can be calculated at a level of 16 percent, falling to a mere 3 percent in 1812 and 6 percent in 1815, before increasing dramatically to 23 percent in 1817 and 44 percent in 1820. During this decade, the average return margin over capital invested amounted to roughly 19 percent.

Since Luanda was the principal center supplying slaves to Brazil in the early nineteenth century, the median profitability level of 19 percent suggests that the Brazilian slave trade as a whole was more profitable than that of any other national slave trade. Brazilian profits appear larger, for example, than the slave trade of the British, whose profitability has been calculated at 9.5 percent, the French (10 percent), or the Dutch (2.9 percent). Profit margins also appear to have been greater than the trade in Europe during the ancien régime, whose profitability was around 5 percent. Moreover, the median net profits of the Brazilian slave trade were higher than returns on capital invested in large slave plantations in Rio de Janeiro, Bahia, and even certain regions of the Caribbean, where profitability has been estimated at between 5 percent and 10 percent. For the Rio merchants who were involved in trade, the Brazilian slave trade was a veritable El Dorado.[25]

Rio's slave trade was marked by rhythms of profitability that varied greatly. On average, profits over initial investments ranged from 3 percent to 44 percent. Such a spread represents these frenetic changes, which explain not only the strong presence of nonspecialized traders during phases of expansion, but also their immediate withdrawal during times of crisis. All in all, rhythms as violent as these denote a market that was structurally both unstable and weak, not to mention dangerous per se. As we shall see below, such a situation turned the traditional slave trader, the typical late 1700s and early 1800s merchant of human beings, into first and foremost an entrepreneur with investments in various sectors.

During the first half of the nineteenth century, two or three out of every ten prominent merchants in Rio de Janeiro, the so-called *homens de negócio de loja aberta* (*varejistas*) or *de sobrado* (*atacadistas*), and the lenders established in the principal streets of the city's historical center were linked to the slave trade. Slave traders also represented almost 10 percent of those merchants who, through coastal maritime commerce, supplied Rio de Janeiro. They owned one out of every ten ships that, laden with consumables such as dried meat, rice, wheat, maize, beans, and cane brandy, arrived at Guanabara Bay from ports within the region or from as far away as Bahia, Rio Grande do Sul, and Santa Catarina.[26]

Although representing only something like 10 percent of the overall number of maritime exporters, the slave traders controlled almost one-third of all vessels with cargoes heading for Europe, Asia, and other parts of the Americas. In the import trade, slave traders dominated between one-fifth and one-third of commerce from ports in Portugal and in Asia. At only slightly lower levels, they dominated commercial exchange with European ports outside Portugal, not to mention Rio de la Plata. The ports in Portugal, Goa, and Macau were centers of Brazilian slave-trading operations; from these ports came a large portion of the goods required to acquire slaves in Africa, particularly fine textiles.[27] Besides the purchase and sale of African slaves, the slave traders were involved in diversified commercial exchanges that supplied internal and external markets. Their businesses took on a truly international profile.

The slave traders were well established in Rio de Janeiro before the Portuguese Court moved there in 1808. At least some of the most prominent of Rio's slave traders operating after 1808 were already dealing in human beings during the eighteenth century. One example confirms the pattern. In 1799 the Portuguese Crown asked the viceroy of Brazil, the Conde de Rezende, to assemble a list of the wealthiest men in Rio de Janeiro. The objective was to create a fund for agricultural development. The viceroy compiled a list of thirty-six names of men endowed with "great capital," all prominent merchants. However, these merchants were opposed to the establishment of such a fund because as lenders they already promoted the development of agricultural activities. Their opposition to the control of the colonial political economy from Lisbon demonstrates the extent of their power. Moreover, by 1811, it is clear that eight of the most affluent merchants were directly or indirectly involved in the commerce of souls.[28] In Rio de Janeiro, the slave-trading hierarchy was clearly embedded in the mercantile elite.

What was the origin of the capital invested in the commerce in human beings, and what was the destination of the profits reaped by the slave traders? To answer these questions, it is necessary to isolate the slave traders in the market, which in turn requires establishing the general profile of this market during the first half of the nineteenth century. The trend in accumulation of the great fortunes in Rio de Janeiro was concentration. Almost half of individuals who left some assets when they died were not particularly well off and collectively accounted for only about 5 percent of the total sum of all inventoried values recorded in wills. The wealthy merchants, on the other hand, never accounted for more than 14 percent of those whose wills have been inventoried, but they accounted for three-quarters of the total value of inventoried wealth (see graph 3).

Hence it is clear that the wealthy merchant elite dominated the economy. In the late eighteenth and early nineteenth centuries, they accounted for 95 percent of all credit transactions, owned almost three-quarters of urban buildings and rural assets, held 70 percent of the currency in circulation, and possessed slightly more than half of all slaves.[29] They virtually monopolized the credit system, urban housing, land, money in circulation, and the black labor force. This elite drove an economy profoundly marked by mercantile forms of capital accumulation, which, it should be noted, was the motor force of economic growth. Because of the high investment required for slaving ventures, the merchants of souls were *negociantes de grosso trato*, that is, merchants of considerable means.

Postmortem inventories show the composition of these fortunes. As can be seen in graph 4, the rising volume of investments in urban buildings from 1800 to 1840 suggests that the process of urbanization was intense. The relatively small amounts of cash in these inventories reflects a situation in which there was relatively low levels of specie in circulation, while, at the same time, jewels and precious metals appear to have been a principal means of hoarding wealth. These data suggest that this was a market with few investment options for those with available resources. Commercial activities and especially loans registered in current accounts, letters of credit, and personal credit lines represented on average one-fourth of wealth. In such a market, commercial exchanges were mixed with interest payments and with usury. While nearly 15 percent of the wealth in these inventories was in rural assets and hence a connection with agrarianism and slavery, mercantile capital dominted the society and economy of Rio de Janeiro.

Some of the postmortem inventories illustrate the investments in the slave trade (see table 4). The trends exhibited by the elite of Rio de Janeiro in general are evident. The participation of the slave traders in the urbanization of Rio was extensive, with a substantial portion of their fortunes invested in urban buildings.

Graph 3
***Distribution (%) of the Wealth between the Richest and the Poorest of the Inventoried of Rio de Janeiro (Urban and Rural Areas), 1790–1835*[30]**

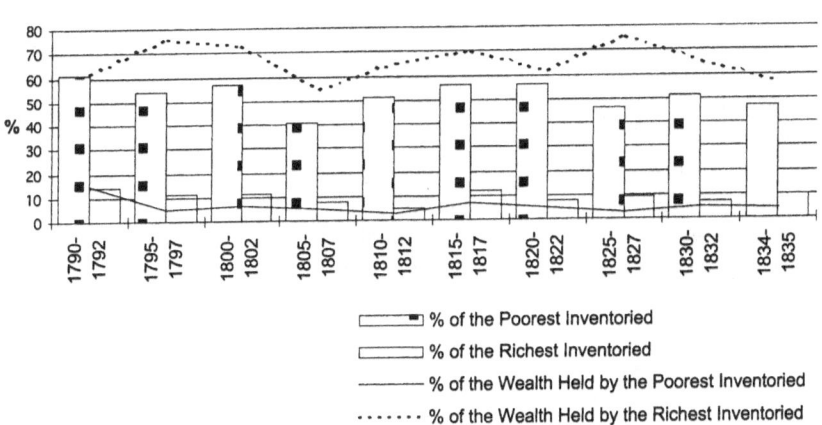

Graph 4
Average Distribution (%) of Economic Activities and Wealth in Postmortem Inventories of Proprietors, Rio de Janeiro, 1800–1840[31]

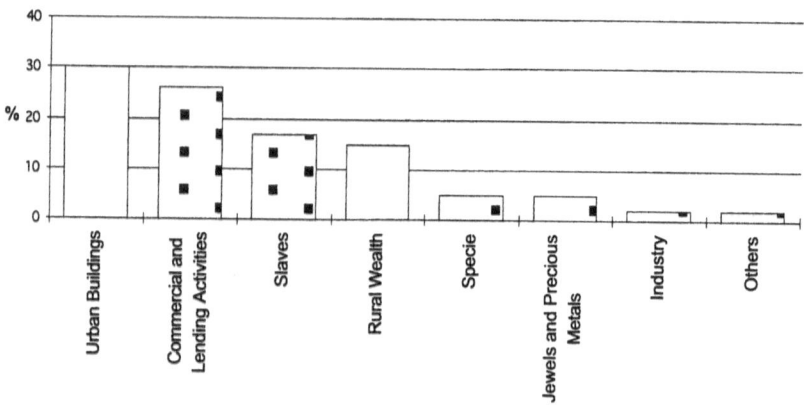

At the same time, investments in jewels and precious metals were greater than cash values, denoting a certain tendency toward hoarding, as well as the fragility of the circulation of cash. Still, the larger portion of fortunes was allocated to commercial and credit activities, although investments in the region's agricultural sector, stock market shares, and insurance policies were also appreciable. Hence is it almost impossible to isolate trade in African slaves from other mercantile activities.[32] Diversified forms of investment, even though some sectors stand out, characterized maritime trade, and slave traders (especially the more prominent ones) invested in various sectors and controlled networks of credit that spread throughout Brazil and beyond. It should be noted that none of the merchants inventoried in table 4 registered a deficit. Elias Antônio Lopes, for example, was involved in business spreading from Rio de Janeiro, Santa Catarina, Bahia, and Pernambuco in Brazil to Lisbon, Porto, London, Hamburg, and Amsterdam, as well as Goa, Luanda, Benguela, and Mozambique.[33]

Investments were both multiple and spread throughout various sectors. Operating within a market that offered few options, the slave-trading entrepreneurs, like the Brazilian mercantile elite in general, sought to diversify their investments not only to guarantee the security of their investments because this was, after all, an unstable market situation by definition, but also to secure the highest possible levels of return. Successful in their undertakings, the prominent slave traders ended up holding a large proportion of the liquidity of the slavocratic economy. They controlled not only the physical replenishment of the slave population but also all the lucrative sectors of the economy.

Florentino: Slave Trading and Slave Traders in Rio de Janeiro 71

Table 4
Percentages of Economic Activities and Wealth in Postmortem Inventories of Slave Traders Established in the City of Rio de Janeiro[34]

Slave Traders	Year	Urban Buildings	Trade	Loans	Shares and Policies	Industrial Activities	Rural Holdings	Slaves	Jewels and Precious Metals	Cash	Other	Total Wealth (1000 réis)
José Francisco do Amaral	1812	37.2	8.3	33.4	—	—	8.6	5.0	0.4	0.1	3.1	153.9
Elias Antônio Lopes	1815	1.3	37.4	40.6	0.9	—	2.8	4.5	2.5	0.1	9.9	235.9
Gertrudes Pedra Leão	1820	—	35.1	15.0	1.3	—	—	4.1	23.0	—	21.5	96.8
João Gomes Barrozo	1829	21.5	19.7	26.9	5.7	—	13.3	7.2	2.6	0.7	2.4	926.7
Leonarda Maria Velho da Silva	1825	18.6	a	a	a	—	33.9	0.9	1.5	—	17.9	285.5
Francisco José Guimarães	1838	40.6	—	48.6	1.5	—	1.9	1.4	—	6.0	231.1	
José Ferreira da Rocha	1820	0.3	7.4	60.2	—	—	10.6	1.6	2.2	17.7	3 6 . 9	
Manoel José Ribeiro Antônio	1831	68.8	—	2.2	—	—	—	3.7	0.1	—	25.4	25.5
José Teixeira	1824	—	—	58.6	—	—	14.3	15.8	1.3	—	10.0	14.1
José Lopes Bastos	1830	26.0	—	—	—	—	38.9	0.7	—	34.4	6.9	

A closer look at the market of Rio de Janeiro during the first half of the nineteenth century indicates that urban real estate attracted most investors and accounted for a large portion of transacted values. Speculation in land, including small rural properties on the outskirts of the city as well as buildings in the center, and the rents from these investements, account for a significant proportion of the economic life of the mercantile community. The elite was preoccupied with commerce and urban real estate rather than agriculture and industry, which suggests that rental, speculative, and mercantile activities were more profitable than truly productive economic activities.[35] Mercantile capital dominated Rio's economy. The rhythms of the market were determined by its operations and the investments that prominent merchants frequently returned to the market under various forms, with rents predominating. Thus the fortunes held by slave traders mirrored the wealth of the merchant elite in general.

As graph 5 shows, the investments of merchants shifted depending upon involvement in the slave trade. The profile of purchases by category of individuals before, during, and after being active in the profession of slave traders reveals that no less than 40 percent of the purchases by subsequent slave traders took place within the urban real estate sector. The second major area of initial capital accumulation was the maritime trade, which centralized one-third of the operations and values inventoried. Other sectors of investment included agriculture and commerce. In general terms, we see that the resource accumulation outlined by this graph conforms even closer to the structural profile of the Rio market. Aggregating the sectors, we find that, according to the hegemony of merchant capital in the general reproduction of the economy, more than 80 percent

Graph 5
Profile of the Purchases by Slave Traders in Rio de Janeiro Before, During, and After Dealing in Africans, 1811–1839[36]

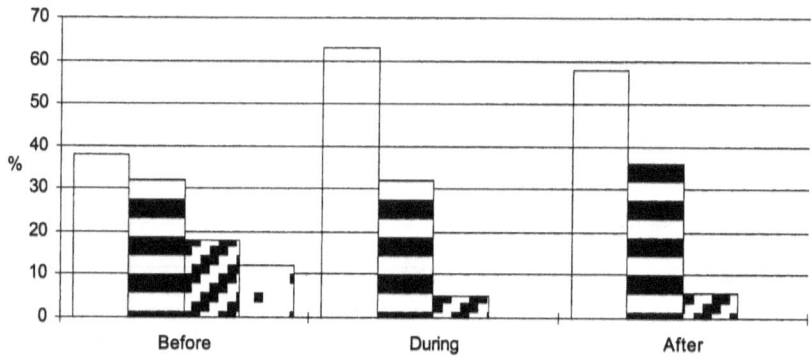

□ Urban Real Estate Sector ■ Ships ■ Rural Real Estate Sector □ Overland Commerce

of the resources invested by future slave traders were directly or indirectly tied to commercial (maritime and terrestrial), speculative, or rental activities (urban real estate). On the other hand, as in the global market, we detect the predominance of wealth accumulation based on the acquisition of urban real estate; but at the same time, given the maritime nature of the slave trade, it should not be surprising to see a large number of the future dealers in human beings also operating in the coastal maritime trade sector. Wealth derived from commerce, speculation, and rents was closely tied to the economic life of the slave trade.

Moving our analysis to the investment profile of the slave traders while operating as such, the results are once again hardly surprising: they reveal the most complete congruency between the logic of the slave-trading entrepreneur and the noncapitalist economy of Rio de Janeiro. At the same time that these slave traders operated in reproducing the business in human beings, they not only diversified their investments but also did so following the patterns of the more ample market.

As one could expect, the data found in graph 5 allow us to conclude that the reinfusion of slaving profits back into the commerce of souls was significant. The purchase of vessels represents about one-third of acquisitions by the slave traders. However, the reinvestment of slaving profits into subsequent ventures in human beings was surely much higher, since the sources upon which graph 5 is based do not inform on the investments required to accumulate the items of exchange necessary for slave trading. In any case, while the portion of investments devoted to acquiring urban real estate assets was highly significant, that directed to the acquisition of land and rural assets was quite small. What is important here, in relation to the returns derived from slaving, is the continuation of investment patterns specific to this market; that is, the search for endogenous spheres of commodity circulation and speculative and rental activities as drainage valves for the dividends obtained from the commerce in human beings.

This pattern maintained itself until after the Atlantic slave trade was legally banned in 1830. We are thus facing extensive proof of a permanent and specific form of macroeconomic calculation of which the slave-trading entrepreneur is a typical example, for he is present in the initial capital accumulation of the commerce in souls and continues into the period following its official end. The wealth obtained from the urban real estate market supported the slave trade and, therein "beefed up," returned to the purchase of further buildings, houses, and other real estate in Rio.

The relationships of the slave traders, over and beyond constituting economic networks, spread into the personal and affective realms, links that again reveal the weight of an archaic structure. The administration of such a business was in many ways familial. Participating in the slave trade were families, among others, such as those of Gomes Barrozo (João Gomes Barrozo, Antônio Gomes Barrozo, and Diogo Gomes Barrozo), Ferreira (Joaquim Antônio Ferreira and João Antônio Ferreira), Rocha (Francisco José da Rocha and Joaquim José da Rocha, nephew), Pereira de Almeida (Joaquim Pereira de Almeida, João Rodrigues Pereira de Almeida, and José Rodrigues Pereira de Almeida) and Velho da Silva (Amaro Velho da Silva and Leonarda Maria Velho da Silva). Of the 279 firms responsible for 1,181 slaving ventures between 1811 and 1830, there were only 14 whose partners were relatives. Although this figure does not seem significant, its larger import becomes more evident when we consider that of the 16 largest firms responsible for nearly half of the slaving ventures between Rio de Janeiro and Africa, no less than 8 were made up of partners related to one another. Of the 559 ventures mounted by this slave trading elite, moreover, entrepreneurial family groups accounted for 324, or 60 percent of the total.[37] To address the requirements of significant, initial investment for slaving purposes, the nondispersal of wealth and, lastly, a market where operations were primarily based upon mutual trust, large business enterprises were principally made up of relatives: brothers such as the Gomes Barrosos; or father, mother, and son like the Velho da Silvas. Within such a small circuit, marriage also functioned as a mechanism to concentrate resources, founding great slave trading fortunes, as in the case of Manoel Guedes Pinto, wedded to a daughter of the matriarch of the

Velho da Silvas.[38] Overall, the personal structure of the slaving business, at least in the case of the major players, led them to draw more upon mutual trust than upon an impersonal capitalist rationale, which created strong ties between the slave traders.[39]

The slave-trading entrepreneur, however, did not increase his range of action and fortune simply through matrimonial and affective alliances. He was also profoundly linked to the State, occupying positions of great importance from which to consolidate his prestige within the high bureaucracy and obtain privileges such as the *arrematações de impostos* (auctioning of taxes) or *sesmarias* (distribution of uncultivated/abandoned lands). His enormous capacity to accumulate financial resources, added to his intimacy with the power structure (the royal family, and especially through membership in the Order of Christ), allowed the slave trader not only to secure the best economic opportunities, but also to confront the key question of the time—the problem created by British pressure to end the slave trade.

Let us look at a few examples. João Rodrigues Pereira de Almeida was from the first decade of the 1800s a *deputado* or member of the Royal Board of Trade and received in May of 1810 the *comenda* or commendation of the Order of Christ. José Luis Alves, in turn, was public attorney of the Municipal Council of Rio de Janeiro and received the Habit of the Order of Christ in September of 1808, along with another slave trader, Joaquim Ribeiro de Almeida, a lieutenant colonel attached to the city's first infantry regiment. The case of the Gomes Barrozo family is, in this respect, exemplary. João Gomes Barrozo received the Habit of the Order of Christ in May of 1808 (one year before Diogo Gomes Barrozo) and had, upon his death in 1829, risen to the position of *comendador* or commander. Coronel Antônio Gomes Barrozo became *comendador* of the same order in October of 1810, while his son later received from Dom João VI the position of *Alcaidaria-Mor* (responsible for policing the city) of Vila de Itaguai. Geraldo Carneiro Belens, grandson through the maternal side of the slave trader Braz Carneiro Leão, was endowed with the Habit, and soon thereafter, the *comenda* of the Order of Christ. This quick ascension was justified as His Royal Highness recognized the fact that Belens had not only "contributed a most extraordinary number of shares for the Bank of Brazil," but that "Casa de Carneiro, Viúva e Filhos was one the most distinguished" businesses in colonial trade.[40]

Another example comes from Amaro Velho da Silva who, during the 1820s, was *viador* (messenger) of His Majesty, *Alcaide–Mor* (official responsible for policing) and Lord-proprietor of Vila Nova de São José, *comendador* of the Order of Christ and of the Order of Nossa Senhora da Conceição, and *deputado* of the Royal Board of Trade. All of his sisters were married to *comendadores*, councillors, and senior magistrates of the High Court; his mother, the Baroness of Macaé, was also a "dame of her Majesty the Empress," or a lady-in-waiting. Manoel Gonçalves de Carvalho, in turn, obtained the Habit of the Order of Christ in September of 1810. In soliciting such a privilege, this self-identified prominent merchant affirmed having contributed financially to the "emergencies of the State, providing what was possible for the *nau* or large ship *Rainha* during the time of Count de Arcádia, the establishment of the *Real Fábrica de Pólvora* [Royal Gunpowder Factory] and the National Bank," as well as "having sent the most vessels under his own consignment and interest to Portugal and the first to have forwarded a ship from Rio de Janeiro to English America, thereby nurturing a trade beneficial to the Royal Treasury through the import-export taxes resulting therefrom."[41]

Finally, we have the well-documented case of Elias Antônio Lopes.[42] Born in Porto, Portugal, he probably arrived in Rio de Janeiro during the last quarter of the eighteenth century. Elias was already a merchant there in 1790 when he received the *patente* (official letter of appointment) of captain and was thenceforth entitled to enjoy "all of the honors, privileges, liberties, and exemptions" that came with the position. But it was only in 1808, upon transferring ownership of the São Cristovão property on the outskirts the city (today the Museu Nacional) to the recently arrived Bragança royal family, that he entered his "golden age." In recognition of the gift, D. João, by virtue of the "well-known altruistic demonstration of loyal vassalage shown to my Royal Person by Elias Antônio Lopes, merchant of this capital, in offering one of his buildings located in São Cristóvão, of distinct and recognized value, for the benefit of my Royal Crown," decided to grant him the *comenda* of the Order of Christ, ownership of the office of *Tabelião Escrivão* (Comptrolling Treasurer) in the Municipal Council, the Almotaçaria of Vila de Parati, as well as the position of *deputado* in the Royal Board of Trade. Two years later, Elias was consecrated *cavaleiro* of the *Casa Real* (Royal House) and made the *Alcaiadaria–Mor* and *Senhorio* (Lord-Proprietor) of Vila de São José del Rei, in Rio de Janeiro, in perpetuity. The emoluments continued when, against the opinion of the Royal Board of Trade, D. João nominated Elias *Corretor e Proveedor* or custodian of the *Casa de Seguros da praça da Corte*, through which he became exempt from paying the one-third rent owed to the same board in 1812, and Councilor in 1811. Spurred by such a close relationship with the power structure, Elias multiplied his transactions with the State. He thus became shareholder of the Bank of Brazil, with shares valued at 1,200$000 *réis*: and, from 1810 to 1814, he secured a large number of *arrematações de impostos*.

The case of Rio de Janeiro inevitably calls into question reductionist views on the nature of modern colonization. To be sure, its slave trade was part and parcel of the "global economy." But at the same time, it also presented many specificities. Thus, if the value of the slave trade during 1797, 1800, 1802, 1805, and 1807, as measured by the price of incoming Africans between twelve and fifty-five years old, corresponded to an average 31 percent of all of Rio's imports from Portugal, in 1810 it was twice as large as the same imports. In isolation, consumables, precious metals, textiles, products from Asia, metals, drugs, and other foreign items never superseded the value of Africans imported during these same years. The value of manufactured goods was greater than that of slave imports in 1797, 1800, and 1802, but during 1805, 1807, and 1810, that of imported slaves was far more significant. Moreover, a comparison of slave imports with sugar exports by value reveals that the latter was higher only in 1805 and 1808; in 1797, 1800, and 1802, the value of slaves imported was greater by 33 percent, 67 percent, and 10 percent, respectively; and in 1810, it was six times over that of sugar exports.[43]

Notwithstanding the crisis then engulfing the metropolis, striking conclusions flow from these figures. In the first place, over and above being more important than exports, the trade in souls roughly equaled the value of manufactured imports in the colonial purchases. Commercial relations with slaving ports in Africa would thus have been as intense as those with European ports. This would suggest a clear redefinition of the place of Brazil's colonial economy in the global market. Its operations would not have been limited to a circuit marked by the capitalist/noncapitalist dichotomy, but increasingly tied to a sphere characterized by archaic economies and societies on both sides of the South Atlantic.

Moreover, having demonstrated above that the Brazilian slave trade was dominated by merchant capital from within Rio de Janeiro and represented one of the most lucrative sectors of colonial commerce, other conclusions are also in order. The first is that, when referring to slave traders, we are actually confronted with the entrepreneurial elite of the colony. Second, if the commerce in souls possessed its own specific dynamic and was controlled internally, it naturally follows that this "periphery" enjoyed an immense degree of adaptation to various international conjunctures, so much so that the South-South sphere of the Atlantic market was, to a certain point, characterized by a large amount of autonomy.[44] Third, the slave trade was important, in and by itself, to sustain the physical reproduction of the labor force and, hence, the most basic social relation. Yet of even greater importance, when analyzing the commerce in souls as a business, is the fact that the principal objective of the colonial economy was not so much the sale of tropical products but, rather, the constant reproduction of a two-sided social differentiation: one, quite obviously, between masters and slaves; and the other, based on slavery, among the free persons.[45]

NOTES

1. Philip D. Curtin, *The Atlantic Slave Trade: A Census* (Madison: University of Wisconsin Press, 1969), pp. 116–19, 207; David Eltis, *Economic Growth and the Ending of the Transatlantic Slave Trade* (New York: Oxford Academic Press, 1987), pp. 243–44.

2. Manolo Florentino, *Em Costas Negras: Uma história do tráfico de escravos entre a África e o Rio de Janeiro (séculos XVIII e XIX)* (São Paulo: Companhia das Letras, 1997), p. 51.

3. See Arquivo Nacional do Rio de Janeiro (ANRJ), Junta do Comércio, hereinafter JCAN: *caixas* or boxes 343 (*pacote* or package 1), 346 (1), 347 (3), 348 (1), 358 (1 and 2), 370 (1), 372 (2 and 3), 374 (1 and 2), 375 (2), 376 (1), 388 (1), 398 (1), 419 (1), 420 (1), 429 (1), 430 (1), 431 (1), 433 (2), 434 (3), and 445 (1); as well as Ofício de Notas, *livro* 217 (pp. 155–56).

4. This is explained by the limited availability of foodstuffs in the ports of Africa, whose supply was prejudiced by cyclical subsistence crises. See Joseph C. Miller, "The Significance of Drought, Disease, and Famine in the Agriculturally Marginal Zones of Western Central Africa," *Journal of African History* 23 (1982): 17–61. The lack of consumables, added to the long amount of time that slave vessels anchored off ports in Africa took to complete their cargoes (4.5 to 5.5 months for slavers in the Congo-Angola zone and 4 to 5 months in the Mozambican zone), greatly increased the cost of slaving ventures: see Biblioteca Nacional do Rio de Janeiro, hereinafter BNRJ, *Jornal do Commércio* from October of 1827 to April of 1830.

5. See BNRJ, *Jornal do Commércio* and *Diário Fluminense* from 1827 to 1830.

6. In 1808, imports at Luanda *direct* from Europe were three times lower that those emanating from de Goa (306,447$600 *réis*). The following year, the figures were 96,328$270 *réis* from Portugal, 63,622$860 *réis* from the rest of Europe, and 244:518$200 *réis* from Goa: see JCAN, caixa 449, pacote 1.

7. See the examples in JCAN: caixas 376 (pacote 1), 445 (1), 374 (1), 388 (1), 433 (1), 431 (1), 430 (1), and 434 (3).

8. JCAN caixa 429, pacote 1; Florentino, *Em Costas Negras*, pp. 254–56; and *Almanak imperial do comércio e das corporações civis e militares do Império do Brasil* (Rio de Janeiro: Plancher-Seignot, 1829), pp. 159–62.

9. See the examples in JCAN: caixas 377, pacote 1, 388 (1 and 2), 387 (2), 378 (3), 356 (2), 346 (1), and 347 (3).

10. JCAN, caixa 398, pacote 1.

11. See, for example, JCAN, caixa 361, pacote 3.

12. Joseph C. Miller, "Mortality in the Atlantic Slave Trade: Statistical Evidence on Causality," *Journal of Interdisciplinary History* 3 (1981): 413–14.

13. During the 1820s, more than 3,000 Africans destined for Rio de Janeiro ended up in the hands of corsairs, resulting in losses of between 700,000$000 and 800,000$000 *réis*: see JCAN, caixa 374, pacote 2; and BNRJ, *Jornal do Commércio* and *Diário Fluminense* from 1825 to 1830. One can estimate from the case of the Companhia do Grão-Pará e Maranhão, which saw one-third of its slaving vessels shipwrecked during the second half of the eighteenth century, that the number of shipwrecks must have been considerable. Antonio Carreira, *A Companhia Geral do Grão-Pará e Maranhão* (São Paulo: Cia. Editora Nacional/Instituto Nacional do Livro, 1988), pp. 112–13.

14. See, for example, BNRJ, *Gazeta do Rio de Janeiro* for 1811, as well as *Diário Fluminense* and *Jornal do Commércio* for 1829.

15. British pressures and the 1815 ban on slaving north of the equator added another risk factor to the operations of the slave traders. Total losses resulting from British actions

amounted to 93,161$989 *réis* in 1815 and 255,519$343 *réis* the following year (JCAN, caixa 369, pacote 3).

16. See, for example, JCAN: *maço* or bundle 657 (*número* or number 9222); 701 (10990); 2314 (1059); and 2332 (591).

17. Data collected from the following newspapers published between 1811 and 1830 in BNRJ: *Diário Fluminense, Diário do Governo, Diário do Rio de Janeiro, Espelho, Gazeta do Rio de Janeiro, Jornal do Commércio*, and *Volantim*.

18. See the newspapers cited in note 17.

19. JCAN, caixas 374, pacote 1; and 372 (3).

20. See the newspapers cited in note 17.

21. Postmortem inventories show that, between 1790 and 1830, slave owners never represented less than 88 percent of the inventoried in the rural areas of Rio de Janeiro: see Manolo Florentino and José Roberto Góes, *A Paz das Senzalas, famílias escravas e tráfico atlântico, Rio de Janiero, c.1790–c.1850* (Rio de Janeiro: Civilização Brasileira, 1997), p. 53.

22. JCAN, caixa 448, pacote 1; 449 (1); and ANRJ, Inventários postmortem, 1810–1820.

23. See Florentino, *Em Costas Negras*, p. 171, based on BNRJ, *Gazeta do Rio de Janeiro* for 1812.

24. See the newspapers cited in note 17.

25. Robert Stein, *The French Slave Trade in the Eighteenth Century (An Old Regime Business)* (Madison: University of Wisconsin Press, 1979); Johannes M. Postma, *The Dutch in the Atlantic Slave Trade (1600–1815)* (New York: Cambridge University Press, 1990); and Roger Anstey, *The Atlantic Slave Trade and British Abolition, 1769–1810* (London: Macmillan Press, 1975).

26. Florentino, *Em Costas Negras*, pp. 178–80, based on BNRJ, *Gazeta do Rio de Janeiro* for 1812 and 1817.

27. Florentino, *Em Costas Negras*, pp. 178–80.

28. See ANRJ, *Códice* or Codex 68, vol. 15, fl. 324; and ANRJ, Graças Honoríficas, Latas Verdes, document 625, henceforth GHAN.

29. João Fragoso, *Homens de Grossa Aventura: Acumulação e hierarquia na praça mercantil do Rio de Janeiro, 1790–1830* (Rio de Janeiro: Arquivo Nacional, 1992), p. 255.

30. ANRJ, Inventários postmortem, 1790–1835.

31. Ibid.

32. The same has been observed in relation to French and Dutch slave traders. See, respectively, Stein, *The French Slave Trade*, p. 138, and Postma, *The Dutch in the Atlantic Slave Trade*, pp. 279–80.

33. JCAN, caixa 348, pacote 1.

34. See ANRJ, Inventários postmortem for the years in question. Note that trade, loans, shares, and policies account for 27.2 percent of the total wealth.

35. ANRJ, Escrituras Públicas de Compra e Venda, 1798–1835, hereinafter EPCV.

36. Florentino, *Em Costas Negras*, pp. 194–204, based on EPCV, 1811–1835, especially *livros* 205, 211, 215, 218, 219, 227, 229, and 230.

37. See the newspapers cited in note 17.

38. ANRJ, Inventários postmortem of João Gomes Barrozo (maço 461, números 1592 and 8821) and of Leonarda Maria Velho da Silva (maço 383, número 4491).
39. See, for example: ANRJ, inventário postmortem de Francisco José Gomes, caixa 476, número 9150.
40. GHAN, documents 625, 857, 1175, 977, 777, 317, and 98; See also the inventory of João Gomes Barrozo cited in note 38.
41. GHAN, document 1464.
42. ANRJ, Ordens Régias, cl. 86, livro 40, fl. 63v; Rui Vieira da Cunha. *Para uma biografia de Elias Antônio Lopes* (Rio de Janeiro: Tipografia do Jornal do Comércio, 1957), pp. 9–22.
43. José J. Arruda, *O Brasil no comércio colonial* (São Paulo: Ática, 1980), pp. 161, 301.
44. As has been shown, in particular, by José C. Curto, *Alcoól e Escravos: O comércio luso-brasileiro do alcoól em Mpinda, Luanda e Benguela durante o tráfico atlântico de escravos (c. 1480–1830) e o seu impacto nas sociedades da África Central Ocidental* (Lisbon: Editora Vulgata, 2002); José C. Curto, "Luso-Brazilian Alcohol and the Legal Slave Trade at Benguela and Its Hinterland, c. 1617–1830," in *Négoce Blanc en Afrique Noire: L'évolution du commerce à longue distance en Afrique noire du 18e au 20e siècles*, ed. Hubert Bonin and Michel Cahen (Paris: Publications de la Société française d'histoire d'outre-mer, 2001), pp. 351–69; and José C. Curto, "Vinho verso Cachaça: A Luta Luso-Brasileira pelo Comércio do Álcoól e de Escravos em Luanda, 1648–1703," in *Angola e Brasil nas Rotas do Atlântico Sul*, ed. Selma Pantoja and José F. S. Saraiva (Rio de Janeiro: Bertrand Brasil, 1999), pp. 69–97.
45. The notion that a slavocratic society defines itself as such on the basis of slave labor reproducing an elite, that is, promoting hierarchical relations between free people themselves, comes from Moses Finley, *Escravidão antiga e ideologia moderna* (Rio de Janeiro: Graal, 1991), pp. 84–85.

4

Retention, Reinvention, and Remembering

Restoring Identities through Enslavement in Africa and under Slavery in Brazil

Joseph C. Miller

This is a speculative inquiry[1] on how scholars might productively understand the experiences of the Africans who through their enslavement connected Africa to America, and America to Africa, during the era of the slave trade—that is, what they may have retained, how they reinvented it in order to do so, and how they remembered what they thus abandoned. I approach this currently animated subject from the methodologically challenging and—as I see it, at least—conceptually radical premise that we do so most productively by exploring the issues as the people forced onto the slavers' ships saw them. This fundamentally historical exercise may strike some methodological purists as also dangerously conjectural, for want of direct verbal witness to what mattered most to, what thus motivated, those enslaved. And so it may be, but the alternatives are even more speculative, because they depend on projecting from the worldviews of the masters or—even worse—from the conceptualizations of the speculators, in the guise of modern historians and theorizers. Close examination of the logic of conventional ways of handling the experience of slavery through sociological and cultural abstractions of dubious relevance to what the slaves experienced reveals no fewer assumptions than those on which this historicized proposal rests, a good many of them highly problematic and less tested than the ones on which I intend to proceed. Raising the problem in the form I propose here is the prerequisite to learning whether diligent researchers can find plausible, even probable answers to it, not by attempting to "read the lips" of those silenced by narrow reliance on the voices audible in written sources but by watching what those who expressed themselves in deeds, not words, did, based on an informed

81

sense of what values they brought with them from Africa that their experience of enslavement most threatened.

What I am wondering about is meant to historicize the discussion currently phrased too often in polarized terms of "survivals" of African culture(s) against "creolization"; that is, the extent to which Africans in the New World drew on unproblematized Old World backgrounds to survive an equally unproblematized brutality of their enslavement and the subsequent exclusions of racism. Tracing selected, abstracted, and reified "traits" from Africa to America, or—and particularly—relying on a similarly obvious "ethnicity" as a kind of humanized proxy for "culture," as the principal aspect of the ways in which Africans identified themselves, that is, sought a measure of respect within the denigration of slavery, have been the dominant strategies followed since Melville Herskovits first insisted on the integrity of ethnicized "cultures" in Africa in the 1930s and their resurrection in the Americas. That is, the debate still draws on the rudimentary understandings of the African past, objectified in order to identify them at all, available at that preliminary phase of modern scholarship on the continent, more than a half-century ago.

We now have that half century of increasingly sophisticated research on histories in Africa and historicized anthropology that, if utilized, allow us to move beyond what Africans may have created to consider how and why they created it, and on that basis, to infer something more complex about the experiences of the enslaved with reasonable, even high, degrees of confidence. We also have learned to read the existing personal accounts of the survivors—and more of them than we once realized—with insight beyond the words they employed when asked to identify themselves before inquisitors, masters, police, and others intending to use whatever they said against them. The singular discourse of ethnic labeling that reached the ears of those who wrote was calculated to tell them what they wanted to hear and to conceal who else the enslaved in fact thought they were and meant to be. Finally, voluminous and creative attention to the experience of slavery itself, in the New World, now allows us to sense, and often to document, how the reported behavior of those enslaved expressed these other meanings of their own, meanings more autonomous and more African than merely reactions to, adaptations of, or assimilation to the norms of their masters, sometimes even when coded in accommodatingly Christian and European terms. Perhaps no historical context is more dependent than slavery on destruction or manipulation of the identities of others—and therefore more conducive to misrepresentation of self—on both sides. I am disinclined to take anybody "at their word" and rather emboldened to interpret the words they used according to the contexts—the "working misunderstandings," which I would extend to emphasize the possibility of "calculated deceptions"—in which people employed them.

The argument here thus considers the perceptions and priorities of the

Africans, hidden beneath, and also appropriating, the ideological conceits of those compelled to assert themselves as "strong," that motivated the actions of those they dismissed as "weak." These motivations of the enslaved centered on the pain of initial isolation, subsequent individuation, and the recurrent—potentially endless—transferability of enslavement in the increasingly commercial world of the Atlantic, as the key deprivation that preoccupied nearly all from Africa who reached Brazil (or anywhere else in the Americas), and thus the violation of their dignity that the slaves sought most intently to overcome.[2] In an age before medical science dreamed of assuring the integrity of the body, integrity of spirit and of community were the only spheres of life over which anyone dreamed of asserting control. Pain and death could not be avoided, but one could seek solace in the company of others. People therefore constructed identities of a primarily social sort, and the identities in Africa that the slaves had lost through capture and forced removal to the Americas were—certainly significantly and adequately for purposes of structuring a coherent interpretation of what they did on the continental scale and over the multiple centuries considered here—thinkable, and attainable, through connections with others. For them, Orlando Patterson's famous characterization of slavery as "social death" conveyed a motivatingly deep sense of personal nonexistence. One thus understands Africans' actions in the Americas as prominently a search to gain recognized places in coherent New World communities, hence as expressed in my subtitle, "restoring identities through enslavement in Africa and under slavery in Brazil."

All slaves, everywhere, built lives of their own under slavery, *if they were allowed to remain long enough in one place to consolidate the social connections that validate anyone's being*—with family, shipmates, master's household, and many others that the people enslaved in Brazil created for themselves. The vulnerability of the people trapped in slavery cannot be equated with passivity, or even victimhood, nor with single-minded strategies of resistance. But in the capitalist environment of the Atlantic their civil and legal status as movable and exchangeable "property" separated them repeatedly through sale or some other form of transfer in pursuit of someone else's economic gain, exposing them over and again to the quintessential vulnerability of their enslavement: of being alone, again, perhaps unable to communicate, unaware of the rules of the game in which they found themselves trapped, ignorant of the factors that impinged on their everyday survival. For the enslaved, survival in more than a minimal physical sense thus meant constant rebuilding of new connections out of the succession of transitory circumstances through which most found themselves propelled, a recurrently thwarted effort to find places of their own, to belong, somehow, somewhere. For them, the burden of commercialized slavery was not bondage in itself, but rather the betrayal of the responsibilities of masters who sold or transferred them for purposes of personal gain.

By tracing the slaves' struggles to reconstitute themselves by building communities as the strategies through which they established their presence in Brazil, in a psychological as well as a historical sense, we can sense them acting independently of—and far beyond merely reacting against—the European minority nominally in charge. By taking account of the enslaved in terms of their strategies, we move toward understanding Brazil's colonial and early imperial eras as "African" in degrees comparable to the emphasis in conventional scholarship on the Portuguese backgrounds of the country's literate elite. By seeing Brazil's "enslaving connection" to Africa as the search of the enslaved for connections of their own, scholars might establish an African presence of an autonomy that can support the full dialectical engagement through which contending Africans and Europeans, embraced in conflict, together worked out the succession of tense accommodations that became "Brazil"—or any other part of the Americas—and underscore the extent to which every identity in the New World was a product of confronting the complex human context of the Atlantic.³

THE PREMISE: *AFRICAN MENTALITÉS*

Confining the elaboration of this process to Brazil, which offers extreme—and therefore analytically useful—instances of demographic tendencies found throughout the relevant parts of the Americas, the story starts by acknowledging that people born and thus formed cognitively in Africa were formative majorities in the most dynamic phases of all the centers where Brazilian identities took shape. The Brazilian frontiers, from the northeast in the sixteenth century through the north and west into the late nineteenth century, thrived on interactions between Amerindians and Europeans,⁴ but—unlike the crucial influence of native American majorities in the construction of modern identities in Mexico and other Hispanic regions of the Americas—the confrontations that became "Brazil" grew out of the masses of enslaved Africans who flooded into and built the sugar and mining captaincies of the Portuguese colony, from Bahia and Pernambuco at the end of the sixteenth century to Minas Gerais and Rio de Janeiro in the eighteenth and (the province of) São Paulo in the early nineteenth. High mortality among the Africans arriving in Brazil, merchant slaving fleets based in America that brought replacements from Africa in significant numbers until the middle of the nineteenth century,⁵ and tendencies to accept survivors and their American-born descendants as Brazilians meant that people born in Africa predominated among those left in slavery to degrees greater than elsewhere in the Americas.⁶ Hence, these *Africans*, as distinguished from their Afro-Brazilian descendants, make Africa and their "enslaving connection" one of the necessary starting points for understanding the formation of Brazil.

Rather than beginning with the struggles of the slaves against their masters, one must therefore start the quest for the strategies of the enslaved by looking at their formative experiences in Africa, at who they thought they had been when they had been sold in Africa, what they had lost, and how they sought to recover from the experience. To see Brazil in these terms as an African country, scholars must see Africa in terms beyond the modernist assumptions that have structured most efforts (outside the most specialist spheres) up to now to understand the history of the continent, by extension also the "black diaspora," and in turn the history of the Americas, and—for that matter—slavery itself everywhere beyond the Atlantic. The myths prevailing in popular culture about Africa, whether racist or romantic, also derive from colonial-era conceptualizations about Africans as either lacking or excelling in the values of modernity and thus offer distractingly limited glimpses of the quite different strategies and perceptions that recent scholarship has revealed among Africans. The coherence of the emerging alternative vision depends on abandoning so comprehensive and politicized a set of assumptions inherited from twentieth-century racist misconstructions that even scholars trained in the styles of history that prevail in other world regions still struggle to understand Africa on terms other than benign glosses on the old, extremely partial, if not broadly misleading, premises.[7]

If we thus reduce the familiar edifice of scholarship to a shambles, looking beyond so much of the modernity that is so large a part of all of us, what are the insights into Africa on which we can begin to construct an inclusive and balanced vision of the full novelty, the formative processes, of Africans' contributions to the formation of Brazil—or, indeed, to any part of the Americas? One begins by understanding how Africans thought of themselves on multiple levels. On only the most general of those did they recognize tendencies that contrasted with the emerging habits of Europeans in ways that distinguished themselves. Africans arriving in Brazil therefore related instinctively to one another only in very limited degrees through these broadly shared sensibilities. It is not a distracting exaggeration to suggest that the more obvious the factors the Europeans saw as unifying them as "Africans," as distinct from themselves, the more transparent, and therefore meaningless, they were to the people from Africa thus distinguished; in the Americas "race" would become a primary (but only later) example of a factor that lay primarily in the eyes of the beholders.

At the same time, sixteenth- and seventeenth-century Africans and the Portuguese in Brazil were more like one another than their modern heirs became, in other ways that are underappreciated in most scholarship that projects modern racialized differences back to times before they were invented.[8] The Portuguese and their Brazilian-born successors in Brazil participated significantly less than the English, Dutch, and French in the currents of thought that, in the course of the eighteenth century, became distinguishably "modern" individualistic senses of identity and civic senses of political "freedom" for individuals.[9] Nonetheless, the commercial habits of the Portuguese, the individualism and universalism of Catholic Christianity, and a political and legal framework based on literate modes of thought and expression set them apart from most of the Africans reaching Brazil as incipiently modern "Europeans."[10] But all differences are relative, and people cluster around very selective criteria they perceive as distinguishing those they embrace as alike from others whom they reject as alien, according to the contexts in which they encounter one another. The Africans' enslavement, the momentary cultural disabilities imposed by relocating in the strange new world of Brazil, and the fears and resentments germane to both sides of the relationship of slavery magnified these marginal distinctions to the dichotomous contrasts that came to dominate the ideologies, hence identities, of both communities there.

At the moment Africans were thrown together in slavery they distinguished no less intensely among themselves according to the flexibly large number of relatively self-contained communities in which they had grown up, signified in the first instance by "country marks"[11] and other symbols of dress and deportment by which they affirmed the small groups to which they felt strong bonds. They had identified themselves by these intimate affiliations. These collectivities were supple groupings that people created, often by intense experiences of personal conversion, to pursue many strategies, from primary affective bonds of family to economic collaboration, social reproduction, personal clientage, political factions, or—for Muslims—affiliation with faith-based communities of worship. They were as much voluntaristic and spontaneous as they were determined by descent. People thought of themselves differently in each of the numerous, intently engaged spheres in their daily lives, naming themselves situationally, and hence differently, in each. Since few of these multiple associations were mutually exclusive, people in Africa claimed as many different connections as their means and interests allowed. The more their memberships, the greater the personal autonomy and advancement they might achieve by playing loyalties claimed in one against challenges or constraints imposed by others. Men had more such ties than women, and adults more than children. The power of old men derived from lifetimes spent building a range of connections. In Africa, therefore, people struggled to define themselves through belonging in multiple ways, through the diversity of the associations they could create.

Their strategies were the exact opposite of the single-minded (or, in the colonial version of the idea, mindless) devotion to unidimensional, homogeneous, comprehending, and stable "ethnicity" that underlies most existing discussion of African identities, old-world or new. The historicizing of such West African stereotypes as "Igbo"[12] and "Yoruba"[13] should extend also to such conventional central African "ethnic" categories as "Bantu," "Congo," "Angolas," and "Benguelas," in Brazil and throughout the Americas.[14] To invoke a single example, worthy of remark because it has become so widespread a cliché in the literature on "African cultures" in the Americas, "Congo" meant one thing in sixteenth-century Lima or São Tomé, something else in Cartagena early in the 1600s, quite another in the late eighteenth century in Rio or Saint Domingue, something else again in New Orleans early in the nineteenth century, and something still different by 1850 or so in Cuba. These differences stemmed in part from the fact that people from the coastlands and adjacent hills on either side of the mouth of the Zaire River, whom modern linguists have classified as "Kikongo"-speaking, found themselves in widely varying contexts in the Americas, in terms of both the ethnic stereotypes with which their masters bought and labeled them and the degrees of difference they recognized between themselves and the other Africans who had preceded them in the enslaved populations they joined. But the differences among "Congo" in the Americas derived further from diverse meanings of "Kongo" in Africa. The term was initially used for the Christian monarchy of the *mani kongo* lords who struggled to consolidate their rule over one part of the region in the sixteenth century.[15] The various later European merchant networks specialized in widely different ports along an extent of coast that ran from very near the equator in the north to Luanda in the south and generically designated as "Congo" speakers of Kikongo who came from specific locations distant from the Kongo "kingdom" and remote from one another. In Africa, the ethno-linguistic abstraction of "Kongo" thus begs specification of the multiple, much smaller, and changing social identities of people it envelopes in a label less evident to them than to outsiders, at least before the twentieth century.

"Ethnicity" in Africa thus provides only the most limited and misleading approximation of the creative, fluid series of identities that people in fact constructed to replace the ties disrupted by their enslavement. The concept has no consistent meaning as scholars have appropriated it for these purposes, though most take varying degrees of linguistic community as proxies for whatever group they might in practice identify.[16] Also, since Africans asserted themselves—in effect "made their histories"—by assembling collectivities, they constantly created new groups of the most flexible, dynamic sorts and used enslavement as a principal means of doing so. In large parts of western Africa only a few of these conformed closely to linguistic boundaries, and most people there spoke several languages in order to function effectively in the complex economies and pluralistic societies in which they lived. In portions of central Africa, though by no means everywhere, linguistic similarities assumed greater—though never exclusive, or even dominating—prominence as markers of collective identities.[17] Thus, although some language-defined communities in Africa persisted for very long times, the speech habits of the people who preserved them evolved constantly as they struggled also to identify themselves by other criteria and spoke in new ways as they reflected on the outcomes of these contests.

PROCESSES OF IDENTITY FORMATION IN BRAZIL—AFRICAN MAJORITIES

In an environment of such close and multiple associations, enslavement deprived people of the social ties that protected them, involuntarily, through abandonment by those otherwise responsible for them, through breakup of communities fleeing drought or disease or assault, or through violent seizures by outsiders. Women, and particularly children, with fewer such social identities were more vulnerable to such isolation than adult males with multiple and strong connections. The individuation that modern thought celebrates as personal "freedom" Africans thus experienced as debilitating loss, and enslavement reduced the multiplicity of connections sought to the singularity of childlike dependence on a master. But Africans responded to enslavement, whatever the purposes—humiliating or privileged—to which new patrons put the dependents they thus acquired, by drawing on skills of social survival that everyone learned as children, to start over, in unknown environments, in their unending quests for connections.[18] Slavery was disruptive and disabling, and enslavement through violence could be physically damaging and even deadly, but it was not the absolute, unimaginable, and irremediable deprivation that modern dependence on civic protections of individuated identity has subsequently made it appear to have been. That is to say that adult Africans reaching Brazil through the transatlantic enslaving connection were usually weakened in body and subjected to gross personal abuses, but they possessed a degree of preparation in spirit to counter their loss of communal identity through enslavement by seeking new identities of a primarily social sort.[19]

The social environment they entered in Brazil during its formative years, like all the regions of the Americas, was a contested site of multiple encounters among strangers, a formative moment that challenged familiar identities, however flexible and multiple, intensified latent differentiation as people discovered who they thought they were in reaction to whom they met, and thus often produced agonized confrontations at unanticipated, and elemental, levels of their identities.[20] The resulting compulsion—even desperation—to redefine selves, individually and collectively, out of encounters with startlingly alien "others" was as intense for Africans as it was for immigrants from Europe or for Amerindians. The dynamics of these encounters then evolved from this amorphousness through the succeeding centuries of Brazil's enslaving connection, through increasingly defined, mostly private, identities reflecting circumstances as they changed in both Africa and the Americas to the public and politicized Brazilian identities of the nineteenth century.[21]

The Africans who redefined themselves in the crucible of Brazilian slavery did so also according to the changing demographic contexts in which the enslaving connection placed them, drawing on the contrasts among the multiple and flexible African identities they brought with them and encountering the increasingly rigid and racialized identities of "European" and "African" constructed out of the confrontations of the New World. They selected, or discovered, aspects of their personal backgrounds to mobilize collective responses to specific immediate challenges according to where and when enough of what sorts of people, from what parts of Africa, found themselves thrown together.[22] Sufficient numbers were the starting point, the sine qua non, to construct communities out of commonalities that they recognized. But the motivation to acknowledge one another in one way rather than in some other, the specific symbols on which they seized to do so, and the purposes for which "countrymen" or "mates" or "brothers" embraced one another by invoking cultural symbols, arose from the specific circumstances that provoked them.

By the time that the broad patterns of Atlantic slaving and general processes of the formation of Brazilian society brought viably large communities of Africans together in Brazil, *and* placed them in contexts where they recognized a need or an opportunity to compete with one another, or to confront their owners or other Portuguese and Brazilians or native Americans, by defining themselves collectively, their "home" backgrounds offered only one option amidst a much wider array of recent and overwhelming experiences that they had shared along the lengthening routes that carried captives from remote interior regions to the coast, during episodes of partial integration into alien communities along the way in Africa, while detained in coastal barracoons where slavers held them awaiting embarkation, in the course of the shipboard Middle Passage, and through contacts formed in Brazil during the succession of transfers from owner to owner that marked the lives of most of the survivors. As slaves they had experienced no single "uprooting" through extraction from a secure, single, stable background in Africa, but rather a series of transfers and partial and ephemeral integrations, all broken again and again by their vulnerability to being transferred.

The extent that these survivors of enslavement subsequently thought of themselves in terms of the lives they had created before their capture and exile depended at least as much on their value to their owners in America as on who they had been in Africa. Beyond language-based ethnicity, they had emphasized other, sometimes primary, qualities of age, gender, professional skills and experience, doctrinal distinctions among Muslims, and social rank. The specific circumstances they encountered in the New World would have turned potential groupings among them toward any of these other identities as bases for forming new connections with their masters, by featuring skills that made them valuable as employees. Knowledge of livestock handling, agricultural techniques, metallurgical and other artisan skills, and hunting were the attributes by which masters recognized the human property they had purchased by their commercial value.

On the other hand, cohorts of new arrivals banded together around their predecessors to establish positions within existing slave communities. The predominance of young males among the arriving Africans would have created a tendency to draw on African initiation rituals for adolescent boys, the principal form of public ceremony that youths would have experienced at the tender ages at which they were captured, and on such military training as older boys might have acquired.[23] Among the slaves, backgrounds in the art of healing appealed especially. The creation of community depended on containing the sense of evil divisiveness that must have overwhelmed people who saw their enslavement in Africa in terms of witchcraft, since people there interpreted involuntary isolation as a breakdown of community integrity, possible only by violations from within, and thus a betrayal by someone within the sacred sphere of trust. They similarly understood the isolation of slavery as vulnerability to predatory strangers—not only their European captors, whom they initially saw as cannibals, but also the alien Africans with whom they found themselves entrapped in the Americas.[24] Without research into the slaves' interpretation of their enslavement as witchcraft, one can only speculate on the suspicions of one another that underlay their terror throughout the Middle Passage and their hindrance to forming effective bonds.[25] It was a contradiction of agonizing proportions that they most suspected the strangers to whom they also had to turn for salvation. At home, they attempted to extirpate this quintessential evil by "eradication movements," healing cults that rallied fraying communities to an intense spirit of collective unity. Under the extreme breach of social faith and vulnerability that followed uprooting and successive transfers, Africans would have united around whatever healing strategies they identified as promising. Since the anticipated efficacy of the antidotes to these very real afflictions of the imagination (as opposed to imaginary afflictions) depended on the promise of novelty, the hopeful potential of the untried (and therefore not yet discredited), preceding generations of captives must have looked to the new arrivals who followed them, particularly those from regions unfamiliar to them, as sources of potential remedies for their misfortune.

Africans thus would have understood European, mostly Christian, "religions" as forms of healing for the social ills that afflicted them—the Church's promise of salvation from the temptations of the devil as equivalent to antiwitchcraft movements they had known in Africa—and would have blended sincere devotion to Catholicism in Brazil into their own ways of combating the isolation of slavery that beset them, covering the underlying strategies with respectable Catholic metaphors as well as tapping whatever potential for social and personal reintegration, in a mundane sense, might lie, unsuspected, behind their masters' corruption of their own spiritual forces to divide rather than to unite.[26] By the early nineteenth century, non-Muslims in some areas embraced Islam for its reputed therapeutic powers. It would be evidence of the efficacy of the slaves' intimate, community strategies for healing the social, and personal, agonies of isolation that their masters recognized very little of their meaning to Africans. Hence, in the masters' records one finds only oblique hints at even their existence. However, their relative invisibility in the literature on slavery in Brazil derives equally, or more, from historians' failure to consider what can be known about the slaves' backgrounds in Africa or to emphasize the specific experience of uprooting that they endured in assessing the reactions of Brazil's enslaved majority.

AN OUTLINE OF VIABLE IDENTITIES IN THE HISTORY OF AFRICANS IN BRAZIL—FORMATIVE YEARS

The first Africans to reach Brazil in the sixteenth century came in numbers too small to give them significant interest in defining themselves as a community in contrast to their European masters.[27] Central Africans had been assembled on the emergent sugar estates of São Tomé earlier in the century, first through Kongo Christian channels that identified them as "Congo," then through competing commercial networks focused along the lower Kwanza River and drawing on military captives taken by forces marshaled there by warlords known as *ngola*, and hence identified as "Angolares." These identities set the initial terms by which the Portuguese later recognized their successors in Brazil. Such identification of slaves in terms of where they were purchased, or who had sold them, as distinct from the radically different identities that the Africans enslaved might have embraced, accurately reflected the commercial terms in which Europeans recognized aliens whom they thought of only as "property" throughout the history of slaving in the Atlantic.

But in northeastern Brazil at that time the Portuguese relied for gang labor not on Africans but rather on Amerindians. They only gradually grew competitive with other, richer, more accessible markets for much costlier labor from Africa in sixteenth-century Iberia and—particularly—in the cities of the silver-mining provinces of mainland Spanish America. Judging from the oblique references to Africans in the records for this early phase of Brazil's enslaving connection, and indeed inferable with some confidence from their very obliqueness, the first Africans brought as slaves came in small numbers, mostly from the Upper Guinea area of West Africa, many of them through Portugal, and were employed in skilled positions and domestic service. In Africa, the first response of individuals isolated was to seek a benign patron, a personal protector who could assume responsibility for the multiple and communal guarantees of personal welfare that they had lost. Such people would have identified more closely with their masters—in European terms, as much in the sense of apprentice as of chattel—than with the native Americans who formed the majority of those forced to toil in the forests and fields.[28] Their influence on the ways in which much larger numbers of Africans in Brazil later distinguished themselves under the very different conditions of gang slavery was, accordingly, extremely limited.

Sometime around the turn of the seventeenth century, Dutch merchants financed the turn toward delivering slaves in numbers socially and culturally viable as "Africans" in Pernambuco and Bahia.[29] The local origins of these people in Africa, and even their numbers, remain unclear, since the Spanish legal authority (the *asiento*) imposed on the Atlantic trade of the Portuguese during the period of the Dual Monarchy (1580–1640) provides the only record of the movements of the ships, and it focused on the captives funneled to Vera Cruz, Cartagena, and the Rio de la Plata (as a gateway to the Andean regions) rather than Brazil.[30] However, inferring from later patterns quietly undertaken in defiance of authorities in Lisbon, Seville, and Amsterdam, Pernambucans in these early years of the seventeenth century would have concentrated the commercial support they obtained from the Dutch in producing sugar and would have ventured independently across the short Atlantic run to buy slaves themselves at Portuguese trading posts along the Upper Guinea coast, thus acquiring the first generation of Africans put out to toil in the canebrakes between the 1590s and 1620s. The Dutch West India Company (WIC) seized the Brazilian sugar captaincies in the 1630s but added only relatively small numbers of slaves in the 1640s, mostly from central Africa.[31] The conflicts of that decade, which finally drove the Dutch out of Brazil in 1654, must have significantly inhibited deliveries of new captives from Africa and contributed to disorders on the plantations that allowed such famed maroon redoubts as the *quilombo* (*kilombo*) of Palmares to flourish there in the 1650s and after.[32] To the limited extent that the overwhelming majorities of new Africans among those enslaved at that time in northeastern Brazil had the luxury of forming communities of any enduring sort, the thriving maroon colonies of the era suggest that they apparently did so mostly through spontaneous, uncoordinated flight into the adjacent forests.

These refugee colonies, to judge from the evidence of recent archaeology at a late phase of the *quilombo* at Palmares, were accordingly mixed in culture, with significant contributions from native Americans, the recent predecessors of the Africans as workers in the cane fields of the Brazilian northeast.[33] The term *quilombo*, of course, entered Brazilian speech from the encounter of other Portuguese with African warrior bands designated thus in Angola, and scholars have long sought continuities in structure from that African precedent to the circumstances in Pernambuco. The Angolan captives whom the WIC brought to Pernambuco in the 1640s provide obvious candidates as bearers of the idea, if not also the practices to which it refers. However, the transatlantic connection lies less in the transfer of an integral set of Angolan practices than in ad hoc strategies of assembling new communities out of refugees of the most disparate backgrounds that the disorders of the warfare attending slaving had provoked long before in Angola. By the middle of the seventeenth century, people in West Central Africa had endured more than a century of dispersal from communities built from ancestral or any other stable ties. Few captives taken from the conflicts there would have been unfamiliar with techniques of assembling refugees in new communities under the tight discipline necessary for self-defense. In the Americas, these included Indians as opportunistically as they also welcomed Africans from Upper Guinea. The terminology may have been Angolan, and *quilombo* may have been the term employed by the Portuguese rather than by the Africans, but at Palmares it referred to experiences in America, not in Africa.

The continuities from Africa to America thus occurred in the strategies and techniques developed in response to parallel experiences, in this case the disruptions, dislocations, and development of new communities under the constraints of slaving and slavery, not in the specific cultural materials that refugees appropriated, ad hoc, in order to realize them in one historical context or another. The heterogeneity of the specific cultural materials on which the fugitives gathered in Palmares drew thus demonstrates the necessarily spontaneous, opportunistic, *bricoleur*-like, integrative quality of constructing new identities under the constraints of slavery in the Americas: desperate people worked creatively with whatever ideas and symbols came to hand, moment-to-moment, since they had so little opportunity to implement more considered strategies. They gave new meanings to old symbols, converting ideas that had differentiated intimates from others in Africa to symbols that united total strangers in America. In the case of the *quilombos* of Angola and Brazil, they (or the Portuguese) reversed even the relations of the Africans and Europeans they employed the term to designate: in Angola, Portuguese military forces had relied heavily on the bands of Africans, called Imbangala (or "Jaga"), who organized in the war camps known as *quilombos*, while in Pernambuco the veterans who gave Palmares whatever African character it exhibited converted strategies that had been developed in alliance in Angola to sustain opposition in America. The connection lay in the continuity of overcoming the dispersal and isolation of slaving and enslavement, not in resurrecting an orderly background in Africa to bring order to lives in America over which the slaves had no inherent control. Continuities in form thus became means to achieve entirely novel effects, both in Africa and in America.

On the plantations of Pernambuco, Portuguese planters faced gaping shortages of labor when they regained control of their own affairs after expelling the Dutch. By that time, southern Brazilians had recaptured Benguela and Luanda, the two principal slaving ports under Portuguese authority in central Africa, after a corresponding period (1641–1648) of Dutch intrusion there. Restoration of Portuguese authority at Luanda positioned the Pernambucans to establish domination over supplies of slaves from there for the remainder of the seventeenth century.[34] Presumably, these Pernambucan interests also sold captives to their counterparts in Bahia to the south during these years, at least in the immediate aftermath of restoration of Portuguese authority in the Brazilian northeast. They would thereby have given planters in Bahia every reason to lessen their dependence for vital supplies of labor on rivals in the neighboring captaincy by supplementing these sources of Angolans with the famous tobacco-for-slaves exchanges at Ouidah and other ports along what they then helped to make West Africa's "Slave Coast" in the 1680s. Bahians distinguished these West Africans by the point of their commodification as slaves, as "Minas," from the name by which the Portuguese knew the entire coastline east of the fortress at São Jorge da Mina that their fifteenth-century predecessors had built on the shores west of the Volta River that the English knew as the "Gold Coast."

The Pernambucans would thus have restocked the labor forces in both Pernambuco and Bahia after 1655, mostly with captives from Angola, many of them taken in the Angolan wars of that era. In Recife, one finds the lethal consequences of introducing large new populations of underfed and overworked Africans in the smallpox pandemic of 1664–1666 and again—more generally—during the 1680s, when droughts in both central and western Africa spawned epidemics that the captives taken in the attendant wars carried to Brazil through the enslaving connection and then fell victim to a devastating outbreak of yellow fever in 1685.[35] Bahia, though not Pernambuco, would have replaced the central Africans lost with West African Minas in the 1680s and 1690s, mostly from the regions just inland from Ouidah then entering the cycle of warfare, characteristic of the slave trade everywhere in Africa, which culminated there when refugees established the Dahomey military state.[36] The mortality suffered in these epidemiological disasters may have been high enough that the ensuing waves of western African Minas in Bahia and Angolans in Pernambuco found themselves in positions to begin over again the process of community formation among the slaves in rural northeastern Brazil.[37]

To the extent that Recife and Salvador, the principal port towns of the captaincies, had by then developed urban communities of slaves, they would have included more acculturated survivors and descendents of the earlier generations, as much Portuguese in culture as specifically African. In early Brazil, arriving captives entered a notoriously mortiferous plantation environment, in which they could have sustained few enduring community strategies as they struggled in isolation for sheer physical survival, collaborating primarily in ephemeral and unstructured ways. Only the fortunate survivors would have built connections, and they tended to elaborate their strategies of doing so mostly in the towns, where veterans of captivity in Brazil congregated in numbers sufficient to work together on a sustained basis. The distinctions between town and country in the ways they struggled for identities, for themselves under slavery, or—from the point of view of the arriving slaves—between the plantations that they sought to escape and the growing port cities on the coast that they might reach became less dramatic in later generations, but in the eighteenth century they remained significant enough that the slaves must have constructed identities and communities according to differing strategies. Their successors turned to still other forms of identity that transcended the rural-urban divide only in the nineteenth century.

The African meanings of the strategies of association that slaves pursued to protect themselves created new identities, in these early phases of slavery in Brazil. By the early eighteenth century, Catholic Church–sanctioned "godparenthood" and marriages had become not uncommon, even widespread, in the urban areas. For Africans held in slavery, both of these bonds, securely sacralized by the Church, inhibited—or at least made disreputable and spiritually dangerous—further sale or transfer by owners whom captives had adopted as patrons, or tied indissolubly through the sacrament of matrimony to slaves held by their own, or other local, master(s). Both these strategies extended African uses of clientage and affiliation through marriage into dominant groups that were basic to building connections and identity. The personal responsibility on the part of the master not to sell the child, or its family, thus taken under the paternalistic umbrella that the slaves secured through "godparenthood" adapted the distinction that Africans observed between slaves affiliated to the community of kin and others held only instrumentally and temporarily, awaiting further transfer.[38] They also seem to build on the strategies of earlier generations of Africans, mostly held in relatively small numbers in skilled and domestic employments, some with backgrounds in Portugal, who had sought to establish social connections by looking less to one another than to the households and workshops of their masters.

Some central Africans had also used Catholicism at home to rebuild communities disrupted by slaving. Several African authorities in the Kongo "kingdom" and in parts of Portuguese-controlled Angola had appropriated missionary efforts to proselytize and baptize to consolidate new, nominally Catholic polities under the protection of the Portuguese. Baptism at Luanda during the process of embarkation landed other slaves, from interior regions beyond the ambitions even of the intrepid missionaries of the seventeenth century, in Brazil already nominally within the Catholic fold, at least in these early eras. Thus baptized, whatever they may have known or cared about Catholicism in any European sense, these slaves would then have taken advantage of their sacramental eligibility to defend themselves against the disabling effects, not to mention the human losses, of further transfers. The sacrament of baptism, extended in Brazil to newborns, recognized the child's parentage and thus established a tie between at least mother and child that masters could subsequently threaten only at the risk of public condemnation and ecclesiastical excommunication. In the patriarchal society of Catholic Brazil, in which planters and merchants built extended households of family and retainers with the support of the Church, marriage, godparenthood, and baptism gave the slaves—particularly women—opportunities to find places of relative security, and thus identities, for themselves. Viewed in terms of the experiences and strategies of the slaves who sought the sanction of the Church, beyond the better-known zeal of the Catholic fathers to save the souls of African heathens and the toleration of the most Catholic Portuguese monarchs, the Catholic rite offered a nascent community of family and added its promise of perpetuating a lineage of their own in the future.

The Catholic sacraments brought stability by confirming women's relations with their masters in private ways, while the other familiar exploitation of Catholicism by male slaves in Brazil appropriated the more public space open to males. The lay brotherhoods, or confraternities (*irmandades*), represented instead the efforts of men in urban parish after urban parish to develop associations among themselves by extending this patriarchal and Christian sort of identification into the streets and markets of the cities. These confraternities, led by assimilated predecessors, would have emerged out of the large assemblages of new enslaved males in the northeast perhaps as early as the 1650s, and certainly by the early eighteenth century there and in Minas Gerais, after about 1710 one of the primary concentrations of the African-born—mostly men—in Brazil. The extent to which slaves of similar backgrounds in Africa congregated in the different brotherhoods, and the degrees of African specificity with which they claimed the similarities around which they congregated, would have derived from the specific concentrations of slaves arriving from contrasting regions in Africa.[39] They reacted more in terms of external contrasts than of internal similarities, more in terms of situations in Brazil than of origins in Africa. The uses of the confraternities to the slaves, according to the demographic concentrations out of which they arose, bear arguable resemblances to the *cabildos* of nineteenth-century Cuba and other urban male voluntary mutual-aid associations that new waves of slaves organized to control work and other opportunities in other colonial cities of the Americas.

Since Africans at home sought identities derived from the solidarity of their ancestral communities, tracing the descendency of the living and linking those present with the others who had gone before, the ultimate assertion of one's self came through dying among one's own, or reuniting with those one had lost through death. The deracination, the "social death," of enslavement left Africans integrated into such originary communities by birth but left alone in Brazil with a lifelong longing to regain connection with their origins, to return "home" in death. Such belief in reunification by "flying back to Africa," and a determination to do so that extended to taking one's own life at moments of greatest and most desolated isolation, is attributed particularly to slaves of Igbo backgrounds in the literature on slavery and reported most often from English-speaking colonies. But the underlying motivation to regain identity—social vitality—in death was more general, and slaves elsewhere acted on it in collective ways by uniting in burial societies that would translate the ubiquitous mortality of enslavement into the final triumph of the enslaved. No one reached Brazil without having witnessed death in the most horrifying immediacy all around him or her, in capture, during transport to the coast, and chained to corpses during the ocean crossing. The isolation and scorn in which captives had seen others die, arbitrarily singled out and killed, bodies abandoned along the trails for animals to consume, remains thrown contemptuously next to the barracoons in rotting heaps, and dumped into the ocean with utter disdain, must have left the survivors resolved, if not obsessed, with converting continuing deaths in Brazil into affirmation of a community who would recognize, and memorialize, them. One must consider the lay brotherhoods as burial societies that offered the prospect of eternal life in terms beyond those in which the Portuguese envisaged a Catholic "heaven," and as predecessors of the more secular and overtly African associations that even small groups of slaves formed out of backgrounds sufficiently similar to share in collective means of integrating themselves into the eternal community of the dead. In Luanda, an ocean closer to the African roots of those enslaved and as much a city of slaves as any city in Brazil, annoyed descriptions of large, noisy funeral gatherings (*entame/entambe*) appear with a frequency that must indicate the preoccupation of the urban population with pervasive death and a response to its presence through collective affirmation of the identity of the deceased. The same people, settled in Brazil in slavery, must have associated with others to restore, in dying, personal identities lost to the living. The restorative impulse may have dominated men, for whom slavery denied any future prospect of ongoing life in the presence of progeny of their own, while women may have used Catholic rites of marriage and baptism to temper their own mortality through the places thus claimed for their children.

The Catholic sacraments restored the hope of personal security, in death as well as in life, that enslavement had cost its victims. Reflecting an era of European religious solidarity that was already dissipating amidst the competitive and individualistic priorities of the Atlantic commercial economy, they would have struck arriving Africans as offering responsible patronage of the sort that enslaved persons might have sought in Africa. The corruption of the commercial slavery in which they found themselves, in Africa as well as in Brazil, lay in the exigencies of the financial credit, rather than personal creditability, that underlay the enslaving connection and might, at any time, force potential patrons or patronesses to save themselves from impending bankruptcy by sacrificing the slave's nascent social bonds, exercising their right as owners to sell them, thus destroying, again, whatever bud of identity within slavery had sprouted. "Trust" kept, in the eighteenth-century English sense of credit entrusted to a debtor, meant the threat of personal trust betrayed to the slave seeking protection from endless transfer.

SLAVES' IDENTITIES IN THE EIGHTEENTH CENTURY

As the seventeenth century ended, and particularly after about 1700, the glitter of the gold in the hills of Minas Gerais ended the era in which religious symbols channeled the strategies of slaves and masters alike in Brazil and also drew men from central Africa, mostly embarked through Luanda and—increasingly— Benguela in the tens of thousands into the 1750s. In Minas Gerais, these central Africans encountered the Mina captives brought there through Bahia from many backgrounds in western Africa. They would have recognized a sense of commonality in terms of their backgrounds only decreasingly through the half century that they poured into the mining regions. Through the middle of the seventeenth century, most had come from Kimbundu-speaking areas subject to Portuguese military intrusions on either side of the lower Kwanza and from the southern part of the Kikongo-speaking region on the turbulent northern frontier of the colony.[40] During the latter decades of the century, captives from the Umbundu-speaking highlands south of the Kwanza joined them in increasing numbers, as well as others taken from the populous southern fringes of the equatorial forest by the emergent Ruund (Lunda) military forces based east of the Kasai. All the language-based communities of the region, from the forest margins to the Kalahari, were relatively diffuse and open, as individuals moved through them, and also in transition as people there formed new communities to defend themselves against slaving or to take advantage of the new opportunities to trade with the Atlantic. Generalized identities as "Bantu" and "Mina" tended to form in Brazil, as much around contrasting commercial origins as around contrasts specific to their backgrounds in western or central Africa.

In central Africa, the Umbundu-speaking highlands passed through a phase of extreme violence during a generation or so after the 1720s as the frontier of slaving violence swept through the region in response to the demand for labor in Minas Gerais.[41] It was also a time of profound realignments in identities within the diffuse linguistic community there as refugees moved to join warlords who might protect them from the raiding and began to regroup themselves according to the political loyalties, and hence identities, that would mature as the "Ovimbundu" states of the later part of the century. Although highlanders shared linguistic and other commonalities, many Umbundu-speakers had been seized in the process of creating these new, often intensely conflictive political identities. Any sense of shared ethnicity on which they might have drawn in Minas Gerais was as divisive in some contexts as it was uniting in others. They may have attained numbers sufficient to produce a coherent and self-conscious "Umbundu" cohort of arrivals, but only in Brazil, largely in contrast to the Africans from other areas whom they met there, and at a level of generality that blurred the sharp, frequently hostile, divisions that they had been defending as "Wambu" or "Mbailundo" in Africa. Since the growing variety of the origins of the central Africans and the instability of political identity in the turmoil of slaving at home, as well as the greater contrast between them and the West African Minas in Brazil, would have promoted only the broadest sense of shared backgrounds, they appropriated the commercial distinction of their masters as "Angolas" or "Benguelas" by their ports of embarkation in Africa. Small groups of countrymen might use specific "ethnic" affinities to collaborate for special purposes, networking ad hoc for mutual protection, but these associations were pragmatic tactics more than comprehensive, even politicized identities.

To the extent that distant African symbols of unity resonated through the distracting clamor of the enslaving connection, these survivors would have heard the echoes of Africa that had entered the popular culture of Catholic Brazil. The prominence, by the late eighteenth century, of the near-legendary king of Congo, at a time when people arriving from the Kongo region knew only deep divisions among many contending claimants to the mantle of the sixteenth-century monarchs who claimed that title, or the legendary reputation of Nzinga, the Imbangala-style leader who had settled at Matamba in the valley of the middle Kwango in the mid-seventeenth century and ended a long and eclectic career as a devout convert to Christianity, at a time when "Jinga" referred to a network of suppliers of captives acquired through Ruund suppliers from far to the east of the Kwango River, would thus have rested as much on their reputations—among the masters as much as among the slaves—as converts to the Christian faith as on any direct memory from Africa.[42] If the slaves gave African memories Catholic form in the sacraments of the Church, they also re-Africanized the Catholicism of the monarchs converted in Africa.

The central Africans, Angolas or Benguelas, who reached southern Brazil in the first half of the eighteenth century also congregated as the founding generation of the slave community in the city of Rio de Janeiro, the rapidly growing port of disembarkation and of resale of the men to buyers who marched them up the trails leading to the mining areas. One would expect the people assembled in Rio to have included a significantly higher portion of women and also of skilled servants familiar with the conventions of domestic service in Luanda and other Portuguese-influenced areas in Angola, commercial towns and military posts along the lower Kwanza, the agricultural estates along the lower Bengo River, and particularly from the compounds of the merchant gentry living in and around Ambaca.[43] These areas were as much Lusitanian in culture as African by the eighteenth century—hence their ambivalent designation in current scholarship as

"Luso-Africans" as well as "Afro-Portuguese."[44] The probably significant numbers of "Luandas" held captive in Brazil thus included a portion—mostly women and children—who experienced Angola's enslaving connection to Brazil as continuity in cultural context, behind disruptions all the more wrenching of successive membership in different households from Ambaca to Luanda to Rio.

To the extent to which Angolans might, in effect, have trained captives, or raised children in their households, for sale as higher-priced domestic servants in the gold-rich urban market that developed in the early eighteenth century in Rio, they would have been continuing the sixteenth- and seventeenth-century Iberian pattern of domestic slavery that had earlier contributed similarly proficient, and acculturated, individuals to the cities of the Spanish mainland and to Recife and Salvador in northeastern Brazil. The most successful of the women enslaved in these cities used their skills to gain control of the marketing of foodstuffs and other domestic provisions and services in the streets, establishing a marked professional identity for themselves in highly stylized dress and behavior, as the famous *quitandeiras* (*kitanda*, "marketplace" in Luanda Kimbundu, where the word and the profession were also basic to the city's life). The word for their profession was African, but produce markets were not characteristic of rural areas in central Africa, and their services were unique to the urban style of Portuguese cities on both ends of Brazil's enslaving connection. How they might have taken in the youthful captives from regions of Africa more remote from Portuguese and Christian influence who also joined them in the households of Rio is a question for the social historians of eighteenth-century Rio to examine.[45]

Similarly awaiting investigation are the commercialized strategies specific to the urban environment of Rio through which male slaves forged bonds of a more public sort. In Brazilian cities skilled males, presumably veterans of slavery who worked as artisans for incomes in cash (*negros de ganho*), generally formed occupational guilds around their professional skills. By the early nineteenth century, the newer arrivals created "nations" (*nações*) that invoked relatively specific linguistic and political backgrounds in Africa, probably reflecting the proliferation of specialized occupations in the increasingly complex urban economy of Brazilian cities.[46] These thus elaborated the commercialized identities, by ports of embarkation, important to their owners to subvert the dehumanization asserted by denominations imposed to emphasize their status as property. One would also consider the utility of *capoeira*, the Rio-centered training regimen based on alleged precedents in central Africa, as a secretive strategy of male discipline and bonding for mutual defense, adapted from the initiation schools for adolescents ubiquitous (at least by the nineteenth century) in the areas east of the Kwango, Kasai, and Kunene rivers, where increasing numbers of the youths taken as slaves to Brazil were originating after the 1750s.[47] These African methods of male bonding, in turn, responded to the massive displacement of populations as slaving developed there and thus as products of the enslaving connection itself, an experience increasingly indistinguishable from "background" in Africa as people moved and reformed themselves throughout the continent in response to the Atlantic commerce. Similarities, rather than connections through "transmission" from Africa and "preservation" in Brazil, may have been simultaneous, parallel elaborations of new ways of bonding refugees from slaving into neighborhood communities sponsored by elders in Africa but as gangs of adolescents under slavery in Brazil.[48]

The increasingly commercialized environment of Brazil's cities in the eighteenth century, as well as the growing significance of secular government guarantees of property, intensified the threat of repeated transfer through sale. The slaves thus menaced appropriated both commercial strategies and the law's protection of property to defend whatever ties of family and patronage they had been able to form by seizing opportunities for manumission. In the Brazilian context of relatively weak institutions of civil governance, slaves thus abandoned to private masters adapted their quests for responsible patronage from the religious sacraments of the seventeenth century to the commercial and civic opportunities of the eighteenth. Masters and mistresses continued to manumit in the name of older pieties of personal patronage, particularly for children of masters born within the patriarchal household to enslaved mothers, but other slaves able to earn cash in the streets of the cities entered into contracts with their owners that obligated the slave to pay a portion of her, or his, earnings, perhaps over many years, against manumission at whatever future time the payments reached an agreed commercial valuation. The price established did not represent a current market valuation, since the arrangement did not so much foresee a severance of the master-slave relationship through sale as it added a financial guarantee that converted the personal connection to a more enduring form of patronage, by—in effect—buying out the master's incentive to realize the slave's cash value by disposing of her or him to strangers. Such a self-purchase contract therefore did not end the connection but rather left slaves as clients in positions of increased autonomy, no longer subject to arbitrary removal but able to engage other patrons through employment or form voluntaristic associations with other slaves in the urban community, as they chose. Manumission brought not freedom in the North American sense of government-guaranteed civil rights but rather the liberty to construct identities by preserving personal networks of one's own.

When the Minas Gerais gold boom died down in the 1760s,[49] rural sugar plantations in the captaincy of Rio de Janeiro became the next region of Brazil in which African men assembled in numbers sufficient to form community identities independent of their masters' households. In numbers that exceeded those of any previous buildup of enslaved populations in Brazil, they came through Luanda and—probably especially—Benguela from the same growing diversity of backgrounds in central Africa as the others who remained in the city of Rio. I am unaware of research that suggests the distinctive sorts of communities that one might expect them to have created at this formative moment of the late boom in Brazilian sugar production, and it may be that the sheer masses of strangers thrown together worked relentlessly during the start-up phases of a new rural industry, on isolated plantations, without predecessors able to broker their relations with the baffling arbitrariness of their masters, and lacking successors, created fewer strategies of their own than their counterparts in the cities of Brazil.[50]

Slavery in Brazil imposed gendered expectations on boys and girls that were different from those that children grew up with in Africa. In Africa, the emphasis on male control of female fertility and reproduction created sharply differentiated, but comparably valued, roles according to sexual function. In Africa, enslavement tended to fall on women, whom men retained for their ability to bear them children without competing loyalties to maternal kin, at least in significant part. The enslaving connection brought males and females to Brazil in imbalanced proportions, perhaps as many as twice as many men as women throughout much of the trade. Beyond commercializing identity, it reduced populations to their productive functions on behalf of others and deprived Africans of their progeny, reproducing them through violence and by purchase.

For females family mattered most, in America as in Africa, and it would have done so increasingly in the nineteenth century as the streams of captives reaching Brazil included more and more youths, even children, without significant experience beyond the hearths of their parents, or of the strangers in Africa who had held them briefly as dependents within their households.[51] The advantage of kidnapping and enslaving children, widely affirmed throughout Africa, was that they grew up without memories of their early backgrounds, identifying themselves completely in terms of connections formed through their enslavement. Could they have remembered, or reconstructed, more in the Americas, under the pressures of slavery? The female minority tended to concentrate in domestic positions, where they were in positions to identify with their masters, if only by overcoming the sterility of enslavement by bearing the children who gave them identities and hopes for the future.

Since the generations born in Brazil included as many females as males, the females among this enslaved population were American, familiar with Africa only through the memories of their mothers. The primarily male populations born in Africa and brought to America were isolated in the fields and in the mines. Women tended to identify as Brazilian, looking forward and orienting their American-born children toward more private, domestic sorts of connections and identities through the rites of the Catholic Church and skills in manipulating the domestic and urban environments. The rural male population, constantly reinforced by new arrivals from Africa, would have appropriated the commercialized ethnicity attributed to slaves from Africa, developed occupational guilds, voluntary affiliations for mutual aid in other forms, particularly to confirm identities through burials that reunited, and ganglike initiatory societies for protection against other Africans. Women and men thus created gendered American identities parallel to those they had known in Africa—women oriented toward their children and men according to occupational skills, community maintenance, and youthful belligerence—but twisted them to draw on the resources available within slavery in Brazil and to survive the constraints of their enslavement.

The contextual, ephemeral, even opportunistic social identities of the sort made necessary by the fragility and transitoriness of personal affiliation within the permanence of slavery would have encouraged slaves to draw on their African sense for the multiple, instrumental identities thus evident in America. It would thus have been possible for the same boy, enslaved in Brazil, to identify himself by his family background to countrymen capable of recognizing the kin he had lost, by the village or region in which he had resided when he found himself in the company of others from the area within which people knew of one another's families, as "Ganguela" (*Ngangela*, the collective term that Kimbundu- and Umbundu-speaking peoples farther west applied to the very fluid and mobile communities who lived sparsely scattered on the dry, sandy plains east of the upper Kwanza and Kunene) when slavers in Angola tied him into a coffle with others of Ruund, or Nyaneka, or Umbundu backgrounds. Later he could be identified as Benguela or Angola or Luanda—depending on the port through which he and the great variety of others bound with him had passed together on their tortured ways to Brazil—when confronting masters, potential purchasers, or legal authorities in Rio de Janeiro or Minas Gerais. Such people were concerned solely with his status as property and more interested in his commercial identity than in personal ancestry, linguistic capabilities, or any other of the many sides that comprised the fully human, multifaceted individual that his life had made him. Men from the deeply rural areas east of the upper Kunene, remote from the missionaries active in Portuguese Angola, baptized in Benguela in only the most cursory fashion, if at all, might equally have sensed the power of the Christian "King of Congo" as a rallying cry under Catholic slavery in Brazil, even if they had never heard of the contenders for this title in Africa.

Slaves would thus have been adept at presenting themselves in terms meaningful in the situations in which they found themselves, particularly in reaction to the powerlessness of their enslavement. Historians should therefore consider the expectations of the author(s) of any source in which they find slaves designated, or designating themselves, by any singular origin in Africa: the sincerest and most calculating claims of a slave in such circumstances would have been guided by a strategy that reflected the nineteenth-century aphorism around which the Portuguese in Brazil also defined themselves, proudly and defiantly, in reaction to the powerful British among them: *para o Inglês ver*, artfully eliding the responsibility implied in saying "as we want the English to see it." Slaves could hardly have presented themselves to their masters with any lesser degree of sensitivity to their dependence.

CIVIC STATUS AND RACE—
THE NINETEENTH CENTURY

Brazil's last frontier of slavery developed in the nineteenth century with the rise of coffee production in the hills of São Paulo, inland from Rio and south of Minas Gerais. Coffee, in turn, supported the consolidation of the civic identity as "Brazilian," distinguished after declaration of political independence in 1822 from Portuguese identity associated with colonial rule and the several diverse captaincies inherited from it, and focused on the independent empire proclaimed. The British, closely involved with Portugal and also major investors behind the growth of new economic sectors in nineteenth-century Brazil, were resented as creditors and as abolitionists contradictorily bent on severing the enslaving connection on which the Brazilians depended to carve coffee estates out of tropical wilderness. Africans, and slaving, thus became a sensitive presence at the core of the formative Brazilian identity.

The demand for labor helped to drive imports of Africans to Brazil to heights never previously approached from the 1790s through the end of the transatlantic trade in 1850 and expanded the enslaving connection to a vast array of new regions in Africa, beyond continuing to exploit established sources of captives closer to Luanda and Benguela. East of Benguela, people in the central highlands acquired their modern identity as "Ovimbundu" in contrast to not entirely dissimilar peoples whom their caravans reached on the margins of the Kalahari Desert, along the upper Zambezi, and in the wooded savannas beyond the Kasai virtually in the center of the continent. They kept many, perhaps most, of the captives they acquired there, and so their new collective identity as Ovimbundu represented the local standards of comportment by which they judged deficient the strangers among them; ethnicity represented the local cultural measures of respectability that distinguished those born to them from immigrants simultaneously identified, and marginalized, as alien. Modern ethnicity in Africa thus drew its urgency from a nativistic reaction to the aliens that slaving introduced everywhere, making collective identities analogous to the "whiteness" achieved in the Americas through barriers raised in terms of race.

Traders at Luanda seem to have tapped the Kikongo-speaking areas to the north of the zone of Portuguese military occupation to an extent greater than they had in the eighteenth century.[52] After withdrawal of the British from the Atlantic trade in 1808, Brazilian slavers flocked to the coasts north of Luanda—Ambriz, the banks of the lower Zaire River, Cabinda, and Malimba and other ports along the Loango Coast—formerly dominated by the British and French. There they also acquired more Kikongo-speakers, or more captives from remote regions in the center of the continent bought from Kikongo-speaking sources than ever before in the history of the trade; for the first time, the area disturbed by slaving extended far up the interior reaches of the Zaire and its principal tributaries.[53] Other Rio slavers began rounding the Cape of Good Hope to buy captives from Quelimane, Inhambane, Delagoa Bay, and trading stations claimed by the Portuguese along the Moçambique coast of southeastern Africa; by the 1820s and 1830s, the "Moçambiques" they brought back with them had become a visible presence in southern Brazil because of their numbers and novelty. The coffee planters, increasingly through the century, built the laboring forces on their estates also by buying slaves, some of West African background and more and more of them Brazilian-born, from the less dynamic economies of northeastern Brazil. The distinctions relevant to this process of mixing tended toward the later inclusive, and generic, identification of the central (and southeastern) Africans as "Bantu."

From northeastern Brazil, the Pernambucans returned—though only on a relatively small scale—to Luanda and the coasts to the north, as did the Bahians, who congregated at the port at Cabinda that the French had abandoned early in the 1790s during the wars that had followed the French Revolution. The Bahians, however, concentrated on their established sources of captives at Ouidah and other ports along the West African Slave (Mina) Coast. As in central Africa, by that time the areas these ports drained of captives extended far inland, reaching the Muslim fringes of the Sahara Desert. In the resulting intense conflicts, characteristic of the initial phases of slaving everywhere in Africa, Muslim clerics there rallied victims and refugees to defend themselves behind the banners of Islam, and so the violence became known as *jihads*, "just wars" fought in the name of Islam. These wars sent the first large wave of Muslims, in unusually high proportions of males, to the ports of the Slave Coast, where the Bahians bought them. The region nearer the coast to the east of Ouidah also fell into an extended period of agonistic warfare at that time, producing a surge of Yoruba-speaking captives known in northeastern Brazil as "Nagôs." Withdrawal from the Niger Delta by the British, where they had concentrated their slaving in the late eighteenth century, opened the trading towns there also to Bahians, allowing them to introduce people from the "Igbo" areas east of the lower Niger—typically including more women than other streams in the Atlantic trade—for the first time. The boys and adolescent males from central Africa, Muslim men from the West African sudan, Yoruba-speakers, and Igbo women and men all arrived as new, self-consciously alien cohorts in slave communities in northeastern Brazil that had begun to blend, through decades of relatively steady arrivals through Ouidah, into a generic Mina population with a growing Afro-Brazilian component of children born and raised in Brazil.

The people arriving from Africa at this late stage in Brazil's enslaving connection thus came from so wide a range of regions that relatively few of them concentrated in numbers sufficient to organize in public, and hence visible, ways based on shared backgrounds. The new arrivals surely created informal networks of countrymen for mutual support in overcoming the isolation of their enslavement, particularly in the cities, but these *nacões* ("nations") were American institutions that, while they surely served newcomers well by functioning in some adaptation of their African maternal languages before they learned Portuguese, did not draw significantly on specific precedents—including local dialects—in the homelands of any of their members. The pragmatic urgency of surviving slavery surely overcame sentimental attachment to the world they had lost, except in the most personal senses. They also faced an early-nineteenth-century world in America in which civil institutions—in particular the police—were supplementing the personal authority of masters in the roles of surveillance and discipline. Hence, strategies in secular and public tones replaced the sacramental idioms in which their predecessors had organized themselves through Church-related *irmandades*, marriages and baptisms, and godparenthood, or the commercial registers in which later generations of human property had negotiated with proprietarial owners. In addition, the established populations of slaves whom arriving Africans joined in Rio and in the older provinces of the northeast included fewer and fewer African-born as reproduction began to generate groups of young Afro-Brazilians. Born into the American cultural milieu, and often connected to patrons among the masters, they were in positions to claim whatever public leadership might be available, and to do so on terms that were increasingly Brazilian.

Africans continued to organize along older lines of identities drawn from their backgrounds on the other side of the Atlantic only where the changing patterns of the Atlantic trade assembled them in new, numerous, and distinguishably different groups. The Moçambiques in southern Brazil appear to have seen themselves as "different" in this sort of practical, implementable sense in the Americas rather than on specific experiences anywhere within the very large portions of southeastern Africa where they had originated, or numerous ports of embarkation scattered along a thousand miles of coastline from Moçambique Island to the bay of Lourenço Marques.[54] In Bahia, the rush of war captives from the conflicts in the Yoruba-speaking regions and from the Muslim areas to the north of the Slave Coast provided the most notorious examples of the catalytic effect—in Brazil—of large numbers of discernibly different newcomers after 1810 and into the 1830s.[55] Unable to find places for themselves, one suspects, in the by-then-established communities of slaves, small parties of these men, perhaps utilizing parochial loyalties formed in the wars that had led to their enslavement, tended to retreat into maroon redoubts or to draw on the common, or at least related, language(s) they spoke to subordinate the enmity in their backgrounds to their need to collaborate in Brazil.[56] The adult male Muslims would have found their shared faith a vehicle, beyond otherworldly salvation, for both solace and self-help in the mundane tribulations of Brazilian slavery. Their skills seem to have led their buyers to employ them in urban pursuits, where—in the most famous, and exceptional, instance of slaves asserting themselves through connections they had brought from their African backgrounds—a group of recent arrivals, augmented through contacts they had developed in other segments of the slave population of Bahia and emboldened by their familiarity with their American circumstances, attempted the famous "Malê" rebellion of 1835.[57] This revolt came at the critical, transitional stage of abandoning Africa and coming to terms with America, a moment sufficiently informed to risk rebellion but insufficiently knowledgeable to appreciate its risks; a little knowledge turned out to be a dangerous temptation, and the revolt failed, betrayed in part by slaves of other persuasions. Igbo-speaking females and youthful central Africans would have tended to blend into the increasingly Afro-Brazilian community their predecessors had established and thus constituted presences less visible by characteristics attributed to Africa.

More commonly, the people enslaved in Brazil in the nineteenth century, apparently particularly in the northeast, turned their strategies of asserting collective identities to resist the cultural Brazilianization that was proceeding everywhere. A growing flow of immigrants from Europe, including many non-Portuguese, forced the heterogeneous mixture of free subjects of the emperors in Brazil to define their public identities in "national" terms, turning to race as what united them. The people of African descent, including greater and greater proportions of children born in Brazil, increasingly sought places for themselves as Afro-Brazilians. They distinguished themselves in broad, autonomous, and fundamentally Brazilian religious societies that featured prominently African idioms, drawing specific metaphors from the Yoruba connection brought by the last wave of slaves imported, new gods creditable by their novelty. These independent successors to the parish-sponsored *irmandades* of the eighteenth century became northeastern Brazil's famed *candomblé* and *umbanda* religio-social communities, and other reinventions of generically African cultural metaphors as symbols of resistance to slavery, inventing identities as African in reaction to racial exclusion in America.[58]

These modern strategies of building community remained inclusive and open, precisely the opposite of the particularity and exclusivity implied by the ethnic specificity of the African metaphors they appropriated: anyone could join, and Yoruba gods in their Brazilian garb stood more for "African" in the emerging generic sense of "Afro-Brazilian" than for any of the Yoruba-speaking communities that the slaves who introduced them had recalled from Africa. As with earlier healing strategies, the novelty of the gods of the Nagô appealed to Afro-Brazilians and to Africans who did not speak Yoruba not because they were old and familiar but precisely because they were new, untested, and therefore full of hope. They also extended the precedents of autonomous, individualized identities created by assimilated city slaves, men and women who had "bought" themselves and formed occupational associations in urban streets to rural plantation workers and, particularly, women as they faced assimilation as subordinated Brazilians. These cultural rallying points accordingly also attracted the larger and larger freed portion of the Brazilian population recognized and excluded as of African descent as slavery wore on toward its final, anticlimactic end in Brazil in 1888. They converted the symbols of their exclusion from the larger community of Brazilians as Africans to intensely collective strategies of surviving their marginalization as Americans. They were suspect in the wider society because they were secret, but they were tolerated because their religious idiom made them appear irrelevantly harmless in an era when political dissent was the most dangerous challenge to the emergent civic community. African religious metaphors had moved from being profoundly threatening in an earlier age of faith to appearing benignly exotic in a secular age of technological progress.

As slavery withered after imports of new people from Africa all but ended in 1850, refined distinctions of skin tone among the "colored" population replaced the former contrast between experienced, Portuguese-speaking, Catholic *ladinos* (acculturated individuals) and untrained, unintelligible *brutos* (nonacculturated individuals) from Africa. The communities and connections that the enslaved had formed were yielding to the permanent affiliations that Afro-Brazilians asserted as "blacks" against the exclusions of the racist order of progress defined in late-century Brazil as European, exclusive of the traditional Africa it defined in contrast, and that those excluded therefore embraced for purposes of their own. For the Afro-Brazilians, born in America, Africa became a memory constructed rather than an experience from which they constructed identities. These strategies, in turn, survived the end of slavery as vital centers of the spiritual, and community, identities of many Brazilians today.

CONCLUSIONS: BRAZIL'S ENSLAVING CONNECTION AS HISTORY AND MEMORY

Progressive heirs of the European Enlightenment consider history as change and its alterations as cumulative and irreversible; we can never go back "home" again. The self, an inherent, stable personal identity, we struggle to realize as growth and development from a formless childishness left behind; of course, we fail. In a capitalist environment, we also accumulate materially to become—in significant degrees—what we own. Africans, in contrast, constructed fluid identities out of the succession of circumstances in which they found themselves, as recognized by the people with whom they could establish secure, unquestionable relations of respect; they "were" the company they kept. They made themselves as centers of the personal networks they could construct. The violence of commercial enslavement reduced them to powerless, anonymous nonentities by making every connection they created arbitrarily severable by others.

Understanding the enslaving connection, as slaves might have experienced it, requires us to extend our suspension of modernist assumptions to the ways in which they reacted to their sudden loss of the familiar and comfortable: by retaining what they could, recreating parts they could not in new forms, and remembering in complex ways, all to restore the social connections that made them who they were. Those born in Africa but uprooted and taken to America might apply shared associations from their lives on the opposite shore of the Atlantic directly to the entirely novel circumstances in which they lived. It is we who try to understand what they did by tracing continuities in form and metaphor from the perspective of the modernist emphasis on history as change, as recreating the past, as experienced, in the present. But it is now becoming clear that Africans experienced the changes that have always occurred in Africa on conceptual premises that reversed this strategy: they encountered change not by an emphasis on the increasing distance from times gone by as loss, adding the roseate overlays of the remembered past that we generate, but rather as an opportunity to preserve continuity, starting from an idealized past to which they must convert the present.[59] The present they thus approached as a restorative challenge rather than lamenting the past as unrecoverable loss. The past they experienced as connection rather than as separation, and the anger of the ancestors always reminded them when they abandoned it. In practice, they realized the past in the present by interpreting the circumstances in which they found themselves as aspects, often subtly camouflaged and difficult to recognize, of where, and when, they meant to be. What they could not adjust, they tended to accept as fate, however inexplicable. The most African aspect of the Africans' struggles for identity under slavery was therefore the adaptability with which they retuned specific echoes of their personal pasts to resonate collectively in the novel circumstances they encountered in the Americas.

Africans and—later—Afro-Brazilians would have connected to an Africa of many different meanings as remembered roots from which they would connect their lives under slavery in America, attempting to restore the ordered continuity that everyone sought to maintain in the face of the arbitrary personal disruptions, the identity crises, of transfers into isolating novelty of terrifyingly relentless, recurrent proportions. Commercial slavery was quintessentially historical in the modern sense of unpredictable, incomprehensible discontinuity. But they would not have depended on preserving the specific metaphors that strike Western modernists as "connecting" slaves in Brazil back to Africa to create a sense of continuity through their enslavement. Rather, as they subtly converted Catholic communion and capitalist ownership to strategies of belonging in an African sense, or adapted African techniques of consolidating bonds of patronage and clientage to counter the ephemerality of their bondage as slaves in Brazil, they struggled in ways they had learned at home to restore a sense of seamless continuity to the rent fabrics of their lives, not for identity in terms of where they came from, for they had irretrievably lost their ancestral origins, except in death, but rather through the new connections they could build to survive, to be recognized, to become visible to one another amidst the disrupted anonymity of slavery in which they lived.

But they confirmed connections, thus establishing identities, by seizing the opportunities offered by the culture of their masters in ways that changed also, from ecclesiastical and sacramental devotion in the seventeenth century to the secular and commercial strategies of the eighteenth and the complementing civic inclusiveness and racial exclusivity of the nineteenth. Before about 1600 in Pernambuco and Bahia, they came mostly as skilled servants who identified themselves more with their masters as patrons than they drew on specific backgrounds in Africa, except as clientage figured in strategies there. When larger numbers of enslaved people arrived directly from Africa in the seventeenth century, the surges of slaves from limited regions there may have allowed them to create senses of community based on selected commonalities in their backgrounds, but they used the sacraments of the church to mask the shift to asserting identities independent of their masters, women in private, domestic modes and men in more public ways. Minas Gerais, followed by the city of Rio and the sugar-growing regions around it, and eventually the cotton-growing north, assembled the laboring majorities who built their economies and populated their societies in much more commercialized ways; there, these founding generations appropriated the laws of property and occupational specializations to carve nascent communities out of the instability of life under capitalist slavery, women converting the domestic ties of their predecessors to contracts of manumission and men grouping around their proprietarial value to their masters. Their masters, in turn, understood their abilities as inherent to fictive ethnic identities that reflected where they had been captured or purchased more than who they had been. In a relationship of theoretically total domination, slaves could create identities for themselves only in ways their masters could not see or by exploiting for their own purposes the identities attributed to them by their masters. What glittered most exotically as "African" often appeared as gold only to those whom slaves fooled.

Brazilianization of the coffee estates of São Paulo and environs symbolized nineteenth-century strategies of constructing a collective memory of an Africa no longer personally recalled by slaves with less direct experience of Africa. By that late stage in the history of Brazil's enslaving connection, fewer and fewer people came from African backgrounds sufficiently similar, or individually stable, to provide unambiguous identities of any sort; slaving spreading throughout Africa was propelling more and more people through bewildering successions of marginal affiliations to communities alien to anything they had ever known and that they understood barely, if at all. The tiny minorities of youths, many of them barely out of severely disrupted childhoods, found few useful, even recognizable, commonalities of background amidst the multiplicity of micro-*nações* in Rio, nor did being vaguely Bantu in the polyglot mixture of West Africans in Bahia mean much to the people who came there from central Africa. The amalgam of Africans relocated to the central provinces of imperial Brazil to plant, tend, and harvest coffee alongside Afro-Brazilians transferred there from the north created a workforce consciousness of a novel, Brazilian sort out of the burdens of toil together on the coffee estates. In the northeast, the ancient religious idiom of forming communities was resurrected once again by applying *candomblé* symbols that relatively coherent recent waves of immigrants had brought from Africa to circumstances in Brazil, as the restraints of slavery eroded and civic senses of society replaced religious conformity. This Brazilianization of Africa met the challenges of growing racial consciousness in Brazil, as Afro-Brazilians generalized the specific elements they appropriated to construct an image of a continent remembered generically and publicly, differently than coherent cohorts of earlier Africans had recalled from their personal experiences of family and other associations there.

As history, the slaves thus adapted their struggles for identity in Brazil to the changing circumstances in which they found themselves: to slavery itself in forms that varied from town to country and region to region, under masters who adapted their strategies from religious to commercial to civic and national frameworks from the sixteenth to the nineteenth centuries, from the many abilities and experiences in Africa of the founding generations of adults to the unformed potential of the children who followed them near the end of the trade, from the relatively narrow range of African regions involved at the start of the trade to the disruptions of continental proportions near its end, from the openness that the founding generations of slaves encountered early in each captaincy of Brazil to the increasingly established slave communities in which later arrivals had to find places for themselves. We are all products of our pasts, as we adapt experience to grasp the circumstances we face in the present as they unfold. In this complex interplay of strategies of retaining what works, recreating it anew to make it work, and remembering it as the past to authenticate it, the first slaves to reach Brazil had only Africa on which to draw; their successors looked back to American precedents, adapting religious connections to commercial purposes, and those in turn to civic claims, each generation remembering Africa in broader and broader terms of what it came to mean to them as slaves in America.

NOTES

1. Therefore presented without a systematic attempt to cite the rich, diverse, and currently very active scholarship on which I draw, from "Atlantic history," the "African diaspora" and the "black Atlantic," Africanist scholarship, poststructuralist efforts to historicize quite unhistorical approaches that have too often passed for "history," and other currents familiar to readers.

I have explored, in a preliminary way, some of these issues as they come up in the historiography of Africa in "History and Africa/Africa and History," *American Historical Review* 104, no. 1 (1999): 1–32. The specific discussion here in part elaborates points sketched in another context in "Central Africa during the Era of the Slave Trade, c. 1490s-1850s," in *Central Africans and Cultural Transformations in the American Diaspora*, ed. Linda Heywood (New York: Cambridge University Press, 2002), pp. 21–69.

2. My emphasis on enslaved Africans' quest for connections historicizes one key term in Orlando Patterson's famous definition of slavery by invoking more recent conceptions of identity, personal and collective. See his *Slavery and Social Death: A Comparative Study* (Cambridge, Mass.: Harvard University Press, 1982), p. 12: "*the permanent, violent domination of natally alienated* [i.e., uprooted] *and generally dishonored persons*" (author's italics, my parenthetical gloss).

My emphasis on this aspect of the enslaving connection has been sharpened by readings of John Edwin Mason's application of Patterson's definition to slaves at the Cape of Good Hope, in *Social Death and Resurrection: Slavery and Emancipation in South Africa* (Charlottesville: University of Virginia Press, 2003), and of Philip Troutman's "Slave Trade and Sentiment in Antebellum Virginia" (Ph.D. diss., University of Virginia, 2000). For a very well developed exploration of the multiplicity and complexity of identity through and under enslavement (though with different emphases), see Paul E. Lovejoy and Robin Law, introduction to *The Biography of Mahommah Gardo Baquaqua*, ed. Lovejoy and Law (Princeton: Markus Wiener, 2001).

3. An epistemological aside: if history proceeds from dialectical confrontations, as I believe it does, rendering one party to the dialectic as primarily, or even significantly, reactive to the other fails to establish the independence of motivation and strategy necessary for a synthesis that goes beyond merely extending the agenda of the dominant party. Without effectively autonomous parties to the dialectic, history remains deterministic and teleological, the story of the "winners" and their victims. In the case of Brazil and Africa, truly historical, unintended outcomes resulted from the not directly competitive struggles between Africans desperate to replace the community they had lost and Europeans struggling to recover from commercial failure.

4. See recent reinterpretations of Palmares that emphasize the native American presence in a mid/early seventeenth-century "maroon" community ordinarily celebrated for the Africans among its residents; e.g., Pedro Paulo Funari, "A arqueologia de Palmares:

sua contribuição para o conhecimento da história da cultura afro-americana," in *Liberdade por um fio: história dos quilombos no Brasil*, ed. João José Reis and Flávio dos Santos Gomes (São Paulo: Companhia das Letras, 1996), pp. 26–51.

5. Manolo Garcia Florentino, *Em costas negras: uma história do tráfico Atlântico de escravos entre a África e o Rio de Janeiro (séculos xviii e xix)* (São Paulo: Companhia de Letras, 1997); Joseph C. Miller, *Way of Death: Merchant Capitalism and the Angolan Slave Trade, 1730–1830* (Madison: University of Wisconsin Press, 1988). For the "illegal trade" of the nineteenth century, see Roquinaldo do Amaral Ferreira, "Dos sertões ao Atlântico: tráfico ilegal de escravos e comércio lícito em Angola, 1830–1860" (Dissertação de Mestrado, Universidade Federal do Rio de Janeiro, Instituto de Filosofia e Ciências Sociais, Programa de Pós-Graduação em História Social, s.d. [1997])

6. Where this fact was also more important than usually appreciated. Since 1998, I have been directing National Endowment for the Humanities Summer Institutes based on the premise that teachers of (north) American history and culture cannot understand the formative years of what became the United States without knowing Africa, and the enslaved Africans who came from there, as well as they understand Elizabethan England; see the Web site for "Roots: The African Dimensions of Early American History and Culture," http://www.virginia.edu/vfh/roots.

I am aware of recent demographic studies that identify late and isolated pockets of population growth achieved by Afro-Brazilians in Minas Gerais and elsewhere; conveniently summarized in Herbert S. Klein, *The Atlantic Slave Trade* (New York: Cambridge University Press, 1999).

7. With due credit to recent efforts by leading scholars of Atlantic and American history to incorporate Africa, whose ways of including the continent do not deserve specific identification in the context of emphasizing their limitations.

Robin Blackburn, *The Making of New World Slavery: From the Baroque to the Modern* (London, New York: Verso, 1996), elegantly traces the contribution of slavery to the making of modernity in Europe and its American dependencies but does not explore the nonmodern premises of the Africans, or native Americans, consumed in the process. An earlier volume in this magnificent series, Blackburn's *The Overthrow of Colonial Slavery, 1776–1848* (London: Verso, 1988), centers on the revolution of emancipation as the slaves made it, but almost exclusively on the modernist aspects of these struggles during and after the North American revolt.

8. As John K. Thornton has emphasized for Europe before the eighteenth century, *Africa and Africans in the Making of the Atlantic World, 1500–1680*, 2d exp. ed. (New York: Cambridge University Press, 1998). However, modern Europeans and Africans are much less unlike than the racial ideologies of the nineteenth and twentieth centuries construed them.

9. Obviously Orlando Patterson's effort to problematize *Freedom in the Making of Western Culture* (New York: Basic Books, 1991), though not all of his specific arguments, contributes to my formulation of the issues in this chapter.

For my preliminary statements on "freedom" as an ideology of modernity, see "Freedom," in *Macmillan Encyclopedia of World Slavery*, ed. Paul Finkelman and Joseph C. Miller (New York: Macmillan/Scribner's, 1998), vol. 1, pp. 344–46, and "Stratégies de la marginalité. Une approche historique de l'utilisation des êtres humains et des idéologies de l'esclavage: Progéniture, piété, production personelle et prestige—Produits et profits des propriétaires," *Déraison, esclavage idelogiques et juridiques et la traite négrière et de l'esclavage*, ed. Isabel Castro Henriques and Louis Sala-Moulins (Lisbon, Portugal, 9–10 December 1998) (Paris: UNESCO Editions, 2002), pp. 105–60.

10. The exceptions were some—though not all—Muslims from West Africa. João José Reis, *Slave Rebellion in Brazil: The Muslim Uprising of 1835 in Bahia*, rev. and exp. ed. (Baltimore: Johns Hopkins University Press, 1993); Paul E. Lovejoy, "Background to Rebellion: The Origins of Muslim Slaves in Bahia," in *Unfree Labour in the Development of the Atlantic World*, ed. Lovejoy and Nicholas Rogers (London: Frank Cass, 1994), pp. 151–82, and Paul E. Lovejoy, "Cerner les identités au sein de la Diaspora africaine: l'Islam et l'esclavage aux Amériques," trans. Raphaëlle Masseaut, *Cahiers des Anneaux de la Mémoire* 1 (1999): 249–77.

11. The bodily scarifications, symbols of identity in Africa, around which Michael A. Gomez has built his intriguing history of Africans in North America; *Exchanging Our Country Marks: The Transformation of African Identities in the Colonial and Antebellum South* (Chapel Hill: University of North Carolina, 1998).

12. David Northrup, "Igbo and Myth Igbo: Culture and Ethnicity in the Atlantic World, 1600–1850," *Slavery and Abolition* 21, no. 3 (2000): 1–20.

13. For example, Robin Law, "Ethnicity and the Slave Trade: 'Lucumi' and 'Nago' as Ethnonyms in West Africa," *History in Africa* 24 (1997): 205–19; J. Lorand Matory, "The English Professors of Brazil: On the Diasporic Roots of the Yorùbá Nation," *Comparative Studies in Society and History* 41, no. 1 (1999): 72–103.

14. Miller, "Central Africa during the Era of the Slave Trade."

15. See the many writings of John Thornton emphasizing the Christianization of Kongo. In the sense in which I understand political processes in the region, "Congo" was redundant on "Christian"; it ought not to go as unremarked as it normally does that the religion dissipated along with the monarchy in the nineteenth century. I sense no other unity among the many groups who defined and redefined themselves in that area throughout its long history of slaving and slave trading.

16. Consider the linguistic hodgepodge of dialect, language, groups of languages at every level from the most closely related to broadly linked families that scholars have appropriated as evidence of commonality. Analogous levels of difference from Indo-European languages—which obviously divide in some contexts but unite in others—would include Brazilian and peninsular Portuguese, Portuguese and Spanish, the Romance-language countries in the European community, western European languages in relation to Slavic, and so on.

17. I have attempted to present Angolan "ethnicity" in these historicized terms in "Worlds Apart: Africans' Encounters and Africa's Encounters with the Atlantic in Angola, before 1800," in *Actas do Seminário "Encontro de povos e culturas em Angola"* (Lisbon: Instituto de Investigação Científica Tropical, 1997), pp. 227–80. See also my general comment on ethnicity in "History and Africa/Africa and History," pp. 16–17.

These African limitations on the utility of "ethnicity" precede most of the considerations that have structured recent, animated discussions of "creolization" and other aspects of slaves' (and modern African Americans') identification with "roots" in Africa. The historical scholarship disputes the degree to which enslaved Africans might have preserved their Africanness (opposing positions: Mintz/Price/Morgan vs. Hall/Chambers) but problematizes what might have composed that "Africanness" only in terms of the conventional ethnic distinctions, for example, whether American terms like "Calabar" or "Congo" refer to African ethnic groups or to ports in Africa through which slaves had passed.

The politics of African Americans' current intense exploration of their identification with Africa, beyond Afrocentrism, have swirled around Henry Lewis Gates's PBS series on the "Wonders of the African World" and most recently in the celebrated reception given Gwendolyn Midlo Hall's database of information on Louisiana slaves as a genealogical resource. To understand the Gates video, one must read the accompanying volume, *Wonders of the African World* (New York: Knopf, 1999); for the discussion, also see critiques assembled in a special issue of the journal *West Africa Review* [online], www.westafricareview. com/war/); also reviews in *AHA Perspectives* 38, no. 5 (2000): 50–53. For Gwendolyn Midlo Hall, see her *Databases for the Study of Afro-Louisiana History and Genealogy, 1699–1860* (Baton Rouge: Louisiana State University Press, 1999), and widespread media publicity. This concern also structured much discussion at the recent Crossing Boundaries conference (New York University, 20–23 September 2000).

18. The basic, and at the same time peripheral, issue around which most attempts to understand slavery in Africa have revolved. Two key contrasting statements are Suzanne Miers and Igor Kopytoff, eds., *Slavery in Africa: Historical and Anthropological Perspectives* (Madison: University of Wisconsin Press, 1977), and Claude Meillassoux, *The Anthropology of Slavery: The Womb of Iron and Gold*, trans. Alide Dasnois, foreword by Paul E. Lovejoy (Chicago: University of Chicago Press, 1991). See also Paul E. Lovejoy, *Transformations in Slavery: A History of Slavery in Africa* (Cambridge: Cambridge University Press, 1983; 2d ed., 2000).

19. Hence the tendency in several parts of the continent to distinguish, with differing terminology, slaves acquired for purposes of integration from others held only temporarily while awaiting further transfer. One also notes the repeated transfers that marked the progress of slaves who eventually reached the Americas and survived to write narratives of their experiences; we have fewer comparable narratives from the descendants of those retained, which would presumably—almost by definition—reveal fewer movements.

20. Blackburn, *Making of New World Slavery*, identifies similarly formative nodes in terms of the heavily capitalized plantations of the (mostly British) Caribbean, but the criterion here is demographic rather than economic.

21. I am thus building on Gomez's sense for how the North American children of Africans exchanged their parents' "country marks" for the complex racial distinctions that emerged as they grew up early in the nineteenth-century United States, but I view the Africans' identities in terms more complex and flexible than Gomez develops.

22. The literature on slavery has made little use of literature on the sociology of groups of strangers forced to live together under severe constraints: refugees, impoverished immigrants, and prison inmates. In all of these cases, mafia-style "gangs" both provide structure within communities living largely outside the framework of the established society and exploit the vulnerability that they also organize. In some plantation contexts and in most situations of urban slavery, including those in Brazil, large enough numbers of slaves congregated sufficiently beyond the reach of direct supervision of their owners to create spaces for secretive voluntary associations of this sort.

23. The latter, principal form of experience that John Thornton has emphasized in a series of careful investigations of the specific African circumstances from which identifiable groups asserted themselves openly in the Americas: see his "African Dimensions of the Stono Rebellion," *American Historical Review* 96, no. 4 (1991): 1101–13; "African Soldiers in the Haitian Revolution," *Journal of Caribbean History* 25, nos. 1–2 (1991): 58–80, and "'I am the Subject of the King of Congo': African Political Ideology and the Haitian Revolution," *Journal of World History* 4, no. 2 (1993): 181–214. All recently framed by Thornton in *Warfare in Atlantic Africa, 1500–1800* (London: UCL Press, 1999).

24. Witchcraft, as the metaphor through which Africans experienced the era of slaving, has only begun to receive the systematic investigation that it merits. See Miller, *Way of Death*, for an initial glimpse of the trade as those enslaved in Angola viewed it; also Gomez, *Exchanging Our Country Marks*, and Rosalind Shaw, "The Production of Witchcraft/Witchcraft as Production: Memory, Modernity, and the Slave Trade in Sierra Leone," *American Ethnologist* 24, no. 4 (1997): 856–67. Elizabeth Isichei has explored the popular consciousness of slaving (and other aspects of modernity) in "Cowries, Statues and Zombis: Some African Representations of Wealth and Death from the Sea," unpublished paper presented at the conference, The Atlantic Slave Trade in African and African American Memory, University of Chicago, 23–25 May 1997. See also Elizabeth Isichei, *Voices of the African Poor* (Rochester: University of Rochester Press, 2002).

25 The indications of terror abound in the studies cited in the preceding note, including their images of Europeans as cannibals (closely akin to witches) and the well-known fright that many Africans experienced upon catching sight of the large copper cauldrons kept on the decks of the ships they were boarding. The ambitious, promising, and very suggestive work of James H. Sweet, "Recreating Africa: Race, Religion, and Sexuality in the African-Portuguese World, 1441–1770" (Ph.D. diss., City University of New York, 1999), probes these and other intimate aspects of Africans' lives under slavery to degrees that should set a broad agenda for further research. For preliminary results, see his "Male Homosexuality and Spiritism in the African Diaspora: The Legacies of a Link," *Journal of the History of Sexuality* 7, no. 2 (1996): 184–202, and "Recreating Africa: Mbundu 'Calundu' Rituals and Portuguese Response in Seventeenth-Century Brazil" (Unpublished presentation, Forum on European Expansion and Global Interaction—Third Biennial Meeting, St. Augustine, Florida, February 17–19, 2000). Also see Eric Taylor, "If We Must Die: A History of Shipboard Insurrections during the Slave Trade" (Ph.D. diss., University of California—Los Angeles, 2000).

26. Another uninvestigated aspect of the slaves' experience of their enslavement is the element of resignation that Africans would have brought from philosophical backgrounds—Muslim and other—that emphasized acceptance and the virtues of clientage to responsible patrons. Assertiveness inspired by a modern sense of righteous individualism would not likely have occurred to people thinking in terms like those that James C. Scott has explored as the *Weapons of the Weak* [*Everyday Forms of Peasant Resistance*] (New Haven: Yale University Press, 1985) utilized by humble people who act, positively and efficaciously, but mostly privately, emerging on the public stage of politics only when authorities of unquestioned legitimacy fail to meet their responsibilities in an accepted *Moral Economy of the Peasant* [*Rebellion and Subsistence in Southeast Asia*] (New Haven: Yale University Press, 1976). Such premises account plausibly for Africans'

"rebellions" in the Americas against personal abuses of slavery that foresaw victory as continuing the enslavement of others.

27. Much of the following builds on patterns of African origins and Atlantic slaving routes elaborated in Miller, "Central Africa during the Era of the Slave Trade."

28. This pattern recurred widely throughout the Americas in the first generation of slaves, in the Iberian colonies as an extension of the prevailing styles of domestic slavery in the Renaissance Mediterranean. Ira Berlin has called attention to it from an English perspective (though to a degree that seems excessive to me) in *Many Thousand Gone: The First Two Centuries of Slavery in North America* (New York: Oxford University Press, 1998), and especially in "From Creole to African: Atlantic Creoles and the Origins of African American Society in Mainland North America," *William and Mary Quarterly* 53, no. 2 (1996): 251–88.

29. A close reading of Stuart B. Schwartz, *Sugar Plantations in the Formation of Brazilian Society: Bahia, 1550–1835* (New York: Cambridge University Press, 1986), reveals the vagueness of this phase of slavery in Brazil. An even greater obscurity envelopes the formative years in Pernambuco, except for the recent Pedro Puntoni, *A mísera sorte: a escravidão africana no Brasil holandês e as guerras do tráfico no Atlântico sul, 1621–1648* (São Paulo: HUCITEC, 1999).

The regional specificity of the enslaving connection, generally throughout the Atlantic trade, has been one of the significant patterns revealed by analysis of the database of slaving voyages; particular parts of the Americas tended to receive slaves consistently from the same parts of the African coast, at least over the short to medium term.

30. This *asiento* trade and its concentration at the government-controlled post at Luanda, in what was becoming the *conquista* (Portuguese-controlled territory) of Angola is much better known. For a summary of this trade, which peaked between 1600 and 1620, see "Central Africa during the Era of the Slave Trade," n. 10.

31. See the attempts to infer these numbers based on quantities of sugar produced in David Eltis, Stephen D. Behrendt, and David Richardson, "A participação dos países da Europa e das Américas no tráfico transatlântico de escravos: Novas evidéncias," *Afro-Asia* 24 (2000): 9–50. Another recent revision of the figures is found in David Eltis, "The Volume and Structure of the Transatlantic Slave Trade: A Reassessment," *William and Mary Quarterly* 58, no. 1 (2001): 17–46.

32. Johannes Postma, *The Dutch in the Atlantic Slave Trade 1600–1815* (New York: Cambridge University Press, 1990); Cornelis Ch. Goslinga, *The Dutch in the Caribbean and in the Guianas, 1680–1791* (Wolfeboro, N.H.: Longwood, 1985); Jonathan I. Isreal, *The Dutch Republic: Its Rise, Greatness, and Fall, 1477–1806* (New York: Oxford University Press, 1995).

33. Readers will sense the implicit doubt that this phrasing casts on the legendarily "Angolan" character of the "state" at Palmares, at least at the time being considered at this point in the argument; skeptics might recall that maroon communities, too, had their histories, and that conditions in the 1630s did not anticipate those that resulted from major changes after 1650 in the origins of the Africans in northeastern Brazil. Until we have evidence that dates these aspects of the history of Palmares, decade by decade, conclusions based on later evidence should be applied only to the subsequent periods they illuminate. For a comparable argument applied to São Tomé, see Jan Vansina, "Quilombos on S. Tomé, or in Search of Original Sources," *History in Africa* 23 (1996): 453–59.

SECTION I: THE LUSO-BRAZILIAN SLAVE TRADE

34. An argument made in Joseph C. Miller, *Way of Death: Merchant Capitalism and the Angolan Slave Trade, 1730–1830* (Madison: University of Wisconsin Press, 1988). I will not make specific references to the numerous premises argued there.

35. Dauril Alden and Joseph C. Miller, "Unwanted Cargoes: The Origins and Dissemination of Smallpox via the Slave Trade from Africa to Brazil, c. 1560–1830," in *The African Exchange: Toward a Biological History of the Black People*, ed. Kenneth F. Kiple (Durham, N.C.: Duke University Press, 1988), pp. 35–109; revised as "Out of Africa: The Slave Trade and the Transmission of Smallpox to Brazil, ca. 1560–ca. 1830," *Journal of Interdisciplinary History* 18, no. 2 (1987): 195–224.

36. Robin Law, *The Slave Coast of West Africa, 1550–1750: The Impact of the Atlantic Slave Trade on an African Society* (London: Oxford University Press, 1991), pp. 282–85.

37. Roughly: a first wave in the 1620s and 1630s, disrupted by Dutch conquest and the wars that restored Pernambuco and Bahia to Portuguese control; a second wave in the 1650s and 1660s, based on Pernambucan control at Luanda; and the third wave of Minas inaugurated by the Bahians in the 1670s and 1680s.

38. See Jan Vansina, *Paths in the Rainforest: Toward a History of Political Tradition in Equatorial Africa* (Madison: University of Wisconsin Press, 1990), for the terminological distinction, correlated to the spread of commercial slaving through central Africa; the difference was also recognized elsewhere, for example, among the Asante. See Larry W. Yarak, "Slavery and the State in Asante History," in *The Cloth of Many Colored Silks: Papers in History and Society, Ghanaian and Islamic, in Honor of Ivor Wilks*, ed. John Hunwick and Nancy Lawler (Evanston, Ill.: Northwestern University Press, 1996), pp. 223–40.

39. João José Reis, "Identidade e diversidade étnicas nas irmandades negras no tempo da escravidão," *Tempo* (Revista do Departamento de História da Universidade Federal Fluminense) 2, no. 3 (1997): 7–33.

40. See Miller, *Way of Death*, esp. chap. 5, for these and other phases of the advance of slaving inland through central Africa; also summarized in Miller's "Central Africa During the Era of the Slave Trade."

41. For the details of this process, see Joseph C. Miller, "Angola central e sul por volta de 1840," in *Estudos afro-asiáticos* (Centro de Estudos Afro-Asiáticos, Rio de Janeiro) 32 (1997): 7–54.

42. This hypothesis interprets John Thornton's insistence on the Catholicity of the Kongo state, as Linda Heywood is now extending the emphasis on the extent of early Christianization in the Ndongo/Matamba areas east of Luanda, as memory in America as well as reality in Africa; it historicizes the enslaving connection to suggest that slaves invented these particular symbols out of the circumstances that they encountered in the mid-eighteenth century in central and southern Brazil, rather than as a direct, mechanical continuity from Africa. See John Thornton, "Kongo and Mbundu Religious Life in the 16th and 17th Centuries," and Linda Heywood, "Portuguese into African: The Eighteenth-Century Central African Background to Atlantic Afro-Creole Cultures"; and Elizabeth Kiddy, "Who Is the King of Kongo: A New Look at African and Afro-Brazilian Kings in Brazil," in *Central Africans and Cultural Transformations in the American Diaspora*, ed. Heywood, pp. 71–90 and 91–113, respectively.

One eagerly anticipates new work from Cathy Skidmore-Hess on the historical Nzinga and from Linda Heywood on this famed monarch's memory in Angola and Brazil.

43. The "Ambaquistas" are beginning to receive closer attention from historians; see Evá Sebestyén and Jan Vansina, "Angola's Eastern Hinterland in the 1750s: A Text Edition and Translation of Manoel Correia Leitão's 'Voyage' (1755–1756)," *History in Africa* 26 (1999): 299–364; also Jan Vansina, "Ambaca Society and the Slave Trade, c. 1740–1840" (Unpublished manuscript, 1998). Also Jill R. Dias, "Estereótipos e realidades sociais: quem eram os 'Ambaquistas'" (Unpublished paper, Seminário—"Construindo a História Angolana: As Fontes e a sua Interpretação," Luanda, 4–8 August 1997) and Jill R. Dias, "Mudanças nos padrões de poder no *hinterland* de Luanda: o impacto da colonização sobre os Mbundu," *Penélope* 14 (1994): 43–91.

44. And known well as it flourished in the first half of the nineteenth century, particularly through the work of Jill R. Dias; a summary in "Angola," in *O Império africano 1825–1890*, coords. Valentim Alexandre and Jill Dias (*Nova história da expansão portuguesa*, vol. 10, dirs. Joel Serrão and A. H. de Oliveira Marques) (Lisbon: Editorial Estampa, 1998), pp. 319–556.

For the eighteenth century, beyond the sketches in Miller, *Way of Death*, see Joseph C. Miller and John K. Thornton, "The Chronicle as Source, History, and Hagiography: The 'Catálogo dos Governadores de Angola,'" *Paideuma* 33 (1987): 359–89 (translated as "A crónica como fonte, história e hagiografia: O *Catálogo dos Governadores de Angola*," *Revista internacional de estudos africanos* 12–13 [1990]: 9–55), and Miller, "Feeding the City: Luanda's *Terreiro Público* in the Eighteenth Century" (draft paper presented at conference on "Africa's Urban Past," London, School of Oriental and African Studies, 19–21 June 1996).

Selma Pantoja is advancing the level of work on eighteenth-century Luanda in "Luanda: relações sociais e de gênero," in *A dimensão atlântica da África* (II Reunião Internacional de História de África, Rio de Janeiro, 30 October–1 November 1996) (São Paulo: CEA-USP/SDG-Marinha/CAPES, 1997), pp. 75–81, and "Traders and Farms: Women and the Food Trade in the City of Luanda from the Eighteenth to the Nineteenth Century" (Unpublished paper, "Bantu into Black: Central Africans in the Atlantic Diaspora," international conference, Howard University, 16–18 September 1999); and other work in progress.

45. Here one eagerly awaits the results of the research of Manolo G. Florentino. In the meantime, see his "About the Slaving Business in Rio de Janeiro, 1790–1830: A Contribution," in *Pour l'histoire du Brésil: hommage à Katia de Queirós Mattoso*, ed. François Crouzet, Philippe Bonnichon, and Denis Rolland (Paris: L'Harmattan, 2000), pp. 394–416; "Biographical Database for Rio de Janeiro" (Unpublished paper, Workshop on Database Construction and the African Diaspora, York University, Toronto, 2–12 July 2002); and with José Roberto de Góes, "L'enfance asservie: les esclaves du Brésil aux XVIIIe et XIXe siècles," in *Déraison, esclavage idéologiques et juridiques de la traite négrière et de l'esclavage*, ed. Isabel Castro Henriques and Louis Sala-Moulins (Paris: Éditions UNESCO, 2002), pp. 349–63.

46. As elaborated in Mary C. Karasch, *Slave Life in Rio de Janeiro, 1808–1850* (Princeton: Princeton University Press, 1987), and numerous supporting smaller studies.

47. For current work, see T. J. Desch-Obi, "Combat and the Crossing of Kalunga,"

in *Central Africans and Cultural Transformations in the American Diaspora*, ed. Heywood, pp. 353–70.

48. Also see Arno Vogel, Marco Antonio da Silva Mello, and José Flávio Pessoa de Barros, *A galinha-d'Angola: iniciação e identidade na cultura afro-brasileira* (Rio de Janeiro: Flacso, 1993).

49. The survivors of slavery in Minas Gerais began to reproduce themselves at that point, and relatively few new captives reached the region. The processes of community formation among the slaves thus would have drawn more and more on the youthful experiences of the generations of locally born Afro-Brazilians, both the changing society that they encountered as adults and their increasingly indirect adaptations of their parents' memories of Africa. Their experiences paralleled those of those enslaved in the United States.

50. One should also take account of the resumption of deliveries of significant numbers of new captives to Pernambuco and the northern captaincies at this time, mostly to toil on new cotton plantations established to take advantage of growing British demand for textile fibers. They have received relatively little academic attention, and works published to date concentrate heavily on the very late phases of slavery there in the nineteenth century. One suspects that slaves from Upper Guinea and Minas from the Slave Coast, delivered through Bahia, would have dominated the initial phase. For the 1750s–1760s chartered "Maranhão Company" that inaugurated these deliveries see António Carreira, *As companhias pombalinas de Grão-Pará e Maranhão e Pernambuco e Paraíba* (Lisbon: Presença, 1983, new edition, revised); and Manuel Nunes Dias, "Fomento ultramarino e mercantilismo: A Companhia Geral de Grão-Pará e Maranhão (1775–1778)," *Revista de história* 36, no. 73 (1968): 71–113.

One indication of the strategies that these slaves adopted might be found in Aldrin Moura de Figueiredo, "Reis de Mina: a Irmandade de Nossa Senhora do Rosário dos Homens Pretos no Pará do século XVIII ao XIX," *Boletim—Museu Paraense Emílio Goeldi (série Antropologia)* 9, no. 1 (1993): 103–21.

51. The starting point for most of the slave narratives from West Africa, particularly of the younger individuals who survived to recall their losses; see, *inter alia*, Philip D. Curtin, ed. *Africa Remembered: Narratives by West Africans from the Era of the Slave Trade* (Madison: University of Wisconsin Press, 1967; reprint Prospect Heights, Ill.: Waveland Press, 1997), including—famously—*Olaudah Equiano: The Interesting Narrative and Other Writings*, ed. Vincent Carretta (New York: Penguin Books, 1995). A revealing testimony to the intensity of these memories for a female in slavery in Barbados is found in Jerome S. Handler, "Life Histories of Enslaved Africans in Barbados," *Slavery and Abolition* 19 (1998): 129–41. For Brazil, see also the structure of the story of Domingos, elaborated in Miller, *Way of Death*, pp. 1–5.

For a recent summary of the statistics, see David Eltis and Stanley L. Engerman, "Fluctuations in Sex and Age Ratios in the Transatlantic Slave Trade, 1664–1864," *Economic History Review* 46, no. 2 (1993): 308–23; and Klein, *Atlantic Slave Trade*.

52. Roquinaldo Amaral Ferreira, "Slavery and the Illegal Slave Trade in Angola, 1830–1860" (Unpublished paper, American Historical Association annual meeting, Seattle, 1998), and other papers showing large proportions of "Congo" in Luanda in the 1840s.

53. Robert W. Harms, *River of Wealth, River of Sorrow: The Central Zaire Basin in the Era of the Slave and Ivory Trade, 1500–1891* (New Haven: Yale University Press, 1981).

54. And they seem to have succeeded in withdrawing to maroon communities, *quilombos*, with greater frequency along the relatively open frontiers of the northern provinces. For the Brazilian west, see Mary C. Karasch, "Os quilombos do ouro na capitania de Goiás," pp. 240–62, and Luiza Rios Ricci Volpato, "Quilombos em Mato Grosso: resistência negra em área de fronteira," pp. 240–62, both in *Liberdade por um fio*, ed. Reis and Gomes; and Mary C. Karasch, "Guiné, Mina, Angola, and Benguela: The Impact of African Cultural Traditions in the Captaincy of Goias, 1780–1835," in *Central Africans and Cultural Transformations in the American Diaspora*, ed. Heywood pp. 117–51.

55. Lovejoy, "Background to Rebellion"; Robin Law and Paul E. Lovejoy, "Borgu in the Atlantic Slave Trade," *African Economic History* 27 (1999): 69–92.

56. For this crucial aspect of *quilombos*, see Flávio dos Santos Gomes, "Ainda sobre os quilombos: repensando a construção de símbolos de identidade étnica no Brasil," in *Política e cultura: visões do passado e perspectivas contemporâneas*, orgs. Elisa Reis, María Hermínia Tavares de Almeida, and Peter Fry (São Paulo: ANPOCS/HUCITEC, 1996), pp. 197–221; and Flávio dos Santos Gomes, "História, quilombo, invenção de cativeiro e liberdade," *Cadernos do CFCH* (Revista do Centro de Filosofia e Ciências Humanas da Universidade Federal do Pará, Belém) 12, nos. 1–2 (1996): 99–140.

57. The definitive, and surely classic, study is Reis, *Slave Rebellion in Brazil*, which elaborates the local circumstances and connections that transcended any simple "ethnic" interpretation of the plot.

58. Kim D. Butler, "Africa in the Reinvention of Nineteenth-Century Afro-Bahian Identity" (Unpublished paper, conference on "Rethinking the African Diaspora"). For the complex interplay of African and Brazilian identities at this late stage in the long and tortured history of Brazil's enslaving connection, see J. Lorand Matory, "The English Professors of Brazil: On the Diasporic Roots of the Yorùbá Nation," *Comparative Studies in Society and History* 41, no. 1 (1999): 72–103.

59. The clearest statement of this insight that I know is in Barbara M. Cooper, *Marriage in Maradi: Gender and Culture in a Hausa Society in Niger, 1900–1989* (Portsmouth, N.H.: Heinemann, 1997), concluding chapter. Note that Cooper came to appreciate this distinction in a Muslim environment. It is my impression that the emphasis I am characterizing as "African" prevails in both Muslim and non-Muslim historical visions, as well as other visions of "history" elsewhere in the world; it is the modern West that is unique.

Section II

*Western Africans in Brazil—
The Fluidity and Evolution of Identities*

Brazil during the 1700s

5

Muitas Línguas

The Linguistic Impact of Africans in Colonial Brazil

Gregory R. Guy

Brazil was the single largest destination of the Atlantic slave trade. It received, according to the most recent estimate, 3,977,100 forced migrants from Africa during the three and a half centuries of the trade.[1] These people amounted to 41.1 percent of the total transatlantic traffic in human beings. The effect of this huge population movement to Brazil, in social, cultural, and demographic terms, is still massively evident in modern Brazil over a century after abolition. One has only to look at the music and the manners, the food and the faces of Brazil today to see the contributions of Africa. The magnitude of this contribution must have been even more apparent in the days when Africans were still arriving in substantial numbers.

Among those millions of people who were taken from their homes and brought across the Atlantic to Brazil, many languages were spoken; indeed, as is common in Africa, many of the individuals involved would have been multilingual. But hardly a handful of them had much prior knowledge of the language of the new colonial masters, the Portuguese. Consequently, the slave trade in Brazil, as elsewhere in the Americas, gave rise to language contact on a massive scale between Lusophone Europeans and an enslaved African majority who were (originally) speakers of Yoruba, Igbo, Hausa, Ewe, Kimbundu, Kikongo, Umbundu, and many other languages. What were the consequences of this contact? What was the linguistic outcome of this unique sociolinguistic situation?

Perhaps surprisingly, answers to these questions have not been obvious in historical linguistic scholarship. There is a distinct dearth of historical documentation on the linguistic usage of enslaved Afro-Brazilians in the colonial and imperial periods. Brazil is not necessarily unusual in this respect: written documents in colonial societies were overwhelmingly produced by the European elite and their descendants, who wrote them in the (European) language and style of their culture and time. The interest of the elite in the language of those whom they considered their racial inferiors was typically slight. Consequently, the voices of Afro-Brazilians are for the most part absent from the written historical records.

Due at least in part to this dearth of documentation, the language of Afro-Brazilians has often been neglected in scholarship on Brazilian linguistic history, and when it has been attended to, the mainstream of scholarly opinion has been to minimize or deny much continuing linguistic impact in Brazil from the history of African enslavement.[2] It is generally conceded that while the slave trade was still underway, African languages were present in some form in Brazil and had some impact on the other languages in use there; however, it is also customarily assumed that the African languages were rapidly lost as the Africans and their Brazilian-born descendants adopted Portuguese. Hence, in this view, the African languages, and the period of contact between them and the dominant Portuguese language, had no lasting impact on the formation of Brazilian Portuguese, and have no relevance to its present-day form. In this account, the many distinctive characteristics of Brazilian Portuguese are either traceable to dialectal features of European Portuguese or are independent developments within Brazil that were *not* triggered by contact with African languages.

For many reasons, this is a surprising and unexpected conclusion. As we have noted, the demographic and sociocultural impact of the African migrants is still highly salient in Brazil. In other places in the Americas where substantial numbers of Africans were present in the founding populations, we find widespread evidence of a linguistic impact. Places like Jamaica, Haiti, and Trinidad are widely recognized as having undergone drastic linguistic transformations as a consequence of African enslavement. The processes involved in these transformations are commonly referred to as pidginization and creolization, that is, the development of a new language from a mixture of languages;[3] they are well enough understood that we can safely say that the parallel social circumstances in Brazil would ordinarily be expected to have produced some creolization; a claim to the contrary would face the large burden of explaining how Brazil could have avoided such an outcome. Therefore, the dominant view of Brazilian sociolinguistic history (minimizing African influence) amounts to a claim that Brazil was historically special, that it was somehow exempted from the operation of the relevant historical sociolinguistic processes as we understand them to have operated elsewhere.

Consequently, Brazilian linguistics is faced with two alternative lines of inquiry. First, if the mainstream opinion is true, that is, if the African languages essentially disappeared without leaving many traces, then we require an explanation of the special historical circumstances that allowed this to happen here, but not in other American locales with similar social histories. Alternatively, the mainstream opinion may simply be incorrect; in other words, it is possible that in fact there were significant African influences on the collective linguistic development of Brazil, and that Brazil was therefore *not* historically special. In this case the research challenge is to explain where these African influences are (or were), and perhaps also why they have not been reported previously.

I adopt this second course here. I believe there is substantial evidence from a variety of sources supporting the hypothesis of lasting African impact on Brazil, including significant survival of African languages in Brazil, and a substantial impact of those languages on the development of Brazilian Portuguese that is still evident in various aspects of current usage. I will present an overview of the kinds of evidence that lead to this conclusion and suggest what this evidence implies about the sociolinguistic history of Brazil. But first I will briefly address the subject of language contact, and more specifically the contact-influenced linguistic developments known as pidginization and creolization.

LANGUAGE CONTACT, PIDGINIZATION, AND CREOLIZATION

Obviously, language contact occurs all the time, in many settings, without necessarily resulting in extensive change in the contacting languages. Tourists normally pass through another linguistic community without leaving a trace. Free immigrants do not often produce dramatic linguistic effects: the many immigrant communities in Toronto, for example, are not causing abrupt and significant change in Toronto English, as far as we know. Typically in such situations, immigrant speakers adopt the dominant language, over the course of a few generations, without influencing it very much, beyond perhaps a few loan words (like Italian *tortellini* and *cappuccino* in English). In such cases, the languages of the immigrants may indeed disappear over time without leaving much of a trace. So why has language contact under slavery often had a different result, namely, creolization, and how can we tell when creolization has occurred?

The distinctive social characteristics that lead to creolization under slavery are as follows. First, the slave-based societies of the Americas typically had a substantial demographic majority of Africans and their descendants so that the speakers of the European language that became the basis of the creole were substantially outnumbered by people who were not speakers of this language. Second, the Africans mainly arrived as adults, and therefore past the childhood age of easy language acquisition. Adults who learn new languages never do so perfectly; they inevitably carry over some traces from their first language. Third, in most Atlantic settings, the slaves were typically drawn from a number of African locales, and hence spoke a variety of different languages. And finally, the European masters did not ordinarily hang around and chat with the newly enslaved Africans so as to facilitate their acquisition of the European language.

All of this meant that new speech communities were formed in the Americas in which the language of the politically and militarily dominant European masters was being acquired by a much larger number of Africans, who were mostly adults, spoke several different African languages, and had limited access to the language they were trying to learn. This is in marked contrast to the sociolinguistic situation of free immigrants, who rarely become demographically dominant (at least prior to linguistic assimilation), include family groups of all ages, and typically have massive exposure to native speakers of the new language, often including formal language instruction. The outcome for immigrants, therefore, is that those who come as children, and descendants who are born in the new country, typically acquire native command of the new language, while the ancestral language often effectively dies away with the original adult migrants. But the outcome for enslaved populations in the Americas was almost always quite different: newly established slave communities normally developed a language variety that was highly divergent from the European target language, transformed in two ways. First, it would show transfer or "substratum" effects, in which linguistic features that were widespread or common in the various African languages were maintained in the creole. Roughly speaking, one could call this the "foreign-accent" effect. And second, the new variety would show evidence of the language-learning strategies of adults who are abruptly obligated to communicate in a new tongue; I will refer to this as the "adult-learner effect." The new language produced by these transformations would then be acquired by the children born into the community; furthermore, it was this language, and not the untransformed language of the European masters, that was transmitted to other people who arrived subsequently from Africa.

The linguistic consequences of these transformative processes are now reasonably well understood. The "foreign-accent" effects differ from creole to creole, depending on which languages were part of the original input, and how similar they were. Grammatical features that are common in the original native languages may be transferred: for example, Tok Pisin (New Guinea Pidgin English) has verbal transitivity markers, which are common in the indigenous languages of New Guinea and Melanesia. Alterations in the sound system are usually evident, to make it more consistent with the sound system of the native languages of the original enslaved population. Thus Saramaccan, an English-based creole of Surinam whose original speakers were maroons who escaped slavery after only a few decades of contact with English speakers, has a system of tones resembling the West African languages spoken by many members of the founding population.

Because the founding populations in creole communities generally included speakers of many different languages, one common result of creolization is the elimination from the creole of typologically rare or unusual features, such as rare speech sounds or uncommon grammatical constructions. This occurs because linguistic diversity of the founding population gives rise to a kind of linguistic "common denominator": of the many "foreign accents" present in this population, those characteristics that are common to most speakers are likely to be preserved, while unusual features found in only one of the substrate languages are unlikely to be reinforced and transmitted to subsequent generations.

The adult-learner effects in creolizing societies are rather more systematic. There are certain common, perhaps universal, strategies that adult second-language learners employ when they must communicate in a language that they know imperfectly, such as minimizing variant structures and concentrating on prominent root forms of words. Morphological alternations in the target language, like the use of affixes, and alternative forms indicating grammatical marking of agreement, case, gender, number, and so on, are typically reduced or eliminated in a creole. Word order in the sentence is often altered and typically becomes more fixed (often in the order of subject—verb—object), and the verbal system often shows alterations in tense, mood, and aspect. Word forms are relatively invariant, and grammatical meanings (like tense and number) are typically expressed by independent words rather than affixes: for example, *boy* (singular) becomes *dem boy* (plural), rather than *boys*. When a target language has alternative stressed and unstressed forms for particular words, the creole will usually select the full stressed form, instead of unstressed, contractible, or clitic forms (e.g., *moi, toi,* in French-based creoles are preferred over *me, te*).

The result of these transformations is therefore a language of everyday interaction for the slave-descended population that is *not* whatever the original target (European) language was; rather, it is a new language, which derives the bulk of its vocabulary from the target language but differs from it in grammar, word-formation, and pronunciation. Often, where speakers of the target language continue to be present and socially dominant, the creole or some of its speakers will go on acquiring standard language features, becoming less divergent. The result of this is that often one finds a continuum of language varieties, with the European standard at one end, and the most divergent creole at the other. Thus in present-day Jamaica, speakers may range from an extreme Jamaican creole to some variety that sounds much like ordinary British English. This sociolinguistic situation is called a *postcreole continuum*.

So let us now apply these observations to Brazil. If a creole language formed in colonial Brazil, we would expect it to show the structural alterations I have described—changes in grammar and phonology, and transferences from the African languages spoken by the founding population. Furthermore, we would expect a range of varieties to be present today, given the long and continuous presence of a dominant group speaking standard Portuguese. Descendants of creole speakers who had extensive contact with standard speakers would experience pressure to acquire standard-language features. To decide the question about the linguistic history of Brazil, then, our strategy will be to look for such traits in the popular language of today, what I will call popular Brazilian Portuguese. If popular Brazilian Portuguese has these traits, they will constitute evidence for a creole history and African influences. If not, one might accept the view that the Africans abandoned their languages for Portuguese, in the way that descendants of free immigrants often do, without showing any significant trace effects of the experience of slavery.

THE SOCIOLINGUISTICS OF POPULAR BRAZILIAN PORTUGUESE

I turn now to a consideration of the sociolinguistic situation in modern Brazil. One of the traits that we have cited as typical of postcreole communities is the presence of a range of varieties. This is manifestly the case in Brazil: the standard Portuguese of the educated upper and middle classes is greatly different from the language of the rest of the population. And this is not merely the ordinary social class differentiation of language that one finds in noncreole communities, like the white population of the United States or Canada. A speaker of standard Portuguese who is unfamiliar with popular Brazilian Portuguese usually finds it nearly unintelligible at first, so great is the difference. And note that the nonstandard speakers are, of course, a substantial majority of the population, and in the areas where African slavery was common, such as Rio, Bahia, Pernambuco, and so on, they are predominantly black. Hence in these respects, Brazil is more reminiscent of Jamaica than of the white ethnic populations of Toronto or Philadelphia. What are these nonstandard features, specifically? Let us consider a brief summary of some of the most important, showing how they are relevant to the issue at hand.

Agreement. Absence of agreement, as we have noted, is a nearly universal trait of creole languages. Standard Portuguese has obligatory number and gender agreement in the noun phrase, and number and person agreement between subject and verb. In popular Brazilian Portuguese, all of these agreement rules are significantly reduced, occurring only variably. I shall describe the two number agreement patterns in some detail. First, noun phrase agreement in popular Brazilian Portuguese is highly variable; plural noun phrases may omit some or even all of the possible plural markers.[4] Thus, where standard Portuguese would have plural markers on all words in a phrase like *as casas brancas* ("the white houses"), the popular dialect allows constructions like *as casas branca* or *as casa branca*. Notably, marking is almost always preserved on the first word of the noun phrase (95 percent according to Gregory R. Guy, in 1981), but rare thereafter (less than 30 percent).

This system has little precedent in other Romance or Indo-European languages. The historical pattern for Latin (and Proto-Indo-European, evidently) was obligatory number agreement throughout all words in a noun phrase. Where this rule has been lost, as in modern English, plural marking is ordinarily confined to a specific word class (just nouns in the case of English). But in popular Brazilian Portuguese, the first word in a noun phrase may be a determiner, adjective, noun, or pronoun, and any of these will bear the nearly obligatory marker, while a word of any of these categories in second or subsequent positions will usually omit marking. This pattern, of designating a particular syntactic position to carry plural marking, is therefore an exceptional innovation in popular Brazilian Portuguese, lacking a European source. Where did it come from? The most likely explanation is that it is a calque, a syntactic carryover from the African languages spoken by the original African Brazilian population. The great majority of Africans taken to Brazil spoke either Bantu languages from Angola and the Congo basin, or Kwa languages from the area of modern Nigeria. Most of these languages use initial position in the noun phrase to mark plurality. In the Kwa languages, like Yoruba and Igbo, number marking is often made by means of a plural word or pronoun that is located at the beginning of the phrase (e.g., *ómò* in Igbo, *awon* in Yoruba). In Bantu languages number is marked by the system of prefixes, again meaning that the first structural position in any noun phrase bears number information.

Therefore, most of the Africans who came into contact with Portuguese in Brazil would have been inclined by their first languages to look for number information in the first element of a noun phrase. As adult second-language learners, they would also be inclined to avoid agreement (multiple redundant markers across the phrase), and to disfavor use of affixes. Hence a proto-Brazilian creole might be expected to show first-position plural marking without agreement, which is basically what we find for many popular Brazilian Portuguese speakers today.

Subject-verb agreement is also highly variable in popular Brazilian Portuguese. The person-number forms of verbs are highly reduced for many speakers, compared to the historical standard. Second-person verb forms (*tu falas, falaste*) are almost completely lost, first-plural forms are often replaced by third singular (*nós fala* or *a gente fala* instead of *nós falamos*), and third-plural subjects commonly occur with singular verbs (*eles fala*, instead of *falam*). Overall, this reduction in the diversity of the verbal paradigm is consistent with the cited tendency of creoles to use invariant word forms. But one of the striking features of this variable agreement deserves further attention. It is apparent, from a number of quantitative studies,[5] that the rate of plural agreement depends strongly on the saliency of the difference between the singular and plural forms. Thus in regular present and imperfect forms, where the singular-plural opposition is just oral vowel versus nasal vowel, rates of agreement are very low (26 percent for first-conjugation verbs like *fala-falam*, 14 percent for the second and third conjugations, e.g., *come-comem*). But for irregular verbs, and preterites, where the singular-plural distinction is marked by a lot more morphological difference, agreement rates are very high (76 percent for *fez-fizeram*, *falou-falaram*, *é-são*, etc.).

This pattern is highly consistent across speakers, appearing reliably in repeated studies. It is thus a systematic feature of popular Brazilian Portuguese. Like the noun phrase number-marking pattern, it lacks European antecedents. How could such a constraint come about? I submit that it is consistent with the creole-origin explanation. The Brazilian proto-creole should have lacked subject-verb agreement, just like other Portuguese-based creoles such as Cape Verdean and São Tomense. Subsequently, speakers who were in contact with standard Portuguese would have learned agreement in the way that is typical of second-language learners: acquire the most obvious features first. It would be highly salient to a standardizing learner that a plural verb like *fizeram* occurs with a plural subject in place of singular *fez*, but rather obscure that plural *comem* is required instead of *come*. Hence, this trait in popular Brazilian Portuguese has a ready explanation in terms of the language-learning strategies that govern creole development. The alternative view, however, which maintains that the history of Brazilian Portuguese was uninfluenced by contact and language acquisition, must treat this as a random, arbitrary innovation, which has little precedent elsewhere in Portuguese, or in other Romance or Indo-European languages.

Negation. Another African calque in popular Brazilian Portuguese is the nonstandard pattern of negation, in which one negator is placed before the verb and another at the end of the clause: for example, *Ele não fala comigo não*. This construction is rare to nonexistent in European Portuguese, but rampant in popular Brazilian Portuguese. It is one of the few features that is actually documented for early slave speech in Brazil. Silva Neto cites a quotation from 1627 attributed to a slave named Bastião that shows this structure: *Não retira não*.[6] It is also found in São Tomense creole, and in Palenquero, a Spanish-based creole spoken in Colombia that is considered to have extensive Bantu influence, as well as in the Afro-Colombian dialect of Chocó, which is described by Schwegler as having a creolized history.[7] According to a number of researchers, the source of this construction is unambiguously African.[8] There are many Bantu languages with this structure, for example Kikongo, in which "the negative is expressed by placing the particle *ke* before the negative clause or verb and *ko* after it."[9] Schwegler reports that the same construction occurs in Kimbundu and in the Kwa group.

Subject and object pronouns. One of the most striking features of Brazilian Portuguese is the pattern of pronoun usage. In Portugal, subject pronouns are optional and more often omitted than not, while object pronouns are nearly obligatory. In Brazil, the reverse is true. Popular Brazilian Portuguese speakers use subject pronouns about 80 percent of the time,[10] while the third-person object pronouns *o* and *a* are almost categorically absent, save for the affixal construction with verbal infinitives (e.g., *contá-lo*). Why the difference? The Brazilian usage is consistent with a creole history. Creoles typically prefer to have overt subjects and disfavor case variation in pronoun forms, and they avoid unstressed variants and replace them by stressed forms. Hence popular Brazilian Portuguese has preserved the stressed subject pronouns (*ele, ela,* etc.) and done away with the unstressed object forms (*o* and *a*). The preference for the stressed forms is so striking in popular Brazilian Portuguese that when an object pronoun must be expressed, it is usually done so with a subject form, as in *Eu vi ele,* "I saw he" (instead of *Eu o vi,* "I saw him"). Such constructions are highly ungrammatical in European Portuguese (just as the equivalent constructions are ungrammatical in English), but routine and unremarkable in popular Brazilian Portuguese. Absent the dramatic upheavals of creolization, it is hard to see how the popular Brazilian Portuguese usage could have evolved from the diametrically opposed European norm in so short a time. Finally, we should note the restriction of subject position. Whereas European Portuguese allows subjects to occur relatively freely before or after the verb, in Brazilian Portuguese subjects are overwhelmingly restricted to preverbal position: more than 95 percent of cases in recent studies by Ana Zilles.[11] This, too, is consistent with a creole history, since creoles typically have subject-verb-object order.

Vocabulary. Finally, one area in which popular Brazilian Portuguese is uncontrovertibly influenced by African languages on a large scale is in its vocabulary. There are an enormous number of words of African origin in common use in Brazil today. In this Brazil is decisively different from other places in the Americas; nowhere else is there such a large African-derived vocabulary. This has been documented by a number of researchers, beginning with Renato Mendonça in 1935, and continuing through more recent studies, such as those by William Megenney and John Schneider.[12] In total, over twenty-five hundred words have been identified in popular Brazilian Portuguese with African etymologies. Remarkably, these words are found across a broad expanse of semantic ranges. Some, of course, are tied to cultural or religious items of African origin, such as the Afro-Brazilian religious groups, who often name their saints after African deities (*Ogum, Exu, Iemanjá* from Yoruba), and use African names for participants (*iaô*) and elements of the ritual. African musical instruments (e.g., *agogô,* Yoruba, *cuica*) and dances (*samba,* Hausa *sambale,* "a young people's dance," or Ngangela *samba,* "leap around"), and African-origin foods (*bolo* "cake," Kikongo *mbolo*, *dendê*, "palm oil," *quiabo*, "okra," *vatapá*), often maintain African-derived names in popular Brazilian Portuguese. But the African lexicon penetrates other areas of the vocabulary as well: *cachimbo*, "pipe" (Kimbundu *kishima*), *quilombo* (Kimbundu *kilombo*, "village"), *xingar* (Kimbundu *xingá*, "to insult"), *tanga* (Kimbundu *ntanga*, "loincloth"), *cachaça*, *moleque*, *camundongo*, "mouse." Strikingly, there are even some African-origin words occurring in some of the semantic areas known as the core vocabulary, which includes the lexical domains that are normally considered the most resistant to borrowing. Two of these core areas, for example, are kinship terms, where Brazilian Portuguese has the African loan word *caçula*, "youngest child" (Kimbundu *kazuli*), and body parts, where the everyday word *bunda*, "buttocks" (Kimbundu *mbunda*), occurs.

To summarize the linguistic evidence, popular Brazilian Portuguese has a massive African-origin vocabulary and shows a range of structural features that differentiate it from its historical source in European Portuguese. Most of these features have straightforward explanations in terms of a creole history, either as transfers from African languages (e.g., the negative construction, the first-position plural marking in noun phrases), or as language-learner effects (the saliency constraint on plural verb marking, the absence of agreement, reduction in the number of verb forms, loss of unstressed pronouns). Some are specifically found in other Atlantic creoles, such as the fixation of subject-verb-object word order.

What would the alternative explanations of these features be if they are *not* due to slavery and creolization? It remains theoretically possible that they could arise through spontaneous innovation. All languages change, and they can do surprising things, even in the absence of any significant language contact. But consider the logical problem that such an account presents. On the one hand, creolization explains all these changes at once. On the other hand, absent a creole history, we would be postulating a whole series of major changes, taking place within a few hundred years, and all just happening to emulate the effects of African contact and large-scale adult language learning. Basic scientific principles like Occam's razor should require us to choose the creole history as more plausible, especially since the African loan words, at least, have *no* possible alternative explanation.

HISTORICAL EVIDENCE

All of this would be more satisfactory if there were at least *some* historical evidence, some fact from the past or surviving relic today that supported this view. Since this is a historical volume, I will conclude with a few pieces of relevant evidence of this kind.

As I have noted, linguists have had little success finding definitive archival evidence bearing on the speech of enslaved Africans in Brazil. It is clear that African languages were known to be used in Brazil at various times in areas where there were substantial concentrations of speakers of a single African language. Hence Yoruba is known to have survived in various sites in Brazil for some time, in part because of its liturgical usage in several Afro-Brazilian religions. The fragmentary representations of slaves speaking some variety of Portuguese are not adequate to decide whether they were using a true creole, but they are usually consistent with the nonstandard features of modern popular Brazilian Portuguese described above.

Nevertheless, there are two historical facts that allow us to infer some creole usage in Brazil for some points in time. First, after a slave revolt in São Tomé in the late 1500s, many planters emigrated from there to Brazil, bringing with them slaves who must have spoken a Portuguese-based creole, which still survives in São Tomé. Second, there is ample evidence to suggest that the creole language Papiamentu, still spoken in the Dutch Antilles (Aruba and Curaçao), originated in a Portuguese-based creole brought from Brazil by the slaves of Dutch planters and their Sephardic Jewish allies who were expelled from northeastern Brazil at the end of a thirty-year interregnum in the 1600s when the Dutch temporarily seized control of parts of northeastern Brazil.[13]

But these facts merely demonstrate that there were once some creole speakers in Brazil, without showing continuity between that time and the present. For this, we must look for communities that have a relevant history. This kind of evidence has recently begun to be discovered. One example is the research done by Alan Baxter in the town of Helvécia in southern Bahia state, which is a black community, descendants of slaves, who were relatively isolated until quite recently. Baxter's description of the language of this community suggests that it had creolelike features, although these are rapidly disappearing as contact with outsiders increases.[14] A number of similar cases, showing rural survivals in isolated, African-descended communities of language varieties that are more extremely divergent from standard Brazilian Portuguese than would otherwise be expected, have been reported by a number of researchers, suggesting that a creole may once have been widespread among Brazilian slaves.

CONCLUSION

Some African influence on Brazilian Portuguese today is incontrovertible, so the only open question is, how much? The most plausible answer is that the influence was massive enough to count as creolization. The extent of this creolization may have been less overall than occurred in places where the Africans formed a higher fraction of the population (e.g., Jamaica and Haiti, with over 90 percent African-origin population, versus a peak of about 70 percent in nineteenth-century Brazil), but the kinds of changes that have occurred in popular Brazilian Portuguese are strongly consistent with creolizing communities.

Why, then, has this African influence not been more widely recognized? Part of the answer is certainly that scholars have been influenced by the lack of archival evidence documenting an earlier Brazilian creole. But another part of the answer no doubt involves the sociology of scholarship itself. Most of the intellectuals and scholars who addressed themselves to these issues were themselves upper class, educated, and white, and speakers of a standard variety of Portuguese that shows little of these African influences. Reflecting on their own language and their own background, they concluded, perhaps correctly, that there was no reason to postulate African influences. In this regard it is best to give the last word to a Brazilian linguist. Renato Mendonça contrasted the denial of African influences by some Brazilian scholars with the enthusiastic attention paid to the influence of indigenous languages. He wrote: "O negro que sua no eito e trabalha sob o chicote não oferece a mesma poesia do índio aventureiro que erra pelas florestas";[15] that is, "The black man who sweats on the plantation and labors under the lash doesn't offer the same poetry as the adventurous Indian who wanders through the forests." Perhaps the weight of accumulating evidence will now move our vision of language in Brazil beyond romanticism to reality.

NOTES

1. David Eltis, "The Volume and Structure of the Transatlantic Slave Trade: A Reassessment," *William and Mary Quarterly* 60 (2001): 17–46. This reassessment falls within the 3.5 to 4 million imports suggested by earlier research. See Philip D. Curtin, *The Atlantic Slave Trade* (Madison: University of Wisconsin Press, 1969), and Maurício Goulart, *A escravidão africana no Brasil* (São Paulo: Editora Alfa-Omega, 1975), pp. 437–54.

2. See, for a recent example, Anthony J. Naro and Maria Marta Pereira Scherre, "Sobre a origem do português popular do Brasil," *Delta* 9 (no. especial, 1993).

3. There are numerous works discussing the processes of pidginization/creolization; two important treatments are Derek Bickerton, *Roots of Language* (Ann Arbor: Karoma, 1981), and Sarah G. Thomason and Terrence Kaufman, *Language Contact, Creolization, and Genetic Linguistics* (Berkeley: University of California Press, 1988).

4. For detailed studies, see Maria Luiza Braga, "A concordância de número no sintagma nominal no Triângulo Mineiro" (Tese de Mestrado, Pontifícia Universidade Católica do Rio de Janeiro, 1977), and Gregory R. Guy, "Linguistic Variation in Brazilian Portuguese: Aspects of the Phonology, Syntax, and Language History" (Ph.D. diss., University of Pennsylvania, 1981).

5. See, for example, Guy, "Linguistic Variation," and Anthony J. Naro, "The Social and Structural Dimensions of a Syntactic Change," *Language* 57 (1981): 63–98.

6. Serafim da Silva Neto, *Capítulos da história da língua portuguesa no Brasil* (Rio de Janeiro: Edições Dois Mundos, 1940).

7. For São Tomense, see Luis I. Ferraz, *The Creole of São Tomé* (Johannesburg: Witwatersrand University Press, 1979); for Palenquero, see Germán De Granda, *Estudios lingüísticos hispánicos, afrohispánicos, y criollos* (Madrid: Gredos, 1978), and Carlos Patiño Rosselli, "El habla en el Palenque de San Basilio," in *Lengua y sociedad en el Palenque de San Basilio*, ed. N. S. de Friedemann and C. Patiño Rosselli (Bogotá: Instituto Caro y Cuervo, 1983), pp. 83–287; for Chocó, see Armin Schwegler, "El habla cotidiana del Chocó," *America Negra* 1 (1991): 11–35.

8. De Granda, *Estudios Lingüísticos*; Armin Schwegler, "Negation in Palenquero (Colombia): Syntax, Functions, and Origin(s)," *Journal of Pidgin and Creole Studies* 6 (1991): 165–214; Luis I. Ferraz, "The Substratum of Annobonese Creole," *International Journal of the Sociology of Language* 7 (1976): 37–47.

9. W. H. Bentley, *Dictionary and grammar of the Kongo language* (London: Baptist Missionary Society, 1887), p. 648, cited by Ferraz, *Creole of São Tomé*, p. 42.

10. Fernando Tarallo, "Turning Different at the Turn of the Century," in *Towards a social science of language*, vol. 1, ed. G. Guy et al. (Amsterdam and Philadelphia: John Benjamins, 1996), pp. 199–220.

11. Ana M. S. Zilles, "A posposiçâo do sujeito ao verbo no português falado no Rio Grande do Sul," *Letras de Hoje* 35, no. 1 (2000): 75–96.

12. Renato Mendonça, *A influência africana no português do Brasil* (São Paulo: Companhia Editora Nacional, 1935); William Megenney, *A Bahian Heritage: An Ethnolinguistic Study of African Influences on Bahian Portuguese* (Chapel Hill: University of North Carolina, Dept. of Romance Languages, 1978); John T. Schneider, *Dictionary of Africanisms in Brazilian Portuguese* (Stanford: Center for the Study of Language and Information, 1992).

13. Morris Goodman, "The Portuguese Element in the American Creoles," in *Pidgin and Creole Languages*, ed. G. Gilbert (Honolulu: University of Hawaii Press, 1987), pp. 361–405.

14. Alan Baxter, "Creole-like Features in the Verb System of an Afro-Brazilian Variety of Portuguese," in *The Structure and Status of Pidgins and Creoles*, ed. Arthur K. Spears and Donald Winford (Amsterdam and Philadelphia: Benjamins, 1997), pp. 265–288.

15. Mendonça, *A influência africana*.

6
"Not a Thing for White Men to See"

Central African Divination in Seventeenth-Century Brazil

James H. Sweet

During the seventeenth and eighteenth centuries, one of the most common ways that Africans explained, predicted, and controlled the world around them was through divination.[1] At its most basic level, divination involved communication between the world of the living and the world of the spirits. Diviners performed a variety of ritual activities to invoke the ancestral spirits and learn their intentions for those on earth. Mediating between the two worlds, the diviner could predict past and future events, uncover the guilt or innocence of suspected criminals, and determine the cause of illness.

Across Africa, the diviner's primary role was to determine the causes of social fissures in society, usually leaving the restoration of balance and harmony to others, particularly village or family elders. The spirit world revealed certain "truths" to the diviner and his clients, but the diviner usually did not pass judgment on the revelation. The interpretation of the revelation was left to the broader community. In this respect, the office of diviner was generally a conservative social phenomenon, reinforcing the public's opinions and broader sense of morality. At the same time, the diviner often acted as a balance against the power of elders, discerning their attempts to deviate from the collective well-being. Diviners also acted as mediators/translators for societies that were undergoing rapid social and political transformations, bridging the gap between tradition and change. In short, the diviner acted as the fulcrum for a balanced and peaceful society, but his or her findings were never completely sacrosanct, requiring affirmation and interpretation from the larger community.[2]

Once Africans became human property and were no longer the masters of their own social and political fates, the African imperatives of divination shifted to accommodate their new condition as slaves in the Western world. On the one hand, social disruption was a common feature of chattel slavery and no doubt provoked an outpouring of appeals by African diviners seeking explanations from the spirit world. The misfortune of enslavement itself begged a spiritual explanation, as did the brutalities, famine, and disease that accompanied the institution. Within the nascent slave communities of the diaspora, Africans utilized diviners in attempts to forge the same types of communal balance that diviners had helped create in their homelands.

On the other hand, the master class often accepted the power of African divination and attempted to co-opt that power as a way of maintaining and affirming white rule. Recognizing the widespread embrace of divination in the slave community, masters often used their African slaves to divine who stole a particular object, who "bewitched" whom, or the whereabouts of runaway slaves. Because divination rituals resonated with most slaves, the divinations were almost always accepted as valid within the slave community, even though peoples of African descent were often implicated. In one respect, this reinforced the institution of slavery, aiding the master in determining the "guilt" of those rebelling against the institution. But it was also an indication of the master class embracing the institution of divination as a way of mediating social unrest. African diviners always maintained control of what they divined and were ultimately accountable to the slave community. Thus, in some instances, Africans were able to seize control of social/judicial inquiries that directly impacted peoples of African descent.

CENTRAL AFRICAN DIVINATIONS IN THE DIASPORA

Central African diviners were particularly adept at seizing control of "criminal" investigations in the slave community, searching for remedies that took into account the interests of both masters and slaves. These investigations usually took the form of ordeals or "trials," in which the diviner invoked the spirit world to reveal the guilt or innocence of suspected criminals. For instance, in Bahia in 1685, a free "Congo" man named Simão was accused of murdering fifteen slaves through the use of witchcraft. The majority of his alleged victims were the slaves of one André Gomes de Medina, a wealthy planter in the parish of Santo Amaro de Pitanga. The only evidence of Simão's guilt was the discovery of pans full of herbs, claws, teeth, and hairs of various animals in his house. In order to find the true identity of the "murderer," André Gomes de Medina ordered that a "trial" be conducted by a "Conga" diviner named Gracia.

Gracia, who was a slave in the parish of Cotegipe, arrived at the property of André Gomes de Medina and began the divination ritual. She put three large sticks on the ground, set a large pot of water on top of them, then kindled a fire underneath the pot, and the water soon began boiling. Gracia threw a rock into the pot and "chanted some words in her language."[3] With the water now at a full boil, Gracia ordered each person who was present, through the interpreters that she brought with her, to put a hand inside the pot and remove the rock, assuring everyone that if they were innocent they would not be harmed. One by one, whites as well as blacks submerged their hands into the boiling cauldron, with each one walking away without so much as a burn. Finally, when it was Simão's turn, he removed his hand from the boiling water, only to find that his hand and arm were completely ulcerated from the burns. For the gathered multitude, Gracia's divination "confirmed the opinion that [Simão] was a witch (*feiticeiro*)."[4]

Simão vociferously denied the charges against him. In his defense, he stated that the "powders" that were found in his house were made from the heads of snakes. The powders were used as antivenom for the bites of other poisonous snakes. Simão claimed that he was taught this remedy by his first master and that many other blacks used these powders for the same effect. Simão also asserted that the witchcraft charges were leveled against him by slaves who were "jealous of his freedom." Simão had recently gained his freedom from the daughter of André Gomes de Medina and was now a free manioc farmer (*lavrador de mandioca*).

Simão's case is a clear example of how African divination operated to achieve balance and harmony in the slave community, from the perspective of both slaves and the master. First, just as in Africa, the divination process was utilized to affirm opinions that were already widely held. Even before the trial, Simão was the primary suspect in the murders of the fifteen slaves. Gracia's divination merely confirmed his guilt. Second, by finding a free person guilty of the crimes, slaves were assured that one of their slave peers would not be found guilty. Finally, Gracia's ritual affirmed the belief that Simão's freedom and economic strivings were the result of some otherworldly force, perhaps even witchcraft.[5] Simão was keenly aware that there were slaves who were jealous of his freedom. From the African perspective, his rapid rise from slavery to economic self-sufficiency was not easily explained. How else could he gain his liberty and become an independent farmer, if not by some strong spiritual power? Certainly Simão was manipulating the spirit world for his own benefit, so why wouldn't he also seek revenge against the master class?

As for André Gomes de Medina, the man who lost fifteen of his slaves to "witchcraft," he, too, benefited from Simão's guilt. He could rest easily with the knowledge that none of his slaves were attempting to undermine his prosperity. Rather, the murders of his bondsmen were the work of a person who was a member of a particularly insidious class of people—free blacks. Throughout the colonial period, free blacks were seen as a threat to the economic and social power of whites, competing with them in business and commerce, as well as stoking the flames of revolt against white rule.[6] Simão's acts of malice came as little surprise to André Gomes de Medina and probably confirmed preexisting stereotypes about the "dangers" lurking in the free black community. Thus, in one deft stroke, Gracia's divination ceremony satisfied the behavioral ideals of both the African and the Portuguese communities, revealing a sort of "résumé of [the] whole social order."[7] The outcome of Gracia's ritual reinforced both African religious beliefs (by revealing the malevolent source of Simão's successes) and Portuguese colonial order (by protecting the master's source of economic power—his slaves—and prosecuting a known danger—a free black).

In spite of this mutually satisfying remedy, Gracia's divination ritual should not be viewed as African capitulation to the colonial order. There clearly was an element of acquiescence in meeting certain Portuguese ideals, but this acquiescence was a pragmatic response to the Brazilian slave setting. As we have already noted, African diviners were mediators during periods of social transformation, and the oppression of chattel slavery in Brazil demanded new divination strategies. Gracia created an ingenious synthesis from the differing Portuguese and central African sociocultural imperatives. By finding a mutually satisfying solution for both master and slaves, Gracia was able to reassert the importance of African divination, even under hostile circumstances. From the African perspective, this ability to adapt to changing social conditions was the hallmark of a good diviner. In the final analysis, central African divination continued to function in Brazil just as it had in Africa—as a "dynamic reassessment of customs and values in the face of an ever-changing world."[8]

The recasting of Gracia's divination ceremony to address new social circumstances also should not obscure the fact that the instrument of justice used in this case was distinctly African. In fact, the ceremony conducted by Gracia was quite common across central Africa during the seventeenth century. At almost exactly the same time that Gracia was performing her ceremony in Bahia, Father Giovanni António Cavazzi, a Capuchin priest in Congo and Angola, described the central African divination, called *jaji*, in the following manner: "The *feiticeiro* lays a rock in a pan of water. . . . When the water boils, the accused is obliged to remove the rock with his hand. If he is burned, he is judged as guilty; if he does not receive harm, each one of those present acclaims him innocent, without any more inquiry."[9]

Other Europeans commented on the same ritual. Father Girolamo Merolla, also a priest in central Africa during the seventeenth century, recalled that the "witch" took the rock out of the boiling water "with his bare hand, ordering the others to do the same; those that take it out without being scalded are presumed innocent, whereas the contrary exposes their guilt."[10]

By comparing the descriptions of Cavazzi and Merolla with the description of Gracia's ritual in Bahia, we can see quite clearly that the religious/judicial apparatus known in central Africa as the ordeal of *jaji* made its way across the Atlantic in a nearly pure structural form. Thus, even as the ritual was transformed to accommodate the slave society in Brazil, it maintained its central African essence. Form was retained, while function was adapted to address new social imperatives.

The transfer of rituals like *jaji* complicates simplistic arguments about African retentions versus African creolization in the Americas. Clearly, African rituals and practices conformed to new social conventions in the Americas, just as they had done when changes occurred in Africa, but this should not divert our attention away from the fact that the rituals themselves remained essentially the same. As anthropologist Wyatt MacGaffey has succinctly argued, "Change must be change in something that itself continues."[11] In Brazil, distinctly central African rituals and practices continued, even as adaptations were made to meet the needs of the slave society.

Another central African divination ordeal, similar to *jaji*, occurred in Bahia on a small island near Ilha de Maré in 1646. In order to find out who stole some cloth on the *fazenda* (agricultural estate) of Duarte Roiz Ulhoa, a slave named Gunza (which comes from the Kimbundu and Kikongo *ngunza*, meaning "prophet")[12] prepared a balm, which he mixed in a dish. When he was finished preparing the balm, he rubbed some on the arm of each person who was gathered to witness the ordeal. After the person's arm was anointed, Gunza took a needle and passed it through the arm. Gunza promised that if the person were not the one who stole the cloth, he would not be harmed. Only the guilty party would bleed. After exhausting all of the suspects who were gathered for the ordeal, including a number of whites, Gunza began conducting the ritual on himself, naming potential suspects who were absent from the gathering. Gunza inserted the needle into his arm over and over, saying "in the name of so-and-so . . . if he stole the cloth then my arm will put forth blood." After sitting through most of the ceremony, our only witness, a thirty-year-old carpenter named Miguel Fernandes, became disturbed with the proceedings and left. As he made his departure, he scolded his white peers, telling them that the ceremony "was not a thing for white men to see." While many whites believed in the supernatural powers of their African slaves, others were sometimes too squeamish to remain complicit in ceremonies that seemed to be the very workings of the devil.[13]

Not all of the divination ceremonies were so offensive to the devout or the faint of heart. Another central African ritual simply involved the use of a cord and a ball. In 1634, Francisco Dembo (Ndembu), a slave on Itaparica Island in Bahia, was called to the house of Roque António Barbeiro to divine who pilfered a dish. Standing up, Francisco took a cord and put it under his foot. He threaded the cord through a ball, which dropped to his feet. Holding the cord near his face, Francisco ordered each person to pull the ball up. As the suspects pulled the ball, Francisco asked the ball if that person took the dish. If the answer was no, then the person was able to pull the ball up to Francisco's face. After some time, a slave from a neighboring property entered. Francisco asked the ball if she stole the dish. Unable to move the ball from its position at Francisco's feet, the woman was revealed as the thief, and she immediately confessed to the crime. Like many other central African "trials" in Brazil, someone from outside the immediate slave community (in this case, a neighboring slave) was ultimately judged to be the guilty party, reinforcing the ritual as a satisfying remedy that balanced the interests of both slaves and masters.[14]

Not all central African divinations operated as trials or ordeals. Some simply functioned as revelations aimed at uncovering the cause of a particular misfortune. Sometimes, these divinations revealed the most intimate and embarrassing details of people's lives. In 1721, Barbara Morais, a white woman in the city of Olinda, had exhausted all pharmaceutical remedies in trying to find a cure for her bedridden husband, who had been suffering from a mysterious illness for more than eight years. Determining that her husband must be suffering from *feitiços* or witchcraft, Morais summoned an "Angolan" named Domingos João Pereira to divine the cause of her husband's illness. Domingos began his divination by drawing a cross in the dirt with his finger. On top of the cross, he put a calabash with various objects inside of it. Domingos tapped on the calabash with his finger and cast some blessings on top of it "in the language of Angola." He then emptied several objects from the mouth of the calabash into the palm of his hand. These objects included "some things like roots" and "a silver coin."

Reading the objects that emerged from the calabash, Domingos informed the sick man that his ailments were "*feitiços* that were given to you by a woman who you had a relationship with before marrying this one; and the cause that she had for this was because she wanted to marry you, and since you left her and married with another, she made this for you to suffer." Skeptical of Domingos's divination, the man wanted further proof that what Domingos said was true. So Domingos prepared a "dance" with three little bottles, and "grabbing one, he danced with it and he showed the bottle suspended in the air." Inside of the bottle "appeared a very old black man with a red belt fastened around his stomach and a shepherd's staff on his shoulder, with some roots in one hand and some coins in the other." The roots and the coin were precisely what had spilled out of Domingos's calabash. When the sick man saw them in the hands of the man inside the bottle, he understood that "that preto was who gave the *feitiços*, and the roots the material from which they were composed, and the coins the payment that he received for the evil." Domingos then reached for another bottle, and again displaying it suspended in the air, there appeared inside of the bottle the mulatta, "who ordered that the *feitiços* be made for the sick man because he rejected her."[15]

All of the elements of Domingos's divination ritual were classically central

African, and more specifically Kongolese. First, the drawing of the cross in the dirt was probably not the Christian crucifix, but rather a Kongo cosmogram. Anthropologist Wyatt MacGaffey has stated that these cosmograms were representative of "God [*nzambi mpungu*] and man, God and the dead, and the living and the dead. The person taking the oath stands upon the cross, situating himself between life and death, and invokes the judgment of God and the dead upon himself."[16] When Domingos set his calabash over the cross, he was invoking the spirits of the dead to reveal the origins of his client's illness. They did so by spilling out only two objects from the array of objects that Domingos had in his calabash.[17] Domingos then "read" the two objects according to their prescribed meanings, determining that the man was bewitched by his former lover.

The bottles that Domingos "danced" with were also very much a part of Kongo cosmology. Various commentators in the eighteenth century noted that the Kongolese and their descendants in the diaspora used bottles to lure and trap evil spirits.[18] Most of these bottles were hung from trees and were used to protect houses and crops from malevolent spirits, but Domingos used his bottles to reveal the evil spirits that were the source of his client's illness. The two evil spirits, the old African *feiticeiro* and the mulatta, revealed themselves inside the bottles, proving their malevolence and their guilt.

As Domingos's ritual reveals, sometimes the outcomes of African divinations did not affirm the expectations of white clients. In some instances, the diviner uncovered compromising information about the master class. In still other instances, African diviners delivered more distressing news to their masters, informing them that they or their loved ones were the guilty party in a criminal act. In 1618, António, a "Guinea" slave in Bahia, looked into a bowl of water in order to divine who had stolen some money and a silver cross from his master. While it is not clear exactly where in Africa António was from, central Africans believed that a body of water separated the worlds of the living and the dead. Diviners could summon their ancestors by peering into water and uttering certain orations. The ancestral spirits would then reveal hidden truths to the diviner. After conducting such a ritual, António determined that the youngest son of his master had stolen the money and the cross. He also revealed that the boy hid the cross in a certain box. When the box was opened, the cross was there, just as António had predicted.[19]

That African diviners sometimes implicated the master class in their ceremonies demonstrates quite clearly that the majority of these rituals did not simply become another tool of the white power structure. On the contrary, white adoption of African forms of divination was an important concession of juridical power. On one level, just by adopting the central African forms of divination, whites diminished the power of their own judicial structures. Some whites obviously found the African judgments more convincing or more efficacious than pursuing potential suspects through the colonial legal system, which was a relatively weak institution in Brazil, especially in rural agricultural areas where there were large numbers of slaves.[20] As long as Africans were finding other Africans guilty in these judgment ceremonies, the rituals could be viewed simply as African forms of justice, "separate from the master's institutions." But as soon as whites accepted the guilt of their own relatives and friends, the power structure was turned completely upside down, turning divination into a potent form of resistance, as whites became the objects of African institutional control.[21] Even though these cases may have been rare, and though whites could always resort to rejecting African religious forms as the work of the devil, the cases demonstrate the extent to which religious and temporal power were contested in Brazil. In every instance that whites consulted African slaves to divine for them, Africans were able to transform religious power into resistance to their enslavement. Some diviners were able to seize more temporal power than others, but the very act of consulting Africans was an admission of African spiritual potency, resulting in small cracks in colonial power and the overall slave regime.

NOTES

1. The phrase "explanation, prediction, and control" is a succinct way of explaining the primary aims of many African religions. I have borrowed this conceptualization from Robin Horton. For a further articulation of its meanings, see the series of essays by Horton, *Patterns of Thought in Africa and the West: Essays on Magic, Religion, and Science* (Cambridge: Cambridge University Press, 1993).

2. René Devisch, "Divination and Oracles," in *Encyclopedia of Africa South of the Sahara*, ed. John Middleton, 4 vols., (New York: C. Scribner's Sons, 1997), vol. 1, pp. 493–97.

3. In nearly all of the Inquisition cases in which central Africans are key figures, there are references to the use of African languages in rituals and ceremonies. Usually these references appear as "in his or her language," or "in the language of Angola." Given the large numbers of Africans who attended these divining and healing ceremonies who apparently understood the orations, it appears that a creolized Kimbundu/Kikongo lingua franca flourished in the slave communities of Brazil. It is likely that this process of linguistic creolization began on the African coast. The differences between Kimbundu and Kikongo were only slight ones. Joseph Miller suggests that Kimbundu supplanted Kikongo at the main slaving port of Luanda during the seventeenth century and after, as Europeans brought large numbers of Kimbundu-speaking slaves from the interior to the coast. Miller, *Kings and Kinsmen: Early Mbundu States in Angola* (Oxford: Clarendon Press, 1976), p. 39; *Way of Death: Merchant Capitalism and the Angolan Slave Trade, 1730–1830* (Madison: University of Wisconsin Press, 1988), p. 403; and "Worlds Apart: Africans' Encounters and Africa's Encounters with the Atlantic in Angola, Before 1800," in Actas do Seminário, *Encontro de povos e culturas em Angola* (Lisbon: Instituto de

Investigação Científica Tropical, 1997), pp. 227–80. Enslavement and the Middle Passage no doubt hastened the search for linguistic common ground.

4. Arquivo Nacional da Torre do Tombo, Lisbon (hereafter, ANTT), Inquisição de Lisboa, Processos, No. 8464. Also see ANTT Cadernos do Promotor No. 59, Livro 256, fls. 130–130v.

5. Wealth and prosperity were considered an indicator of religious strength, but overabundance (in the case of a slave community, a relative "overabundance") was very likely believed to be the result of malevolence or witchcraft. For an articulation of the link between "modern" wealth and witchcraft, see Peter Geschiere, *The Modernity of Witchcraft: Politics and the Occult in Postcolonial Africa* (Charlottesville: University of Virginia Press, 1997).

6. A. J. R. Russell-Wood, *The Black Man in Slavery and Freedom* (New York: Macmillan, 1982), pp. 45–46, 51–52, 134–35.

7. Henri Junod, *The Life of a South African Tribe*, vol. 2: *Mental Life*, 2d ed. (London: Macmillan, 1927), p. 571, as quoted in *African Divination Systems: Ways of Knowing*, ed. Philip M. Peek (Bloomington: Indiana University Press, 1991), p. 69.

8. Philip M. Peek, "African Divination Systems: Non-Normal Modes of Cognition," in *African Divination Systems*, ed. Peek, p. 195. This dynamism in the function of central African divination rituals is reflective of the "historicizing" of slave culture called for by Joseph C. Miller in his contribution to this volume.

9. Padre Giovanni António Cavazzi, *Descrição Histórica dos Três Reinos do Congo, Matamba e Angola*, ed. and trans. Padre Graciano Maria de Leguzzano, 2 vols. (Lisbon: Junta de Investigações do Ultramar, 1965), vol. 1, p. 109.

10. Father Girolamo Merolla, *Breve e succinta relatione del viaggio nel regno di Congo nell'Africa Meridionale* (Naples, 1692), p. 98. Antônio de Oliveira de Cadornega also describes this ritual in his *História Geral das Guerras Angolanas*, 3 vols. (Lisbon: Agência Géral das Colônias, 1940–42), vol. 3, pp. 319–20.

11. Wyatt MacGaffey, "Dialogues of the Deaf: Europeans on the Atlantic Coast of Africa," in *Implicit Understandings: Observing, Reporting, and Reflecting on the Encounters between Europeans and Other Peoples in the Early Modern Era*, ed. Stuart Schwartz (New York: Cambridge University Press, 1994), p. 255.

12. Rev. W. Holman Bentley, *Dictionary and Grammar of the Kongo Language* (London: Baptist Missionary Society, 1887; reprint, London: Gregg Press, 1967), p. 375.

13. ANTT, Inquisição de Lisboa, Cadernos do Promotor No. 29, Livro 228, fls. 10–11.

14. ANTT, Inquisição de Lisboa, Cadernos do Promotor No. 18, Livro 219, fls. 305–13. This same ceremony with the cord and ball was still practiced by the Ndembu and Lunda in the middle of the twentieth century. See Victor Turner, *Revelation and Divination in Ndembu Ritual* (Ithaca, N.Y.: Cornell University Press, 1975), p. 337.

15. ANTT, Inquisição de Lisboa, Cadernos do Promotor No. 92, Livro 285, fls. 396–401.

16. MacGaffey as quoted in Robert Farris Thompson, *Flash of the Spirit: African and Afro-American Art and Philosophy* (New York: Random House, 1984), p. 108. The cross is to be read as a symbol—with God at the top, the dead at the bottom, and water in between.

17. Divination by casting lots with various symbolic objects was, and continues to be, common throughout central and southern Africa. For the most detailed description of these divinations and the symbolic meanings of the objects, see Turner, *Revelation and Divination in Ndembu Ritual.*

18. Thompson, *Flash of the Spirit,* pp. 142–45.

19. ANTT, Inquisição de Lisboa, Livro 784, fls. 113–14.

20. Stuart Schwartz has noted that colonial justice in Brazil was constantly threatened by "an unruly colonial society, great power in the hands of individuals and families, and broad sectors of the population unable or unwilling to comply with the social norms." In addition, he has written that the law applied to slaves "more as an object lesson than as the application of justice." See his *Sovereignty and Society in Colonial Brazil: The High Court of Bahia and its Judges, 1609–1751* (Berkeley: University of California Press, 1973), pp. 246–47.

21. Such cases challenge the assertions of scholars like Sidney Mintz and Richard Price, who argue that the institutions of slaves took "shape within the parameters of the master's monopoly of power, but separate from the master's institutions." See their *The Birth of African-American Culture* (Boston: Beacon Press, 1992), p. 39. For a broader articulation of the relationship between African religions and resistance to slavery, see James H. Sweet, *Recreating Africa: Culture, Kinship, and Religion in the African-Portuguese World, 1441–1770* (Chapel Hill: University of North Carolina Press, 2003).

7

Ethnicity and Family Formation among Slaves on Tobacco Farms in the Bahian Recôncavo, 1698–1820

Linda Wimmer

To what extent did slaves reproduce and form families in the Bahian Recôncavo, the area around the Bay of All Saints, on which Salvador is located, during the eighteenth century? How did ethnicity intersect with reproduction and family formation? Until recently, it was generally accepted that slaves engaged in plantation labor in the Americas did not experience natural increase, except in the United States. Explanations of the aberrant pattern in the U.S. South have been many but inconclusive, although important factors appear to include climatic factors, disease environment, and the work regime required by the crop being grown.[1] Unlike the United States, the slave-based export economies in the Caribbean and Brazil experienced depressed reproductive rates, since they relied on the continued existence of the Atlantic slave trade to maintain and replenish the slave population.

A negligible rate of reproduction did not, however, characterize Brazil as a whole throughout the entire colonial period. Conditions varied at different times as well as between and even within regions. For example, Stuart Schwartz found that during the eighteenth century, Sergipe del Rey, the captaincy (administrative division) north of Bahia, whose economy combined cattle raising, sugar cultivation, and subsistence production, was less reliant on the African slave trade than Bahia. Sex ratios in the slave population in Sergipe del Rey were higher than the two-to-one average normal in sugar production. Correspondingly, the rate of slave reproduction was higher than that in Bahia.[2] Clotilde Paiva and Douglas Libby examined documents concerning the slave labor force in Minas Gerais in the nineteenth century and also found a significant rate of reproduction there.[3]

149

SECTION II: WESTERN AFRICANS IN BRAZIL

This chapter examines the ethnic identity and familial relationships of slaves on tobacco farms in the Bahian Recôncavo during the eighteenth and early nineteenth centuries. Only in the past decade have scholars begun to focus specifically on the lives and identities of slaves engaged in tobacco production. Catherine Lugar, Giancarlo Belotti, and Jean Baptiste Nardi studied primarily tobacco farmers in colonial Brazil, rather than their slaves.[4] More recently, B. J. Barickman has undertaken a demographic analysis of the slave labor force on Bahian tobacco farms during the late colonial and early national periods. He found that the slave labor force at this time was predominantly Brazilian-born, and he suggested that it was largely self-sustaining on tobacco farms. He speculated that the transition from an imported to a native-born slave force might have occurred in the 1750s or the 1760s.[5]

My analysis is based on 221 probate inventories of tobacco farmers located in the municipal archive (Arquivo da Prefeitura Municipal) of Cachoeira,[6] the center of tobacco production, and in the state archive (Arquivo Público do Estato) of Bahia in Salvador.[7] The sample includes the earliest extant inventories dating from the end of the seventeenth century. All available, legible inventories before 1750 were examined, along with at least fifteen inventories for each decade thereafter, to 1821. These inventories accounted for a population of 4,134 slaves, all of them from Africa or of African descent. The inventories included in the sample could be positively identified as belonging to tobacco growers through the presence of elements (such as tools, tobacco fields, slaves skilled in cultivating or processing tobacco) within them indicating the cultivation of tobacco.[8]

The inventories normally include the name, ethnic group, occupation, and price of each slave. The ethnic labels indicate a particular slave's perceived ethnic affiliation in Brazil, as assigned by planters taking the inventory. Sex, household, and age group can be deduced from the information.[9] Moreover, identification of parent-child, marital, and sibling relationships occurs consistently throughout the inventories, indicating the existence of families, their size, and their structure.

Inventories and the data extracted from them contain certain inherent disadvantages. First, inventories were produced for the purposes of planters and familial inheritance. As such, the documents show a planter's perspective on slaves. They do not contain the voices of the slaves themselves, nor their views on their own families or ethnic identities. Nevertheless, the labels, descriptions, and other information included to justify the price assigned to particular slaves can also be used to examine slaves' reproduction and family formation. Second, the sample was chosen from extant documents. No inventories dated before the turn of the eighteenth century were found; therefore, an examination of the ethnicity and family formation among slaves involved in tobacco production in the seventeenth century cannot be undertaken here. In the initial phases of the establishment of commercial tobacco cultivation, Amerindian individuals from Tupi-speaking groups may have been enslaved and used as forced labor, as happened in the case of sugar cultivation.[10] However, indigenous slavery had largely ended in Bahia by the third decade of the seventeenth century.[11] Thus, even the earliest surviving inventories, dating from the end of the seventeenth century, contain no evidence to support this possibility. In spite of these limitations, the inventories can be analyzed productively to discern patterns of reproduction, ethnicity, and family formation.

All tobacco farmers in the sample owned slaves. The number of slaves varied widely among the holdings, from as few as 1 to as many as 165. The mean size of slave holdings also varied widely by decade, ranging from a low of 11 to a high of 30. The eight largest holdings in the period under study contained more than 60 slaves. This finding emphasizes the great variety of farmers and labor arrangements engaged in tobacco production in the Bahian Recôncavo during the eighteenth century.

In the first decades of the eighteenth century, the majority of slaves on tobacco farms had come from West and central Africa, rather than having been born in Brazil. African slaves are never described as *africanos* in the inventories. Instead, a wide variety of specific ethnic or regional designations were attached to them. Similarly, slaves born in Brazil (*crioulo*) are also frequently described by a wide variety of designations often based on perceived parentage and physical appearance including shade of skin color, such as *pardo* and *mulatto*.

Slaves with a wide variety of ethnicities appear in the inventories, and their relative proportions in the slave population on tobacco farms changed over the course of the eighteenth century. These changes reflect the shifting importance of sources of slaves and slave ports during this period.[12] At the start of the eighteenth century, the largest single ethnicity represented on tobacco plantations was "Mina" from Ouidah and adjacent parts of the Bight of Benin, followed by Angola. From the 1750s, significant numbers of "Gege" (Gbe), "Tapa" (Nupe), and "Nagô" (Yoruba) slaves appeared. In the second half of the eighteenth century, "Gege" and "Angola" became the most well-represented ethnicities, reflecting changes in the sources of slaves due to the internal dynamics of western African politics. Hausa slaves, who were nearly all male, first appeared in the tobacco inventories at the end of the eighteenth century, and their presence increased markedly in the first decades of the nineteenth century, as wars in their home region produced captives who were sold into the Atlantic slave trade.[13]

In the first decade of the eighteenth century, slaves designated by African ethnicities outnumbered Brazilian-born slaves on tobacco farms by nearly a two-to-one margin. The gulf narrowed, however, to three-to-four in the 1710s and the 1720s. The 1730s saw Brazilian-born slaves increase their proportion of the slave population of tobacco farms to 51 percent. Following a small decrease in the 1740s to 49 percent, the Brazilian-born segment of the slave labor force then rose again to 58 percent during the 1750s. The middle decades of the eighteenth cen-

SECTION II: WESTERN AFRICANS IN BRAZIL

Table 1
African to Brazilian Slave Ratios, by Decade

1700s	1710s	1720s	1730s	1740s	1750s	1760s	1770s	1780s	1790s	1800s	1810s	1820s
178	745	141	98	102	80	54	45	34	55	48	42	45

tury represented an important demographic transition. In the 1760s, nearly 60 percent of the holdings of tobacco farms included twice as many Brazilian-born as African slaves, and this proportion increased to 69 percent in the 1770s and 1780s.

Only in the 1790s did Brazilian-born slaves again make up less than 60 percent of the total slave labor force, an occurrence that probably reflects the resurgence of the Bahian sugar industry due to the Haitian revolution and the subsequent demise of St. Domingue as a sugar-producing colony.[14] This revival caused an accompanying rise in the numbers of newly imported slaves from Africa. Although most of these slaves ended up on sugar plantations, the increase in the quantity of slaves available in the Bahian slave markets inevitably appeared on tobacco farms as well. Consequently, because the majority of those shipped from Africa were males, the sex ratio became increasingly unbalanced at this time. Nevertheless, throughout most of the eighteenth century, tobacco farmers relied on natural reproduction more than the slave trade to maintain the size of their slave holdings.

Technically, it is not necessarily correct to speak of slaves as forming households. Slaves could be housed in common quarters that offered rude shelter, little space, and even less privacy. They may well have had little choice of where or with whom they would live.[15] Typically, slave quarters listed in the inventories were described as rough, dilapidated constructions and were assigned a minimal monetary value. Even the largest holdings listing a hundred or more slaves rarely had more than six or seven such structures. Nevertheless, within these quarters, slaves on eighteenth-century Bahian tobacco farms married and formed families over which they exercised some degree of choice.

The inventories record marriages among slaves over the course of the eighteenth century. Such marriages were undoubtedly consensual, rather than formally recognized by the Church. One hundred and sixty-three couples are listed as married. Eighty-six, or over half of them, had children. Choice of marriage partners among slaves involved ethnicity as well as place of birth.[16] In the first four decades of the eighteenth century, two patterns are evident. First, slaves from Africa who had the same ethnic designation intermarried. Second, individuals of certain ethnicities also intermarried, particularly Mina, Gege, and Angola. These unions may reflect the availability of potential marriage partners among the ethnic designations present on a particular plantation. In the 1740s and 1750s, exogamous African marriages, that is, unions between Africans of different ethnicities, predominated.

Interestingly, no unions between African and Brazilian-born slaves occurred until the 1730s. Initially, this trend paired African men with Brazilian-born

Table 2
Ethnicity of Marriage Partners

Endogamous African	Endogamous Brazilian	African-Brazilian	Mina-Gege
33	35	39	6
Mina-Angola	Angola-Gege	Other Exogamous African	Unclearly Identified
10	6	25	9

Source: See notes 6 and 7.

women, who, particularly on smaller holdings, were the only women available. In the 1730s, all but one of the Brazilian-born spouses were female. Until the 1760s, the frequency of these marriages lagged well behind the frequency of exogamous marriages between individuals of African ethnicities. However, such unions became common from the 1760s on. In the 1760s and 1770s, approximately half of these marriages involved African women and Brazilian men, as did all three of the African-Brazilian unions that occurred in the 1810s. This trend may reflect the preference of Africans to marry Brazilian slaves rather than Africans of other ethnicities or regions.

None of the African-Brazilian unions involved lighter-skinned Brazilian-born slaves, designated as *pardo* or *mulatto*, who were a clear minority within the Brazilian-born population.[17] Without exception, these slaves married other Brazilian-born slaves, usually also of lighter skin color. This finding supports the contention of earlier work that Brazilian-born, light-skinned women married "up" in the established racial hierarchy, preferring men of lighter skin color to darker or African men.[18]

In the 1760s, marriages between slaves born in Brazil occurred more frequently than any other type. Marriages between African-born slaves of the same and of different ethnicities and between African- and Brazilian-born slaves were also common. The increasing involvement of Brazilian-born individuals in marriages reflects both the maturation of the Brazilian-born population and the stagnation of purchases of slaves imported from Africa.

Both absolutely and proportionately, the number of endogamous Brazilian marriages increased over the course of the eighteenth century, reflecting the growth and maturation of the Brazilian-born slave population. However, in absolute terms, African-Brazilian marriages also occurred more frequently than endogamous Brazilian unions. This may reflect the influence of sex ratios, which were significantly more skewed among the African-born slaves than within the Brazilian-born population. Interestingly, from the 1760s forward, African-

Brazilian marriages occurred at the same or greater rates than exogamous African marriages. The popularity of African-Brazilian marriages suggests that greater animosity may have existed among different African ethnic groups than between African- and Brazilian-born slaves, or that the latter were seen as more suitable marriage partners. Acculturated slaves may have been preferred as suitors over recently arrived, or *boçal*, Africans, or those of different ethnicities, regions, or religious belief systems.

The proximity of tobacco farms and sugar and cattle areas in the Recôncavo theoretically allowed slaves to visit and to find mates among slaves on different farms. However, there is little direct evidence in the inventories to support this possibility. Cases in which slaves married persons off the plantations were rare, lending further weight to arguments that slaves' choices of sexual partners were limited to their own plantations.[19] Only one slave, a male, was noted as *casado de fora*, married to an unidentified person beyond the plantation. In two other cases, slaves are noted as married to a slave of a godchild. In these cases, close affiliations among the owners may have reduced the likelihood of conflict involving issues of ownership. In the vast majority of cases, slaves were limited to choosing partners from among slaves on their own plantations. Similarly, only one marriage between a slave and a freed slave (*forro*) occurred in this sample. Whereas other scholars have found that 20 to 25 percent of slave marriages in Bahia and Vila Rica involved *forro* spouses,[20] this pattern is not evident among slaves on tobacco farms. So few slaves designated as *forros* are present in the sample, however, that this finding is inconclusive at best.

The inventories of eighteenth-century Bahian tobacco farms shows that 44 percent of slaves were members of families of one sort or another, including two women listed as widows who, without other surviving family members, were incorporated into other units. This rate is considerably higher than the one-third that João Fragoso and Manolo Florentino found among slave families in Paraíba do Sul in the nineteenth century.[21] Families were a feature of slave life on tobacco farms throughout the eighteenth century, and particularly from the 1730s to the 1780s. They occurred in a wide variety of forms, including both nuclear and extended. In some cases, families involved three generations and more than ten members. A marked decline in the occurrence of families happened after the 1780s. This finding may reflect the resurgence of the African slave trade, which brought more adult males to the farms and created an imbalance in the sex ratio.

The size of the slave force on farms affected the rate of natural increase among slaves. Families occurred with greater frequency on farms with more slaves, where slaves had greater opportunities to find potential mates.[22] In general, as might be expected, the larger the slave holding, the greater the frequency of families. Large families of more than four members also occurred with greater frequency on these farms. However, some plantations holding as many as twenty-six slaves had no

Table 3
Numbers of Slave Families, by Family Structure

Childless Couple	77
Two Parent	78
Single Mother	310
Single Father	3
Parentless Siblings	28
Three Generations including Two Parents	11
Three Generations including Single Mother/Grandfather	8
Three Generations including Single Grandfather	1

families listed. Conversely, on a farm listing a mere four slaves dating from 1698, three of them belonged to a family: a mother, a father, and a son.[23] Families with one or two children occurred most frequently, but families with four or five children were not uncommon. The inventories indicate that childbearing tended to be concentrated among a few female slaves on a given plantation, rather than uniformly distributed among the female slave population as a whole.

Slaves forming family ties and kinship networks did so in the hope that they would not be separated from their relatives. Studies of slave family formation among slaves during the nineteenth century, such as in João Fragoso and Manolo Florentino's study of Paraíba do Sul, have suggested that families were relatively stable.[24] Similarly, Robert Slenes's study of slave families in Campinas in the nineteenth century found that slaves on larger holdings formed stable sexual unions and that the majority of slave children grew up in two-parent families. He suggested that these conditions characterized Rio de Janeiro and São Paulo.[25] Similar conditions existed in Lourena at the turn of the nineteenth century.[26]

In contrast to the findings of these studies, the evidence in the inventories of tobacco farms suggests that the hopes of slaves to form stable families were often dashed in the eighteenth-century Bahian Recôncavo. Most families on tobacco farms were incomplete. While a variety of family forms occur in the inventories, families headed by single women were the most common. Three hundred twenty-one women are listed as single mothers with at least one child. Eleven of them were grandmothers. Only four single fathers with children appear in the inventories, one of them also a grandfather. Circumstances for families in the Recôncavo contrasted sharply with conditions elsewhere during the nineteenth century. This divergence suggests that planters may have placed greater emphasis on encouraging family formation and maintenance in conjunction with the end of the slave trade to Brazil in the mid-nineteenth century.

Parentless families also appeared in significant numbers in the sample, and they are fairly evenly distributed across decades. A total of ninety-eight children, occurring in twenty-eight groups, are listed without parents. Some of these appar-

Table 4
Numbers of Slave Families, by Number of Children

Number of Children	1	2	3	4	5	6	7	8	9	10	11	12
Number of Families	202	97	48	25	24	11	5	3	4	0	0	1

ently unattached children may be listed as such due to unclear identification of the children with a parent in the inventory. However, they are invariably referred to as brothers and sisters (*irmão* and *irmã*) rather than child (*filho* or *filha*), suggesting that their primary kinship was to a sibling, not a parent. In addition, the significant number of parentless siblings demonstrates the existence of a population of incomplete families in which parents are absent. Some parents may have died, but many of these absences were likely due to sale. It is also possible that the high proportion of single mothers listed may have been at least partly due to a practice of selling productive adult male slaves to other tobacco farmers, or more likely to sugar planters, who had sufficient capital to offer high prices for them.

Twenty-three percent of the total slave labor force was composed of children. This rate is high compared to the negative reproduction that characterized sugar plantations,[27] but low when compared to studies of nineteenth-century subsistence areas.[28] As might be expected, a nearly perfect sex ratio of 97 existed among the children in the sample. Of the 486 females who had been born on Bahian tobacco farms in the eighteenth century, 365 were not yet of productive age at the time they were inventoried, as compared to 385 of 473 males. These figures may indicate that a local slave market redistributed slaves from the land holding on which they were born, married, or formed families to others when they were of productive age.

Another telling indication of the precarious fate of slave families occurs in the inventories themselves. Of all of the slaves listed, only two are evaluated together: Dominga, *crioula* (Brazilian-born, of African descent), and her husband Gonçalo, *cabra* (having a black mother and probably a mulatto father), slaves of Rosa Maria Pereira in the first decade of the eighteenth century. This joint evaluation suggests that they were to be sold or inherited together.[29] The absence of such arrangements in all other inventories examined implies that slaves could be and commonly were sold or inherited individually, rather than as families.

Proving that reproduction occurred among the slave force on Bahian tobacco farms does not explain the reasons behind it.[30] Over the eighteenth century, the presence of equipment for processing manioc flour in the inventories indicates that tobacco farmers usually produced at least some *farinha* (flour). In addition, they sometimes produced other subsistence crops, such as beans and maize. Such practices may have meant that slaves on tobacco farms, at least in some cases, had greater access to a diet adequate in caloric content and richer in necessary nutrients than their counterparts on sugar plantations.

Over and above the varied diet, the work required in tobacco cultivation was less harsh than that involved in the growing and refining of sugar. While the growing cycle and processing of tobacco required painstaking and continual labor, the miserable, backbreaking conditions of work in the cane fields, and the hellish conditions involved in extracting, boiling, and refining the cane juice had no equivalent on tobacco farms.[31] Therefore, the potential for accidents was lower and the tasks involved in tobacco cultivation, while monotonous and intensive, were not as exhausting.

Perhaps the factor most crucial to explaining natural reproduction during the eighteenth century is the sex ratio. The ratio of men per 100 women on tobacco farms was 129 during the period from 1700 to 1821. This sex ratio was relatively balanced compared to slaves on Bahian sugar plantations, where it was as high as 275.[32] Presumably this divergence reflects the greater reliance of sugar plantations upon the slave trade. The resulting uneven sex ratio depressed rates of natural reproduction on large sugar plantations. The sex ratio of slaves on tobacco farms more closely resembled that of their counterparts belonging to cane farmers (*lavradores de cana*). The cane farmers, like tobacco farmers, represented a less capitalized sector of agricultural production. Their buying patterns likely favored less expensive slaves, resulting in a higher proportion of women, a circumstance conducive to natural reproduction.[33]

Natural increase among slaves involved in tobacco cultivation began early in the eighteenth century. For most of the century, the sex ratio consistently dropped. However, the ratio shows a sustained rise from the 1780s through 1821. This finding reflects the resurgence of the African slave trade during this period due to the recovery of the sugar sector. The demand of sugar planters for more slaves, particularly males, brought a new influx of captives from Africa. Tobacco farmers may have benefited from the greater availability of slaves in the region by being able to purchase male slaves in greater numbers during the late eighteenth and early nineteenth centuries.

Aside from the relatively balanced sex ratio, the slave force exhibited another unusual characteristic striking for an area engaged in the production of agricultural exports. Slaves on tobacco holdings had a ratio of marginally productive individuals (children, invalids, and elderly) per 100 productive adults (of working age) of 170: 158 for females, and 181 for males. This rate is significantly higher than the rates of other regions producing agricultural exports and resembles that of subsistence areas.[34]

Several factors may explain this occurrence. One is the nature of tobacco work. Tobacco included many tasks that, while tiring and repetitive, did not require great physical strength.[35] Women, children, and marginally productive

Table 5
Sex Ratios of Slaves by Decade
(Number of Males per 100 Females)

1700s	1710s	1720s	1730s	1740s	1750s	1760s	1770s	1780s	1790s	1800s	1810s	1820s
124	129	147	143	130	120	121	114	130	133	141	140	146

men could play significant roles in tobacco production. Children weeded and picked bugs off tobacco leaves. Inventories commonly attached occupational descriptions to older male and female slaves and gave no indication that they were not continuing to fulfill their tasks in the field or the household. Tobacco farmers, who generally had less access to capital and credit than sugar planters, bought less expensive slaves, such as female or older slaves, to provide labor in the various tasks involved in the cultivation of tobacco.[36]

The relatively small presence of productive slaves on tobacco farms reflects in part the increasing numbers of slave families and slave children over the course of the eighteenth century. The slave trade from West Africa to Bahia brought primarily adult men, both as a result of the preferences of sugar planters and as a reflection of the captives produced by West African wars.[37] These factors raised the number of adult men on sugar plantations.[38] On tobacco farms, in contrast, from the 1730s forward, the slave population began to experience self-sustaining reproduction. In its initial stages, this phenomenon was undoubtedly encouraged by the relatively even sex ratios that characterized slave populations on these farms even before the 1730s.

Judging from the evidence contained in the inventories, tobacco farmers purchased larger numbers of female slaves due to their lower prices and to the fact that such slaves could adequately perform some of the tasks involved in tobacco farming. The availability of potential marriage partners encouraged the start of reproduction. As the labor force on tobacco farms reproduced with increasing frequency, reproduction became self-reinforcing: the sex ratio became increasingly balanced, which in turn facilitated a greater rate of reproduction. This trend stands in sharp contrast to patterns in the sugar industry, where planters relied heavily on purchases of slaves imported from Africa and bought a greater number of males than females as their laborers. Their preference resulted in significantly skewed sex ratios. On tobacco farms, the reproduction that began in the first half of the eighteenth century and was well-entrenched by the 1750s meant that a sizable population of Brazilian-born slaves existed. This trend reversed only in the late eighteenth century, when Hausa male slaves imported from West Africa appear in significant numbers on tobacco farms.

How much choice and control did slaves have over their family lives, and how much influence did slave owners and structural factors exert? The nature of the sources is not conducive to such an inquiry, for they were written by masters rather than by slaves, and by slave owners and evaluators concerned with economic values rather than with human lives and their emotional content. In her study of eighteenth-century Minas Gerais, Alida C. Metcalf has suggested that economic changes and structural circumstances determined the potential for slave families. Slaves attempted to form families on their own initiative, but were subject to the acts of their masters. In turn, these acts were influenced by cycles of economic expansion and contraction.[39]

The great variety in the size of slave holdings on tobacco farms meant that circumstances varied greatly among them, making it difficult to draw generalizations. Masters may also have exerted varying degrees of control over marriage and choice of spouse.[40] However, there is no direct evidence of influence on the part of owners on these decisions in the inventories of individual tobacco plantations. On the whole, it appears that slaves chose to reproduce when they were given conducive circumstances to do so, such as the availability of potential marriage partners of compatible ethnicities. Tobacco farmers certainly permitted, and may well have encouraged, both stable marriages and short-term unions, relying on natural increase as an economically feasible way to swell the size of their slave force.

The slave force on tobacco farms in the Bahian Recôncavo was characterized by relatively balanced sex ratios, a low productive-adult to dependent ratio, significant rates of reproduction, and significant family formation. These features resemble those found among slaves in subsistence areas, or in former export areas with weak ties to the export sector, rather than areas producing agricultural products for export. Along with structural conditions dictated by the nature of a crop, and the production arrangements developed to cultivate it, personal circumstances, such as relationships with other slaves and with masters and overseers, may have also played a significant role.

The rate of formation of families on Bahian tobacco farms likely also reflects larger factors. The depression in the second half of the eighteenth century may have limited the purchase of new slaves and thus encouraged a more balanced sex ratio, which in turn had a positive effect on reproductive rates.[41] However, if structural circumstances facilitated the formation of families, they also seem to have encouraged familial separation, particularly in the second half of the eighteenth century, when a local market for slave exchanges existed. Whereas studies have shown two-parent families to have been the norm in subsistence areas during the nineteenth century, on eighteenth-century Bahian tobacco farms families headed by a single mother were by far the most common kind, followed distantly by two-parent households, childless couples, parentless siblings, and single fathers. It is important, however, not to lose sight of the role of human agency in determining the circumstances of individual slaves. Slaves on tobacco farms not only reproduced, but they also attempted to construct and maintain stable families even in circumstances in which they or their kin were liable to be separated through sale. Nevertheless, slaves engaged in tobacco cultivation persisted. Through their efforts, they succeeded in changing their own demographic composition by the middle of the eighteenth century.

NOTES

1. Magnus Morner, "Comprar o Criar: fontes alternativas de suministro de esclavos en las sociedades plantacionistas del nuevo mundo," *Revista de Historia de America* (Mexico) 91: 37–81.
2. Stuart B. Schwartz, *Sugar Plantations in the Formation of Bahian Society, 1550–1835* (Cambridge: Cambridge University Press, 1985), pp. 351–52.
3. Clotilde A. Paiva and Douglas Cole Libby, "The Middle Path: Slavery and Natural Increase in Nineteenth-Century Minas Gerais," *Latin American Population History Bulletin* 23 (spring 1993): 13.
4. Catharine Lugar, "The Portuguese Tobacco Trade and Tobacco Growers of Bahia in the Late Colonial Period," in *Essays Concerning the Socioeconomic History of Brazil and Portuguese India*, ed. Dauril Alden and Warren Dean (Gainesville: University Press of Florida, 1977), pp. 27–71, especially 54 ff.; Giancarlo Belotti, "Le tabac, brésilien aux XVII et XVIII siecles" (Ph.D. diss., Université Paris X-Nanterre, 1973), pp. 13–56; Jean-Baptiste Nardi, "Le tabac brésilien et ses fonctions dans l'ancien système colonial portugais (1570–1830)," (Ph.D. diss., Université d'Aix en Provence, 1990), vol. 1, pp. 50–86.
5. B. J. Barickman, *A Bahian Counterpoint: Sugar, Tobacco, Cassava, and Slavery in the Recôncavo, 1780–1860* (Stanford: Stanford University Press, 1998).
6. Arquivo da Prefeitura Municipal da Cachoeira (hereinafter APMC), Secção Jurídica, Inventários 01/11/11/79-B, 01/70/70/554, 01/70/70/557,01/71/71/560, 01/71/71/564, 01/72/72/570, 01/72/72/574, 01/72/72/505, 01/73/73/577, 01/73/73/576, 01/74/74/588, 01/74/74/594, 01/75/75/601, 01/75/75/602, 01/66/66/507, 01/75/75/595, 01/66/66/508, 01/66/66/506, 01/66/66/503, 01/66/66/510, 01/66/66/511, 01/67/67/520, 01/69/69/536, 01/69/68/543, 01/65/65/492, 01/65/65/489, 01/73/73/580, 01/73/73/581, 01/37/37/285, 01/37/37/286, 01/39/39/301, 01/45/45/347, 01/45/45/342, 01/45/45/349, 01/47/47/366, 01/47/47/370, 01/47/47/371, 01/48/48/373, 01/58/58/452, 01/58/58/451, 01/56/56/440, 01/50/50/395, 01/74/74/593, 01/74/74/594, 01/74/74/585, 01/75/75/606, 01/75/75/601, 01/75/75/598, 01/75/75/599, 01/73/73/580, 01/73/73/581, 01/72/72/567, 01/72/72/569, 01/71/71/558, 01/70/70/553, 01/65/65/491, 01/65/65/496, 01/69/69/537, 01/69/69/535, 01/69/69/542, 01/69/69/541, 01/69/69/539, 01/10/10/64, 01/10/10/67, 01/13/13/89, 01/13/13/101, 01/08/08/41, 01/45/45/354, 01/50/50/404, 01/50/50/400, 01/49/49/389, 01/48/48/384, 01/48/48/374, 01/47/47/367, 01/46/46/359, 01/56/56/427, 01/57/57/448, 01/56/56/431, 01/52/52/414, 01/53/53/416, 01/55/55/425, 01/62/62/472, 01/61/61/467, 01/59/59/454, 01/60/60/463, 01/60/60/458, 01/47/47/365, 01/31/31/252, 01/31/31/255, 01/30/30/124, 01/30/30/250, 01/36/36/283, 01/28/28/241, 01/27/27/234, 01/25/25/210, 01/23/23/194, 01/19/19/161, 01/17/17/144, 01/13/13/85, 01/13/13/89, 01/13/13/86, 01/44/44/335, 01/31/31/251, 01/15/15/118, 01/16/16/127, 01/16/16/131,

01/16/16/133, 01/16/16/134, 01/18/18/147, 01/13/13/99, 01/07/07/35, 01/08/08/41, 01/08/08/43, 01/09/09/52, 01/09/09/46, 01/10/10/63, 01/14/14/108, 01/13/13/85-B, 01/19/19/158, 01/19/19/165, 01/21/21/180, 01/21/21/178, 01/21/21/183, 01/20/20/169, 01/24/24/207, 01/26/26/221, 01/26/26/223, 01/26/26/218, 01/27/27/235, 01/28/28/237, 01/29/29/245, 01/03/03/18, 01/01/01/06, 01/01/01/08, 01/01/06-B, 01/01/01/5, 01/04/04/19-B, 01/04/04/25, 01/22/22/187, 01/45/45/342-B.

7. Arquivo Público do Estado da Bahia, Salvador, Secção Jurídica, Inventários 02/676/1135/5, 02/635/1090/2, 02/674/1133/5, 02/648/1105/2, 02/638/1093/3, 02/637/1132/1, 02/634/1088/1, 02/638/1092/1, 02/635/1089/4, 02/638/1093/2, 04/1699/2169-B, 02/648/1105/3, 02/635/1089/3, 04/1474/1943/0, 02/702/1103/0, 02/635/1089/1, 02/638/1092/5, 04/1829/2300/4, 02/638/1093/4, 06/2796/01, 02/766/1132/0, 02/913/1592/0, 01/639/1094/0, 02/635/1090/0, 02/638/094/05,0 02/777/0244/0, 02/702/1163/0, 02/698/1160/0, 02/690/1150/0, 02/674/1133/0, 02/76/1233/0, 02/922/1391/0, 02/924/1393/0, 02/777/1244/0, 02/676/1135/0, 02/675/1134/0, 03/1282/1751/0, 02/634/1088/1, 02/675/1134/0, 02/700/1161/0, 02/6336/1091/0, 02/649/1106/0, 02/636/1091/0, 02/639/1095/0, 02/638/1092/0, 02/634/1088/0, 02/675/1134, 02/634/1088/0, 02/638/1092/1, 08/3466/20, 02/673/1132/0, 02/641/1096/0, 02/649/1106/0, 02/677/1137/0, 04/829/2300/0, 02/638/1092/4, and 02/772/1238/0.

8. These clues included the designation of slaves as *fumeiros* (those who dried, cured, and processed tobacco), *enroladores* (those who formed tobacco into the large rolls in which form it was transported), or simply as working with tobacco; the presence of crops in the ground; equipment needed to process tobacco into rolls; and/or tobacco sales, receipts, or debts to local merchants.

9. While few of the inventories give ages for slaves over ten years old, by comparing the price of a particular slave with others within the inventory and considering comments concerning health and age of particular slaves, it is possible to group slaves into three general categories: 0–14; 14–45, the productive stage of adult life; and over 45. As might be expected, distinctions blur at the borders of each category.

10. Schwartz, *Sugar Plantations*, pp. 51–72.

11. Ibid., p. 338.

12. Katia Mattoso, *To Be a Slave in Brazil, 1550–1888* (New Brunswick: Rutgers University Press, 1989), pp. 12–13.

13. Patrick Manning, *Slavery and African Life: The Occidental, Oriental, and African Slave Trades* (Cambridge: Cambridge University Press, 1990), pp. 137–38.

14. Schwartz, *Sugar Plantations*, pp. 422–24.

15. I am indebted to Ana Rios for bringing this point to my attention. "The Politics of Kinship. *Compadrio* among Slaves in Nineteenth-Century Brazil," Unpublished paper.

16. Schwartz finds that slaves on sugar plantations tended to marry within their own ethnic groups or regions of origin, and that African and Brazilian-born slaves tended not to intermarry. Schwartz, *Sugar Plantations*, p. 392.

17. These findings concur with those for slaves on Bahian sugar plantations. Ibid., p. 349.

18. Ibid., p. 392.

19. Ibid., p. 358.

20. Ibid.; Iraci Nero da Costa, *Vila Rica: Populacão, 1719–1826* (São Paulo: Universidade de São Paulo, 1979), pp. 34–36.

21. João Fragoso and Manolo Florentino, "Marcelino, Filho de Inocencia Criola, Neto de Joana Cabinda: Um estudo sobre famílias escravas em Paraíba do Sul (1835–1872)" *Estudos Econômicos* 17, no. 2 (1987): 151–73.

22. The regressive correlation of the number of famlies to plantation size is 0.917, indicating a strong relationship between the two.

23. APMC, Secção Jurídica, Inventário, 01/11/11/79-B.

24. Ibid. Fragoso and Florentino found that families tended to be preserved when sold or inherited. See their "Marcelino, Filho de Inocencia," pp. 151–73.

25. Robert W. Slenes, "Escravidão e família: padrões de casamento e establilidade familiar numa comunidade escrava: Campinas, século XIX," *Estudos Econômicos* 17, no. 2 (1987): 212–27.

26. Iraci del Nero da Costa, Robert W. Slenes, and Stuart B. Schwartz, "A família escrava em Lourena (1801)," *Estudos Econômicos* 17, no. 2 (1987): 267–68.

27. Schwartz found that about 14 percent of the population of six *engenhos* (sugar plantations) in the early eighteenth century were children under the age of eight. Schwartz, *Sugar Plantations*, p. 350.

28. Costa, Slenes, and Schwartz, "A familia"; see also Horacio Gutierrez, "Demografia escrava numa economia não-exportadora: Paraná, 1800–1830," *Estudos Economicos* 17, no. 2 (1987): 297–314.

29. APMC, Secção Jurídica, Inventário, 01/96/78/422.

30. Barickman, *A Bahian Counterpoint*, pp. 158–61. Barickman attributes the phenomenon of reproduction among this slave population in his period of study to the nature of the work, a greater quantity and variety of food, and a more balanced sex ratio.

31. Schwartz, *Sugar Plantations*, pp. 139–59.

32. Ibid., p. 348.

33. Ibid.

34. Elizabeth Kusnesof finds a ratio of 167 adults per 100 dependent slaves in São Paulo in 1798, before the beginning of coffee cultivation in the region. In 1828, when coffee was well established as the major economic activity, she finds the ratio of 232. She explains the abrupt rise as ". . . due to the increased importation of slaves for use in the sugar and coffee plantations." Elizabeth Anne Kuznesof, *Household Economy and Urban Development in São Paulo: 1755 to 1836* (Boulder: Westview Press, 1968), p. 83.

35. For a more complete description on tasks involved in tobacco cultivation see Antonil, *Cultura e Opulencia do Brasil por suas drogas e minas*, ed. Andree Mansuy (Paris: Institut des Hautes Études de l'Amérique Latine, 1968).

36. Compare Barickman, *A Bahian Counterpoint*, pp. 158–61.

37. Manning, *Slavery and African Life*, pp. 30–48.

38. Schwartz, *Sugar Plantations*, p. 346.

39. Alida C. Metcalf, "Família escrava em Santana de Parnaíba," *Estudos Econômicos* 17, no. 2 (1987): 242.

40. Schwartz, *Sugar Plantations*, p. 386; Mattoso, *To Be a Slave in Brazil*, pp. 110–11.

41. Compare Schwartz, *Sugar Plantations*, pp. 351–53.

8
Guiné, Mina, Angola, and Benguela
African and Crioulo Nations in Central Brazil, 1780–1835

Mary C. Karasch

In research that is carried out over many years, an idea sometimes lurks in the back of our minds that we play with, bring out, examine now and then, and return to a dark corner of our memory. Such an idea is the concept of *nação* (nation) that first surfaced in *Slave Life in Rio de Janeiro* when I struggled to identify the ethnic origins of enslaved Africans and kept coming up against slave trade ports as African identities.[1] As I have moved into research on central Brazil in the late colonial period, I have encountered similar national identities in a place as remote as the captaincy (administrative division) of Goiás, now the modern states of Goiás and Tocantins in central Brazil. Similar uses of the concept of nation in Rio, Salvador, and Minas Gerais led me to look more carefully at the documentation I have been collecting on the captaincy of Goiás. My initial research on the region had focused on the Amerindians of the region, that is, the short biography of Damiana da Cunha and the study of Indian policy in Goiás in *História dos Índios*.[2] When working on Indian policy in particular, I noted the use of nation as well as terminology such as *gentes barbaros* ("barbarous peoples"), *gentios* ("barbarians"), and *nações de gentio* ("nations of barbarians"). A colleague at Oakland University, Professor Ronald Finucane, referred me to the similar usage of *barbaras gentes et nationes* ("barbarous peoples and nations") in the Roman Empire for the people who lived in a border region near the city of Palmyra in the province of Phoenicia.[3]

The idea of nation was now more complicated. Not only did Africans have nations but so, too, did the Amerindian populations of central Brazil, who lived far from the coast and slave trade ports. Enslaved Amerindians were also known by their nations, since they were commonly captured by *bandeiras* (exploring, slave-raiding, or prospecting expeditions) and taken to the mining towns or branded, bought, and sold to be traded north to Belém via the Tocantins River. Hence individuals identified as *cativo* (captive) or *agregado* (household dependant) of the Xavante nation were not African but Amerindian in origin. These insights, as well as concepts of nation, are summarized in "Minha Nação: Identidades Escravas no Fim do Brasil Colonial," an essay recently published in Brazil.[4] At the time I wrote that essay in 1996, I had not yet done the analysis of the census nor the tax records to document ethnicity, nor the preliminary work on the black regiments, the Henriques. What the present essay will develop, therefore, are the results of this new research to date.

The first part of the chapter will present the census data and the specific ethnic and national identities based on the *meia-sisa*, the tax imposed at the time of slave sales. Unlike other parts of Brazil where the tax records were destroyed at the time of the abolition of slavery, provincial authorities in Goiás carried out only a token burning of some of the documents in the governor's office. Obviously, these were identities imposed by bureaucrats on enslaved Africans at the time of sale or on the occasion of a census; but now and then a specific name, such as Muteco, Nagô, or Ussá, reminds us that the enslaved Tio, Yoruba, and Hausa did not live or work only in Salvador and Rio de Janeiro. They had also been enslaved in Natividade and the city of Goiás, which were months of travel from coastal ports. As this essay will demonstrate, the great majority of slaves were born in Brazil by 1832, and the word "nation" was commonly used together with the word *crioulo*, or black born in Brazil.

What is missing from these bureaucratic records is the identity constructed by the enslaved Africans or Amerindians or the meaning attached to *nação crioulo* ("creole nation") or *nação Angola* ("Angola nation"). We can, however, tease some meaning from other types of documents, such as those dealing with the black regiments, which help to document the transition from a majority African population in the eighteenth century to a second/third-generation creole population by 1832.

THE SLAVE POPULATION OF GOIÁS, 1779–1832

In the captaincy of Goiás in 1779, almost two-thirds of the population was defined as *prêto* (or black), presumably slaves (table 1). In contrast, more than fifty years later only one-fifth of the population was still enslaved in 1832 (table 2 gives slave populations). Obviously, the institution of black slavery had eroded as the mining economy collapsed. What had been a tragedy for the mine owners, however, was a liberation for the enslaved African miners, who bought their

Table 1
Goías Census of 1779

Julgados (Jurisdictions)	Whites	Pardos	Blacks	Total	% Black
South					
Vila Boa	1,460	1,003	4,491	6,954	64.6
Anta	602	689	1,377	2,668	51.6
Meia Ponte	1,809	1,581	4,495	7,885	57.0
Santa Luzia	490	717	2,177	3,384	64.3
Santa Cruz	562	268	704	1,534	45.9
Pilar	576	930	3,650	5,156	70.8
Crixá	219	348	2,247	2,814	79.9
Subtotal	5,718	5,536	19,141	30,395	63.0
North					
Traíras	679	1,398	3,176	5,253	60.5
Tocantins	276	985	3,042	4,303	70.7
São Félix	387	682	2,681	3,750	71.5
Cavalcante	142	168	974	1,284	75.9
Arraias	156	164	762	1,082	70.4
Natividade	555	656	1,980	3,191	62.1
Carmo	84	202	885	1,171	75.6
Palma	530	240	716	1,486	48.2
S. Domingos	118	219	281	618	45.5
Pontal	87	150	653	890	73.4
Paraná de Cima	198	283	585	1,066	54.9
Subtotal	3,212	5,147	15,735	24,094	65.3
Total	8,930	10,683	34,876	54,489	64.0

Source: Arquivo Histórico e Geográfico Brasileiro (IHGB), Rio de Janeiro, Arq. 1.2.7, "Estatística, Ofício de Luiz da Cunha Menezes á Martinho de Mello e Castro, remetendo o Mapa da população da Capitania de Goiáz, com distinção de classes," Vila Boa, 8 de julho de 1780, fl. 246. Another version of this census was published in Portuguese as *Liberdade por um fio: História dos quilombos no Brasil*, ed. João José Reis e Flávio dos Santos Gomes (São Paulo: Companhia das Letras, 1996), p. 242.

freedom and continued to mine for gold as freedmen. In fact, one Portuguese bureaucrat, Antônio Luis de Souza Leal, even blamed these freed miners for the "decadence of the *quinto*" (the tax on gold production). He complained that "freedmen, *pardos* [people of mixed ancestry], and blacks" did not work and lived in "inaction," which he argued was the true reason why gold production

Table 2
Slaves in the Captaincy of Goiás, 1783–1832

	1783	1789	1792	1804	1825	1832
South						
Vila Boa	4,689	9,200	8,568	4,432	3,274	3,073
Meia Ponte	1,682	4,777	4,855	2,282	1,842	1,800
Santa Luzia	899	2,960	2,491	1,264	741	741
Santa Cruz	723	1,223	1,153	997	887	1,094
Pilar	1,567	1,967	3,839	1,575	969	1,033
Crixás	1,207	2,444	2,045	634	699	384
Rio das Velhas	299	277	2,261	—	—	—
Desemboque	—	—	—	660	—	—
Carretão	—	—	—	—	—	5
Traíras	—	—	—	2,807	—	—
Subtotal:	11,066	22,848	25,212	14,651	8,412	8,130
North						
Vila de São João	—	—	—	—	78	228
Traíras	3,790	6,245	5,328	—	1,493	1,441
Cavalcante	923	993	950	1,209	456	474
Flores	—	—	—	—	478	561
São Félix	648	2,707	2,599	641	142	231
Arraias	363[a]	1,198	1,198	469	765	792
Conceição	—	986	908	684	271	156
Natividade	923	2,332	2,338	1,529	904	879
Porto Real	—	—	—	—	376	325
Carmo	—	—	—	844	—	—
Carolina	—	—	—	—	—	39
Duro	—	—	—	—	—	5
Subtotal:	6,647	14,461	13,321	5,376	4,963	5,131
Total:	17,713	37,309	38,533	20,027	13,375	13,261[b]

Sources: Gilka V. F. de Salles, *Economia e Escravidão na Capitania de Goiás* (Goiâna: CEGRAF/UFG, 1992), p. 277; Arquivo Histórico Ultramarino (AHU), Lisbon, caixa 35, Goiás, 1790–1798, "Mappa em que Tristão da Cunha Menezes... apresenta ao Real Ministerio... até o prezente anno d' 1789," 19 October 1790; ibid., "Mappa em que o Governador, e Capitão General da Capitania de Goyaz Tristão da Cunha Menezes aprezenta ao Real Ministerio...," 29 July 1792; AHU, Cód. 2109, "Reflexoens Economicas sobre as Tabellas Statisticas da Capitania de Goyaz Pertencentes ao anno de 1804 e feitas no de 1806," Biblioteca Nacional de Rio de Janeiro (BNRJ), Manuscript Section, 11,4,2, "Estatistica da Provincia de Goyáz remettida á Secretaria de Estado dos Negocios do Imperio...,1825"; and Arquivo Nacional de Rio de Janeiro (ANRJ), Cód. 808, v. 1, Goiás "Censo da População da Provincia de Goyaz [1832]," fl. 96.

a. The manuscript copy of the census of 1793 gives 364 rather than 363.

b. The overall population for the captaincy of Goiás was 59,287 in 1783; 58,504 in 1789; 60,428 in 1792; 50,365 in 1804; 62,478 in 1825; and 68,497 in 1832.

had declined. After accusing them of laziness, he then gave an example of how the freedmen mined gold. They formed a society of sixty freedmen, forty of whom worked in mining while the other twenty raised food crops to sustain the miners. Afterward, the gold was divided "equally" among them, obviously leaving nothing for the king's share of the gold, the *quinto*.[5] That the majority of freedmen in 1825 were males (1,539) rather than females (1,441) is testimony to their success in mining and a sharp contrast to coastal patterns in which two-thirds of those freed were female.[6]

The first obvious conclusion, therefore, is that the enslaved population of late colonial Goiás was small in number in contrast to the thousands of slaves who labored in Minas Gerais or in the plantation economies; that is, the captaincy had less than 40,000 slaves at the height of recorded slavery in 1792 (table 2). Even during the mining boom of the earlier eighteenth century, the Portuguese had documented only 10,000 to 20,000 slaves between 1735 and 1750—numbers that are suspiciously low given the productivity of the mines and local traditions.[7] After the alleged decline of the mines as measured in the drop in the *quinto* that reached Portugal, however, the number of documented *prêtos* rose to almost 35,000 in 1779 (64 percent). Partial records on slaves in 1783 are obviously incomplete since the sum total was only 17,713; more useful information from 1783 is the relative importance of the slave population. The largest centers of slavery were Vila Boa (the capital of the captaincy), Traíras, and Meia Ponte. Six years later in 1789 the slave population for the captaincy was counted at 37,309, or 64 percent enslaved, a percentage comparable to that of the *prêtos* in 1779. The next census of 1792 also recorded that 64 percent of the population was still enslaved. The total number of slaves was 38,533, the largest number thus far documented for the captaincy of Goiás (table 2). Such a large number of enslaved blacks suggests that the mining economy was still going strong contrary to complaints from Lisbon.

Since the census of 1798 was incomplete—or missing—the next census of 1804 recorded a sharp decline in the slave population by nearly 50 percent. Only 20,027 slaves were counted in 1804, and they made up only 40 percent of the population (table 2). The censuses of 1792 and 1804 record, therefore, the period of decline in the slave population—in particular the dying off of the elderly African men who had been imported in the eighteenth century and who were not replaced with new Africans in the early nineteenth century. Furthermore, the two censuses of the early national period (1825 and 1832) document yet another decline to 13,375 and 13,261, or to 21 and 19 percent of the population (table 2). The census of 1832, which divided the slave population by birth in Brazil or Africa, confirms the drop in the enslaved African population (table 4). By 1832 only 17 percent of the enslaved black population had been born in Africa; these numbers exclude the *liberto* (freed) population, which unfortunately was not dis-

Table 3
Goiás Census of 1825

	Whites	Ing.- Lib.[a]	Slaves	Indians	Total
South					
Cidade	2,527	8,366	3,274	—	14,167
M. Ponte	2,767	4,842	1,842	—	9,451
S. Luzia	1,113	2,777	741	—	4,631
S. Cruz	2,083	2,895	887	—	5,865
Pilar	380	2,038	969	—	3,387
Crixás	270	1,031	699	—	2,000
São José	—	—	—	125	125
Carretão	—	—	—	198	198
Subotal	9,140	21,949	8,412	323	39,824
North					
Palma	34	288	78	—	400
Traíras	395	4,321	1,493	—	6,209
Flores	210	2,701	478	—	3,389
São Félix	44	680	142	—	866
Cavalcante	163	1,448	456	—	2,067
Arraias	267	2,505	765	—	3,567
Conceição	50	979	271	—	1,300
Natividade	157	1,977	904	—	3,038
Porto Real	35	1,137	376	—	1,548
Duro	—	—	—	300	300
Subtotal	1,355	16,036	4,963	300	22,654
Total	10,495	37,985	13,375	623	62,478

Source: BNRJ, 11,4,2, "Estatistica da Provincia de Goyáz," 1825.

a. *Ingenuos e Libertos* (Free People of Color and Freedpersons)

---

tinguished by birthplace. In other words, the census of 1832 suggests that the key period of transition from an African-born to a Brazilian-born slave population took place in Goiás between the 1790s and the 1830s. By 1832, officials and priests identified most slaves as *crioulos* or *pardos*. The census records establish, therefore, that the captaincy of Goiás was one region of Brazil where the native-born slave population outnumbered those born in Africa in the 1830s.

MEIA-SISAS

Unfortunately, however, most censuses reveal little about ethnicity or additional color distinctions within the slave population. We must utilize other sources for such insights. Since the census data is so rich for the early nineteenth century, we have turned to a similar period for which the sales taxes on slaves survive, that is, 1810–1824. What is particularly useful is that sales taxes exist for all regions of the captaincy of Goiás for that period of time, except for Vila Boa de Goiás. Later tax records survive, however, for the city of Goiás (the new name of Vila Boa) in the 1830s. The lack of *meia-sisas* for Vila Boa in the late colonial period is indeed unfortunate, since so many slaves were sold in the city of Goiás. In 1810, for example, the total income from the *meia-sisas* in Vila Boa was 408$431 *réis* compared to Meia Ponte, which was 159$937 *réis*. In third place was Traíras with 88$837 *réis*, and a distant fourth was Santa Luzia with 53$840. At the bottom in terms of income were Pilar at 26$137 *réis*, Crixás at 20$280, and Santa Cruz at 12$000.[8] The wealth generated by slave sales in Vila Boa was substantial in contrast to Santa Cruz, but what survives are the documents from Santa Cruz rather than Vila Boa. Since so much of the archive of the Museu das Bandeiras is still uncataloged, the *meia-sisas* may yet be discovered if they were not lost in the move of the state archive to Goiânia. Since scholars have generally not had access to *meia-sisas* for studies of the slave population in Brazil, I would like to explain what they were and clarify their usefulness and limitations for studies of slave identities. In the captaincy of Goiás, slaveowners had to pay a sales tax in gold or *mil-réis* upon the purchase of a *ladino* (acculturated) slave as opposed to a new imported African. This sample excludes, therefore, the new Africans, who were taxed upon their arrival in the captaincy. The scribes recorded the following information for each of the mining towns: the date, amount of the *meia-sisa* in gold, the name of the slave with color or African nation indicated, and the price paid by the new master. The *meia-sisas* also document the manumission of slaves who paid for their liberty, since each newly freed slave also had to pay the tax. Thus, the *meia-sisas* permit some insights into patterns of self-purchase throughout the captaincy. They also document the auction and sale of slaves as *bens do vento* ("property of the wind"). These were the blacks who were found in Brazil, presumed to be slaves, and sold as unclaimed slaves.[9] Obviously, the *meia-sisas* also include valuable price data on slaves, which is beyond the scope of this essay.

What the *meia-sisas* reveal is that the ethnic and national identities of the slaves of Goiás in the late colonial period varied from the Comarca do Norte (a judicial district roughly equivalent to the state of Tocantins) to the Comarca do Sul (the modern state of Goiás). Table 5 reveals that the northern Comarca, had received a majority of its Africans from West Africa, who were usually identified

Table 4
Black Slaves in Goiás, 1832

	Brazilians			Africans			
	Male	Female	Total	Male	Female	Total	Total
South							
Goiás	892	774	1,666	373	150	523	2,189
Meia Ponte	511	465	976	214	90	304	1,280
Santa Luzia	250	241	491	62	44	106	597
Santa Cruz	388	381	769	138	57	195	964
Pilar	525	300	825	125	83	208	1,033
Crixás	139	170	309	53	22	75	384
Carretão	2	2	4	—	1	1	5
Subtotal	2,707	2,333	5,040	965	447	1,412	6,452
North							
Palma	100	128	228	—	—	—	228
Traíras	702	607	1,309	69	63	132	1,441
Cavalcante	218	200	418	36	20	56	474
Flores	329	216	545	13	3	16	561
São Félix	109	112	221	10	—	10	231
Arraias	328	353	681	100	11	111	792
Conceição	90	66	156	—	—	—	156
Natividade	340	359	699	100	80	180	879
P. Imperial	177	148	325	—	—	—	325
Carolina	14	12	26	3	2	5	31
Duro	2	2	4	1	—	1	5
Subtotal	2,409	2,203	4,612	332	179	511	5,123
Total	5,116	4,536	9,652	1,297	626	1,923	11,575[a]
			83.4				16.6

Source: Cód. 808, v. 1, Goyaz, Censo da População de Goyaz, fl. 96.

a. The total slave population was 13,261, including 1,686 *pardos* (807 males and 879 females); the overall population in 1832 was 68,497.

as "Mina," except for a minority of "Nagô" (Yoruba) and "Guiné." Additional ethnic groups from West Africa also appear on table 5 and further document the prevalence of West Africans in the north. In other words, 61.7 percent of the enslaved Africans in the north had come from West Africa. These national identities conform to the internal slave trade to the North, which flowed directly from Salvador across the backlands to Barreiras and then to Natividade. The appearance of Guiné, however, raises questions. A regimental list of the black troops in the Henriques from São José de Tocantins gives an even more prominent place to the people of Guiné. According to the roster of black soldiers and their officers, which had been compiled sometime before 1799, only six soldiers were Guinés, but many of the other soldiers were the sons of mothers and/or fathers born in Guiné.

All of the other men, if African, were listed as "Mina" (table 6). What did "Guiné" mean in the late colonial period? Were these the Africans sold from Guinea-Bissau in the late eighteenth century to Belém and Maranhão? Guinea-Bissau was the site of a Portuguese fort and trading factory, which sent many enslaved Africans to Brazil.[10] Because of the geographical proximity of Maranhão and Goiás, the presence of the Africans known in Goiás as "Guiné" points to another internal trade in Africans that ran from Maranhão south to the captaincy of Goiás or from Belém to the northern Comarca.[11] The regimental list also suggests that enslaved Africans known as "Guiné" were more common in the eighteenth century, since the parents were more often described as "Guiné." At least the older generation had maintained an identity as a nation distinct from that of the "Mina" nation.

The northern Comarca also had enslaved Angolans, one "Benguela," and two "Mutecos." The populations of West Central Africa were less numerous and less well known to the scribes of the northern Comarca. Since Salvador also imported so many enslaved Africans from what is now the modern country of Angola, it is hardly surprising to find some specific names, such as "Cabundá" or "Muteco." The tax records reveal, however, that most Africans from West Central Africa who lived in the north were identified as Angolans (table 5).

In contrast, the Comarca do Sul, excluding, of course, Vila Boa de Goiás, had a smaller percentage of West Africans (37.2 percent) and a higher percentage of West Central Africans (61.7 percent). Angolans were far more significant in the south than in the north; and they frequently appear, along with Congos, in other types of documentation, such as *irmandade* (Catholic lay brotherhood) registries, inventories, manumissions, and parish registers. The Comarca do Sul evidently received more of its enslaved Africans via the trade route from Rio de Janeiro, Minas Gerais, Meia Ponte (now Pirenópolis), and Vila Boa. The merchants based in Rio and Vila Boa commonly moved enslaved Africans from as far away as Rio de Janeiro to the gold mines of Goiás in the eighteenth century,

Table 5
Africans Sold in the Captaincy of Goiás, 1810–1834

	South	%	North	%	Total	%
West Africa	*35*	*37.2*	*66*	*61.7*	*101*	*50.3*
Mina	27		53		80	
Mina Segodetodo[a]—		1		1		
Nagô (Yoruba)	7		4		11	
Nagano	—		1		1	
Guiné	1		2		3	
Tapa (Nupe)	—		1		1	
Ussa (Hausa)	—		1		1	
Busa	—		1		1	
Cobû	—		1		1	
Sabarú	—		1		1	
West Central Africa	*58*	*61.7*	*33*	*30.8*	*91*	*45.3*
Angola	41		28		69	
Congo	2		—		2	
Benguela	5		1		6	
Banguela, Banguella3	—			3		
Bonguela	1		—		1	
Banguita	1		—		1	
Cabundá	—		1		1	
Camundá	1		—		1	
Comunda	1		—		1	
Canjongo	—		1		1	
Muteca, Muteco—		2		2		
Mofumbe	1		—		1	
Cassange	1		—		1	
Songa	1		—		1	
Ladinos[b]	*1*	*1.1*	*8*	*7.5*	*9*	*4.5*
Sum Total:	94		107		201	

Source: Arquivo do Museu das Bandeiras (AMB), City of Goiás, Livros de Meia Siza dos Escravos Ladinos, numbers 167–175, 1810–1822, and 1824 for Flores. The complete tables organized by julgados are in my "Central Africans in Central Brazil, 1780–1835," in *Central Africans and Cultural Transformations in the American Diaspora*, ed. Linda M. Heywood (New York: Cambridge University Press, 2002), pp. 117–51.

a. A Mina who was totally blind.
b. Presumed to be acculturated Africans, but Amerindians were also called *ladinos*.

Table 6
Birthplace of the Black Troops and Their Parents, São José de Tocantins

	Sons	%	Fathers	Mothers	Total	%
Africa	39	33.9	91	90	181	78.7
Guiné	6		20	19	39	
Mina	33		71	71	142	
Brazil	65	56.5	16	15	31	13.5
Crioulos	—		16	15	31	
São José	54					
Arraias	1					
Traíras	1					
Vila [Boa?]	1					
Bahia	3					
Minas [Geraes?]	3					
Gerais [backlands?]	1					
Sabará	1					
Illegible/Uncertain	11	9.6	9	9	18	7.8
Total:	115					

Source: Arquivo da Curia, Diocese de Goyaz, Sociedade Goiâna de Cultura, Goiânia, Registros, Lançamento das cargas, lista da Companhia de Infantaria, Capitão Luis Gonçalves dos Santos.

while other central Africans came from neighboring captaincies. The percentages in tables 5 and 7 should not be regarded as exact proportions because of the large number of unknowns (see "unknown color" in table 7). In many cases, slave-owners identified a slave only by the term *escravo* (slave) or *prêto* (table 7). The term *prêto* usually identified Africans, but many Africans may have been included in the "unknown" category. This is an important consideration when one attempts to define percentages of Africans in the population, and the *meia-sisas* may not be the best measure of the exact proportion of Africans to Brazilian-born slaves.

The tax records also provide additional information on those born in Brazil, that is, what might be termed the "nations of color" (table 7). Unlike the city of

Rio de Janeiro where "nation" was rarely used with color terms, in Goiás *"crioulo* nation" was an ordinary usage. Why? If we understand nation in its archaic sense as a foreign people, then why did slaveowners and scribes think of their slaves as belonging to the *crioulo* nation? Were such individuals still so linked to the cultures of their parents and grandparents that they followed a more African cultural and religious tradition? The links with African parents on the part of the *crioulos* in the Henriques regiment of São José de Tocantins are notable. They were clearly second-generation *crioulos*, whose parents were listed as either "Guiné" or "Mina." In contrast, their sons had been born in São José or elsewhere in Brazil. The expression *"crioulo* nation" also occurs commonly in the *irmandade* registers from the captaincy of Goiás. Whatever the cultural context of *"crioulo* nation," the *meia-sisas* clarify that the great majority of slaves sold, who were Brazilian by birth, were *crioulos*, that is, 627 (table 7). Another 177 were defined as *cabras*. Who or what a *cabra* was in late colonial Goiás is uncertain. The baptismal registers for Vila Boa of the early nineteenth century list *cabra* infants of African mothers. By the 1870s and 1880s, *cabra* usually defined a person of mixed ancestry, and *cabras* appear on some registers with their African mothers. Perhaps they were dark mulattos.[12] The *meia-sisas*, however, did not usually record the color or nation of both mothers and children. Many children were simply identified as *crias* (offspring) when they were sold. Since the tax records distinguished between *cabras* and other racially mixed individuals, such as *mestizos*, mulattos, and *pardos*, the scribes apparently had another identity in mind for those they defined as *cabras*. The third most numerous group were those termed mulatto, that is, only 77, while another 11 were called *pardo*. Finally, 6 *mestizos* were openly sold, which may reflect the enslavement of Amerindians in the captaincy. Such individuals were probably children of captive indigenous mothers and white fathers. Two other individuals were of unknown color (table 7).

Of all the slaves sold in Goiás in the early nineteenth century, more than half were identified as black (*crioulo* and African), with another 18 percent racially mixed. The indigenous captives do not obviously appear in the tax records, unless they were counted as *pardos, mestizos,* and/or *crias*. The large number (417) who appear in the unknown category as *escravos* could be such individuals. To locate the Amerindian captives in the documentation for Goiás, we must turn to other sources. As of the Carta Regia (royal letter of instructions) of 1811, it was legal to enslave Indians; but before that date the frankest discussion of Amerindian slavery in the captaincy appears in the 1805 report of Antônio Luis de Souza Leal, who wrote that elite families were allocated "Indios" as *agregados* (household dependents), who were not free to change service or masters. The only census for Goiás that lists *agregados* as a census category is the Census of 1783. What is of particular interest is that all social classes, including free men

Table 7
Slaves Sold in Goiás by Color, 1810–1824

	South	North	Total	Percentage
Blacks	301	527	828	54.6
Africans	94	107	201	
Crioulos	207	420	627	
People of Color	108	163	271	17.9
Mulattos	38	39	77	
Pardos	7	4	11	
Cabras	61	116	177	
Mestizos	2	4	6	
Unknown color	1	1	2	0.1
Escravo[a] or other	213	204	417	27.5
Sum Total:	623	895	1,518	

Source: AMB, Livros de Meia Siza dos Escravos Ladinos, numbers 167–175, 1810–1822, and 1824 for Flores.
a. Slave.

and women of color, had *agregados* attached to their households; but in addition to *agregados* and slaves, they also possessed individuals known as *pessoas de obrigação* (obligated persons). Amerindians held as *agregados* were also listed in the death registers for Natividade; some of them were children, suggesting recent capture and enslavement in the frontier wars. Because Natividade was located near the region, where settlers were then at war with the Xavante, at least one Xavante Indian was recorded in Natividade (table 8). There is no doubt that the settlers of Goiás treated Amerindians as slaves, hiding such practices behind the term of *agregado*.[13]

In summary, therefore, census and tax records reveal that the identity and nations of the slaves of the captaincy of Goiás ranged from the Xavante to the *cabra, criVlo,* "Angola," "Mina," and "Guiné." The enslaved Africans of the captaincy had come from many parts of Africa, from Guinea-Bissau to Benguela in southern Angola and Mozambique in East Africa. The majority were identified as black, yet *crioulos* clearly differentiated themselves and their nation from the African nations. Mulattos also valued their color and social background, but they were a minority.[14] *Cabras* may have had a separate identity and some sense of cultural ties with their African mothers, but did they value it as did the *crioulos* and mulattos? The sources consulted do not include petitions by *cabras*, which might provide some insight into their sense of identity.

THE BLACK REGIMENTS

To establish more about the Africans and their descendants, we have a limited number of sources, in part due to the remote location of the captaincy of Goiás. Among the most important are the documents of the black regiments of the late colonial period. In 1812 there were twelve Henriques regiments in the captaincy of Goiás. They were usually composed of freed blacks, in particular *crioulos*. The regimental and household lists of the 1820s that record the men in the Henriques suggest that only *crioulos* served in the nineteenth century; but those lists do not match the eighteenth-century São José regimental list for its richness of data and insight into the identity and social status of the black troops.[15]

First, the regimental list reveals that the militia force comprised 115 men, headed by Captain Luis Gonçalves dos Santos, "Lieutenant Gabriel Rodrigues de M.ca" ("Mendonça"?), and Second Lieutenant Roque de Oliveira. In addition, there were a sergeant, a *furriel* (lance corporal), a flag bearer, five *cabos* (corporals), and a drummer. Presumably all the rest of the men were soldiers. Someone, most likely the governor, had required the sending of this regimental list to Vila Boa in order to demonstrate the military readiness of the captaincy. After the document had served its purpose, it had been discarded, apparently given to a priest, which is why it survives in the Archive of the Curia in Goiânia.[16] What makes this regimental list so significant, however, is what it reveals about a small black community in São José de Tocantins (now Niquelândia), a rich mining town of the late eighteenth century. Moreover, it may be the only surviving Henriques list for the eighteenth century; the others thus far located are from the 1820s.

Second, the regimental list reveals that all 115 men were not enslaved, since almost all had surnames without any indication of the slave status. Furthermore, 26 of them owned slaves. The census of 1798 for São José de Tocantins recorded a total of 229 free black males living in São José, and about half of the males served in the regiment (table 9). Thirty-nine of the men were Africans by birth. The scribe had recorded not only their nation (33 "Mina" and 6 "Guiné") but also that of their fathers and mothers. Ninety-one fathers and 90 mothers had been born in "Guiné" or "Mina." Apparently, the scribe was making a distinction between those from the Costa da Mina, that is, modern Benin and neighboring

Table 8
Slaves, Freedpersons,[a] and Amerindians
Buried in Natividade, 1801–1805

	Number	Percentage
Africans	*23*	22.3
Mina	21	
Mina *prêto forro*	1	
Nagô	1	
Brazilians	*21*	20.4
Crioulos	9	
Crioulos forros	8	
Pardos	2	
Cabras	2	
Amerindians	*7*	6.8
Mamaluca	1	
Indios	6	
Unknown/uncertain	*52*	50.5
Escravos	35	
Forra	1	
Prêtos	6	
Prêtos forros	10	
Sum Total:	103	

Source: Biblioteca de Fundação Educacional da Cidade de Goiás, City of Goiás, Livro de Obitos, Nossa Senhora do Monte do Carmo, Natividade, 1801–1805.
  a. *Forro* or *forra* in Portuguese.

countries, and Upper Guinea, from which Africans were exported via Cacheu or Bissau in Portuguese Guinea. These 39 men had been enslaved in Africa, transported across the Atlantic, traded from Bahia, Maranhão, or Belém, and walked to a small town in central Brazil. By the time they appeared on the regimental list, they had earned their freedom, formed families, and become men of property and status within the black community. Other than 11 individuals whose birthplace is unknown or uncertain, the rest of the men, or 65, had been born in Brazil. The majority were natives of São José (54): the others came from Arraias (1), Traíras (1), Vila [Boa?](1), Bahia (3), Minas [Gerais] (3), Geraes [the backlands?] (1), and Sabará (1) (table 6). These numbers hold no surprises; they merely support the usual *crioulo* identity in Henriques forces. What is unique, however, is the additional data recorded here. Since the scribe also noted the birthplace of the parents of each soldier, we can use this list to document that 70.8 percent of the *crioulos* were second-generation Brazilians, whose parents had been born in Africa. Thirty-eight *crioulos* had "Mina" parents; eight had "Guiné" parents. Two *crioulos* had a *crioulo* father and a "Mina" mother, another two had "Mina" fathers with a *crioula* mother and a mother of unknown nation. Only 12 *crioulo* men had been born of *crioulo* parents. Thus, the children of African parents were especially important in the Henriques regiment. When we combine the 39 African men with the 46 of the second generation, we can establish that at least 85 men (73.9 percent) were closely linked to African identities. By the 1820s, a generation later, the regimental list for São José would be composed of different men, identified as *crioulos*, including their *crioulo* captain, Luis Gonçalves dos Santos, who was then a tailor, and who was incapable of fighting because of his advanced age of seventy-eight.[17]

The eighteenth-century list also recorded data by age (table 10). When we divide the age data by African or *crioulo*, there is a notable difference in age structures. The Africans were all over thirty years of age, while the *crioulos* spanned the years from twelve to eighty. As table 10 reveals, there were no Africans between the ages of ten and twenty-nine. Seven were in their thirties, but all the rest were above age forty. Twelve were in their forties, and 16 in the fifties. Only 1 African was sixty. This is exactly the age profile one would expect to find in the late eighteenth century in Goiás. These 39 men had probably been imported in their teens or twenties and set to work in gold mining with the obligation to hand in a *jornal* (a daily amount) in gold dust; the total daily amounts were due to their master at the end of each week. After they had paid the *jornal* to their master, they could keep the rest and use at least part of their gold to purchase their freedom. By the time they were enrolled in the Henriques, they were over age thirty-five. The *crioulos* were obviously much younger, and thus table 10 clarifies that 26 *crioulos* were between the ages of ten and twenty-nine. As opposed to only 2 Africans in their early thirties, there were 16 *crioulos* between

Table 9
Free Blacks in São José de Tocantins, 1783 and 1798

1783

Africans and Crioulos			Total
Married			23
Single			131
Total:			154[a]

1798

Ages	Males	Females	Total
1 to 7	31	15	46
7 to 15	21	11	32
15 to 60	164	209	373
60+	13	29	42
Total	229	264	493
% of total[b]	12.0	19.5	15.1

Sources: BNRJ, Cód. 16,3,2, Notícia Geral da Capitania de Goiás, 1783; and AMB, no. 342, Mappa das Pessoas que contem a Freguezia de São José de Tocantins no anno de 1798.
  a. Total population of 341.
  b. In 1798 the total population was 3,261, including 1,909 males and 1,352 females. The scribe also recorded an additional 50 male births and 42 female births. The captives comprised 917 males and 441 females.

---

thirty and thirty-four. In contrast, there were only 5 *crioulos* in their early fifties as opposed to 13 Africans. What this small sample suggests is that the older generation included African men who had won freedom for themselves and their *crioulo* sons. It is most likely that the Africans were all freedmen who had purchased their freedom, while many of the *crioulos* were born as free blacks who owed their free status to their father's hard work in mining gold or their mother's food and drink vending.

The link of African fathers and *crioulo* sons to gold mining is obvious from the property ownership and occupations listed for the militia men. Almost half

(53) had *lavras* (goldworks), where they panned for gold; and one was identified as a miner. Far fewer (21) had *roças* (small plots of land used for food production).[18] In addition to the blacks who worked in mining and on food crops, the scribe also listed the black artisans and craftsmen of São José. The town must have been a center of clothing production since 14 were tailors and 8 were shoemakers. Another 8 worked in iron as *ferreiros* (iron workers) and 7 were *carapinas* (carpenters). Only 1 pursued the occupation of *mascate* (peddler). Militia forces in Brazil typically drew on artisans and craftsmen, and São José was no different than other towns.

Finally, the scribes recorded marital status. Not too surprisingly, the majority who were married were *crioulos* (12), followed by 7 "Mina" and 2 "Guiné." The small number of married blacks was probably due to the unbalanced sex ratio, as well as the mining economy in which single men outnumbered single women. In 1798 when a priest reported on his parishioners in São José, he recorded 1,146 free and enslaved black men as opposed to only 705 women (table 9). Such a disproportion may explain why only a minority of the men were married, but on the other hand, some of the Africans may have refused to convert and marry in a Catholic ceremony, especially if they came from Muslim societies in West Africa.

Thus, the census of 1798 and the regimental and household lists for São José de Tocantins identify a free black community whose men served in an Henriques regiment, while being men of property and skilled craftsmen. They were apparently the most important men within the black community, and the older officers may have been the leaders of their community. These documents, however, reveal almost nothing about the religious life of the blacks of São José. The 1820s household list records that some of the troops lived on the Beco do Rosário, suggesting that they lived close to the black church of Our Lady of the Rosary.[19] Since there seem to be no surviving brotherhood charters for São José, we cannot also use them to define ethnicity or national identitites in the mining town.

In Salvador and Rio de Janeiro, membership in the brotherhoods of the Rosary or Santa Efigênia was often linked to ethnicity. However, the registries of brotherhood officials from the captaincy of Goiás did not limit membership in a specific brotherhood to one ethnic group or nation. The brotherhoods included both *crioulo* and African-born individuals, usually identified as Angolan or Mina. For example, two Minas, nine Angolans, and one Conguinho served on the board of Rosário in the city of Goiás between 1826 and 1841. In 1788, however, the charter of Our Lady of Mercies "of the Captives" of the mining town of Cocal required that the king and queen be "prettos" (Africans) in one year and "creoulos" in the next year. As in Bahia, the brotherhood alternated the leadership between Africans and *crioulos*, thus suggesting divisions within the brotherhood based on birth origin.[20]

An earlier charter of Our Lady of Mercies, which was written in 1772, how-

Table 10
Age and Nationality of the Black Troops in the Henriques Regiment of São José in the Late Eighteenth Century

Ages	Africans		Crioulos	Unknown	Total
	Guiné	Mina			
10–14	—	—	2	—	2
15–19	—	—	8	—	8
20–24	—	—	11	—	11
25–29	—	—	5	1	6
30–34	—	2	16	1	19
35–39	—	5	3	—	8
40–44	1	7	5	1	14
45–49	2	2	1	—	5
50–54	2	11	5	—	18
55–59	—	3	5	1	9
60s	—	1	2	1	4
70s	—	—	—	—	—
80s	—	—	1	—	—
Unknown	1	2	7	—	10
Total:	6	33	71	5	115
%	5.2	28.7	61.7	4.3	

Source: Arquivo da Curia, Goiânia, uncatalogued documents, Diocese de Goiás, Registros, Lançamento das cargas, lista da Companhia de Infantaria, Capitão Luis Gonçalves dos Santos.

ever, recorded another identity for its members. The document opens with a deferential statement in which the brothers identify themselves as "the miserable, and most humble natives of Ethiopia, slaves of your Majesty." They sought royal protection, in particular from a local priest who demanded exorbitant fees in gold for his services. After their appeal to the monarch, they made certain that the reader knew that they were the ones who had built the "spacious chapel" dedicated to Our Lady of Mercies in Cocal. Historically, the brotherhood of Our Lady of Mercies was linked to liberating Christian captives in Muslim North Africa, and their choice of this patronness suggests that they were seeking her protection and assistance in obtaining freedom from captivity. Our Lady of Mercies was also a popular brotherhood in Minas Gerais that was especially associated with *crioulo* slaves.[21] In this case, however, the brotherhood had African members due not only to their self-identification as "natives of Ethiopia," that is, Africa, but also to the subsequent division of leadership roles between blacks and *crioulos* that appears in the second revised charter of 1788.

These fragmentary sources, that is, censuses, tax records, and regimental lists, document outsider constructions of the frontier identities of African nations with occasional registries of specific ethnicities. The north, or the modern state of Tocantins, clearly drew most of its Africans from West Africa, while the south, or the modern state of Goiás, received the majority of its Africans from West Central Africa with a minority from Mozambique. By the 1830s, however, their descendants were blacks born in Brazil (*crioulos*), who defined themselves differently than the Africans in the black brotherhoods. In at least one brotherhood in Cocal, they self-identified themselves as Ethiopians, a sophisticated Atlantic construct. Whatever their national identities, however, the sources pinpoint that the key period for central Brazil in which creole identities emerged was that of 1790 to 1832, although a small number of enslaved Africans would continue to enter the province until the abolition of the African slave trade in 1850. Their presence in the province of Goiás may have helped to preserve many Afro-Brazilian cultural traditions that continue to be celebrated at present.

NOTES

1. Mary C. Karasch, *Slave Life in Rio de Janeiro, 1808–1850* (Princeton, N.J.: Princeton University Press, 1987).

2. Mary Karasch, "Damiana da Cunha: Catechist and *Sertanista*," in *Struggle and Survival in Colonial America*, ed. David G. Sweet and Gary B. Nash (Berkeley: University of California Press, 1981), pp. 102–20; and "Catequese e cativeiro: Política indigenista em Goiás, 1780–1889," in *História dos Índios no Brasil*, ed. Manuela Carneiro da Cunha (São Paulo: Companhia das Letras, 1992), pp. 397–412.

3. Benjamin Isaac, *The Limits of Empire: The Roman Army in the East* (Oxford: Clarendon Press, 1990), p. 397. Similar usages of barbarian nations for Goiás are cited in my "Catequese e cativeiro," *História dos Índios*, p. 403.

4. Mary Karasch, "Minha Nação: Identidades Escravas no Fim do Brasil Colonial," trans. Angela Domingues, in *Brasil: Colonização e Escravidão*, ed. Maria Beatriz Nizza da Silva (Rio de Janeiro: Editora Nova Fronteira, 2000), pp. 127–41.

5. Lisbon, Arquivo Histórico Ultramarino (henceforth AHU), Goiás, "Relatório de Antônio Luis de Souza Leal sobre o estado geral da capitania," Vila Boa de Goiás, 2 March 1805 (formerly *caixa* [box] 50).

6. Census of 1825, Biblioteca Nacional do Rio de Janeiro (henceforth BNRJ), Seção de Manuscritos, 11,4,2, "Estatistica da provincia de Goyáz remettida á Secretaria de Estado dos Negocios do Imperio... , 1825."

7. Slaves before 1779: Gilka V. F. Salles, *Economia e Escravidão na Capitania de Goiás* (Goiânia: Universidade Federal de Goiás, 1992), p. 276.

8. Income from *meia-sisas*: Arquivo Nacional do Rio de Janeiro (henceforth ANRJ),

IJJ9-493, pacote 1811, Rendimento das Sizas, que se tem recolhido aos cofres, pertencente ao anno de 1810.

9. *Bens do vento*: Robert E. Conrad, *Children of God's Fire* (Princeton, N.J.: Princeton University Press, 1983), p. 323.

10. Guiné: Joel Serrão, "Guiné," in *Pequeno dicionário de história de Portugal*, ed. Joel Serrão (Porto: Figueirinhas, 1987).

11. David Michael Davidson, "Number and Origin of African Slaves Imported to Belém do Pará, 1757–1804," in his "Rivers and Empire: The Madeira Route and the Incorporation of the Brazilian Far West, 1737–1808" (Ph.D. diss., Yale University, 1970), pp. 477–84.

12. Luis da Camara Cascudo, *Dicionário do Folclore Brasileiro*, 5th ed. (Belo Horizonte: Editora Itatiaia, 1984), pp. 167–68. He includes the definition of *mulato escuro*.

13. Karasch, "Catequese e cativeiro," p. 402; and AHU, Goiás Souza Leal, 2 March 1805; and BNRJ, Cód 16.3.2., "Notícia Geral da Capitania de Goiás, 1783."

14. Petition by *pardos*: AHU, Goiás, Vila Boa, 5 February 1803 (formerly *caixa* 41).

15. Henriques: BNRJ, 9,2,10, [Luiz Antônio da Silva e Souza], "Memoria sobre o Descobrimento, Governo, População, e cousas mais notaveis da Capitania de Goyaz, Vila Boa, 13 [?] August 1786 [1812]," fls. 37–39; Arquivo Histórico do Estado de Goiás (henceforth AHG), Goiânia, Documentação Diversa, no. 68, Correspondência Dirigida do Comandante das Armas, Raymundo José da Cunha Mattos, "Relação da População do Arraial de São José de Tocantins [1823–1824]," fls. 123–42; and ibid., "Relação da Companhia de Henriques do Quartel no Arraial de São José, Santa Rita, e Amaro Leite," Quartel de São José, 12 October 1823.

16. Arquivo da Curia, Goiânia, Diocese de Goyaz, Registros, Lançamento das cargas, lista da Companhia de Infantaria, Captain Luis Gonçalves dos Santos and his men, c. 1799. He headed the regiment in São José de Tocantins before 1799 and in the 1820s. Furthermore, most of his *crioulo* men were born in São José; and a few of the same surnames appear on all three lists, such as Alvares Cardoso and Gonçalves dos Santos. Captain Gonçalves dos Santos also appears on a household list of the 1820s, which records him as living on the Beco do Rosário. He was then seventy-eight years old, a property owner, who was married to Dona Micaela Lopes, age fifty, with two sons and one daughter. See note 15 above.

17. AHG, "Relação da Companhia de Henriques," 12 October 1823.

18. AHG, "Relação da População do Arraial de São José, [1823–1824].

19. I was unable to find *irmandade* charters for São José at the Arquivo da Curia in Goiânia or Rio de Janeiro. Possibly the reason the brotherhood's papers have not survived in archives is due to the ruin of the church of Rosário in São José by 1893. Paulo Bertran, who has located much documentation on São José for the eighteenth century, did not report on any surviving papers for Rosário, although he found documents on other *irmandades*, such as Boa Morte, and photographed the church of Santa Efigênia. See his *Memória de Niquelândia* (Brasília: SPHAN próMemória, 1985), pp. 40–44. My thanks to the author for a copy of his book.

20. The brotherhood records of Our Lady of the Rosary for the City of Goiás, as well as for Natividade, are both in the Biblioteca de Fundação Educacional da Cidade de Goiás, Cidade de Goiás. Used here to check for ethnicity were the Livro dos Termos de

Meza, 1826–1840, and the Compromisso of Our Lady of the Rosary of the City of Goiás and fragments of a livro or livros dos termos and asentos of Our Lady of the Rosary from Natividade, 1786–1801. The two compromissos for the Irmandade de Nossa Senhora das Mercês dos Captivos from São Joaquim do Cocal (1772 and 1788) are at the Arquivo da Curia, which is now housed with the Sociedade Goiana de Cultura. None of the brotherhood records were cataloged as of 2000. For a similar rotation between the African-born and *crioulos* in Salvador, see Kim D. Butler, *Freedoms Given, Freedoms Won* (New Brunswick, N.J.: Rutgers University Press, 1998), p. 53.

21. Julita Scarano, *Devoção e Escravidão* (São Paulo: Companhia Editora Nacional, 1976), p. 39.

Section III

The Impact of Brazil and Afro-Brazilians upon Western Africa

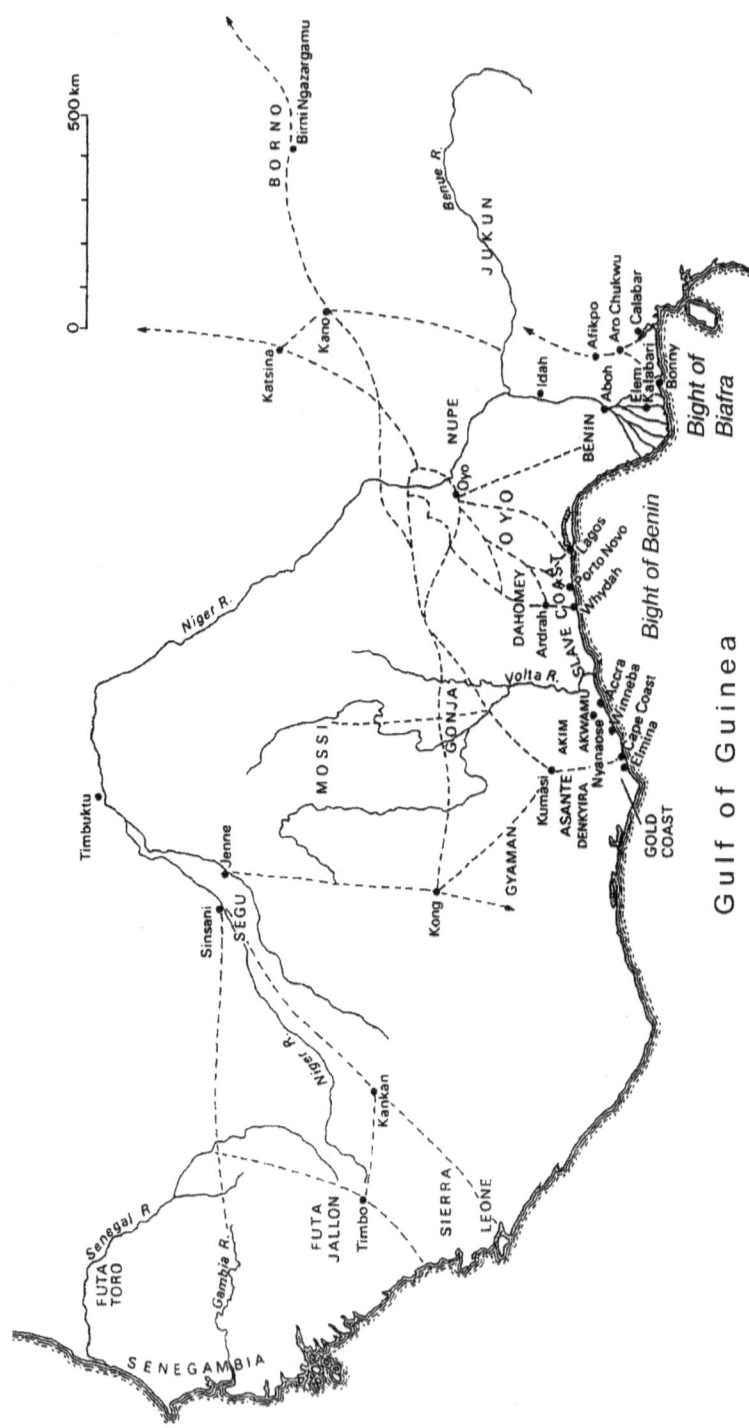

The slave trade in eighteenth-century West Africa

9
Francisco Felix de Souza in West Africa, 1820–1849[1]

Robin Law

The career of the Brazilian slave trader Francisco Felix de Souza, alias "Chacha," highlights the important interaction between the Bight of Benin and Bahia. In the early nineteenth century, he was the largest dealer in slaves and maintained close relationships with the merchants in Bahia. In 1818, he was involved in the coup d'état that overthrew the reigning monarch of Dahomey and installed Gezo as king. As Chacha, he served as the principal agent for the king. De Souza married locally, and his family formed part of the wealthy and influential elite of the lagoon-side towns of the Bight of Benin, from Lagos in the east as far as Accra in the west. His career is therefore important in itself but also because it reveals considerable insights into the interrelation between Brazil and West Africa in the early nineteenth century, and especially in the movement of Brazilians, including those of Portuguese descent, former slaves, and mulattos, to West Africa, where they constituted a commercial and intellectual elite in coastal society often referred to as "Afro-Brazilians" or "Aguda." The purpose of this chapter is not to attempt a complete account of de Souza's career but the more preliminary venture of exploring certain key aspects of it, with particular reference to the obscurities and contradictions in the available evidence.[2] Special attention is paid to British antislavery records, which have hitherto been little exploited for this purpose.

De Souza was a central figure both in the operation of the transatlantic slave trade and in the history of Ouidah, the West African coastal community in which he eventually settled (and, beyond Ouidah, in that of the kingdom of Dahomey to which it belonged). These two roles were evidently interconnected; the wealth

187

derived from his transatlantic trading formed a principal basis of his local position in Africa; while conversely, the large household (based on polygamous marriages and the accumulation of slaves) and the networks of local business and political connections that he built up in Africa facilitated his overseas commercial operations. They represent, nevertheless, what were to some extent distinct spheres of activity. Previous studies of de Souza's career have emphasized primarily its local West African dimension.

It is difficult for the historian in retrospect to fit these two dimensions of his career together, because of the character and limitations of the available evidence. Any attempt to trace and explain de Souza's career must be based on a combination of contemporary European sources and retrospective accounts recorded in local oral traditions. The contemporary sources illuminate primarily the international dimension of his career and say little about his local position, beyond generalized assertions of his influence with the reigning Dahomian king Gezo; in effect, the local basis of his position is taken as given, rather than explicated. For example, the locally resident Afro-French trader Nicolas d'Oliveira, whose own career prefigured that of de Souza, and who according to tradition played a critical role in the latter's definitive establishment in Ouidah in 1820, is nowhere mentioned in contemporary sources.[3] The indigenous Dahomian merchants who supplied slaves to de Souza in Ouidah—Adjovi, Boya, Codjia, Gnahoui, Hodonou, Quénum—are likewise invisible in the contemporary record until after his death.[4] Conversely, the local traditions say little about de Souza's involvement in the overseas slave trade, beyond generalized assertions of his preeminence; in this case, it is his international connections that are taken as given, rather than being explained.

Beyond this, the evidence available for de Souza's career suffers from more basic limitations, due to its fragmentary and uneven character. A critical deficiency is the nonsurvival of any papers of de Souza himself. Some other Ouidah families of Brazilian origin preserve written material from their early history: notably the dos Santos family, which holds correspondence of its founder José Francisco dos Santos (d. 1871).[5] A parallel case outside Ouidah is the "Great Book" of the Afro-British Lawson family of Little Popo (Aného), containing (inter alia) commercial correspondence from the period 1841–1853.[6] No comparable material, however, is preserved in the possession of the de Souzas. It may be that none ever existed. One trader who dealt with de Souza in 1830 noted that he declined to read an invoice presented to him, and inferred that he was illiterate; and while this was certainly untrue, other contemporary testimony asserts that de Souza himself kept no accounts, probably as an expression of a self-consciously "aristocratic" code of business behavior, in which verbal agreements were considered adequately binding.[7] However, a few items from his hand do survive outside Ouidah, especially in British archives, among papers found in illegal slave ships captured by the British navy.

It may be further noted that personal documentation is lacking for the Brazilian side of de Souza's career. For two of the leading Brazilian merchants on the West African coast of the following generation, Joaquim d'Almeida (d. 1857) and Domingos José Martins (d. 1864), their wills made out in Brazil prior to their definitive settlement in Africa have been traced and published.[8] No comparable will of de Souza has been found, however. This may be because he was a poor man prior to his settlement in Africa;[9] and after making his fortune there, unlike d'Almeida and Martins, he did not subsequently return, even briefly, to Brazil. De Souza family tradition maintains that he did, in fact, own property in Brazil, but the papers relating to it were destroyed in a fire in the factory of his eldest son, Isidoro, at Little Popo shortly after his father's death in 1849.[10] However, stories of the destruction of papers (especially relating to property claims) are a stereotype in oral tradition in Ouidah and should be treated with reserve. The Lawson papers at Little Popo do include a text purporting to represent the will of Isidoro de Souza, made out shortly after his father's death (and shortly before his own removal from Popo back to Ouidah) in 1849; but this was evidently copied long after the event, is of dubious authenticity, and in any case relates only to his property in Popo, with no reference to anything in Brazil.[11]

The versions of family history, including accounts of the founder, given by the de Souzas in recent times appear to be based mainly on oral traditions, although sometimes these are conflated with material from published sources. Early (late nineteenth-century?) versions of the story of the founder were transcribed into the Lawson papers.[12] A fuller account was published by his grandson (and successor to his position as "Chacha," or head of the family) Norberto Francisco de Souza, in 1955. A more recent publication by Simone de Souza (a Frenchwoman, married into the de Souza family) is largely a compilation of previously published accounts, but includes a fair amount of additional material (some derived from unpublished manuscripts, though these seem to be based on tradition rather than contemporary sources).[13] These accounts contain many contradictions and implausibilities, and demand careful interpretation and evaluation.

The deficiencies of the local sources are paralleled and compounded by the limitations of contemporary material generated by outside visitors to and temporary residents in Ouidah. The correspondence and accounts of the three European forts at Ouidah, which give detailed evidence for the eighteenth century, ceased with the abandonment of these forts, in consequence of the legal abolition of the slave trade: the French fort had been abandoned in 1797, the English fort in 1812, while communication between the Portuguese fort and the colonial authorities in Brazil to which it was subordinate lapsed from c.1807. At the same time, first-hand accounts by visitors to Ouidah are rare, except for the last years of de Souza's life, from 1843 onward; the only extended firsthand account of de Souza of any great value before this is by Henry Huntley, an officer in the British navy's antislaving squadron in the 1830s.[14] Although these later accounts contain allusions to de Souza's earlier career, some deriving from statements by de Souza himself, these are generally fragmentary, and sometimes obscure and even contradictory. For the 1820s and 1830s, the most informative material is that deriving from judicial proceedings relating to illegal slave ships intercepted by the British navy. But these, too, present considerable difficulties, since details of ownership of ships and cargoes in them were frequently falsified or contested. Moreover, "de Souza" is a common Portuguese name, and there were several persons of this surname active in the slave trade at this time (including at least two with identical forenames); some of whom were totally unrelated to the famous de Souza of Ouidah but were sometimes confused with him in the commentaries of the British authorities.

EARLY YEARS (c. 1792–1820)

The contradictions surrounding de Souza's career begin with his place of origin. He is generally held to have been born in Brazil; according to family tradition specifically in Bahia, although some contemporary testimony suggests that he came from Rio de Janeiro.[15] However, one British trader who dealt with de Souza in the 1830s understood him to be "a Spanish nobleman, who possessed estates in Havana";[16] and this assertion also appears in the (notoriously unreliable, and probably largely fictitious) memoirs of the self-styled illegal slave trader Richard Drake, who claims to have traded with de Souza at Ouidah in 1839, and, although acknowledging his ultimate Brazilian origins, to have recognized him as a man with whom he had dealings earlier in Cuba.[17] This attribution of a Cuban connection may be simply a confusion, since there was a second Francisco Felix de Souza involved in the slave trade at this time, who was resident in Matanzas, Cuba.[18] But de Souza himself may have contributed to the belief, since according to the British merchant Thomas Hutton, who knew him during the last ten years of his life, he liked to give the impression that he was "a Spaniard by birth."[19] This mystification of his origins may have reflected embarrassment on de Souza's part about his earlier career, since (as noted below) other evidence suggests that the circumstances of his arrival in Africa were disreputable.

The early stages of de Souza's career, prior to his definitive settlement at Ouidah in 1820, are obscure, because most of the source material comprises accounts recorded retrospectively, mainly from the 1840s onward, and including traditional accounts recorded in the twentieth century. Although these sources broadly agree in identifying a range of episodes in his early life in West Africa, they disagree about their chronological ordering.

First, various dates have been given for his arrival in Africa, the question being complicated by the fact that he came more than once. He told an English visitor in 1847 that he had originally come to the coast in 1793 and had lived there continuously since 1800;[20] and the date of his first arrival is roughly confirmed by Hutton, who says that he first came to Ouidah in 1792, when he was age twenty-three,[21] and stayed three years before returning to Brazil (although, as noted later, it is doubtful whether on this first visit he in fact resided specifically at Ouidah). The date commonly given in de Souza family tradition, 1788, must be discounted.[22] The date of his second, definitive arrival is confirmed as c.1800 by several contemporary accounts; for example, a British expedition that visited Ouidah in 1825 understood that he had been "resident at Whydah and Popoe upwards of twenty-five years"; and two French visitors in 1843 wrote that he had been living locally for either forty-two or forty-three years.[23] The date 1800 is also commonly given in family tradition.[24]

The circumstances as well as the dates of de Souza's successive arrivals in Africa are disputed. Hutton reports him as saying that he originally came out, in 1792, to serve as secretary in the Portuguese fort at Ouidah; the story is improved in subsequent family tradition, to assert that he arrived as governor of the fort.[25] But it must be supposed that Hutton misunderstood what he was told, because surviving records of the Portuguese fort document de Souza's presence there only in the later period, after 1803. More probably, therefore, his first visit to Africa, c.1792–1995, was as a private trader. Family tradition suggests that he traded on this first visit at Badagry, east of Ouidah, where he built a factory called Ajido.[26]

It also seems clear that when he returned to Africa in 1800, this was again initially as a private trader, and that he took service in the Portuguese fort at Ouidah only when his commercial affairs proved unsuccessful.[27] There was, however, apparently a legal/political as well as a commercial context to his return to Africa. The earliest contemporary account of his activities after his later resettlement at Ouidah so far traced, in a British report of 1821, describes him as "a renegado . . . banished from the Brazils"; and an account recorded shortly after his death states that he had been exiled from Brazil for "some political crime."[28] The circumstances of this banishment, however, are obscure. The notorious illegal slave trader Theophilus Conneau (alias Theodore Canot), who traded with de Souza at Ouidah in 1830, claimed that the latter had come there after involvement in the Brazilian war of independence (1822–1823), having enlisted in the army of the secessionist emperor Dom Pedro at Rio de Janeiro, but subsequently deserted.[29] This story, however, certainly cannot be true, since as seen earlier de Souza had come to the coast c.1800, long before the Brazilian secession (and in any case, his "banishment" from Brazil is already reported in 1821). There was an earlier, unsuccessful nationalist insurrection in 1798 (though this was at Salvador, Bahia, rather than Rio), and it is perhaps conceivable that Conneau's story is a muddled allusion to involvement by de Souza in that episode. But alternatively, his status as an outlaw may have related to his involvement in the slave trade, which had been technically illegal (north of the equator) for Portuguese citizens since 1815; or more likely, it arose from unknown circumstances.

The sources are also contradictory over where on the coast de Souza settled on his return to Africa, though it was probably not (as assumed by Ross) at Ouidah.[30] An account recorded from the de Souza family in the 1880s says that he settled in 1800 initially at Badagry.[31] This, however, may involve confusion with his earlier visit to Africa in the 1790s. More recently recorded versions of family tradition generally state that he settled in 1800 at Little Popo, to the west, where he established a second factory called Ajido. He certainly maintained connections with Little Popo in this period, since it was evidently around this time that he married Jijibou, daughter of Comlagan, chief of Little Popo, who, according to family tradition, bore his first son, Isidoro, in 1802.[32] But it is possible that now, as later, he maintained establishments at more than one place on the coast.

Within a short period, in any case, his commercial operations ran into difficulty, and he enlisted in the Portuguese fort at Ouidah. This had occurred by 1803, when he is documented in the capacity of scribe and bookkeeper of the fort; and he was still at the fort in 1806, then acting as storekeeper.[33] The last formally appointed governor of the fort, Jacinto José de Souza, sent out from Bahia in 1804, was his brother; a later account alleges that Francisco procured his brother's appointment.[34] Jacinto de Souza, however, died soon afterward, as did his immediate acting successor; and with the death of his superiors, Francisco de Souza himself assumed the governorship of the fort.[35] Subsequently, however, he abandoned the fort to set up as an independent trader in the still flourishing although now illegal slave trade to Brazil and Cuba.

Where on the coast he settled in this period is, again, disputed; according to the English missionary Thomas Birch Freeman, writing after de Souza's death, it was at Ouidah; and a slave ship partly owned by him that was taken by the British navy in 1816, the *Dos Amigos*, had taken its slaves at Ouidah.[36] Some versions of more recent tradition, however, say that it was at Little Popo; perhaps he maintained residences, or at least business establishments, at both places. He subsequently became involved in a dispute with King Adandozan of Dahomey, and in consequence supported the coup d'état by which the latter was dethroned in favor of his brother Gezo in 1818. Although this story is fully told only in traditional accounts recorded after his death, there seems no reason to question its essential accuracy.[37] In reward for his support, de Souza was then invited to resettle at Ouidah by the newly installed king Gezo. According to family tradition, he moved back from Popo to Ouidah in September 1820;[38] and this is consistent with the contemporary record, in which his presence there is first attested in 1821.

DE SOUZA AS "CHACHA" OF OUIDAH

The received account posits that when de Souza returned to Ouidah, this was not merely as a trader, since he was appointed by King Gezo to an official position: in Ross's formulation, for example, he became "a Dahomian chief... [with] a special title... the Chacha of Whydah."[39] But this is an oversimplification. The contemporary evidence shows that initially de Souza did not in fact intend to settle permanently in Ouidah, since in April 1821 he obtained a passport to return to Brazil from the Portuguese authorities in Rio de Janeiro.[40] Evidently, his evolution into a "Dahomian chief" was not originally envisaged, but took place over time; and certainly the appellation "Chacha" was in origin a personal nickname, which became transformed into a title of office only retrospectively, when it was inherited by his sons after his death.

Why de Souza did not in any event return to Brazil is unclear. According to a story recorded by Freeman, he did in fact intend to leave for Brazil in a slave ship called the *Prince of Guinea*, but this was captured by the British navy; and British documents do record the capture of a ship of this name, bound from Bahia for Ouidah with a cargo consigned to de Souza, in August 1826.[41] But this leaves unclear why he did not repeat the attempt. It may be that he was prevented from leaving by the Dahomian authorities: Huntley in the 1830s understood that he was forbidden to leave Ouidah by King Gezo, although he also suggested that this precaution was no longer necessary, since de Souza was by then reconciled to continuing to live there.[42] It is also possible that his plans were affected by the independence of Brazil from Portugal in 1822. As noted earlier, one account of the circumstances of his alleged "banishment" from Brazil claims that he was a deserter from the army of the emperor Dom Pedro at the time of Brazilian independence; and although this cannot be literally true, it might represent a garbled recollection that he at first supported but later broke with the new regime in Brazil. The secession of Brazil had repercussions in Ouidah, where the title to the Portuguese fort was disputed between Portugal and Brazil but confirmed to the former in the agreement recognizing Brazilian independence in 1825; a later account (recorded in the 1860s) says that de Souza offered the Ouidah fort to the Brazilian government but received no reply.[43] A contemporary report of 1823 confirms at least a temporary breach between de Souza and the new government in Brazil, which had seized two of his ships, with more than one thousand slaves.[44] The suggestion of alienation from Brazil is also given circumstantial support by evidence relating to the education of de Souza's sons. Although his eldest son, Isidoro (born in 1802), was sent for education in Brazil, this was evidently before independence, since he is said to have returned to Africa in 1822; while a younger son, Antonio "Kokou" (born 1814), was educated instead in Portugal.[45] It is also noteworthy that de Souza continued to assert his own status as a Portuguese national after 1822; and although (as explained below) there were practical advantages in this, in relation to his illegal slaving activities, it may also have represented a more positive political statement. Although the quarter of Ouidah which de Souza founded was later called "Brazil" (as it remains, in Fon "Blézin"), it is doubtful whether any inference about his political allegiance or identity can be based on this, since this name is not in fact attested during his own lifetime, when his household seems to have been called (like the factories he had founded earlier in Badagry and Little Popo) Ajido.

The nature of de Souza's position at Ouidah is often misrepresented in local tradition as that of "viceroy of Whydah, chief of the whites"; and this perception has been consolidated in the wider world through the historical novel by Bruce Chatwin, which is closely based on the career of the historical de Souza.[46] The misrepresentation, however, goes back to his own lifetime. One of the British naval officers testifying before the 1842 Parliamentary Committee, for example, said that "Mr De Souza is [the king's] viceroy, he has the power of life and death"; and although this was contradicted by another officer, who observed that the "*caboceer* [chief]" of Ouidah was "a native," he, too, opined that this chief was "completely under" de Souza, and implied that the latter had some sort of official position, since he could allegedly raise a large force of soldiers.[47] In fact, the position of Yovogan or "Viceroy" of Ouidah remained distinct, and in the hands of a native Dahomian, who for most of this period was Dagba.[48] The continuing primacy of Yovogan Dagba is clear from accounts of European visitors to Ouidah in de Souza's last years, such as the missionary Freeman (1843) and the explorer Duncan (1845), who upon arrival visited the Yovogan to explain their business first, and talked to de Souza only subsequently.[49] It is entirely likely that de Souza himself was formally appointed a *caboceer* of Ouidah, which among other things involved an obligation to provide military forces; however, this was not unique to him, but normal practice with regard to leading merchants of Ouidah generally (including later, for example, Domingos Martins).

It is clear, in fact, that de Souza's position was essentially commercial rather than political, functioning as the king's agent at Ouidah; although Europeans tended to exaggerate his status in Dahomey, because it was with him rather than directly with the king that they normally dealt on matters of trade. Even his commercial position was often misunderstood and exaggerated; although commonly represented as enjoying a "monopoly" of trade, this is not strictly correct.[50] The reality was that, in his capacity as the king's agent, he enjoyed the royal privilege of first refusal of trade. As an account of 1839 explicitly noted, "the other factors had only what he didn't want for himself."[51]

One thing that clearly emerges from the contemporary record, as opposed to the local traditions, is that de Souza's position at Ouidah derived its legitimacy and authority from his European/international connections, as well as (and perhaps initially, more than) his appointment by the king of Dahomey.[52] Upon his return to Ouidah, as has been seen, he contacted the Portuguese authorities in Brazil in order to obtain a passport to return there. This passport authorized de Souza to bring with him to Brazil the slaves that he owned in Africa, and he seems to have represented this as an authorization to continue trading in slaves, until he returned to Brazil. A British report of 1823 noted that he "confidently states that he has permission from the king of Portugal to realize his property in any way, either by shipping slaves or otherwise."[53] He also now reasserted his claim to be governor of the Portuguese fort at Ouidah, and hence to official status as a representative of the Portuguese Crown. Another British account of 1821 notes that de Souza "assumes the rights and privileges of a person in authority, granting papers and licences to all the slave traders, in all the form and confidence of one empowered to do so, by the Portuguese government";[54] and later sources make explicit that this claimed authority was based on continuing governorship of the Portuguese fort. Huntley in the 1830s, for example, noted that he "by no means disconnected himself from his position of a governor, whenever it became necessary to assume it upon any ground of policy with reference to natives or others."[55]

This assertion by de Souza of Portuguese nationality may have been merely prudential, an attempt to secure for the slave ships in which he had an interest the partial immunity from arrest by the British navy that Portuguese vessels enjoyed until the British Equipment Act of 1839, prior to which they could be taken only if they actually had slaves on board. The issuing of papers mentioned in 1821 probably relates to the common practice of providing false passports authorizing ships to take slaves south of the equator, where the slave trade remained legal for Portuguese nationals until 1836; in consequence of which, ships that traded at Ouidah were safe from arrest, even with slaves on board, if they could make the short passage south to the equator. Further, the claim to be the legal governor of the Portuguese fort was probably related to the argument that Ouidah was a Portuguese possession, in which the British had no right of pursuit or arrest. In 1827, for example, when a Brazilian vessel was seized at Ouidah, its master protested that "he verily believes that the said vessel and cargo are protected by the treaty or convention," because his ship had been taken while at anchor "under the fort ... the said fort being in the possession of the Crown of Portugal"; though the British authorities declined to accept de Souza's continuing occupation of the fort as having any official standing. Again in 1839 when the ship *Emprehendedor*, which was owned and commanded by Joaquim Telles de Menezes, a son-in-law of de Souza and like him resident in Ouidah, and which sailed under Portuguese colors (though adjudged by the British to be Brazilian), was taken at Ouidah, de Menezes claimed that "his vessel was Portuguese, and was improperly captured under the guns of the Portuguese fort at Whydah."[56]

It is clear, however, that de Souza did not reside in the Portuguese fort, which was reported in 1825 to be serving as a lodging house for visiting Portuguese captains; Huntley in the 1830s noted that he was living in "a well-constructed mansion, erected by himself."[57] According to local tradition, he originally lodged with Nicolas d'Oliveira; and when he established his own household, which became the center of the "Brazil" quarter of the town, this was on the opposite (west) side of the town from the Portuguese fort.

De Souza's claim to be governor of the Portuguese fort presumably ended when it was officially reoccupied by the Portuguese authorities on the island of São Tomé in 1844, and he is said to have handed over the keys of the fort to the new governor.[58] By then, the utility of claiming a Portuguese connection had in any case largely disappeared with the Equipment Act of 1839. It seems likely, therefore, that the perception of de Souza as essentially a "Dahomian chief" reflects conditions in his final years, in the 1840s, when the overseas dimension of his activities had been attenuated.

DE SOUZA AS SLAVE TRADER: SOME NEGLECTED DIMENSIONS (c. 1820–1840)

With regard to de Souza's operations in the international slave trade, as noted earlier, a wealth of detailed information exists in the records relating to the pursuit and arrest of illegal slavers by the British navy. Although this material has been commonly used for the more general study of the illegal slave trade, its potential value for understanding de Souza's individual career has been largely neglected.[59]

One area where this material is especially valuable is in identifying other individuals who were engaged in the slave trade at Ouidah, whether in association or in competition with de Souza. Whereas local tradition gives the impression that de Souza was the only significant slave trader prior to the 1840s, the contemporary material supplies the names of others who resided there, temporarily or longer term, for purposes of trade. Although many of these names occur without sufficient detailed context (or corroboratory reference in other material) to identify them or establish their precise role and importance, in a few cases they emerge more clearly from the record. For example, one important associate of de Souza documented in the British records was Joaquim Telles de Menezes, mentioned earlier, who settled in Ouidah around 1830 and married one of de Souza's daughters. He is first mentioned in 1835, as the owner of a slave ship intercepted by the British navy; and subsequently as both owner and master of two other captured slave ships, in 1836 and 1839. De Menezes himself, in the consequent judicial proceedings, gave contradictory testimony about his origins, describing himself as born either on Prince's Island or in Pernambuco, Brazil; but, like de Souza himself, he consistently asserted Portuguese nationality. His final appearance in the contemporary record was in 1841, when he was a passenger on a suspected slave ship bound from Bahia to Prince's Island.[60] De Menezes presumably operated in partnership, or at least in cooperation, with his father-in-law; indeed, one of the ships of which he was owner, the *Emprehendedor*, had originally belonged to de Souza, from whom de Menezes purchased her in 1837, the transaction being registered at Prince's Island. De Menezes is not remembered, however, in local tradition in Ouidah, presumably because he left no descendants there.

Another important slave dealer who settled in Ouidah in this period was Juan José Zangronis (or Sangron), the son of a leading merchant of Havana, who supplied slaves for his father (and later, for his brother) in Cuba. In the contemporary record, Zangronis is first attested at Ouidah, taking delivery of goods shipped from Cuba, in 1834; and subsequently recorded as the consignee of cargoes from or supplier of slaves to four other vessels trading to Ouidah between 1835 and 1839.[61] He died at Ouidah in 1843.[62] The missionary Freeman, who met Zangronis shortly before his death, described him as "in rank and influence ... second only to de Souza."[63] Unlike de Menezes, Zangronis did leave descendants in Ouidah; a "half-caste" son of his, Francisco Zangronis, is noted incidentally, attending the royal court at Abomey, in 1864.[64] Indeed, the family survives to the present, although its name is now given a Portuguese form, Sangronio, and its founder (whose name is recalled as José Sangron) is wrongly remembered as having been "a Brazilian of Portuguese origin," rather than as Spanish from Cuba; this confusion evidently reflecting the family's subsequent absorption into the larger Brazilian community.[65] In British records, Zangronis is regularly mentioned together with de Souza in terms that imply that they were associates, rather than rivals in trade; for example, the ship *Emprehendedor*, arrested at Ouidah in 1839 (commanded by de Souza's son-in-law de Menezes) according to some testimony had previously been owned jointly by de Souza and Zangronis. Another of his sons, Ignacio José Sangron, married one of de Souza's daughters, but this was later, in the 1870s.[66]

A second aspect of de Souza's operations that emerges from the British records is that he frequently shipped slaves for sale in the Americas on his own account, rather than merely supplying them to ships in Africa; in Bahia, the merchant Andre Pinto da Silveira operated as his agent in such sales in the 1830s.[67] He also owned several ships employed in transatlantic slaving. At least one of these was built to his order in America: the *Principe de Guiné*, which was built at Philadelphia and sailed from there to Ouidah en route to Bahia in 1825 was, according to the testimony of its American master, the property of de Souza, who had supplied the money for its construction; although when this ship turned up again on the coast in the following year, to trade with de Souza at Ouidah, its papers showed it as owned by a Bahia merchant, Antonio Pedroso de Albuquerque.[68] Others were purchased in West Africa. For example, the *George and James*, arrested off Ouidah in 1825, had originally been owned by the London firm of Mathew Forster & Co., and engaged in legal trade, but had been sold in West Africa to its mate, Mr. Ramsay, who then took it on a voyage to Bahia and back; but the British held that the real owner was de Souza, who was believed to have given Ramsay the money for its purchase.[69] De Souza also purchased condemned and confiscated slave ships for reemployment in the slave trade; in 1828 he had an agent in the British colony of Freetown, Sierra Leone, for this purpose.[70] Other ships taken by the British that were owned (or partly owned) by de Souza included the *Legitimo Africano* in 1835, the *Don Francisco* and the *Florida* in 1837, and the *Fortuna* in 1839.[71] Others, although not owned by de Souza at the time of their capture, had been his property earlier: the example of the *Emprehendedor*, purchased by his son-in-law de Menezes from de Souza (or from de Souza and Zangronis jointly) in 1837, was mentioned earlier.[72] Other ships also, as has been seen, were owned by de Menezes, perhaps acting in association with or as proxy for his father-in-law. Most of these ships owned by de Souza and de Menezes in the 1830s had been purchased in West Africa, generally at Ouidah, though in some cases at Prince's Island; but one, the *Legitimo Africano*, had reportedly been built locally at Ouidah. This ownership of ships by merchants resident in Africa was, in fact, a general pattern in the period of the illegal trade, but de Souza appears to have been a pioneer in it; while the construction of ships on the African coast, either by assembly from imported prefabricated parts or from scratch from local materials, was likewise an occasional practice in the illegal trade.[73]

A further feature of de Souza's commercial operations that is clearer from the contemporary record (although acknowledged in local traditions also) was his exploitation of canoe-borne communication along the lagoons to other ports to the east and west of Ouidah. Although such lagoon links were by no means new in the trade of Ouidah,[74] they acquired an enhanced significance in the illegal slave trade as a means of evading the British naval squadron. Given the notoriety of Ouidah itself as a slave port, it attracted the particular attention of the British, and slaves were therefore, even if originally bulked up at Ouidah, frequently moved along the lagoon to be embarked at other, less well-known places. As Huntley noted, for example, in the 1830s: "If ... a [British] cruiser was known to be off Whydah, de Souza would order the slaver to go to some other anchorage, and then send the Negroes by the canoes upon the lagoon, who would be relanded, travelled across the strip of land [between the sea and the lagoon] ... instantly embarked, and the slaver would proceed on her voyage."[75]

To the west of Ouidah, as has been seen, de Souza's principal base before 1820 had been at Little Popo. After his removal to Ouidah, he seems initially to have intended to maintain his influence in Popo; in 1822–1823 he supported the prominent trader George Latty Lawson in a civil war against its ruler, Comlagan, who was driven out.[76] But in the event, he did not maintain his factory there; local tradition in Little Popo records that after his departure to Ouidah the houses he had built there were neglected (and indeed "fell down"), until they were reoccupied many years later by his son Isidoro.[77] The reason for this abandonment is unclear, although it may be that communication between Ouidah and Little Popo was disrupted as a result of the civil war of 1822–1823, after which the defeated faction settled at Agoué to the east. Isidoro's reoccupation of the factory is dated by tradition to 1840, and this is consistent with the contemporary record, in which his presence at Little Popo is likewise first attested in that year;[78] this was probably a response to increasing pressure from the British navy following the Equipment Act of 1839, which encouraged further the dispersal of slave embarkations from Ouidah.

In the 1820s and 1830s, de Souza seems to have paid more attention to the lagoon route to the east. Local tradition in Ouidah recalls that he had the lagoon to the east dredged, in order to allow canoes to go as far as Cotonou.[79] East of Ouidah, the lagoon was separated from Lake Nokoué by a sandbank at Godomey, and it was presumably this obstacle which de Souza now (temporarily) cleared. From its strategic situation in the lagoon system, Godomey played a central role in communication between Ouidah and Porto Novo and Badagry to the east. But it was also connected by an overland path to its own roadstead on the seashore. According to tradition, Godomey was the site of the former slave port of Jakin, destroyed by the Dahomians in 1732; but it was reestablished in this period to serve as an outport of Ouidah. At least one recorded slave ship in 1830, after landing its cargo at Ouidah and purchasing slaves from de Souza there, proceeded east to embark them at Jakin.[80] Its alternative (and perhaps new) name Godomey is first attested in the contemporary record in 1843, when de Souza was reported to have gone there "on business."[81]

Cotonou was situated on the southern shore of Lake Nokoué, at the point where its waters approached most closely to the sea, thus maximizing the advantage of water transport. Traditions of its foundation attribute it to King Gezo, acting on the advice of de Souza, who was seeking an alternative point of embarkation for slaves, less familiar to and therefore less subject to harassment by the British navy than Ouidah.[82] The implied date seems here, too, to be after the Equipment Act of 1839, and this is supported by the fact that in contemporary sources the earliest allusion to trade at Cotonou seems to be in an account by a British naval officer who served in the West African squadron in 1839–1841, who observed that a blockade of Ouidah would be ineffective, because slaves could be sent for shipment instead at Ekpe ("Apee"); this probably alludes not to the Ekpe that had been a port of embarkation for slaves in the eighteenth century, but to a distinct place further west called in other sources "Appi Vista," which was an alternative name for Cotonou.[83] After de Souza's death, control of Godomey and Cotonou initially remained in the hands of his family; in 1852 the former was reportedly a monopoly of his eldest son (and successor as Chacha), Isidoro, and the latter of Isidoro's younger brother Antonio.[84]

Godomey and Cotonou, like Ouidah, belonged to Dahomey; but de Souza's operations to the east also extended beyond Dahomian territory. In particular, he reestablished links with Badagry, in whose territory he had briefly maintained a factory earlier. According to family tradition, when his eldest son, Isidoro, returned from Brazil in 1822, he was sent by his father to trade at Badagry, from which he returned to Ouidah c.1834.[85] The de Souza factory, Ajido, was actually some miles east of Badagry. It is mentioned in records of the illegal slave trade during 1826–1827, although these make no reference specifically to the de Souzas; one ship taken off Lagos in 1826 had earlier called at Ajido, to purchase provisions and other goods, and another was taken off Ajido itself with slaves on board in 1827.[86] The traditions explain the abandonment of this factory in the 1830s as due to losses incurred from fire and theft, and by implication attribute the failure to Isidoro's youth and inexperience. But it may be that broader geopolitical factors were also involved; it is suggestive that Isidoro's installation at Badagry roughly coincided with the establishment there of Adele, the exiled king of Lagos further east, under whose rule the town achieved an enhanced commercial importance, as the principal outlet for the trade of Oyo in the interior; but conversely, the return of Adele to resume his throne at Lagos c.1835 probably marked the end of this flourishing.[87] De Souza continued, however, to do some trade at Badagry; in 1836, for example, a ship from Bahia trading at Ouidah carried tobacco and other goods for de Souza to Porto Novo and Badagry.[88]

The contemporary evidence also shows de Souza in the 1830s maintaining commercial links further east along the coast to Lagos. Two of the ships which de Souza himself owned, the *Florida* in 1837 and the *Fortuna* in 1839, did their trade at Lagos rather than Ouidah. One of those owned by de Menezes in 1835 likewise sailed from Ouidah to Lagos to take in slaves there; and a second in 1836, commanded by de Menezes in person, went even further afield, taking in its slaves at Old Calabar.[89] It also appears that their ships regularly called at Prince's Island to obtain passports from the Portuguese colonial authorities there, and one of them, the *Fortuna*, carried a passport issued at Luanda, Angola.

De Souza's commercial operations thus transcended his base at Ouidah, involving not only operations across the Atlantic, but also links to other ports on the African coast, including places beyond Dahomian jurisdiction, Little Popo to the west and Porto Novo, Badagry, and Lagos to the east; and legal dealings with Portuguese colonies in Africa. Again, the implication is that, rather than being a specifically "Dahomian" figure, he operated, at least down to the 1830s, on an international scale.

DE SOUZA IN ECLIPSE? (c. 1840–1849)

Although de Souza lived on until 1849, he had lost his dominant position within the Ouidah trade before then. By 1845, as he told Duncan, he was doing "very little [slave trading] compared with what he formerly did."[90] In part, this was simply a reflection of his advancing age. As late as 1843, he was still traveling to Abomey to participate in the king's "Annual Customs," accompanying the French agent Brue in that year; but in 1845 Duncan found him bedridden with sickness and consequently unable to accompany him to the capital.[91]

The physical decline of the head of the family led to the passing of leadership in it to the younger generation of de Souzas. As seen above, his eldest son, Isidoro, had traded on his behalf in Badagry earlier and in 1840 was sent to reestablish his factory at Little Popo. A younger son, Antonio "Kokou," was also involved in the trade along the lagoon to the west, being mentioned along with Isidoro in the Lawson correspondence, as doing business at Agoué and Little Popo, from 1843 onward; and also traded in Ouidah, where the correspondence of José Francisco dos Santos records three transactions involving payments to him, one of them explicitly for slaves, during 1846–1847.[92] Antonio also appears as the owner of a suspected slave ship, the *Galliana*, arrested by the British off the West African coast in early 1849 (though eventually released for lack of conclusive evidence). This ship had been built to Antonio's order, at Oporto in Portugal, and sailed from Portugal first to Bahia, where it was met by another of the de Souza brothers, Francisco, who served as supercargo on the voyage to Africa.[93] Another brother, Ignacio, is also mentioned in 1848, attending the royal court in Abomey; in 1849 he was named along with Isidoro and Antonio as being "weathy and slave-merchants," and presumably he also had begun his trading operations before their father's death.[94] Tradition indicates that these and other de Souza sons traded "each on their own account," rather than as a family collective; after the father's death, all three competed for the succession to his title of Chacha, and the family property in Ouidah was partitioned among them.[95]

More was involved in de Souza's decline, however, than his retirement through old age. By the 1840s his commercial operations were running into difficulties, and he was heavily in debt; at the time of his death in 1849, he was described as "almost a pauper." When the king sent officials to seize his property, they found "neither money, nor goods, nor anything of value," only "a little furniture and some plate"—though, very likely, his family would have removed or concealed any movable items, to avoid the royal inheritance tax—and his son Ignacio had to borrow money to pay for his funeral ceremonies. His debts were mainly to merchants in Brazil and Cuba; but he also owed $80,000 to King Gezo, and shortly before his death had been obliged to send his silver coffin as a pawn to the king.[96]

Some versions of tradition in Ouidah blame de Souza's impoverishment on King Gezo, who allegedly became jealous of his wealth and sought deliberately to ruin him by making excessive demands on his resources, including failing to pay for goods supplied on credit; these accounts attribute de Souza's death to his despair at his loss of royal favor, or even insinuate that he was poisoned on Gezo's orders.[97] The contemporary accounts, however, do not support this. It seems more likely that his ruin was due principally to the losses which he incurred through the activities of the British antislaving squadron; he told Duncan in 1845 that the British had captured twenty-two of his ships.[98] He is also said to have lost property to the value of $100,000 in a fire at Ouidah in c.1836–1837.[99] Some contemporary comment suggests that his difficulties were compounded by his own extravagance and mismanagement, especially his reckless acceptance of goods on credit; and one does refer to his "having been over liberal in his presents" to the king.[100] But the claim that he was ruined by Gezo's failure to pay for goods is contradicted by the contemporary evidence cited earlier, that in fact de Souza owed money to Gezo rather than vice versa. The traditional account probably represents a reading back into the first de Souza's times of the circumstances of the 1880s, when the then Chacha, another of his sons called Julião, was liquidated and his property confiscated by Gezo's successor King Glele.

Whatever the cause, de Souza's commercial difficulties prompted Gezo to reorganize the trade, depriving him of his position as sole royal agent. According to Hutton (writing shortly after de Souza's death), following representations from his creditors in Brazil and Cuba, "it was arranged that agents from the Havana and Brazils might settle at Whydah, and Da [sic] Souza should give up shipping slaves, but to receive a commission of a doubloon for every slave that was shipped."[101] This account presents a number of difficulties, most obviously that no precise date is indicated; although an allusion to "a more rigid law ... respecting the capture of slave-trading vessels" seems to point to the period after the Equipment Act of 1839. It might be objected that some other agents for the slave trade had been able to settle in Ouidah earlier than this, notably the Cuban Zangronis in the early 1830s; but he, as seen earlier, traded in association rather than in competition with de Souza. Conversely, de Souza was still shipping slaves as late as August 1839, when he is recorded as the owner of the captured slave ship *Fortuna* and the consignee of its cargo. More probably, therefore, the change occurred in the 1840s.

The wording of Hutton's account of the new commercial arrangements is also ambiguous and open to different interpretations. Ross reads it to mean that de Souza ceased trading altogether, becoming instead "a functionary levying a tax ... on every slave exported."[102] But a more natural interpretation is that he continued to supply slaves to other merchants in Ouidah, the payment of one doubloon ($16) per slave being his commission on such sales. It is clear, moreover, that de Souza, as well as his sons, continued to sell slaves, at least occasionally. Dos Santos in 1847 complained of the high prices demanded for slaves bought from "the old man," referring evidently to de Souza: "he says he wants 80 pesos [dollars] apiece because the whites purchase at 70 pesos outside and pay *caranquejo*," the meaning of this last word (perhaps miscopied) being obscure, but perhaps referring to de Souza's "commission" on slave sales.[103] De Souza also, in common with other Brazilian slave traders, engaged in the new trade in palm oil, which expanded rapidly at Ouidah from the mid-1840s, being reported to have loaded five ships with oil during the year 1846.[104]

One of the new dealers who were able to enter the slave trade at this time was Joaquim d'Almeida, whose principal base was at Agoué, to the west, rather than in Ouidah itself.[105] Local tradition in Agoué claims that he first came there in 1835, and contemporary British records confirm that he was trading there by 1840;[106] but he settled definitively in Africa, after returning to Brazil, only around the beginning of 1845.[107] At some point he secured from King Gezo permission to trade at Ouidah; in fact, one later account links the breaking of de Souza's monopoly specifically with d'Almeida's entry into the trade there.[108] By 1849, if not earlier, he maintained a residence at Ouidah, as well as at Agoué, and was indeed accounted "the richest resident in Whydah," outshadowing any of the second-generation de Souzas.[109] According to tradition in Ouidah, d'Almeida's principal business associate there was Azanmado Quénum, formerly a client of de Souza, but who now broke away to trade independently; indeed, it was Quénum who persuaded Gezo to trade with d'Almeida and to allow him to settle in Ouidah.[110] By implication, he received slaves from Gezo through Quénum rather than through the de Souzas. D'Almeida's household in Ouidah was situated in the quarter of his business partner Quénum, immediately south of de Souza's "Brazil" quarter, out of which it had been carved.[111]

Even more important among the new generation of slave traders was Domingos José Martins (alias Domingo Martinez).[112] Martins had originally come to Africa c.1833, as a member of the crew of a slave ship consigned to de Souza; the ship was captured and the crew put ashore at Ouidah, where Martins lived for some years "upon the charity" of de Souza.[113] In the late 1830s he moved to Lagos, where he became the leading slave merchant. After briefly returning home to Bahia, he returned to Africa in early 1846, and this time established himself at Porto Novo, east of Ouidah.[114] Martins was the most important slave trader in this period; in 1849 he was described as "the richest merchant in the Bights."[115] He settled in 1846 not in the capital of the kingdom of Porto Novo (the modern city) to the north of the lagoon, but on the seashore to the south, at the village to which the name "Porto Novo" had been originally applied (modern Sémé). This was in fact now under the effective control of Dahomey rather than of Porto Novo, and it was to the former rather than the latter that Martins paid tribute.[116] He also received his main supply of slaves from Dahomey. Later in 1846 he visited King Gezo at Abomey and told him "that he need not fear a demand ceasing for slaves; that he could take all that he, the king, could send him."[117] This wording implies that Martins traded directly with Gezo, rather than through the de Souzas. Probably much of this trade bypassed Ouidah altogether, slaves being taken overland to the northwest shore of Lake Nokoué, and then by canoe (through the port of Abomey-Calavi) across the lake to Sémé. But Martins also did business through Ouidah; by 1849 he, too, had an establishment there, which, consistent with his superior wealth, was judged to be "the best building in town."[118] This was situated on the east of the town, close to the Portuguese fort, again outside the de Souza quarters.[119] Although Martins eventually formed a connection with the de Souza family, marrying one of the founder's daughters, this was apparently only after the latter's death in 1849.[120]

In addition to these traders whose main bases were outside Ouidah, others were able to set up in the slave trade in this period inside the town, in more direct competition with the de Souzas. One of these was José Francisco dos Santos, whose correspondence documents his activities from 1844 onward. According to tradition, dos Santos was originally in the service of the de Souza family (as a tailor), and indeed married Francisco Felix de Souza's eldest daughter, Francisca.[121] Ultimately, however, he (or at any rate his descendants) settled in Tové quarter, in the northeast of Ouidah, implying some degree of independence from the de Souzas.[122] His correspondence shows him selling slaves both on his own account and as agent for traders in Brazil, and shipping slaves from Agoué and Little Popo to the west, as well as from Ouidah itself. In his business operations along the lagoon to the west, he collaborated, at least occasionally, with Isidoro de Souza at Little Popo, as well as with d'Almeida at Agoué. Within Ouidah, although he bought some slaves from Antonio de Souza, as noted earlier, he records buying others directly from the king.[123]

It would appear, however, that conventional perceptions of the eclipse of de Souza's influence (as reproduced, e.g., by Ross) are exaggerated;[124] they are not supported by the contemporary evidence from the 1840s, but are principally based on Hutton's retrospective account, which may have been colored by the decline in the de Souza family fortunes after the founder's death. The principal significance of the commercial reorganization of the 1840s, it may be suggested, was the restriction of de Souza's activities to Ouidah, as opposed to the transatlantic shipping of slaves in which he had earlier engaged. Together with his loss of the titular governorship of the Portuguese fort in 1844, this represented the curtailment of the international dimensions of his position, which now much more than previously did indeed become that of a "Dahomian chief."

EPILOGUE (1849)

De Souza died on May 8, 1849. The misunderstanding (or mythologization) of his position at Ouidah persisted to the end. The British assumed that his death was a severe blow to the slave-trading interest in Ouidah and would clear the way for the negotiation of an antislave trade treaty with Dahomey;[125] whereas in fact, as has been seen, he was by now no longer actively involved in the slave trade, and the leading role in it had passed from the de Souzas to Martins and d'Almeida. (And in any event, the attempt to negotiate an antislave trade treaty with King Gezo in 1849–1859 was a fiasco.) Contrariwise, however, the later allegation that de Souza had lost royal favor is belied by the fact that King Gezo gave him an official funeral appropriate to a major Dahomian chief; the ceremonies even included, despite the protests of his sons, the offering of human sacrifices (normally a royal prerogative).[126] His status as a naturalized Dahomian was also emphasized when, as noted earlier, Gezo claimed his estate, as customary in the case of senior officials, sending agents to seize his property in order to exact the royal inheritance tax, and assumed the prerogative of determining the succession to the headship of his family, which was conferred on his eldest son, Isidoro. De Souza's transformation from an expatriate merchant into an African chief was thus consummated and formalized in his death.

NOTES

1. This paper is a by-product of a wider project of research on the social history of Ouidah in the eighteenth and nineteenth centuries. An earlier version was published in Portuguese translation, "A carreira de Francisco Félix de Souza na África Ocidental (1800–1849)," *Topoi: Revista de História* (Universidad Federal do Rio de Janeiro) 2 (2001): 9–39. Some of the factual material included here is also to be found in my article, "The Evolution of the Brazilian Community in Ouidah," *Slavery and Abolition* 22, no. 1 (2001): 22–41. My thanks to Silke Strickrodt for assistance in tracing relevant source material.
2. For previous studies, see David Ross, "The First Chacha of Whydah: Francisco Felix de Souza," *Odu*, 3d series, 2 (1969): 19–28; also Pierre Verger, *Flux et reflux de la traite des nègres entre le Golfe de Bénin et Bahia de Todos os Santos du XVIe au XIXe siècle* (Paris: Mouton, 1968), pp. 460–67; Jerry Michael Turner, "Les Brésiliens: The impact of former Brazilian slaves upon Dahomey" (Ph.D. diss., Boston University, 1975), pp. 88–98. The treatment in the recent work of Milton Guran, *Agudás: os "brasileiros" do Benim* (Rio de Janeiro: Editora Nova Fronteira, 1999), pp. 20–31, follows these earlier studies. Previous studies have not been entirely successful in resolving some of the key questions related to his career, or indeed in engaging effectively with some important aspects of it. In part, the deficiencies of earlier work derive from failure to take account of the entire range of source material available; but they also reflect the problematic char-

acter of this material and the difficulty of synthesizing information relating to different aspects of de Souza's career.

3. The earliest allusion to him is from local tradition, as recorded in the 1890s: Edouard Foà, *Le Dahomey* (Paris: A. Hennuyer, 1895), p. 22.

4. See also Robin Law, "The Origins and Evolution of the Merchant Community in Ouidah," in *Ports of the Slave Trade (Bights of Benin and Biafra)*, ed. Robin Law and Silke Strickrodt (Stirling, Scotland: Centre of Commonwealth Studies, University of Stirling, 1999), pp. 55–70.

5. Published in French translation, in Pierre Verger et al., *Les Afro-Américains* (Dakar: IFAN, 1953), pp. 53–100.

6. Adam Jones, "Little Popo and Agoué at the End of the Atlantic Slave Trade: Glimpses from the Lawson Correspondence and Other Sources," in *Ports of the Slave Trade*, ed. Law and Strickrodt, pp. 122–34.

7. Theophilus Conneau, *A Slaver's Log, or 20 Years' Residence in Africa: The Original 1853 Manuscript* (London: Robert Hale, 1977), p. 202; UK Parliamentary Papers (PP), Papers Relative to the Reduction of Lagos, 1852, inclosure in no.8, Thomas Hutton, Cape Coast, 7 August 1850. For de Souza's "aristocratic" business ethics, see Ross, "First Chacha," p. 22.

8. Texts (in French translation) in Verger, *Flux et reflux*, pp. 425–27, 475–77.

9. De Souza himself, in later life, recalled that on his first arrival in Ouidah he had supported himself by pilfering cowries from offerings at religious shrines: Thomas Birch Freeman, "West Africa" (typescript of book, c.1861, in Wesleyan Methodist Missionary Society Archives, London), p. 251.

10. Foà, *Le Dahomey*, p. 27.

11. Jones, "Little Popo and Agoué," p. 130.

12. Grand Livre Lolamè, in the possession of the Lawson family, Aného (GLL), "The History of Francisco F. de Souza." The material recorded in the 1890s in Foà, *Le Dahomey*, pp. 19–22, seems to be closely related to that in the Lawson papers.

13. Norberto Francisco de Souza, "Contribution à l'histoire de la famille de Souza," *Etudes dahoméennes* 13 (1955): 17–21; Simone de Souza, *La Famille de Souza du Bénin-Togo* (Cotonou: Les Éditions du Bénin, 1992).

14. Sir Henry Huntley, *Seven Years' Service on the Slave Coast of Western Africa* (London: Thomas Cautley Newby, 1850), vol. 1, pp. 113–24.

15. For example, Conneau, *Slaver's Log*, p. 202.

16. PP, Report of the Select Committee on the Coast of West Africa, 1842, Minutes of evidence, 2286–87, Capt. Henry Seward.

17. Richard Drake, *Revelations of a Slave Smuggler* (New York, 1860), excerpt in George Francis Dow, *Slave Ships and Slaving* (Salem, Mass.: Marine Research Society, 1927), pp. 234–36, 252. For the spurious nature of Drake's account, see T. C. McCaskie, "Drake's Fake: A Curiosity Concerning a Spurious Visit to Asante in 1839," *History in Africa* 11 (1984): 223–36.

18. A ship engaged in the slave trade to Cuba, taken by the British navy off Gabon in 1839, was according to its documents owned by Francisco Felix de Souza. The British authorities assumed that this was de Souza of Ouidah, but the master stated that "de Souza, the owner, was a resident of Matanzas": PP, Papers Relative to the Slave Trade 1839–1840, Class A, no.44, case of the *Tejo*.

19. PP, Lagos, incl. in no.8, Hutton, 7 August 1850.
20. Archibald Ridgway, "Journal of a Visit to Dahomey," *New Monthly Magazine* 81 (1847): 195.
21. De Souza family tradition dates the founder's birth to 4 October 1754, which would make him around thirty-eight in 1792. Contemporary observers in the 1840s give differing estimates of his age, but agree in making him substantially younger than the traditional account suggests.
22. First in Paul Hazoumé, *Le Pacte de sang au Dahomey* (Paris: Institut d'Ethnologie, 1937), p. 28, n.1; also Norberto de Souza, "Contribution," p. 15.
23. Public Record Office, London (PRO), ADM55/11, Journal of Hugh Clapperton, November 1825; Brue, "Voyage fait en 1843, dans le royaume de Dahomey," *Revue coloniale* 7 (1845): 56; Prince de Joinville, *Vieux souvenirs (1818–1848)* (Paris, 1894), quoted in Verger, *Flux et reflux*, p. 463.
24. Norberto de Souza, "Contribution," p. 18. Other versions give the date as 1798.
25. PP, Lagos, incl. in no. 8, Hutton, 7 August 1850; [Gavoy], "Note historique sur Ouidah (1913)," *Etudes Dahoménnes* 13 (1955): 6; Norberto de Souza, "Contribution," p. 17.
26. Norberto de Souza, "Contribution," p. 17.
27. As stated in traditions recorded in the 1880s: Augusto Sarmento, *Portugal no Dahomé* (Lisbon: Livraria Tavares & Irmao, 1891), p. 59.
28. PRO, FO84/19, Sir G. R. Collier, "Report upon the Coast and Settlements of Western Africa," 27 December 1821; Frederick E. Forbes, *Dahomey and the Dahomans* (London: Frank Cass, 1966 [1851]), vol. 1, pp. 106–107.
29. Conneau, *Slaver's Log*, p. 202.
30. Ross, "First Chacha," p. 19.
31. Sarmento, *Portugal no Dahomé*, p. 59.
32. Norberto de Souza, "Contribution," p. 18.
33. Verger, *Flux et reflux*, pp. 240, 460.
34. *Royal Gold Coast Gazette* (Cape Coast), 15 April 1823; reflected in a distorted form in later tradition, which says that Francisco appointed his brother (who is given the incorrect name Ignacio) to succeed him as governor of the fort when he himself left Ouidah: Norberto de Souza, "Contribution," p. 2.
35. Huntley, *Seven Years' Service*, vol. 1, p. 113.
36. Freeman, "West Africa," p. 170; Verger, *Flux et reflux*, p. 638.
37. First told by Freeman, "West Africa," pp. 169–73. For a synthesis of the traditional accounts, see Moussa Oumar Sy, "Le Dahomey: le coup d'état de 1818," *Folia Orientalia* 6 (1964): 205–38.
38. GLL, "History of Francisco F. de Souza."
39. Ross, "First Chacha," pp. 20–21.
40. Verger, *Flux et reflux*, p. 462.
41. Freeman, "West Africa," p. 255; PP, Slave Trade 1827, Class A, no. 49, case of the *Principe de Guiné*.
42. Huntley, *Seven Years' Service*, vol. 1, p. 115.
43. Carlos Eugenio Corrêa da Silva, *Uma viagem ao estabelecimento portuguez de S. João Baptista de Ajudá em 1865* (Lisbon: Imprensa Nacional, 1866), pp. 59–60.

44. *Royal Gold Coast Gazette,* 15 April 1823.
45. Norberto de Souza, "Contribution," pp. 18–19; Simone de Souza, *La Famille de Souza,* p. 59.
46. Foà, *Le Dahomey,* p. 22; Bruce Chatwin, *The Viceroy of Ouidah* (London: Jonathan Cape, 1980).
47. PP, Select Committee on West Africa, 4063, Lieutenant Reginald Levine; 2461–64, Commander Henry Broadhead.
48. Dagba was appointed Yovogan in 1823 and retained the office until his death in the 1870s, founding a family which still exists in Ouidah: see Léon-Pierre Ghézowounmè Djomolia Dagba, *La Collectivité familiale Yovogan Hounnon Dagba de ses origines à nos jours* (Porto Novo: l'Imprimerie Rapidex, 1982).
49. Thomas Birch Freeman, *Journal of Various Visits to the Kingdoms of Asante, Aku, and Dahomi* (London: Frank Cass, 1968 [1844]), pp. 239–40; Duncan, *Travels,* vol. 1, pp. 117–19.
50. See further Robin Law, "Royal Monopoly and Private Enterprise in the Atlantic Trade: The Case of Dahomey," *Journal of African History* 18 (1977): 555–77.
51. N. Broquant, *Esquisse commerciale de la Côte occidentale d'Afrique* (Paris, 1839), quoted in Verger, *Flux et reflux,* p. 463.
52. In qualification of the argument of David Eltis, *Economic Growth and the Ending of the Transatlantic Slave Trade* (New York: Oxford Academic Press, 1987), p. 57, that de Souza and other Brazilian traders of this period "had none of the European political ties" of earlier European establishments in the area.
53. *Royal Gold Coast Gazette,* 15 April 1823.
54. PRO, FO84/19, Collier, 27 December 1821.
55. Huntley, *Seven Years' Service,* vol. 1, p. 114.
56. PP, Slave Trade 1827, Class A, no. 57, case of the *Trajano*; 1839–1840, Class A, no. 77, case of the *Emprehendedor.*
57. PRO, ADM55/11, Clapperton journal, November 1825; Huntley, *Seven Years' Service,* vol. 1, p. 116.
58. Corrêa da Silva, *Uma Viagem,* p. 79.
59. However, Eltis, *Economic Growth,* is illuminating on the general context of de Souza's career, with occasional allusions to his activities specifically.
60. PP, Slave Trade 1836, Class A, no. 59, case of the *Thereza*; no. 69, case of the *Joven Carolina*; 1839–1840, Class A, no. 77, case of the *Emprehendedor*; 1842, Class A, no. 79, case of the *Galliana.*
61. PP, Slave Trade 1836, Class A, no. 50, case of the *Mosca*; 1837, Class A, no. 39, case of the *Latona*; no. 41, case of the *Carlota*; 1840, Class A, no. 47, case of the *Jack Wilding.* Among papers found on this last ship, belonging to a passenger, Antonio Capo, was an account of goods delivered at Ouidah by the latter, when commander of the *General Manso* in 1834, to Zangronis and de Souza.
62. Freeman, *Journal,* p. 258 [3–4 February 1843] (referring to "Mr. Zangronies, one of the principal slave-dealers in Whydah").
63. Freeman, "West Africa," p. 241.
64. Richard Burton, *A Mission to Gelele, Kingdom of Dahomey* (London: Tinsley Brothers, 1864), vol. 2, p. 258 ("Francisco Zangrony").

65. Simone de Souza, *La Famille de Souza*, p. 71.
66. Their eldest child was baptised in 1876: ibid., pp. 71, 244, 277.
67. PP, Slave Trade 1835, Class B, no. 107, Mr Parkinson, Bahia, 10 December 1834.
68. PP, Slave Trade 1826–1827, Class A, no. 8, J. T. Williams, Sierra Leone, 1826; 1827, Class A, no. 49, case of the *Principe de Guiné*.
69. PP, Slave Trade 1826–1827, Class A, no. 38, George Randall, Sierra Leone, 30 March 1826.
70. Christopher Fyfe, *A History of Sierra Leone* (London: Oxford University Press, 1962), pp. 196.
71. PP, Slave Trade 1835, Class A, no. 54, case of the *Legitimo Africano*; 1837, Further Series, no. 13, case of the *Don Francisco*; no. 14, case of the *Florida* (owned jointly by de Souza and its master, Alexandre Balbino Proença of Havana); 1840, Class A. no. 61, case of the *Fortuna*.
72. Another case was the *Atrevido*, arrested in 1834, whose master claimed to have purchased her from de Souza in 1831: PP, Slave Trade 1835, Class A, no. 52.
73. Eltis, *Economic Growth*, pp. 158, 182.
74. For the wider context, see Robin Law, "Between the Sea and the Lagoons: The Interaction of Maritime and Inland Navigation on the Pre-Colonial Slave Coast," *Cahiers d'études africaines* 29 (1989): 209–37.
75. Huntley, *Seven Years' Service*, vol. 1, pp. 115–16.
76. Nicoué Lodjou Gayibor, *Le Genyi, un royaume oublié de la Côte de Guinée au temps de la traite de Noirs* (Lomé: Éditions Haho, 1990), pp. 189–201.
77. GLL, Judgement in the case of Kain versus Chico d'Almeida, Little Popo, 2 March 1893.
78. PP, Slave Trade 1840, Class A, no. 85, case of the *Plant*.
79. Gavoy, "Note historique," p. 61.
80. PP, Slave Trade 1830, Class A, no. 33, case of the *Veloz Pasagera*.
81. PRO, CO96/12, J. H. Akhurst, Agoué, 25 September 1843.
82. Jacques Lombard, "Cotonou, ville africaine," *Etudes dahoméennes* 10 (1953): 30.
83. PP, Select Committee on West Africa, 3997, Lieutenant Levinge; compare Slave Trade 1855–1856, Class B, no. 38, Consul Campbell, Lagos, 6 January 1856.
84. PRO, FO2/7, "Commercial Report," encl. to Vice-Consul Frazer, Fernando Po, 15 May 1852. Later in the 1850s Cotonou passed into the control of Domingos Martins.
85. Norberto de Souza, "Contribution," p. 19. He then spent six years at Ouidah before being sent to Little Popo, which (on other evidence) was in 1840.
86. PP, Slave Trade 1827, Class A, no. 51, case of the *Hiroina* (referring to "Judo, a place between Badagry and Lagos"); also no. 54, case of the *Venus* ("Ajudo," identified in these documents, wrongly, as Ouidah). Ajido was also visited by Richard Lander, walking overland from Badagry, in 1826–1827: Richard Lander, *Records of Captain Clapperton's Last Expedition to Africa* (London: Henry Colburn & Richard Bentley, 1830), vol. 2, pp. 265–66, 269 ("Adjeedore").
87. Robin Law, "The Career of Adele at Lagos and Badagry, c.1807–c.1837," *Journal of the Historical Society of Nigeria* 9, no. 2 (1978): 35–59 (though this does not note the de Souza connection).

88. PP, Slave Trade 1837, Class A, no. 39, case of the *Latona*.

89. PP, Slave Trade 1835, Class A, no. 59, case of the *Thereza*; 1836, Class A, no. 69, case of the *Joven Carolina*.

90. PP, Report of the Select Committee on the Slave Trade, 1848, Minutes of Evidence, 3055, J. Duncan.

91. Brue, "Voyage," p. 56; Duncan, *Travels*, vol. 1, p. 203.

92. Jones, "Little Popo and Agoué," p. 131; Dos Santos correspondence, in Verger, *Les Afro-Américains*, nos. 44, 52, 80 [28 December 1846, 19 February and 1 December 1847].

93. PP, Slave Trade 1849–1850, Class A, no. 98, case of the *Galliana*. The Francisco de Souza mentioned here was probably the one surnamed "Chico," who was later Chacha (1860–1880) in succession to Isidoro.

94. Blancheley, "Au Dahomey," *Les Missions catholiques* 223 (1891): 536; PP, Slave Trade 1849–50, Class B, incl. 10 in no. 9, Lieutenant Forbes, 5 November 1849.

95. Norberto de Souza, "Contribution," p. 20; Foà, *Le Dahomey*, pp. 26–27; Gavoy, "Note historique," pp. 68–69.

96. PP, Lagos, incl. in no. 8, Hutton, 7 August 1850; Slave Trade 1849–1850, Class B, no. 7, Duncan, 22 September 1849; incl. 10 in no. 9, Forbes, 5 November 1849.

97. Foà, *Le Dahomey*, p. 23; Hazoumé, *Le Pacte de sang*, p. 109.

98. Duncan, *Travels*, vol. 1, p. 204.

99. PRO, CO96/12, Thomas Hutton, Cape Coast, 17 March 1847.

100. PP, Slave Trade 1849–1850, Class B, incl. 10 in no. 9, Forbes, 5 November 1849.

101. PP, Lagos, incl. in no. 8, Hutton, 7 August 1850.

102. Ross, "First Chacha," p. 25.

103. Dos Santos correspondence, no. 54 [19 February 1847].

104. PRO, CO96/12, Thomas Hutton, Agoué, 7 December 1846; compare Eltis, *Economic Growth*, p. 171. This casts doubt on the assessment of Ross, "First Chacha," p. 22, that de Souza failed to make the transition to combining the slave and oil trades, as done by the newer Brazilian traders such as Domingos Martins; in fact, here, too, he seems to have been a pioneer.

105. Turner, "Les Brésiliens," pp. 102–105.

106. PP, Slave Trade 1841, Class A, no. 109, Case of the *Gratidão*, arrested in October 1840: papers found on this ship showed that a passenger on it, Tobiaz Barreto Brandão, had been involved in the slave trade over the previous two years, trading at Agoué with d'Almeida, among others.

107. He made out his will in Bahia, prior to returning to Africa, in December 1844: text in Verger, *Flux et reflux*, pp. 475–77.

108. Foà, *Le Dahomey*, p. 23.

109. PP, Slave Trade 1849–50, Class B, incl. 10 in no. 9, Forbes, 5 November 1849.

110. Foà, *Le Dahomey*, p. 23; [Reynier] "Ouidah: organization du commandement [1917]," *Mémoires du Bénin* 2 (1993): 63; Maximilien Quénum, *Les Ancêtres de la famille Quénum* (Langres: Dominique Gueniot, 1981), pp. 60–61.

111. Reynier, "Ouidah," p. 66.

112. David Ross, "The Career of Domingo Martinez in the Bight of Benin, 1833–1864," *Journal of African History* 6 (1965): 79–90.

113. PRO, CO96/12, Hutton, 17 March 1847.
114. Dos Santos correspondence, in Verger, *Les Afro-Américains*, no. 28 [3 March 1846].
115. PP, Slave Trade 1849–1850, Class B, incl. 10 in no. 9, Forbes, 5 November 1849.
116. PP, Slave Trade 1854–1855, Class B, no.21, Campbell, Badagry, 1 November 1854.
117. PRO, CO96/12, Hutton, 17 March 1847.
118. PP, Slave Trade 1849–1850, Class B, incl. 10 in no. 9, Forbes, 5 November 1849.
119. Burton, *Mission*, vol. 1, p. 72.
120. Martins' child by Maria Felix de Souza was baptized in 1853: Simone de Souza, *La Famille de Souza*, pp. 254, 273.
121. Simone de Souza, *La Famille de Souza*, pp. 51–53.
122. Reynier, "Ouidah," p. 48.
123. Dos Santos correspondence, in Verger, *Les Afro-Américains*, no.52 [19 February 1847].
124. Ross, "First Chacha," pp. 27–28.
125. PP, Slave Trade 1849–1850, Class A, incl. 2 in no. 9, Commodore Fanshawe, 9 September 1849.
126. PP, Slave Trade 1849–1850, Class B, incl. 14 in no. 9, Duncan, 18 September 1849.

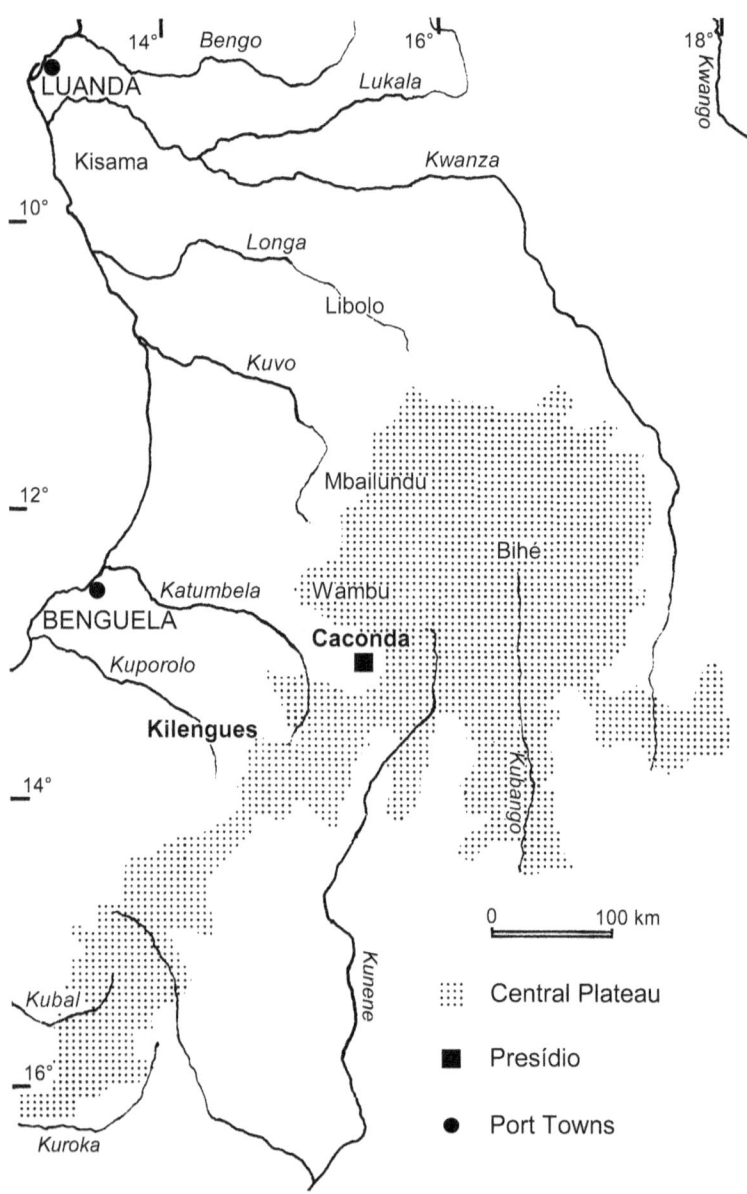

Central Angola during the late eighteenth century

10
"Afro-Brazilians" of the Western Slave Coast in the Nineteenth Century[1]

Silke Strickrodt

During the era of the slave trade, the western Slave Coast was normally marginal to European economic interest on the West African coast. The commercial value of the ports in this area was eclipsed by that of the ports situated further to the east, such as Ouidah, Lagos, and the ports in the Bight of Biafra, which provided a more abundant and consistent supply of slaves. It was only in the era of the illegal slave trade, in the nineteenth century, that the western Slave Coast rose in importance. This was due to the enforcement of the antislave trade legislation by the British Royal Navy, especially after the Equipment Act of 1839, which gave the cruisers the right to detain Portuguese vessels that carried equipment for the trade. This made necessary a decentralization of the slave trade at Ouidah and caused the traders there to shift their activities to less well-known places to the west and east. At about the same time, the Slave Coast experienced a large-scale immigration of liberated slaves from Brazil, who tended to settle at certain ports: Agoué on the western Slave Coast and Ouidah, Porto Novo, and Lagos further to the east. They associated with the slave traders and, helped by the shared Portuguese language and Catholic religion, merged with them into an economic, political, and cultural elite that historians and anthropologists have come to refer to as "Afro-Brazilians" (in French, *Brésiliens*), even though some actually came from Cuba and elsewhere and included former slaves, free mulattos, and whites.

The object of this chapter is to discuss the activities of the Afro-Brazilians on the western Slave Coast in the precolonial period. The Afro-Brazilians have been studied extensively, but not with a focus on this particular region and period.² My interest is in the first generation of the Afro-Brazilians, the people that immigrated and settled in the area in the nineteenth century. As this is a very large subject, I will concentrate on two aspects: first, the identification of the slave traders who were active in the region and, second, the liberated slaves at Agoué. I am also dealing with these two dimensions because a large amount of source material is available, some of which has never been used before. An appendix provides a list of liberated slaves who settled at Agoué.

For the purpose of this chapter, the western Slave Coast is defined as the part of the West African coast that extends from west of Ouidah to Porto Seguro (modern Agbodrafo), comprising parts of the coastal area of modern Benin and Togo. The outstanding topographical features of this region are, on the one hand, a complete lack of natural harbors and a heavy surf and, on the other hand, an extensive system of coastal lagoons that stretches from east of Porto Seguro to Ouidah and beyond to Lagos. Both of these features played an important role during the era of the illegal slave trade. The lack of natural harbors meant that there was no point particularly favorable for the shipment of slaves; they could be shipped from anywhere. The lagoons greatly facilitated transport and communication along the coast and made possible the swift movement of slaves by canoe from Ouidah into the region to any point of embarkation where the cruisers of the British anti–slave trade squadron were not patrolling.

In the nineteenth century, there were four major settlements in this area, which were, from west to east, Porto Seguro, Little Popo (modern Aného), Agoué, and Grand Popo. Of these places, Grand Popo and Little Popo were long-established trading ports, whereas Agoué and Porto Seguro were nineteenth-century creations. Agoué was founded in 1821 after a civil war at Little Popo, when the victorious party, led by the wealthy trader Akuété Zankli, alias George Lawson, drove out their opponents. The latter settled some ten kilometers further east on the beach where they founded Agoué. The origins of Porto Seguro are not clear due to the lack of sources. According to some traditions, it was founded in 1835 following another war at Little Popo, while others state that it was founded by a trader from Little Popo seeking to maximize his trade.³ Little Popo, Agoué, and Porto Seguro were all situated in the area that, nominally at least, was controlled by the king of Ge (Genyi/Guin), who resided at the town of Glidji, some five kilometers north of Little Popo. However, by the early nineteenth century the king's authority over the port towns was much weakened and did not exist in any real sense.⁴ Grand Popo formed part of another kingdom, which to Europeans was known as the kingdom of Grand Popo and whose capital, Agbanaken, was situated some three kilometers inland on the western bank of the River Mono.

As to the size of these settlements and the number of their inhabitants in the period, this is difficult to determine since there is very little reliable data. Little Popo was, initially at least, the largest of these towns, followed and eventually overtaken by Agoué, whose population increased dramatically from the 1840s due to the immigration of liberated slaves from Brazil and Cuba. Thomas Birch Freeman, a missionary of the Wesleyan Methodist Missionary Society who visited the area in 1843, called them both "second class towns."[5] He estimated the number of inhabitants at Agoué at 1,500 to 1,600, but gives no estimate for Little Popo. John Duncan, a British explorer who passed through the area in 1845, gives "about 5,000" as the number of inhabitants at Little Popo.[6] According to Pierre Bouche, who worked as a missionary of the Société des Missions Africaines at Agoué in 1874–1875, Agoué's inhabitants had numbered 6,000 in 1873 before a smallpox epidemic killed 1,500 of them.[7] There is little information for Grand Popo, which attracted very few European visitors. An officer of the Royal Navy, who in 1852 went there to conclude an anti–slave trade treaty with the chiefs, referred to it as a "town" and eight years later another officer, who visited the place to remind the chiefs of the treaty, called it "a large town."[8] Porto Seguro was probably the smallest of these places. Although in 1845 John Duncan called it "a town of considerable size," in 1863 another visitor described it as "a small village."[9] In 1884, a German journalist visited all four settlements and gave the following estimates: 1,200 inhabitants at Porto Seguro, 4,000 at Little Popo (excluding the quarter Adjido), 9,000 at Agoué, which according to him was after Ouidah the most populous place on the Slave Coast, and 1,500 at Grand Popo.[10]

THE SOURCES

Although there are a variety of sources for Afro-Brazilian activity on the western Slave Coast in the nineteenth century, authors who have previously dealt with the subject have often relied to a large extent on retrospective accounts recorded in local and family oral traditions. In this chapter, I will focus on contemporary sources, some of which have been not been used to this purpose before and, indeed, do not seem to be known to scholars working in the field.

The sources can be grouped into two broad categories, external and internal sources. The external sources comprise documents that were produced by people or agencies outside of Afro-Brazilian society, and internal sources are those that were produced by the Afro-Brazilians themselves. It is clear, however, that this distinction is not always clear-cut.

External Sources

Among the most important documents in this group are the records of British government agencies that were engaged in the suppression of the slave trade, including the Royal Navy and the consular agents.[11] Among the records of the Royal Navy, two groups of documents are especially informative. First, there are the documents relating to ships that had been arrested on suspicion of being engaged in the slave trade and that subsequently had been adjudged by the Mixed Commission's Courts at Sierra Leone, Luanda, or St. Helena. Second, there is the correspondence of Royal Navy officers, which includes accounts of visits to the coastal settlements, reports of captures of slave ships, and annual reports on the state of the trade. The consular correspondence also contains valuable information about the Afro-Brazilians. From 1849 to 1852, the British had a vice consul for the kingdom of Dahomey who resided at Ouidah, and subsequently there was a British consul for the Bight of Benin who was based at Lagos. Furthermore, there are also a number of published accounts, such as those by the explorer John Duncan (1847), the naval officer Frederick E. Forbes (1851), and Richard Burton, consul for the Bight of Biafra (1864).[12]

The records of the various missionary societies that were active in the region in the period are also important. First, there are the papers of the Wesleyan Methodist Missionary Society, which became active in the region in the 1840s and in 1858 briefly established itself at Agoué. The papers include the correspondence of various missionaries and, most important, the papers of Thomas Birch Freeman, who visited the region several times in the 1840s and 1850s.[13] Second, there are the records of the Catholic missions, whose followers were mostly Afro-Brazilians. The first Catholic priests to come to the area were the priests from the seminary at São Tomé who were attached to the Portuguese fort at Ouidah.[14] They visited Agoué, Little Popo, and Porto Seguro from 1846 to 1860 and carried out baptisms of the children and slaves of the Afro-Brazilians. They were followed by the missionaries of the Société des Missions Africaines of Lyon, which established itself at Ouidah in 1861. In 1874, the Société established a mission at Agoué.

Apart from the baptismal registers, which arguably are an internal source since they come from within the Afro-Brazilian community and therefore will be discussed below, the Catholic missionaries produced a large number of accounts. Some of these were published as books, such as those by Francesco Borghero, Irenée Lafitte, and Pierre Bouche, others in the form of articles in the publications of the Missions Africaines.[15] Apart from these published works, there presumably exists a large body of unpublished material in the archives of the Société des Missions Africaines, only a small part of which has been uncovered by historians so far. Among these are the writings of Isidore Pelofy, who between 1911 and 1946 was curate at the Catholic Mission at Agoué. One of Pelofy's works, which has recently been published, is a manuscript of a history of Agoué.[16] It comprises abstracts of ten chapters discussing Agoué's evolution from its foundation in 1821 to the colonial partition of the West African coast in 1885, when the town became part of the French colony Dahomey, and contains information about Afro-Brazilians, the Portuguese, Brazilian, and Spanish traders as well as the liberated slaves. Pelofy's manuscript formed the basis of another manuscript history of Agoué, written by a French colonial administrator, Jean Pierucci (1953).[17] Pierucci's manuscript includes interesting additional information, such as lists of the various town quarters and the names of their inhabitants. However, one drawback of Pelofy's and Pierucci's manuscripts is that they do not indicate their sources of information. They obviously used a mixture of written and oral sources, the former including mainly the writings of the French Catholic missionaries mentioned above. The oral sources presumably comprise accounts given to them by the inhabitants of Agoué during their stay there, including descendants of the slave traders and liberated slaves. These texts need to be interpreted carefully, even skeptically.

Internal sources. The most important documents in this group are the baptismal registers of the Catholic Missions at Agoué. I have not seen the original registers for the period before 1896, but parts of them have been reproduced in the works of various authors.[18] Most important, Isidore Pelofy compiled a register of families who had come to Agoué from Brazil, Cuba, and Sierra Leone.[19] This register, which contains almost 150 entries (i.e., family names), gives mainly genealogies of the Afro-Brazilian families, including the name of the returnees, their ethnic origin, the quarter of the town they settled in, and the names of their descendants. Sometimes there is additional information, such as the profession of the returnees and/or their descendants, and names of family members who had returned with them. This is a unique source, providing a wealth of information about the first generation of the returnees at Agoué.

Simone de Souza, in her work about the de Souza family, also reproduces extracts from the baptismal registers from Agoué.[20] Among others, she gives a list of names of Afro-Brazilians at Agoué in 1863, which she compiled from the first baptismal register of the Missions Africaines at Ouidah.[21] It is clear that lists of this kind, which consist exclusively of people's names with very little explanatory information, are intrinsically problematic and unreliable. Nevertheless, de Souza's list is useful, not least for clarifying the provenance of the information about the returnees' ethnic identity that is given in Pelofy's register. The fact that she, too, gives this information indicates that it appears in the baptismal registers.

Besides the baptismal registers, there are other important "internal" documents, such as wills and business correspondence. Among these are the wills of Joaquim d'Almeida (d. 1857) and Antonio d'Almeida (d. 1890), both of whom were liberated slaves from Brazil who settled at Agoué and Ouidah.[22] The will of the former, which was made at Bahia in 1844 shortly before he finally returned to Africa, throws light on his career up to this point but gives little information about his activities on the West African coast. The will of Antonio d'Almeida was written at Ouidah in 1864 and is more informative as regards his life at Agoué and Ouidah. The business correspondence of José Francisco dos Santos, part of which has survived and was published in a French translation by Pierre Verger, is another valuable source.[23] Dos Santos was a Brazilian slave trader who was based at Ouidah but in the 1840s extended his activities to the western Slave Coast. His correspondence includes three letters written by him at Agoué (November 1844) and five letters at Little Popo (August 1847 and December 1847), apart from a number of letters that were written elsewhere but refer to his affairs at these places. Another important source is the business correspondence of the Lawson family of Little Popo, part of which has been preserved in the "Grand Livre Lolamé" (GLL).[24] The Lawsons were a major factor in the economic and political life of the region, and their business partners and acquaintances included, among others, the de Souzas, Joaquim d'Almeida, José Francisco dos Santos, and João Gonçalves Baeta.

As can be seen from this overview, there is a large variety of documentary material that allows us to study the activities of the Afro-Brazilians on the western Slave Coast in the precolonial period.

SLAVE TRADERS ON THE WESTERN SLAVE COAST

After the implementation of the Equipment Act in 1839, a number of the slave traders at Ouidah shifted their activities to the western Slave Coast; that is, they branched out. They kept their establishments at Ouidah, which remained the center of the illegal trade, but established secondary establishments and agents in the region. From Ouidah, the slaves were moved in canoes along the coast by means of the lagoon and embarked from any point that was not watched by the cruisers. Initially, shipments took place mainly from the larger settlements, that is, Little Popo, Agoué, and Grand Popo. After 1852, however, when the British concluded anti–slave trade treaties with the chiefs of these places, this became more difficult because the chiefs were liable to punishment for breaking the treaty. The threat of bombardment by the cruisers was a very real one for the settlements in the region because, unlike Ouidah, they were situated on the beach. Therefore, slaves were increasingly shipped from places outside these settlements, which the chiefs claimed to lie beyond their authority.[25] For example, in 1853, Sekko, some five kilometers to the east of Agoué, became a notorious point of embarkation.[26] In 1856, shipments were reported to have taken place from a beach between Little Popo and Agoué, and in the following year Praya Nova, between Grand Popo and Ouidah, was said to be a new place for shipping slaves.[27]

The first of the traders from Ouidah that extended their activity to the western Slave Coast was Francisco Felix de Souza, the Chacha of Ouidah (d.

1849). This is no coincidence, given that he was the most influential of the traders on the coast in the period and able to draw on old connections with Little Popo. He had been based there earlier in the century, first after his arrival on the coast around the turn of the century and then again in the 1810s after a dispute with the Dahomean king Adandozan. He had returned to Ouidah probably in 1820, but still owned a property at Little Popo. This was a peninsula opposite the town on the northern bank of the lagoon, which according to local traditions had been given to him by Sekpon, the chief of the place.[28] It was called Ajido, like his establishments at Ouidah and Badagry. His eldest son, Isidoro (d. 1858), had been born there, his mother being the daughter of Akué, a local chief. Furthermore, de Souza entertained good relations with George Lawson, the de facto ruler of Little Popo whom he had supported in the civil war of 1821.[29]

Francisco Felix de Souza did not himself go to Little Popo but sent Isidoro to act as his agent there. Isidoro, who after being educated in Brazil had served his father at Badagry and Ouidah, reoccupied the factory at Adjido apparently in 1840.[30] He was based there until his father's death in 1849, when he returned to Ouidah to become the latter's successor to the office of Chacha. While he was at Little Popo, other traders were reported to be active there, probably in cooperation with him: Felis Cosme Madail, Joseph Moreyra Sampayo, and José de Taparica.[31] No details are given in the records regarding the former two, but the latter can probably be identified with João Pinheiro Taparica, a son-in-law of Francisco Felix de Souza who is mentioned by both Richard Burton and Simone de Souza. According to Burton, who included him in his list of slave traders at Whydah in 1863–1864, he was a Brazilian.[32]

Another trader who was said to have had close connections to Isidoro at Little Popo was Thomas Sastre, a Spaniard from the Canary Islands. Few facts are known about him, since he does not appear in the contemporary records except once in 1839. At this time, he was apparently based at Occo, a small port on the eastern Gold Coast some miles to the west of the River Volta, and it appears that he, or the people for whom he acted as an agent, were engaged in trade at Little Popo.[33] Sastre's connection with Little Popo is supported by information recorded by Simone de Souza. According to her, Sastre's son, João ("Tutu"), was born at Little Popo about 1835 and grew up at Adjido among the children of Isidoro, who was his godfather. João is said to have gone to Grand Popo about 1850 and subsequently to Agoué, where he married (among others) one of the daughters of Francisco Felix de Souza.[34] However, if he was engaged in the slave trade, then it was probably only small-scale, since there are no references to him in the records of the Royal Navy.

Another son of Francisco Felix de Souza, Antonio, was also active on the western Slave Coast in the 1840s, both at Little Popo and at Agoué. De Souza had several sons by the name of Antonio, but most likely it is Antonio Felix

"Kokou" who is referred to here.³⁵ Recently recorded family tradition recalls that his mother was Ahossi, a "princess of Glidji," but Burton noted that she was "a large woman from Agwe, dashed to the old Chacha. Her name was Akho-'si, that is, King's Wife, but she had no connection with royalty."³⁶ From the contemporary sources it appears that Antonio oscillated between Ouidah, Little Popo, and Agoué, presumably as an agent for his father. Letters in the Lawson correspondence show that he was at Little Popo in October 1843 and in January 1844, and at least on the former occasion he stayed with the Lawsons rather than with his brother Isidoro at Adjido.³⁷ However, the good relations with the Lawsons seem to have suffered from an incident in 1849 after which George Latty Lawson complained that "Mr. Antonio left here day before yesterday, he has bid adieu for life. I was very glad when he was going, in fact nobody could get any peace from him, playing about the town the whole day and the night through."³⁸

It is not clear when the de Souzas first became active at Agoué, but by 1844 they had a house there in which Antonio appears to have resided at least from time to time.³⁹ This house was presumably situated in the Zomayi quarter, which also belonged to the de Souzas. According to Pierucci, this quarter had been founded by Francisco Felix de Souza, who stopped there sometimes during his trips from Ouidah to Little Popo and also used it to bulk his slaves before shipping them.⁴⁰ It seems likely that it was one of his sons rather than Francisco Felix de Souza himself who founded the quarter, but apart from this the account certainly makes sense, given also that the quarter bears the same name as one in Ouidah that had been established by Francisco Felix de Souza.⁴¹

In the period before Francisco Felix de Souza's death, the de Souzas exercised great influence over the western Slave Coast. If they did not actually monopolize the trade in the region, then they had at least a large share of it.⁴² However, after the death of Francisco Felix de Souza in 1849 the family lost a considerable part of their wealth, due to the Dahomean inheritance tax, and consequently lost part of their influence. Furthermore, with Isidoro's return to Ouidah, they seem to have lost interest in the region and focused on the ports to the east. By 1852, Isidoro was reported to have monopolized the trade of Godomey and Antonio that of Cotonou.⁴³

There were other traders besides the de Souzas who became active on the western Slave Coast in the 1840s. Among them was José Francisco dos Santos ("Alfaiate"), a Brazilian who traded as an agent for merchants in Bahia and Rio, as well as on his own account. He was based at Ouidah, but letters in his business correspondence show that in the mid-1840s he also shipped slaves from Little Popo and Agoué.⁴⁴ One of these letters describes the capture of the Spanish vessel *Pepito* with four hundred slaves on board, which had been embarked at Agoué.⁴⁵ Letters in the GLL show that he was friendly with the Lawsons at Little Popo.⁴⁶

Another slave trader who was active on this part of the coast is Domingo

Mustich. He was a Spaniard who worked as an agent for a Barcelona firm by the name of Vidal (at least for a period the 1850s) as well as on his own account.[47] He is reported to have had "a slave factory" at Little Popo by 1847–1848. Subsequently he based himself at Agoué but possibly kept his establishment at Little Popo.[48] His name appears in the documents until 1857, after which no more mention is made of him.[49]

However, the most important trader in the region in the period, beside the de Souzas, was Joaquim d'Almeida (d.1857), a liberated slave from Brazil. D'Almeida, or "Zoki Azata" as he was called on the coast, was a Mahi from Hoko who as a child had been captured by the Dahomeans and sold into slavery.[50] He had been shipped to Bahia, where he had been purchased by Joaquim Manoel d'Almeida, the captain of a slave ship who traded between Brazil and the West African coast. Joaquim d'Almeida had been employed in this trade and became a trusted servant of his master, whose name he later assumed. After being liberated, he continued to trade between Bahia and the Bight of Benin. In 1840 he appears in the records of the Royal Navy for the first time, when he was said to engage in the slave trade at "Agui" together with several other traders: Tobias Barretto Brandão, Elias Domingo de Carvalho, Antonio Caetano Coelho, Seçar Medair, and Antonio Verra dos Santos.[51] In 1845 he finally returned to the West African coast and settled at Agoué, where he founded his own quarter, Zokikome ("Zoki" or "Joqui" being a short form for Joaquim).[52] He was only one of a large number of liberated slaves who settled at Agoué in the period and engaged in the illegal trade there. However, he was exceptional in that he was the only one of them who entered the overseas dimension and came to the notice of the Royal Navy, shipping slaves himself rather than just buying and reselling them locally on a small scale.

D'Almeida's success in the trade seems to have led to strained relations with Francisco Felix de Souza.[53] This is indicated by the tradition of the Quénum family of Ouidah, which says that the family's founder, who had been an associate of de Souza, had convinced Gezo to break the latter's monopoly of trade at Ouidah by allowing d'Almeida to trade there. D'Almeida was granted the favor and, in cooperation with Quénum, traded very successfully, much to the dislike of the Chacha. It is not clear when exactly this happened, but a letter in the Lawson correspondence indicates that by 1848 d'Almeida had established himself at Ouidah.[54] In 1849, after the death of Francisco Felix de Souza, a visiting naval officer described d'Almeida as "a slave-merchant on an extensive scale" and "the richest resident in Whydah."[55] In the following year, the same officer referred to Agoué as a "slave-port, almost a monopoly of José [sic] d'Almeida."[56]

Letters from the Lawson correspondence show that in the late 1840s d'Almeida collaborated with other traders on the western Slave Coast, such as the Lawsons of Little Popo and João Gonçalves Baêta.[57] Baêta was a trader from

Bahia who was then active at Atoko in the Volta region.[58] In 1850, however, when the British took possession of the Danish settlements on the West African coast, among them Fort Prinzenstein at Keta, he was forced to move further east. It appears that first he moved only a few miles, just out of the reach of the British authorities, to Elmina Chica. By 1856, however, he, too, was established at Agoué.[59] While he was based in the Volta region, Baêta had apparently employed Francisco Olympio da Silva (d.1907), a Brazilian who had come out with him to the coast.[60] Later Olympio was established at Porto Seguro, and it seems likely that he went there as Baêta's agent when the latter relocated to Agoué. Olympio, too, eventually moved to Agoué, but this was probably only after the end of the illegal slave trade. This is indicated by the accounts of Borghero and Burton, according to which he was still established at Porto Seguro in 1863 and early 1864, respectively.[61] Borghero, who during his visit there was received in Olympio's house, noted that Porto Seguro, due to its isolated situation, had often been chosen as a point of embarkment for slaves.

Slaves were also shipped from Grand Popo. In 1850, the town was reported to be "almost a monopoly" of Joaquim Antonio, a Spanish trader who was based at Ouidah.[62] By 1852, a "Senôr Carvallio" was established at Hévé ("Guévé" or "Quw-vay"), a village some miles east of Grand Popo near the entrance of the lagoon into the sea ("Bouche de Roi").[63] Hévé was still "Mr. Carvalho's place" three years later, in 1855, when the Wesleyan Methodists were requested to open a school there.[64] There are a couple more references to a "Mr. Carvalho" in the records of the Royal Navy, one dating from 1859 and mentioning his engagement in the slave trade at Ouidah and Porto Seguro. The other, from December 1863, is more intriguing. It refers to "Mr. Carvalho, until recently well-known as a slave dealer at Whydah and Godomey, now settled at Porto Novo," who had allegedly given up the slave trade and, out of spite, denounced to the Royal Navy some of the people still engaged in it, among them José Francisco Medeiros, João Pereira Soares, and Samuel da Costa Soares (see below).[65]

It is not perfectly clear who this Mr. Carvalho was since there were at least two Carvalhos active in the region in the period, both of whom resided at Agoué for at least some time (and who furthermore shared the same initials). There was José Pereira Monteiro do Carvalho, who in 1860 acted as agent for the "Companhia União Africana" at Agoué and probably on the western Slave Coast more generally.[66] According to information given by the British Consul at Lagos, the Companhia was "a Brazilian one originating at Bahia; the Agents are said to do a good deal of legal trade . . ." Its principal agent on the Slave Coast, José Maria C. Brandão, was believed to reside chiefly at Ouidah.[67] According to Brandão, the Companhia had "the sum of twenty-two thousand dollars [at Agoué] invested in various kinds of goods landed from various ships of the Company."[68]

More plausible, however, is the identification with Manoel Joaquim de Carvalho, who according to Pelofy was a "white Portuguese" who was married to Maria Balbina de Amor Divino, a liberated slave from Brazil at Agoué, and had three children with her.[69] According to Newbury, he was a Brazilian slave trader and subsequently became Régis's agent at Porto Novo.[70] It is his connection with Régis that suggests that he was the Carvalho who was at Hévé in 1852, because subsequently Régis established a factory there. Furthermore, in 1863 Manoel Joaquim de Carvalho signed the French Protectorate treaty with Porto Novo, which fits in with the Royal Navy's information from the same year that the Carvalho who denounced other slave traders was resident at Porto Novo.[71]

During the 1850s there was a decline in the slave trade due to the closure of the markets in Brazil and Cuba. Many of the slave traders on the coast went into the palm oil trade. In May 1857, the commander of the Bights Division of the Royal Navy reported that the slave trade was practically finished on the Slave Coast, but singled out Agoué as one of the places most likely to ship a cargo of slaves if opportunity offered:

> I really do not think any slaves have been shipped to windward of Lagos for the two last years. This I attribute to two reasons: first (and the principal one) the closing of the ports in Brazil and Cuba to the importation of human cargoes, and the strong measures taken by Brazil at the instigation of the English government; and secondly, the very great increase in the demand of palm oil. . . . There cannot be said to be any regular Slave Trade dealers in the Bight of Benin now, but doubtless many individuals at present engaged in the oil trade would ship a cargo of slaves with the greatest willingness, could they obtain a market for them. I believe the most likely places for shipping at the neighbourhoods of Aghwey and Jaboo . . .[72]

In the same year, however, a new impetus was given to the illegal trade due to a brief revival of the Cuban market. This new Cuban trade was organized in a different way from the trade before. It was carried on by organizations in Cuba with ramifications in the United States, which used American vessels and the American flag to elude the search of the British cruisers. One such organization that came to the notice of the Royal Navy in the Bight of Benin was the "Expedicion por Africa."[73] The new trade apparently also involved a change of traders on the African coast, with new people moving in and replacing the established traders, who one by one disappear from the records of the Royal Navy in this period. This was due to various reasons: while some of the established traders presumably died, such as Joaquim d'Almeida in 1857, others, such as José Francisco dos Santos, gave up the slave trade and went into the palm oil trade. Others again left the coast, such as João Gonçalves Baêta, who by 1862 had apparently returned to Bahia where he became an agent for dos Santos.[74]

The most prominent of the new slave traders on the western Slave Coast was

Francisco José de Medeiros (d. 1875), who settled at Agoué. He was a Portuguese from the island of Madeira who had been based for a long time in Cuba, where he had engaged in the slave trade. He had first come to the notice of the Royal Navy in 1842, when he was the master of a vessel from Havana that had been detained on suspicion of being engaged in the trade. On this occasion he had stated that he had been living in Havana for five years, that is, since 1837.[75] At Agoué, he is first documented in November 1859.[76] According to local tradition as recorded by Pierucci, he had bought Baêta's house and continued his trade, which is plausible since Baêta is last documented there earlier in this year.[77] De Medeiros worked in cooperation with Samuel da Costa Soares and João Soares Pereira.

Samuel da Costa Soares (d.1894), who was Portuguese by origin and a naturalized citizen of the United States, was apparently one of the old traders on the coast, based at Ouidah. He is first mentioned in the records in 1857, when he appeared "to act as a general agent for the Slave Trade at Wydah and the adjacent shipping ports," which presumably included Agoué. He was thought to be "the only of the numerous old slave-dealers, residing in the King of Dahomey's territories, who has not embarked in the palm-oil trade."[78] According to the tradition of the da Costa Soares family as recorded by Turner, he had first established himself at Agoué before settling at Ouidah, but there is no record of this in the contemporary sources.[79]

João Soares Pereira, also a Portuguese, was the associate of Francisco José de Medeiros at Agoué. It is not clear when he arrived on the coast. The first reliable reference to him in the records dates from 1863. However, there is also a reference from 1859 to a person called "Swarey," who was said to be a slave trader and living with de Medeiros at Agoué.[80] Although this is ambiguous and could mean either João Soares Pereira or Samuel da Costa Soares, it seems likely that it is the former who was later closely associated with de Medeiros. By 1863 Pereira Soares also had an establishment at Ouidah.[81]

The illegal slave trade in the Bight of Benin effectively ended in 1863. The last successful shipment was made from Godomey, to the east of Ouidah, in October of that year. The last confirmed shipment on the western Slave Coast took place at Agoué on 20 October 1862, when about 1,100 slaves where shipped.[82] However, according to the Royal Navy the slave traders kept hoping and trying for some time after this. In 1864, Commodore Wilmot reported that

> slaves are as numerous as ever, but the slave dealers are afraid to purchase, in consequence of the great risk to be incurred, and the almost certainty of capture. Hundreds of slaves have been kept waiting [for] an opportunity of shipment in the neighbourhood of the principal depôts on the coast, and constantly marched from place to place as the chances of embarkation seemed to offer, according to the plans of the slave dealers, but without success, which has led to great mortality amongst them, from privations and diseases of every kind.[83]

According to him, in May 1864 a suspect steamer, supposed to be the *Ciceron*, had attempted to communicate by signal with Porto Seguro but was prevented from doing so by one of the cruisers. Another suspect vessel, "a screw-steam barque," appeared off Little Popo in June of the same year but left after "reconnoitering the cruisers."[84] A third incident occurred in March 1866, when the Portuguese barque *Dahomey* was taken at Agoué by the Royal Navy on the suspicion of intending to ship six hundred slaves. However, the evidence for this was very thin and the owners/master were subsequently acquitted by the Mixed Commission at Sierra Leone.[85] Nevertheless, the fact that de Medeiros and Soares Pereira, "the last of the rich traders," kept their establishment at Agoué until 1867 suggests that they did not give up trying, or at least hoping, until then. In 1867 they finally reduced their establishment at Agoué and relocated to Ouidah. De Medeiros reportedly explained to a naval officer, "[t]he Slave Trade is finished for the present, so I am going into the legal trade; your cruisers have not stopped it, but there is no demand from Cuba."[86]

LIBERATED SLAVES FROM BRAZIL AND CUBA AT AGOUÉ

In this section, I focus on Agoué, which in the nineteenth century experienced a large-scale immigration of liberated slaves from Brazil and Cuba and became one of the centers of Afro-Brazilian settlement in the Bight of Benin. The large part of the returnees from Brazil, who were later joined by those from Cuba, came to the Slave Coast after the slave revolt of 1835 in Bahia, which became known as the Malê revolt.[87] Although some of the former slaves returned to their places of origin in the interior, the large majority established itself in the settlements on the coast. These offered better opportunities for trade, which is what most of them did to earn a living. Also, a return to their places of origin in the interior would have meant exposing themselves to the risk of being enslaved again.[88]

We do not know when exactly the settlement of the liberated slaves at Agoué began, due to the lack of contemporary sources.[89] According to Pelofy, the liberated slaves began to arrive during the reign of Chief Toyi (Yaovi Siko), who is said to have ruled from 1835 to 1844.[90] According to the tradition of the d'Almeida family of Agoué, the founder of their family, Joaquim d'Almeida, first arrived there in 1835, and the same date is given as the time of arrival of Francisco da Silva Pereira, another liberated slave from Brazil.[91] However, although this is possible, there is no evidence in the contemporary records to support these accounts. D'Almeida is first documented at Agoué in 1840.[92] It seems likely that the returnees settled there in sizable numbers only after the implementation of the Equipment Act in 1839, when Agoué gained importance as a trading port due to the increased activity of the Portuguese and Spanish slave traders there. By 1843 it boasted a "Portuguese town," which implies that by then a sizable number of liberated slaves from Brazil had established themselves there.[93] Twenty years later, when the Catholic missionary Francesco Borghero visited the place, he observed that there were "some hundred Christians, all returned from Brazil after their liberation."[94] According to Pierucci, about one hundred families arrived at Agoué between 1835 and 1870.[95] On the basis of Pelofy's "Familles d'Agoué venues du Brazil et de Cuba et de Sierra Leone," I have identified sixty liberated slaves from Brazil and seven from Cuba that settled at Agoué, a list of whom is given in the appendix. Remarkably, although according to Borghero "almost all" of the returnees at Agoué were Yorubas ("nangos"),[96] only twenty-three of the sixty-seven returnees that I have listed are identified (and presumably identified themselves) as such. The others comprised thirteen Mahis, nine Hausa, four Fon, and one each of the following: Nupe ("Atakpa"), Bariba, Dassa, Egba, and Sehoue. One person was identified as both Hausa and Mahi on different occasions, and no ethnic identification is given for twelve people.

At Agoué, the returnees founded new quarters, where they settled largely according to their ethnic origin. Fonkome was settled by Fon, Mahis, and Yorubas; Diata (or Idi-Ata) by Yorubas; and Hausakome by Hausa, Mahis, and Yorubas.[97] Pierucci and Akibode both state that the returnees erected two mosques, one in Diata and one in Hausakome, but it is not clear when they were built and whether this happened in this period. Bouche says that the Muslims had their own quarter, but does not mention a mosque.[98] Furthermore, there was Zokikome, the quarter of Joaquim d'Almeida, the most successful and prominent of the returnees. The settlement in several quarters according to ethnic origin is remarkable, especially in comparison with Ouidah, where the returnees settled in only one quarter, called Maro. An explanation is perhaps that Agoué was only a recent foundation and a small town when the liberated slaves immigrated, and that the number of the immigrants in proportion to that of the indigenous inhabitants was comparatively large. Besides these four quarters settled by the returnees from Brazil and Cuba, which formed part of "Portuguese town," there was also one that had been established by immigrants from Sierra Leone, who were called Saro or Salo and belonged to "English town."

Trade was the main occupation of the returnees. This was observed by Borghero, who in 1863 noted that they "tend to become the masters of the trade."[99] Many, if not all, engaged in the slave trade, although on a small scale rather than a large one, buying slaves and reselling them as opportunity offered. According to Pierucci, "most of the liberated slaves engaged in this trade.... The main markets for the purchase of slaves were Lagos, Ouidah, Atakpame, and Salaga. Many of the young people from Ouidah and Agoué went to Atakpame with bags of salt, which they bartered for slaves.... These they re-sold to the slave-traders at Agoué."[100] The most successful of the returnees became very wealthy and were able to establish large farms north of Agoué on the other side of the lagoon. Apart from Joaquim d'Almeida, these included Antonio d'Almeida (who in Brazil had served the same master as Joaquim), João do Rego, Tobias Borges de Souza, and Francisco da Silva Pereira, whose farm was still said to be cultivated by slaves in 1931.[101] On these farms, oil palms, which produced palm oil for export, were grown as well as vegetables for the supply of the returnees' own wants. This is shown by the will of Antonio d'Almeida, which says that d'Almeida, who by 1864 had moved to Ouidah, still owned a farm (roça) at Agoué that supplied his household with vegetables and cereals. It was tended by eighteen male slaves and six female slaves.[102] The number of domestic and field slaves that some of the returnees owned was considerable, as can be seen from the baptismal registers. Joaquim d'Almeida, for example, had seventy-three slaves baptized in 1855, and Agostinho de Freitas twenty-two in 1855 and sixteen in 1857.[103]

The returnees who were less successful probably attached themselves to the wealthy traders and became their clients. Patron-client relationships are documented at Ouidah, such as in the case of Francisco Felix de Souza and Sabino Vyeira.[104] Unfortunately, there is very little documentation for such relationships at Agoué. However, some indication for their existence can be gleaned from the sources. For example, some association seems to have existed between Joaquim d'Almeida and José Pereira de Paixão, which is indicated by the fact that the latter established himself in d'Almeida's quarter.[105] Another case seems to be that of Juba Bramfo and Justino Bandeira. According to the family tradition of the Bandeiras, the founder of their family, Justino Bandeiro, arrived destitute at Agoué and was given a piece of land by Juba Bramfo. After the death of Bandeira's wife, Bramfo also gave him a female slave, with whom Bandeira later had a son.[106] Some returnees also entered the service of the Portuguese and Spanish slave traders that were established at Agoué. Others had come out to the coast with their masters, such as Sallustro de Adaões, who is reported to have been the cook of a Portuguese trader, João da Cruz. Francisco José Gonçalves Baêta is said to have been employed by Joaquim Garcia, a Portuguese who before his settlement at Agoué had been working on a slave ship, and from Baêta's name it appears that there was also a connection to João Gonçalves Baêta.[107]

The cultural impact of the liberated slaves from Brazil and Cuba on the indigenous societies on the Slave Coast has been discussed widely in the literature.[108] Two of the most important aspects were the establishment of schools and the introduction of the Catholic religion. At Agoué, the liberated slaves founded a school where their children were taught Portuguese and received religious instruction. They brought a schoolmaster from Brazil, who was assisted by some of the liberated slaves or their children.[109] The school was subsidized by Francisco José de Medeiros, who is remembered as a "generous Portuguese."[110] Borghero, who visited the school in 1863, reports that it was attended by thirty children but he was not impressed with the results of their instruction: "alas, the children... did not know one prayer or one article of the catechism."[111] This suggests that it was either a secular school or not a very good religious one. Bouche seems to point to the latter, noting (with reference to the state of affairs ten years later) that it was in fact a religious school: "Agoué also had a master of the Brazilian school; he taught the elements of the Christian doctrine."[112]

The returnees also brought with them the Catholic religion. According to Bouche, who arrived at Agoué in 1874, the first Catholic chapel had been built there in 1835 by a liberated slave from Brazil, a woman. It is said to have been abandoned after being destroyed in a fire.[113] A "Portuguese chapel" at Agoué is documented in 1843, referring presumably to this chapel.[114] Better known is the chapel that was erected by Joaquim d'Almeida and opened for service in 1845. According to Borghero, it was situated in d'Almeida's house and "lavishly decorated for this country, nothing was missing." D'Almeida "had brought or made come from Brazil all that is necessary for establishing a church, even the bells."[115] It had been the latter's intention to build another, larger church in the town itself for the use of the public, but he had died before he was able to do so. Borghero also reported that the returnees were eager for missionaries to establish themselves at Agoué. "They asked for missionaries with great desire."[116] Since the mid-1840s, Agoué had been visited (in irregular intervals) by the priests from the seminary at São Tomé who were attached to the Portuguese fort at Ouidah and who had carried out baptisms of the children and slaves of the returnees.[117] These had been replaced in the early 1860s by the missionaries of the Société des Missions Africaines, which in 1861 had established itself at Ouidah. In 1874, Agoué became the headquarters of the newly established "Dahomian" mission of the Société (i.e., separate from Lagos).

The question why so many liberated slaves chose to settle at Agoué remains open to discussion. One possible explanation is that it was the presence of the Portuguese and Spanish slave traders there that attracted the returnees, many of whom had no firsthand experience of Africa but had been born in Brazil. They shared the Portuguese language and Catholic religion with the slave traders, who provided a familiar cultural environment in the strange country to which they had "returned." Another explanation, which is related to this one, is that Agoué was a young town and its burgeoning economy, based on the illegal slave trade and the trade in provisions, offered possibilities to the returnees that were not available at the more established places where political power was more strictly controlled by the indigenous authorities. Finally, the personal influence of Joaquim d'Almeida, the central figure at Agoué in the 1840s, may have also played a role.

Obviously, the Afro-Brazilian settlement at Agoué was in its origins connected with the slave trade. However, it continued to thrive beyond the end of this trade because many of the former slave traders who had relocated elsewhere maintained their connection with the town, where they still had their houses and families, and some returned after they had retired. In 1884, this prompted the German journalist Hugo Zöller to observe that "for the former slave traders who have retired from business, Agoué plays exactly the same role as Wiesbaden [a spa town in Germany] for retired officers," namely, that of a retirement home.[118] The connection with the slave trade was over for the Afro-Brazilian community at Agoué, but the initial investment in property and houses after the return to the Bight of Benin meant that it was difficult for families to move away. Individuals might seek employment elsewhere, but the family homes remained as a place for retreat and, ultimately, retirement.

APPENDIX: LIBERATED SLAVES FROM BRAZIL AND CUBA WHO SETTLED AT AGOUÉ

The following list gives the names of liberated slaves from Brazil and Cuba who settled in Agoué in the nineteenth century. It is based mainly on Isidore Pelofy's "Familles d'Agoué venues du Brésil et du Cuba et du Sierra Leone."[119] Some information has been added, too, from Jean Pierucci's *History of Agoué* (1953). Information from other sources is indicated by notes.

This list is not complete or representative, for various reasons. First, Pelofy's register is based on the baptismal registers of the Catholic missions at Agoué and Ouidah. Therefore, only those returnees appear in his register (and, consequently, in my list) who either were Catholics or had Catholics in their family. However, a number of the returnees were Muslims. Sometimes Muslims, too, had their children baptised at the Catholic mission, but not always, and therefore it can be assumed that there were more Muslim "Brésiliens" at Agoué than appear in this list. Second, the entries in Pelofy's register represent families rather than individuals. The liberated slaves often returned together with other members of their family, parents, partners, or children, rather than on their own. Pelofy, however, does not usually list all the members of a family that settled at Agoué but only the head of the family, who often, though not always, is the eldest male family member. Therefore, women are not usually listed in his register. Third, in the compilation of this list I have been exclusive rather than inclusive, that is, I have extracted from Pelofy's register only the names of those people who are explicitly stated to have come from Brazil or Cuba. Pelofy gives some 150 names altogether, not all of which, however, are clearly identified as belonging to "Brésiliens." Apart from the Sierra Leoneans and Europeans, there are also a number of people about whom no information is given apart from the name and sometimes a date. These people, who usually either had no descendants or did not stay at Agoué, I have not included.

Some remarks concerning the organization of the information are necessary. The list consists of five columns, the first of which gives the name of the returnees. The second column gives the date of the earliest record of the person at Agoué, which if not otherwise indicated is the date of a baptismal register. Thus, this column does not give the date of arrival of the person at Agoué but only the time by which he or she had arrived. The third column gives the ethnic origin of the returnees. This information is taken from Pelofy, who apparently copied it from the baptismal registers. Originally it supposedly comes from the returnees themselves, which is interesting in light of the fact that some of those who are identified with an African ethnic group were born in Brazil, such as Maria Balbina de Amor Divino, Manuel Cardozo dos Santos, and Manuel Maceido. Even more remarkable is the case of Felipe de Santiago (dos Santos), who reportedly was a mulatto but is nevertheless identified as "Nagô" (Yoruba). The fourth column gives the quarter in which the returnees were reported to have settled. This information is taken mainly from Pelofy and sometimes from Pierucci, but it is not clear where it originally came from. Since it is not likely that it is given in the baptismal registers, it could be supposed that Pelofy and Pierucci obtained it from inquiries among the descendants of the returnees. Another possibility is that they just noted the quarter where the descendants lived, on the assumption that the families had stayed at their original place of settlement. Therefore, this information is not absolutely reliable. The last column gives additional information concerning the returnees' lives and careers. In some cases, this includes information concerning their religious affiliation. This information comes from Pelofy, who in his register only notes the Muslims and Protestants, everybody else being by implication Catholic. I have followed this practice.

Table 1. Returnees from Brazil

Name	Date	Ethnic Origin	Quarter	Remarks
1. de Adaões, Sallustro	1858	Nagô	Diata	He was the cook of João da Cruz ("Kokê"), a Portuguese trader at Agoué. His son became a Muslim.
2. da Alcantara, Maria Pedro	1846			She had two children with Eleuthério da Silva Vasconcellos (see below).
3. d'Almeida, Antonio		Nagô	Fonkome	d. 1890 in Ouidah Like Joaquim d'Almeida, he had been a slave of Manoel Joaquim d'Almeida in Brazil. He had come

				to Agoué with his son Bernadino (b. 30 June 1830). By 1864 they had moved to Ouidah.[120]
4. d'Almeida, Joaquim ("Zoki Azata")	1846	Mahi	Zokikome	b. in Hoko (Mahi), d. 1857 in Agoué[121]
5. de Almoral, Venancio	1855	Mahi	Fonkome	
6. d'Alveira, Francisco	1873	Nagô	Diata	His son became a Muslim.
7. de Amor Divino, Maria Balbina	1858	Hausa		b. 1832 in Brazil, d. 1894 in Agoué She was the sister of Manuel dos Reis (see below) and the wife of Joaquim Manoel Carvalho.[122]
8. de Araujo-Braga, Antonio Quaetano/ Gaetano		Mahi	Hausakome	He had come from Brazil with two sons, Veríssimo, and Passion. Antonio Quaetano, Verríssimo, and the latter's son Fortunato were shoemakers.
9. Bahia, Ricardo		from Séhoué ("Sahué")[123]	Fonkome	He had arrived in Agoué about 1870.
10. Bandeira, Justino[124]	1871	Mahi (Savalu)	Hausakome	b. in Savalu, d. 1887 in Agoué, about 90 years old
11. Barboza, Romão		Hausa	Hausakome	Muslim
12. Borges de Souza, Tobias	1866	Nagô	Hausakome	He had come from Brazil with his daughter, Joanna.
13. Cacia, Bonfim[125]	1855	Atakpa from Bida[126]	Hausakome	He was married to Jesuína de Boa Morte.
14. Cardozo dos Santos, Manuel	1870	Fon	Fonkome	b. 1847 in Bahia, d. 1882 in Agoué
15. de Conceição, Maria	1858			b. c.1832 in Brazil, d. 1887 in Agoué
16. da Costa, Adriano		Nagô	Hausakome	Muslim
17. da Costa, Antonio[127]	1874	Nagô		
18. da Costa, Carlos	1855	Bariba[128]		He had come from Brazil with his son, Thomé, who had been born during the passage. [Therefore, he presumably also brought his wife.]
19. da Costa, Clemente	1877	Nagô		He had been a slave of Captain Clemente da Costa.
20. da Cruz, Ephigenia		Dassa[129]		Her husband was Dassa too, but is not named in the register.
21. Eduard, João	1866	Egba	Hausakome	Muslim

SECTION III: THE IMPACT OF BRAZIL AND AFRO-BRAZILIANS

22. de Freitas, Agostinho	1855	Mahi	Salo/ Fonkome	He had possibly brought his son Ildefonso (b. 1848, d. 1886) with him from Brazil.
23. Geraldo, ... [?]	1855	Nagô	Zomayi	He left some children in Brazil and had three children, Dionysio, Pedro, and Bento, at Agoué.
24. Geraldo, Manoel			Hausakome	His family comprised "Muslims and some rare Christians."
25. Getayi, Domingo Friz Pinto	1858		Diata	b. in Bahia He had come to Agoué with Magdalena da Gloria, who was possibly his daughter. He was schoolmaster at Diata.
26. da Gloria, Daniel ("Bêlu")		Nagô	Diata	Muslim He had come to Agoué with his son Adriano, who had been born in Brazil (d. 1909). The imam of the quarter Diata is chosen from this family.
27. da Gloria, Dionysio		Nagô		
28. Gonçalvez Baêtas, Francisco José		Nagô	Fonkome	d. 1907
29. Gonzallos[130]		Nagô	Hausakome	possibly Muslim His son Jibila was a Muslim, and so were his grandchildren, who nevertheless were baptized.
30. Henriquy (João?)		Nagô	Zomayi	
31. de Jesus, Felicianna Theresa	1846			She had come from Brazil with her daughter, Felicianna Prudentia, and her granddaughter, Vénussa.
32. de Lima, Estevão	1855	Hausa	Hausakome	
33. de Maceido, Manuel		Mahi	Fonkome	b. 1844 in Bahia, d. 1912 in Agoué He had come to Agoué in c.1863, with his father.
34. de Mascarenhas, João	1860	Mahi or Nagô[131]	Fonkome	
35. Maria, José	1858	Hausa	Hausakome	Muslim He had come with his son Joachim Pedro, who had been born in Brazil.
36. Maria, José	1866		Hausakome	mulatto He had come from Brazil with his elder brother, Romualdo.

37. de Mello, Sophia	1869		Hausakome	Wife of Juba Bramfo, who had come from Cuba (see below). She had probably come to Agoué by 1850 (her grandchild was baptized in 1869).[132]
38. de Merelho Mothão, Joachim	1865		Diata	
39. Monteiro, José Manuel		Nagô		
40. Napier, Francisco Diogo	1858	Nagô	Diata	He, or at least his descendants, were Muslims. He had been a cook in Brazil.
41. de Nascimento, Martins		Mahi		
42. Paraizo, Aureliano		Nagô	Diata	Muslim
43. Pereira da Paixão, José	1855	Mahi	Zokikome	b. in Agonlin,[133] d. by 1855
44. Pereira dos Santos, Antonio	1855	Nagô	Diata	Muslim He had come to Agoué by 1843, when his daughter was born. He was the husband of Francisca Iya Mondukpê.
45. Pio, José	1872	Nagô	Hausakome	He was at Agoué by 1875.
46. Pio, Manuel	1874	Nagô	Diata	
47. do Rego, João[134]	1864	Hausa	Hausakome	possibly Muslim He left a "large family of Muslims, Catholics, and Protestants." His first son, Apollinario, was born at Ouidah.
48. dos Reis, Manuel José	1858	Hausa[135]		d. 1881 in Porto Seguro He had come from Brazil with his sister M. B. de Amor Divino (see above).
49. Ribeiro, Alvez	1863	Mahi	Fonkome	
50. de Santa Cunha, Estevão	1858		Hausakome	
51. Santa Lopez, Francisco Pereira	1874	Mahi		He had come from Brazil with two sons, Emiliano (Géminiano [?]) and Demas [sic?] Pereira.
52. Santanna de Souza, José[136]		Mahi	Fonkome	d. 1874, 80 years old
53. de Santanna, José Maria	1860[137]	Hausa	Hausakome	

54. de Santiago, Felipe[138]	1858	Nagô	Diata	mulatto, d. 1895 He had come from Brazil with his son Leandro, who was baptized at Agoué in 1858.
55. de Serra, Rufino	1864	Nagô	Yakome	
56. da Silva, Antonio Manuel	1846	Nagô	Fonkome	He had come from Brazil with his son, Thomé, who had been baptized there.
57. da Silva Pereira, Francisco	1858	Fon from Avlékété[139]	Ayelekome	d. 1858 He had come to Agoué in 1835.[140]
58. da Silva Vasconcellos, Eleuthério	1846	Fon	Fonkome	He had come from Brazil before 1845.
59. Vieyra da Silva, Antonio[141]	1860[142]	Nagô	Hausakome	Muslim His brother Silvestre was also at Agoué and had many children baptized.
60. Zinsu, Michel		Mahi	Kpota	

Table 2. Returnees from Cuba

Name	Date	Ethnic Origin	Quarter	Remarks
1. André	1868	Hausa	Hausakome	He, or some of his descendants, were Muslims.
2. Bramfo, Juba[143]	1869	Mahi	Hausakome	He had probably come to Agoué by 1850 (his grandchild was baptized in 1869).
3. Domingo[144]	1887			
4. Gozegan, José ("Charuteiro")	1857	Fon	Fonkome	He came from Havana, where he had been employed producing cigars.
5. Perico and Victorin				They had come from Havana.
6. Soarez, Domingo	1869	Hausa	Hausakome	

NOTES

1. This chapter is the by-product of my research for a Ph.D. dissertation on Afro-European trade relations on the western Slave Coast in the precolonial period (submitted at the University of Stirling/U.K. in December 2002). The chapter has benefited greatly from the advice and support of Robin Law, to whom I offer my profound thanks. I also want to thank the participants in the conference "Enslaving Connection: Africa and Brazil

during the Era of the Slave Trade" (York University, Toronto, 12–15 October 2000) for their helpful and encouraging comments.

2. See, for example, Pierre Verger, *Flux et reflux de la traite des nègres entre le golfs de Bénin et Bahia de todos os santos du XVIIe au XIX siècle* (Paris: Mouton, 1968); Jerry Michael Turner, "Les Brésiliens—The Impact of Former Brazilian Slaves upon Dahomey" (Ph.D. diss., Boston University, 1975); Pierre Verger, "Identidade étnica na África-Ocidental: o caso especial dos afro-brasileiros no Benin, na Nigeria, no Togo e em Gana nos séculos XIX e XX," *Estudos Afro-Asiáticos* 28 (October 1995): 85–99; Manuela Carneiro da Cunha, *Negros, estrangeiros; os escravos libertos e sua volta à África* (São Paulo: Editora Brasiliencé, 1985); and Milton Guran, *Agudás: os "brasileiros" do Benim* (Rio de Janeiro: Editora Nova Fronteira, 1999). There are also a number of articles that deal with individual Afro-Brazilians: David Ross, "The Career of Domingo Martinez in the Bight of Benin, 1833–1864," *Journal of African History* 6, no. 1 (1965): 79–90; David Ross, "The First Chacha of Whydah: Francisco Felix de Souza," *Odu* 2, 3d series (1969): 19–28; D. E. K. Amenumey, "Geraldo da Lima: A Reappraisal," *Transactions of the Historical Society of Ghana* 9 (1968): 65–78; and the chapter by Robin Law in this volume.

3. For a detailed discussion, see Silke Strickrodt, "Afro-European Trade Relations on the Western Slave Coast, Sixteenth to Nineteenth Centuries" (Ph.D. diss., Stirling University, Scotland, 2002), chap. 5. See Nicoué Lodjou Gayibor, "Les conflits politiques à Aného de 1821 à 1960," *Cahiers du CRA* (Centre de recherches africaines) 8 (Paris, 1994): 202.

4. For a discussion of the political situation in the kingdom of Ge in the period, see Nicoué Lodjou Gayibor, *Le Genyi, un royaume oublié de la Côte de Guinée au temps de la traite de Noirs* (Lome: Éditions Haho, 1990), pp. 179–201, 212–17; Adam Jones, "Little Popo and Agoué at the End of the Atlantic Slave Trade: Glimpses from the Lawson Correspondence and Other Sources," in *Ports of the Slave Trade (Bights of Benin and Biafra)*, ed. Robin Law and Silke Strickrodt (Stirling, Scotland: Centre of Commonwealth Studies, University of Stirling, 1999), pp. 122–34; Strickrodt, "Afro-European Trade Relations," chap. 5.

5. Wesleyan Methodist Missionary Society London, Archives (hereafter: WMMS), Special Series, Biographical, West Africa: Papers of Thomas Birch Freeman: Thomas Birch Freeman, "Journal December 1842—December 1845," p. 166.

6. John Duncan, *Travels in Western Africa in 1845 and 1846* (London: Frank Cass, 1968), vol. 1, p. 101.

7. Pierre Bouche, *Sept ans en Afrique Occidentale: la Côte des Esclaves et le Dahomey* (Paris: Plon, 1885), p. 301.

8. Public Record Office, London (PRO), FO84/893, incl. in Hamilton [London], 10 April 1852, Lieutenant T. G. Forbes, HMS *Philomel*, at Whydah, 5 February 1852; PRO, FO84/1124, Admiralty [London], 13 July 1860, Commander W. Bowden, *Medusa*, Whydah, 31 January 1860.

9. Duncan, *Travels*, vol. 1, p. 147; Francesco Borghero, *Journal de Francesco Borghero, premier missionnaire du Dahomey, 1861–1865* (Paris: Karthala, 1997), p. 124.

10. Hugo Zöller, *Das Togoland und die Sklavenküste*, vol. 1 of *Die Deutschen Besitzungen an der westafrikanischen Küste* (Berlin and Stuttgart, 1885), pp. 147, 176, 182, 191. For a French translation, see Hugo Zöller, *Le Togo en 1884 selon Hugo Zöller*,

trans. K. Amegan and A. Ahadji, ed. Y. Marguerat (*Les chroniques anciennes du Togo* 1, Lomé 1990).

11. The original documents produced by the Royal Navy and the consular correspondence are preserved in the PRO in the ADM, FO2 and FO84 series. A large number of them have been published, although sometimes in abridged form (which is not indicated), in the Parliamentary Papers (PP), Slave Trade (ST) Series.

12. Duncan, *Travels*; Frederick E. Forbes, *Dahomey and the Dahomeans* (London: Frank Cass, 1966 [1851]), 2 vols.; Richard Burton, *A Mission to Gelele, King of Dahomey* (London: Tinsley Brothers, 1864), 2 vols.

13. The papers of the Wesleyan Methodist Missionary Society are kept in the Society's archives at SOAS in London. The papers of Thomas Birch Freeman include journals, letters, and an unpublished manuscript of a history of Africa. Parts of his journal have been published in an edited form, in which a reference to Agoué had been deleted: Thomas Birch Freeman, *Journal to Various Visits to the Kingoms of Ashanti, Aku, and Dahomi in Western Africa* (London: Frank Cass, 1968 [1851]), 2 vols.

14. For a brief summary of the Catholic missionary activity on the western Slave Coast, see Robert Codjo Sastre, *Le premier siège de la préfecture apostolique du Dahomey: Survol de l'histoire religieuse d'Agoué* ([Mission d'Agoué], 2000).

15. Borghero, *Journal*; Abbé Lafitte, *Le Dahomé, souvenirs d'un voyage et de mission* (Tours: A. Mame, 1876); Bouche, *Sept ans*. These works have been quoted extensively by Verger. See, for example, his "Retour des 'Brésiliens' au Golfe du Bénin au XIXème siécle," *Etudes Dahoméennes* (October 1966): 24–25; also his *Flux et reflux*, pp. 600–602.The articles were published in *Echo des Missions Africaines* and *Annales de la Propagation de la Foi*. See Sastre, *Le premier siège*, pp. 3, 8–10.

16. Isidore Pélofy, *Histoire d'Agoué (République du Bénin)*, ed. Régina Byll-Cataria (Leipzig: University of Leipzig Papers on Africa [ULPA], History and Culture Series no. 8, 2002). I am very grateful to Mrs. Régina Byll-Cataria of the Université Nationale du Bénin/Benin, who made Pelofy's and Pierucci's works available to me while she was engaged in editing them.

17. Archives Mgr. Robert Codjo Sastre, Lokossa/Benin: Jean Pierucci, "Histoire d'Agoué" (ms, 1953, 48pp.).

18. The earliest of the baptismal registers that I saw during my visit to the Catholic Missions at Agoué in 2000 starts from the year 1896. According to information from the local Abbé, Benjamin Ãdodo Gaglozoun, this is the earliest of the registers that are preserved at Agoué. The registers before 1874, when a mission was established at Agoué, are presumably at Ouidah. It is a mystery to me where the registers from 1874 to 1896 are.

19. Archives Mgr. Robert Codjo Sastre, Lokossa/Benin: Isidore Pelofy, "Familles d'Agoué venues du Brésil et du Cuba et du Sierra Leone." This list was apparently written in 1931, with additional information being added subsequently. The latest date mentioned in it is 1843. For published version, see Pélofy, *Histoire d'Agoué*, pp. 13–32: "Liste des Brèsiliens et affranchis résidant à Agoué."

20. Simone de Souza, *La famille de Souza Bénin-Togo* (Cotonou: Les Éditions du Bénin, 1992).

21. Ibid., pp. 295–96.

22. The wills of Joaquim d'Almeida and Antonio d'Almeida as well as that of their

former master, Manoel Joaquim d'Almeida, were published by Pierre Verger (*Os libertos. Sete Caminhos na Liberdade de Escravos da Bahia no Século XIX* [São Paulo: Corrupio, 1992], pp. 114–24). Joaquim d'Almeida's will has also been published in French translation: see Verger, *Flux et reflux*, pp. 540–41.

23. Pierre Verger, *Les afro-américains* (Dakar: IFAN, 1952), pp. 53–100.

24. The "Grand Livre Lolamé" (GLL) is currently being edited for publication by Adam Jones and Peter Sebald: *An African Family Archive: Correspondence and Other Writings of the Lawsons of Little Popo/Aneho (Togo), Mainly from the Victorian Era* (Oxford, forthcoming). For a description, see Jones, "Little Popo and Agoué," pp. 125–34; Peter Sebald, "7,5 Kilogramm westafrikanische Korrespondenz 1843–1887: Der Foliant der Königsfamilie Lawson, Aneho, Togo," in *Sprachkulturelle und historische Forschungen in Afrika: Beiträge zum 11. Afrikanistentag in Köln 1994* (Cologne, 1995), pp. 267–81.

25. PRO, FO84/950, no. 21, Consul Campbell, Lagos, 12 August 1854.

26. PRO, FO84/920, incl. no. 5 in Vice Consul Fraser, Lagos, 24 March 1853 and Lagos, 21 March 1853; PRO, FO84/926, incl. in Under Secretary of State, London, 25 October 1853, "Journal kept by C.G. Phillips, Esq. Commander of HMS Sloop *Polyphemus* & Senior Officer of the Bights Division from 25 April to 30 June 1853."

27. PRO, FO84/1002, no. 26, Consul B. Campbell, Lagos, 18 August 1856; FO2/20, incl. in Consul B. Campbell, Lagos, 7 March 1857, Commander George H. Day, HMS *Firefly*, off Whydah, 24 February 1857; PRO, FO84/1040, incl. in Under Secretary of the Admiralty [London], 9 October 1857, Lieut. Commander J.R. Pike, HMS *Antelope* at Sea, 2 July 1857. For a more detailed discussion of the illegal slave trade in the region, see Strickrodt, "Afro-European Trade Relations," chap. 6.

28. Gayibor, *Le Genyi*, p. 168.

29. Agbanon, *Histoire*, pp. 47, 65–66; Norberto Francisco de Souza, "Contribution à l'Histoire de la Famille de Souza," *Etudes Dahoméennes* 13 (1955): 17–21. According to Agbanon, *Histoire*, p. 47; F. F. de Souza and George A. Lawson were brothers-in-law, both being married to daughters of Akué. De Souza's wife, Jijiabu, died soon after giving birth to Isidoro, who is said to have been brought up by Adolévi Apé, Jijiabu's younger sister and wife of George Lawson. Isidoro and Latévi Agamazon, Lawson's son, "were considered like twins."

30. See the chapter by Robin Law in this volume. For a contemporary description of Isidoro's house at Adjido, see Duncan, *Travels*, vol. 1, p. 102. Shortly before Isidoro left for Ouidah, his house had been accidentally destroyed by a fire and its remains plundered. See Jones and Sebald, eds., *An African Family Archive*, George Latty Lawson to Capt. Jno Marmon, 10 May 1849.

31. PP, ST, 1840, Class A, no. 85: case of the brig *Plant*; PP, ST 1844, A, no. 73: case of the Spanish brigantine *San Pedro*.

32. Burton, *A Mission*, vol. 1, p. 74: "João Pinheiro de Souza, commonly called Taparica." According to de Souza, *La famille*, p. 45, "João Tapariga" had been given a piece of land at Adjido after his marriage to Joanna, one of F. F. de Souza's daughters.

33. PP, ST, 1840, A, no. 47: case of the schooner *Jack Wilding*. Among the papers found on board, there was a letter addressed to "Jozé Mora, or Don Thomas Sastre, at the Port of Occo," dated 24 March 1839, in which reference is made to trade at "Popo." It is probably

Little Popo that is meant here, since it was usually referred to by the abbreviated form in the period, having completely eclipsed Grand Popo in the trade. It appears that Grand Popo became interesting again to European traders only after the Equipment Act of 1839.

34. De Souza, *La famille*, p. 243. According to de Souza's account, João Sastre had settled at Agoué by 1868, when his first child with Judith Félix de Souza was born. See Turner ("Les Brésiliens," pp. 131–32), for a version of the story as recorded in the tradition of the Sastre family. They have apparently forgotten about the founder of their family and only remember his son (although not his first name). According to Turner, the family residence was established in Grand Popo and later additional compounds were constructed at Agoué and Little Popo.

35. According to the naval officer Frederick E. Forbes, who visited the coast in 1849, three of the Chacha's sons were "wealthy and slave-merchants": Isidoro, Antonio "Kokou" ("Cockoo"), and Ignatio (PP, ST 1849–1850, B, incl. 10 in no. 9: Lieutenant Forbes, *Bonetta*, at sea, 5 November 1849). According to de Souza, *La famille*, p. 46, another son, called San Antonio, was also engaged in trade at Little Popo, but there are no references to him in the contemporary records.

36. De Souza, *La famille*, p. 59; Burton, *Mission*, vol. 1, pp. 105–106 incl. notes. According to de Souza (p. 18), Antonio was born of the same mother as Ignacio. Norberto de Souza, however, states that "Ahosi Zanglanmio" was the mother of Maria and Ignacio but he does not mention Antonio in this context.

37. Jones and Sebald, eds., *An African Family Archive*, J. H. Akhurst, Ahguay, 1 October 1843; James W. Hansen, Ahguay, 31 October 1843; Ahguay, 12 November 1843; Ahguay, 23 October 1843; Ahguay, 4 January 1844; Ahguay, 10 January 1844.

38. Ibid., George Latty Lawson, Little Popo, 30 March 1849.

39. WMMS, Special Series, Biographical, West Africa: Papers of Thomas Birch Freeman: Revd. Wiliam Allen to T. B. Freeman, Ahgnay [*sic*], 18 January 1844, quoted in Thomas Birch Freeman, "West Africa" (unpublished ms), p. 248.

40. Archives Mgr. Robert Codjo Sastre, Lokossa/Benin: Pierucci, "Histoire d'Agoué," pp. 9–10. According to Pierucci, a daughter of Antonio, Rita Ajisen, also lived in this quarter. She married Joaquim Garcia, a Portuguese seaman who had been working on a slave ship and who after her death inherited the quarter (pp. 9–10, 26–27).

41. Zomayi literally means "fire prohibited." See Robin Law, "Memory, Oblivion, and Return in Commemoration of the Atlantic Slave Trade in Ouidah (Republic of Bénin)," in *The Atlantic Slave Trade in African and African-American Memory*, ed. Ralph Austen and Kenneth Lowrie (Durham, N.C.: Duke University Press, 2003), p. 12.

42. In 1850, F. E. Forbes observed that Little Popo "is almost a monopoly" of Isidoro de Souza (PP, ST 1849–1850, incl. 2 in no. 220, Journal of Lieut. Forbes [4 July 1850]). The great influence of the de Souzas is also shown by the fact that in 1843, when the factory of the British trader Thomas Hutton at Agoué was destroyed in a fire, Francisco Felix de Souza was asked by the British governor at Cape Coast Castle to use his influence to help find the guilty person. See PRO, CO96/2, incl. in Thomas Hutton, Cape Coast Castle, 24 October 1843, George Maclean, Cape Coast Castle, 10 October 1843.

43. PRO, FO2/7, incl. in no. 3, Louis Fraser, Fernando Po, 15 May 1852, Commercial Report.

44. The number of slaves that dos Santos annually shipped from Ouidah, Agoué, and

Little Popo rose from 27 in 1844 to 296 in 1847. See Verger, *Les afro-américains*, pp. 53–86; Jones, "Little Popo and Agoué," p. 130.

45. Verger, *Les afro-américains*, p. 61 (no. 5, J. Dos Santos to Sr Manoël Pereira [Bahia], Ouidah, 25 March 1845). For alternative accounts of this event, see PRO, FO84/610, incl. in Hamilton [London], 5 June 1845: Commander H. B. Young, HMS *Hydra*, off Quitta, 7 March 1845; Duncan, *Travels*, vol. 1, p. 142.

46. Jones and Sebald, eds., *An African Family Archive*, George Latty Lawson to Senhor Jose F. dos Santos, New London, Popo, 6 August 1848; to Mr Jose F. dos Santos, New London, Popo, 20 August 1848. See also Jones, "Little Popo and Agoué," p. 130.

47. PP, ST 1855–1856, B, no. 9, Consul Campbell, Lagos, 28 August 1855.

48. PRO, CO96/23, incl. in no. 87, Stephen Hill, Cape Coast Castle, 24 November 1851, Deposition of George Latty Lawson, 12 and 14 November 1851. According to Lawson, Mustich had left Little Popo for Agoué by 1851, but this statement is not reliable since it was in Lawson's interest to convince the British authorities that he had severed all connections to the slave trader. According to the British Consul at Lagos, Mustich had establishments at both Agoué and Little Popo in 1855 (PP, ST 1855–1856, B, no. 9, Consul Campbell, Lagos, 28 August 1855).

49. See PP, ST 1854–1855, B, no. 17: Consul Campbell, Lagos, 12 August 1854; PP, ST 1855–1856, B, no. 9: Consul Campbell, Lagos, 28 August 1855; no. 30: Consul Campbell, Lagos, 1 February 1856; no. 31, Consul Campbell, Lagos, 18 August 1856; PRO, FO84/1031, incl. in no. 35: Consul B. Campbell, Lagos, 5 September 1857, Report on slave vessels and cruisers in the Bight of Benin.

50. Verger, *Os libertos*, pp. 43–44. Verger gives "Gbego Sokpa" as Joaquim d'Ameida's original name. For a discussion of d'Almeida's career on the coast, see Turner, "Les Brésiliens," pp. 102–105; Guran, *Agudás*, pp. 85–87.

51. PP, ST 1841, A, no. 109: case of the Brazilian schooner *Gratidão*.

52. According to family tradition, Joaquim d'Almeida first arrived at Agoué in 1835, but there is no evidence of this in the contemporary records. The date is inscribed in a memorial plaque that has been erected by the family at Agoué. For a photograph, see Guran, *Agudás*, p. 87.

53. The Quénum tradition exists in several versions that vary in the details but agree in the essence. See Edouard Foà, *Le Dahomey* (Paris: A Hennuyer, 1895), p. 23; Reynier, "Eléments sur la réorganisation du commandement indigène à Ouidah (1917)," *Mémoire du Bénin* 2 (Cotonou, 1993): 63; Maximilien Quénum, *Les ancêtres de la famille Quénum* (Langres: Dominique Gueniot, 1981), pp. 60–61.

54. Jones and Sebald, eds., *An African Family Archive*, George Latty Lawson, New London, Popo, 14 August 1848. According to local tradition as recorded by Agbanon, the enmity between Joaquim d'Almeida and the de Souza family was overcome in the 1850s, after F. F. de Souza's death. D'Almeida and Chico de Souza, who later became Chacha III, are said to have been good friends (Agbanon, *Histoire*, p. 81).

55. PP, ST 1849–1850, B, incl. 10 in no. 9: Lieutenant Forbes, "Bonetta," at sea, 5 November 1849.

56. Forbes, *Dahomey*, vol. 1, p. 102.

57. Jones and Sebald, eds., *An African Family Archive*, George Latty Lawson, New London, Popo, 14 August 1848; Andreas Malm to Senhor J.G. Baeta, Popo, 3 January

18[49]; George Latty Lawson to Mr. Joaquin Almada, New London, Popo, 21 March 1849.

58. PP 1850 [1171] XXXVIII, Papers respecting the Cession to Great Britain of the Danish Possessions on the Coast of Africa, 5 (Journal of Governor Winniett, 10 March 1850).

59. PRO, CO96/22, no. 30, J. Bannerman, Cape Coast Castle, 7 April 1851; PP, ST 1855–1856, B, no. 30, Consul Campbell, Lagos, 1 February 1856.

60. For versions of the traditions of the Olympio family, see Alcione M. Amos, "Afro-Brasileiros no Togo: a história da família Olympio, 1882–1945," *Afro-Ásia* 23 (1999): 175–97; Guran, *Agudás*, pp. 56–68. It is said that Francisco Olympio da Silva dropped the "da Silva" from his name in an attempt to fool the officers of the Royal Navy (p. 57).

61. Borghero, *Journal*, pp. 124–25; Burton, *A Mission*, vol. 1, p. 74.

62. PP, ST 1859–1850, Class A, incl. 2 in no. 220: "Journal of Lieutenant Forbes" [4 July 1850]; ibid., incl. 10 in no. 9, Lieutenant Forbes, "Bonetta," at sea, 5 November 1849. In the "GLL," there is also a reference to "Antonio" who was buying palm oil at Grand Popo, dating from 1848 (Jones and Sebald, eds., *An African Family Archive*, George Latty Lawson, Popo, 7 November 1848). However, it seems likely that it is Antonio de Souza rather than Joaquim Antonio who is meant here, since the former is often referred to as "Mr. Antonio" in the correspondence. To add to the confusion, there apparently was yet another Antonio at Grand Popo or Hévé, who had died by 1855. This is indicated by a reference in the correspondence of the Wesleyan Methodist Missionary Society to "the late Antoney De Tesyar's mother" (WMMS: West Africa Correspondence: Joseph Dawson, Little Popo, 23 February 1855).

63. PRO, FO84/893, incl. in Hamilton [London], 10 April 1852, Lieutnant T. G. Forbes, HMS *Philomel*, at Whydah, 5 February 1852. For Hévé, see Félix Iroko, "Gahu et Kposu d'Abomey et de Hêvê des origines à nos jours," *Cahiers du C.R.A.* 8 (1994): 108 n. 3.

64. WMMS: West Africa Correspondence: Joseph Dawson, Little Popo, 23 February 1855.

65. PRO, FO84/1221, Consul G. Stanhope Freeman, Lagos, 8 January 1864. A similar occurrence had happened in 1857 when a "Señor Monteiro" (n.b. the "Monteiro" in the name of José Pereira Monteiro do Carvalho) allegedly renounced the slave trade and provided information to the Royal Navy concerning the organization of the new Cuban trade. See PRO, FO84/1040, incl. in Admiralty [London], 18 November 1857, Commander G. F. Burgess, HMS *Hecate*, Whydah, 12 August 1857.

66. PRO, FO84/1115, Consul G. Brand, Lagos, 2 May 1860. For a more detailed discussion, see Strickrodt, "Afro-Brazilians," pp. 9–10.

67. PRO, FO84/1115, Consul G. Brand, Lagos, 2 May 1860.

68. Ibid., incl. in Consul G. Brand, Lagos, 2 May 1860, José Maria C. Brandão, 30 March 1860.

69. Pelofy, *Histoire d'Agoué*, p. 14.

70. C. W. Newbury, *The Western Slave Coast and Its Rulers: European trade and administration among the Yoruba and Adja-speaking peoples of South-Western Nigeria, Southern Dahomey, and Togo* (Oxford: Clarendon Press, 1961), pp. 63–64, 68n., 69.

71. See Turner, "Les Brésiliens," pp. 223–35. In September 1864, he was expelled from Porto Novo through the influence of the French and in December 1864 was resident at Lagos. This means he is not identifiable with "M. D. Joaquim Carvalho, called Breca," who according to Burton died at Ouidah in January 1864 (PP, ST 1864, B, Consul Burton, Bonny River, 23 March 1864).

72. PP, ST 1857–1858, A, no. 155, Commander Hope, 23 May 1857. Jaboo (Ijebu) lies northeast of Lagos on the eastern limits of the Slave Coast.

73. PRO, FO84/1040, incl. in Admiralty [London], 18 November 1857: Commander G. F. Burgess, HMS *Hecate*, Whydah, 12 August 1857.

74. The dos Santos correspondence comprises nine letters addressed to "J. Gbr. Baêta." If this refers to João Gonçalves Baêta (as Verger assumed), this would mean that Baêta had returned to Bahia between July 1859 (when he was last recorded at Agoué by the Royal Navy) and 1862 (the date of the first letter to him at Bahia). The letters show that Baêta was not only dos Santos's agent and sold palm oil and kola nuts for him, but also a trusted friend who took care of his mother. See Verger, *Les afro-américains*, pp. 53–100.

75. PP, ST 1842, A, no. 54, case of the brig *Fortuna*. Burton, *A Mission*, vol. 1, p. 74 n., lists him as a Brazilian, adding that "some say he is a Portuguese, born in the United States."

76. PRO, FO84/1123, incl. no. 2 in: Secretary of the Admiralty [London], 29 February 1860: Commander Bowden, Lagos, 21 November 1859.

77. Archives Mgr. Robert Codjo Sastre, Lokossa/Benin: Pierucci, "Histoire d'Agoué," p. 26.

78. PP, ST 1857–1858, B, no. 19, Consul Campbell, Lagos, 27 July 1857.

79. Turner, "Les Brésiliens," pp. 125–26. Guran, *Agudás*, p. 21, repeats this information.

80. PRO, FO84/1123, incl. no. 2 in: Secretary of the Admiralty [London], 29 February 1860: Commander Bowden, Lagos, 21 November 1859.

81. Burton, *A Mission*, vol. 1, p. 74 n.

82. PRO, FO84/1175, incl. in: Secretary of the Admiralty [London], 25 January 1864: Rear Admiral B. Walker, *Narcissus*, Simons Bay, 17 November 1863. According to the British Consul at Lagos, another shipment of 650 slaves had been made from Agoué in late 1863, but there is no confirmation of this in the records the Royal Navy. See PRO, FO84/1221, Consul G. Stanhope Freeman, Lagos, 8 January 1864.

83. PP ST 1864–1865, A, no. 151, Commodore Wilmot, *Rattlesnake*, at Ascension, 1 December 1864 (annual report on the Slave Trade on the West Coast of Africa).

84. Ibid.

85. PRO: FO84/1267, incl. in Secretary of Admiralty [London], 12 April 1866: Commander M. S. L. Peile, HMS *Espoir*, Lagos, 7 March 1866; PP ST 1867, A, no. 48, Commodore Hornby, Sierra Leone, 12 February 1867.

86. PP ST 1867, A, no. 65, Commodore Hornby, Elephant Bay, 7 June 1867.

87. Verger, "Retour des Brésiliens," pp. 7–9.

88. See Carneiro da Cunha, *Negros, Estrangeiros*, pp. 106–107.

89. Agoué, which had been founded in the 1820s, appears in the documents only in the 1840s. One early exception dates from 1836, when the Royal Navy recorded the capture of a slave ship between "Aqué" and Whydah. See PP, ST 1936, A, no. 45: case of the Spanish brig *El Esplorador*.

SECTION III: THE IMPACT OF BRAZIL AND AFRO-BRAZILIANS

90. Pelofy, *Histoire d'Agoué*, pp. 6–7. For Toyi's reign, see Bouche, *Sept ans*, p. 302; Strickrodt, "Afro-European Trade Relations," p. 211.

91. This information is given by de Souza, *La famille*, p. 295, and comes apparently from the baptismal register of the Catholic Mission at Ouidah.

92. PP, ST 1841, A, no. 109, case of the Brazilian schooner *Gratidão*.

93. PRO, CO96/2, incl. in W. B. Hutton, London, 20 December 1843, Chiefs of Agoué, Ahguay, 8 October 1843.

94. Borghero, *Journal*, p. 123.

95. Archives Mgr. Robert Codjo Sastre, Lokossa/Benin: Pierucci, "Histoire d'Agoué," p. 25. Pierucci based his estimate on Pelofy's "Familles d'Agoué," which is based on information from the baptismal registers.

96. Borghero, *Journal*, p. 123.

97. See appendix to this chapter and Archives Mgr. Robert Codjo Sastre, Lokossa/Benin: Pierucci, "Histoire d'Agoué," p. 13. For more detail about Agoué's quarters, see Imbert B. Oswin Akibode, "Contribution à l'étude de l'histoire de l'ancien royaume d'Agoué (1821–1885)" (mémoire de maîtrise, FLASH [Faculté des lettres, arts, et sciences humaines], Université Nationale du Bénin, 1989), pp. 20–29; Strickrodt, "Afro-European Trade Relations," appendix 4.

98. Archives Mgr. Robert Codjo Sastre, Lokossa/Benin: Pierucci, "Histoire d'Agoué," pp. 11–12; Akibode, "Contribution," p. 27; Bouche, *Sept ans*, p. 302.

99. Borghero, *Journal*, p. 124.

100. Archives Mgr. Robert Codjo Sastre, Lokossa/Benin: Pierucci, "Histoire d'Agoué," p. 16.

101. Pelofy, *Histoire d'Agoué*, p. 25, 27, 29.

102. See Verger, *Os libertos*, p. 123.

103. Sastre, *Le premier siège*, p. 6; Pelofy, *Histoire d'Agoué*, pp. 13, 18.

104. Turner, "Les Brésiliens," pp. 116–18.

105. Pelofy, *Histoire d'Agoué*, p. 22; Archives Mgr. Robert Codjo Sastre, Lokossa/Benin: Pierucci, "Histoire d'Agoué," p. 24.

106. Guran, *Agudás*, pp. 82–83.

107. Pelofy, *Histoire d'Agoué*, pp. 18–19; Archives Mgr. Robert Codjo Sastre, Lokossa/Benin: Pierucci, "Histoire d'Agoué," pp. 26–27.

108. See the works by Verger, Turner, Akibode, and Guran.

109. Bouche, *Sept ans*, p. 267.

110. Archives Mgr. Robert Codjo Sastre, Lokossa/Benin: Pierucci, "Histoire d'Agoué," pp. 17–18.

111. Borghero, *Journal*, p. 276.

112. Bouche, *Sept ans*, p. 267. According to Pelofy, *Histoire d'Agoué*, pp. 7, 22, the schoolmaster was Micer Gonsallos, "a black Brazilian priest who lived at Fonkomé, [and] occupied himself mainly with the catechism and the Portuguese school." He died "about 1870," "leprous and venerated by all."

113. Bouche, *Sept ans*, p. 266; Pelofy, *Histoire*, p. 7.

114. PRO, CO96/2, incl. in W .B. Hutton & Sons [London], 20 December 1843, J. H. Akhurst, Ahguay, 3 October 1843.

115. Borghero, *Journal*, pp. 123, 251.

116. Ibid., p. 251.
117. Four priests visited Agoué between 1846 and 1860 and administered baptisms: 30 in 1864, 247 in 1855 (among which were 22 children and 73 slaves of Joaquim d'Almeida), 174 in 1857–1859, and 36 in 1860. See Sastre, *Le premier siège*, pp. 5–6.
118. Hugo Zöller, *Das Togoland*, p. 182 (my translation).
119. Published as "Liste des Brésiliens et affranchis résidant à Agoué" in Pelofy, *Histoire*, pp. 13–30.
120. See Antonio d'Almeida's will, which was published by Verger (*Os Libertos*, pp. 121–24). For a discussion of the will and some family history, see ibid., pp. 48–54. According to Verger, Antonio had settled in Zokikome. His name also appears in Burton's list of Afro-Brazilians established at Ouidah in early 1864 (Burton, *A Mission*, vol. 1, p. 74 n.).
121. Verger, *Os libertos*, pp. 43–48. For a copy of Joaquim d'Almeida's will, see ibid., pp. 116–21. This will has also been published in a French translation: see Verger, *Flux et reflux*, pp. 540–41.
122. See the inscription on her tombstone in the cemetery of the Catholic Mission in Agoué: "In loving memory of/Maria Balbina de Carvalho/born in Bahia March 31st 1832/died March 8th 1894 . . ."
123. Séhoué lies between Allada and Abomey.
124. For an account of Justino Bandeira's settlement at Agoué as recorded in the family's tradition, see Guran, *Agudás*, pp. 81–84.
125. Could he possibly be identified with "Bonfim José Garcia," who appears in de Souza's, *La famille*, p. 296?
126. "Takpa" or "Tapa" is the Yoruba/Dahomian term for the people who call themselves Nupe.
127. This is possibly Antonio José da Costa, who is buried in the cemetery of the Catholic Mission in Agoué. The inscription on the tombstone reads: "In Memoriam/Antonio José da Costa/Né au Rio de Janeiro (Brésil)/le 3 Janvier 1833 et décédé/à Agoué, le 19 Mars 1939/R.I.P."
128. "Bariba" is the Yoruba/Dahomian term for the people of Borgu, who call themselves Baatonu (pl. Batomba).
129. Dassa is a Yoruba-speaking group and was among those that were subject to attack by Dahomey. For a contemporary description of the country and people, see John Duncan, *Travels*, vol. 2, pp. 192–201. The modern town of Dassa lies some eighty-five kilometers to the north of Abomey.
130. Could he possibly be identified with "Gonçallo José Gomes Laranjeira," who signed the letter from the inhabitants and merchants of Agoué to the British Consul at Lagos in 1860? See PRO, FO84/1115, incl. in Slave Trade no. 30, Consul G. Brand, Lagos, 2 May 1860: Letter from the inhabitants and merchants of Agoué, Agoué, 5 March 1860.
131. Pelofy, *Histoire d'Agoué*, pp. 20, 31, was apparently doubtful as to de Mascarenhas's ethnic origin. He gives both Mahi and Nâgo, the latter with a question mark. Although de Mascarenhas also appears in de Souza, *La famille*, p. 296, she gives no information concerning his origin, which indicates that the baptismal registers 1863–1874 do not mention it either. According to Pierucci, *Histoire d'Agoué*, p. 12, he was Nagô.

132. According to the family tradition of the Bandeiras, the wife of Juba Bramfo was a cousin of Justino Bandeira and came from the same village in Mahi/Savalu as he did. This would mean that Sophia de Mello was Mahi. See Guran, *Agudás*, pp. 82–83.

133. Agonlin is a place northeast of Dahomey, south of Mahi, and was also subject to attack by Dahomey. See Albert Nouhouayi, "Zagnanado (Agonlin) et la Route de Esclaves," in *Le Bénin et La Route de l'Esclave*, ed. Elisée Soumonni et al. (Cotonou, n.d.), pp. 113–17.

134. He is possibly the same person as "João Antonio de Rego, of Whydah," a slave trader who is mentioned in the records in 1840 and who also appears in Burton's list as one of the "Africans or Brazil liberateds" that were established at Ouidah in early 1864. See PP, ST 1841, A, no. 109, case of the Brazilian schooner *Gratidão*, 13 October 1840; Burton, *A Mission*, vol. 1, p. 74 n.

135. According to de Souza, *La famille*, p. 295, Manuel José dos Reis was Nagô.

136. See FO84/1115, enclosure in Slave Trade no. 30, Consul G. Brand to Lord Russell, Lagos, 2 May 1860: Letter from the inhabitants and merchants of Agoué, Agoué, 5 March 1860: "José Maria da Santa Anna."

137. Ibid.

138. See ibid., "Felippe Santiago dos Santos."

139. Avlékété/Avrékété is a settlement on the coast about fifteen kilometers east of Ouidah.

140. De Souza, *La famille*, p. 295.

141. According to Burton, *A Mission*, vol. 1, p. 74 n., Antonio Vieira da Silva was a Portuguese who in early 1864 had establishments at Ouidah, Little Popo, and Agoué.

142. FO84/1115, enclosure in Slave Trade no. 30, Consul G. Brand to Lord Russell, Lagos, 2 May 1860, Letter from the inhabitants and merchants of Agoué, Agoué, 5 March 1860.

143. For Juba Bramfo, see also Guran, *Agudás*, pp. 82–84.

144. A "Mr. Domingo" at Agoué is mentioned in a letter in the Lawson correspondence: Jones and Sebald, eds., *An African Family Archive*, J. H. Akhurst to George Latty Lawson, Ahguay, 7 November 1848.

11
The Saga of Kakonda and Kilengues
Relations between Benguela and Its Interior, 1791–1796

Rosa Cruz e Silva

In the late eighteenth century, central Angola was essentially dominated by military actions launched from Portugal's colonial administrative center at Benguela against African polities in that region. The main objective of these actions was to capture slaves for export to Brazil. This chapter focuses on the conflicts that broke out during the period, which saw Benguela, then the second-largest colonial Portuguese slave port on the Angolan coast, experience a veritable boom in its exports of human merchandise.

The city of Benguela is old. It was founded in 1617, some four decades following the founding of its sister port, Luanda, to the north. Benguela was governed by military commanders until November 1779, when the first governor, António José Pimentel Castro e Mesquita, took office. In the meantime, this urban center became increasingly important as a source of enslaved Africans destined for Brazil. The Benguela authorities often employed methods of obtaining slaves by inciting conflicts in the interior, and Brazilian slave traders contributed as much as the Portuguese to these disputes. Most especially, conflicts between the Benguela government and the autonomous African states of Kakonda and Kilengues between 1791 and 1796 can be identified as the cause of the sudden increase in the number of exports in these years. Brazilian traders established in Benguela had a decisive impact in these conflicts and therefore also on the sociopolitical changes that took place in central Angola.

The study of trade at Benguela is, from the Angolan side, hampered by a lack of documentation.[1] The *Arquivo Histórico Nacional de Angola*, the nation's most important and central archive, holds eighty-nine manuscript volumes on the

245

colonial administration of this urban center before the early 1900s; the first dates only from 1761, when the first statistics are available on the transatlantic slave trade, as Joseph Miller has observed.[2] The Benguela archive was only organized in 1791, when the then governor implemented a secretariat.[3] However, many of the records of the secretariat were subsequently lost.[4] Given these conditions, it is unlikely that many more documents will be found for the early history of Benguela. The few documents that exist for the late eighteenth century are the subject of analysis in this study. They were written within a context of administrative autonomy. When, in 1791, the administrative center of Benguela acquired a charter that ended its subordination to Luanda, it was placed on equal footing with the colony of Angola, with communications established directly with Lisbon. The extant primary sources include the reports of the governors of Benguela and their instructions to the *presídios* (military-administrative units) in the interior that contain information on the actions of African rulers.

The political and economic context of this documentation was the slave trade and the need to satisfy the strong demand for human merchandise in Brazil especially, which wanted cheap labor to work its gold mines and plantations. Not infrequently, the Benguela authorities reported contraband trading on its shores by French, Dutch, and British ships.[5] Slaves were clearly the most important contribution to the Crown's revenues, as one governor asserts in a letter to the Portuguese court:

> The Commerce of this Country is active, there occurring in the Backlands all of its transactions at great risk due to the disloyalty and insurgency of the majority of the *Sobas* or Chiefs, sometimes instigated by the urgencies with which the Europeans, who abound in the same Backlands, challenge them; at other times due to their natural agitation whose procedures for the most part are based on the laws of nature and the law of force . . . [T]he goods exported are limited to slaves, ivory, and wax, with the first leaving substantial profits for Your Majesty due to the tariffs paid, whose collection is carried out by the three Inspection Boards of Pernambuco, Bahia, and Rio de Janeiro, where their navigation is most convenient.[6]

Once the Portuguese Crown ended its monopoly on the slave trade in 1769, private traders engaged in the traffic in human beings. The door was opened to all sorts of merchants who subsequently poured into the African markets in pursuit of the wealth that the slave trade promised. As we will see, private initiatives to promote the trade rarely followed the recommendations of the Crown.

There is no doubt as to the motivations behind the development of Lisbon's policy at Benguela, which was essentially to promote the transatlantic slave trade, which could generate revenues that no governor could disregard, in view of the lack of alternative goods. The slave trade filled the coffers of the Portuguese Crown and the pockets of governors themselves, who devised all kinds of strategies to sustain the commerce. The establishment of colonial power structures in the Benguela region was the responsibility of representatives of the Portuguese government. These individuals, belonging to the army's military structure, became governors in order to further the plan to occupy African territory, a policy that was intermittently promoted since the beginning of the seventeenth century. Men such as these included Francisco Paim de Câmara y Ornelas, whose administration lasted from 17 May 1791 to 25 May 1796 and was marked by disagreements with the local colonial magistrates, due not only to the character of each of the protagonists but also to the private interests that opposed them, as Ralph Delgado has observed.[7] The local magistrates had autonomous powers that often clashed with the equally independent powers of the governor. Thus, the motivations that overshadowed the climate in which these structures competed with one another through the performance of their duties are therefore implicit. Francisco Paim was succeeded by Alexandre José Botelho de Vasconcelos, who governed the colony from 25 May 1796 to 14 January 1800, under a similar climate.[8]

There was no effective legal means of containing this friction between the governors and the local magistrates. Moreover, *presídio* commanders were given free rein in their jurisdictions and were primarily concerned about safeguarding their own interests. As a result, they resorted to unethical practices for personal gain, often using force to achieve their objectives, which did little to benefit trade in the interior, even the capture of slaves. *Presídio* commanders sometimes tried their hand directly at the slaving business, even if they had to exceed their official functions and clash with the interests of the governor. The governors also had to contend with a corrupt judiciary, which resulted in removing judges from office and conveying them back to Portugal. These frictions within the colonial state were particularly serious during the administration of Francisco Paim, who complained of the difficulties he encountered when attempting to end the misrule of commanders who did everything they could to flout his authority.

Benguela's relations with Brazil are best understood through the royal charter of 11 January 1758, which guaranteed that slaves dispatched from the port of Benguela would be sent exclusively to Brazil, specifically Rio de Janeiro, Bahia, and Pernambuco.[9] The relative proximity of Benguela to Brazil made contact between Lisbon and Luanda less frequent. When sailing from Benguela to Lisbon, ships stopped at Pernambuco, Bahia, or Rio de Janeiro, and only afterward went to Portugal, so that the Crown received news from the Benguela government in this circuitous manner. Travel via Brazil was the fastest way to reach Lisbon. This pattern is explained by the economics of commercial navigation in the South Atlantic.[10] Such a close relationship is further demonstrated in the fact that even damaged ships registered in Benguela were taken to Brazil for repair.[11]

This dependency on Brazil dates back to the reestablishment of Portuguese control of Angola in 1648, when the military intervention of Correia de Sá from Brazil ended the period of Dutch rule. From that time, a strong Brazilian presence in the trading ports along the Angolan coast was not uncommon.[12] At Benguela, the influence of Brazil was not only a continuation of this pattern but also more intense than elsewhere. When Francisco Paim's administration asked Lisbon for permission to increase the number of soldiers in the army of his captaincy, the request was satisfied by the dispatch of troops from Pernambuco, Bahia, and Rio de Janeiro. This reliance on Brazilian soldiers also reflected the desire of Brazilian authorities to get rid of people who were considered "very dusky and rebellious" and hence presumably better suited for Benguela due to the services required there.[13] The governors also looked to Brazil for settlers to augment the population of Benguela. In 1796, Governor Alexandre Botelho de Vasconcelos asked the Crown to help restore a population severely reduced by high mortality rates. As mortality statistics for Benguela reveal, the death rate among Europeans from Portugal was particularly high, and hence the governor was willing to accept Brazilian convicts: "Therefore, I beg Your Excellency to send me eighty couples from Rio de Janeiro, where there are over seven hundred prisoners, Bahia and Pernambuco, and that they be *pardos* [brown skinned] to better survive here and increase this population so that in the course of a few years, this city will be like Brazil."[14] Such individuals included people convicted of involvement in the abortive 1789 rebellion in Minas Gerais. For example, we know that one of these, Sergeant Major Francisco António de Oliveira Lopes, was sent to Benguela, bound for Bié, in the interior. However, when he was delivered to the local colonial magistrate, he was encouraged to remain in Benguela, which concerned the governor of Angola in Luanda, although apparently without further consequences.[15]

Thus, a population was formed whose occupations supported the slave trade. The Brazilians who moved to both Benguela and Caconda were predominantly male, as well as being mulatto and black. The census material for seventeen extant years between 1798 and 1832 records an annual average of eight Brazilian civilians enumerated by colonial officials as residing in the *presídio* of Caconda. They were almost exclusively men, and almost all were either mulatto or black.[16] In the twelve years between 1798 and 1819 for which there is census data, there was an annual average of eighty Brazilian civilians, twelve females and sixty-eight males, resident in Benguela: of these, fourteen were classified as white, thirty-five as mulatto, and thirty-one as black.[17] As a result, there naturally emerged a class of merchants who would contribute to the growing trade in that area. Brazilian merchants, particularly traders from Rio de Janeiro, not only took slaves from Benguela at the height of the slave trade but also covered the gap left by Luanda when Portugal attempted to suppress the Angolan slave trade during the 1830s and 1840s. Moreover, Brazilian merchants active in Benguela further drew upon dependent compatriots to scour the backlands, where they competed with their Portuguese partners in the slave trade.

During the 1780s, with the slave export trade from Benguela expanding at an unprecedented rate, most of the Brazilian traders there operated around three or four large firms with close commercial ties to Rio de Janeiro. According to a contemporary chronicler of colonial Angola, these merchants dominated most of the commerce carried out in and from the town.[18] Among them were probably many of the known traders living in Benguela in 1791, including António Jozé da Costa, António de Souza Vale, António Jozé de Barros, António Jozé Pinto Sequeira, Antonio Felype Calderone, Fructuozo Jozé da Cruz, João Pedro Barrocas, Jozé Maria Arcenio de Lacerda, Jozé António da Costa, Ignacio Jozé de Souza, Jozé da Costa, Joaquim Mendes Bicho, Jozé Ferreira Gomes da Silva, Lourenço Pereira Tavares, Lourenço de Carvalho Gameiros, Manuel Jozé da Cruz, Nuno Joaquim Pereira e Silva, and Sebastião Gil Vaz Lobo.[19] One was surely António Jozé de Barros, still a resident there when the south side of the town was enumerated in November of 1797. White, single, and about thirty-five years of age, de Barros was one of Benguela's most affluent inhabitants. He owned fourteen male and eight female slaves, as well as an unspecified number of two-story buildings adorned with red-clay shingles, some of which were still unfinished. De Barros happened to be away in Rio de Janeiro on business in November 1797 when the census of southern Benguela was carried out.[20] Another may well have been António de Souza Vale, who seems to be the same person as Valle, who is listed in 1797 in the north side of Benguela as owning the sixth *senzala* (residential area for free, freed, and enslaved Africans) with a total of twenty round homes. Apparently, Valle at this time was deceased.[21] Exact statistics on the overall number of Brazilian traders in the Benguela hinterland are not, at the moment, available for the period being studied. Nevertheless, as the Caconda census material suggests, the total was appreciable.

Very few of the Brazilian traders residing in this central Angolan port town around 1791 were still there toward the end of 1797. One cause of the high turnover within this commercial community was certainly the disease environment in Benguela, which exacted a steep death toll among all foreigners. If they survived, the Brazilian representatives dispatched to Benguela eventually returned to Rio de Janeiro, replaced by fresh recruits. Whatever the case, few of these individuals ever became permanent residents of this urban center. We can see in this interaction between Brazil and Benguela the meshing of gears involving the migration of enslaved people from West Central Africa to Brazil and the return of *pardos* and people of other hues to Benguela to reinvigorate the slave trade. This cycle clearly involved people of very different social categories, arising from the genetic interaction between black and white progenitors, thereby representing the mixed society of Brazil. The historic process that returned people to Benguela, even if only on a semipermanent basis, effectively shaped the dynamics of colonial development. This was particularly evident during the first half of the 1790s when Rio's demand for slaves from Benguela reached its height: the unprecedented requirement for the semipermanent Brazilian residents to meet the needs of their backers spurred local Portuguese colonial authorities into similarly unparalleled military ventures in the interior to produce exportable captives.

We are therefore observing a range of factors that effectively explain how Brazil came to dominate the social and even political makeup of Benguela's slaveocratic society. Although it is sometimes maintained that slaves resulted from internal conflict, drought, and disease within the African interior, the 1791–1796 documentation on Benguela clearly shows that the Portuguese authorities consciously aggravated local conditions as a means of encouraging enslavement. In fact, this age-old method was utilized whenever the interests of the authorities or their peers in this business required it. Conflicts between Portuguese and African rulers were premeditated and designed to capture slaves. This policy of intervention in the backlands furthered the production of merchandise for the slave market and violated the terms of several agreements signed with the indigenous peoples. The overriding aim was taking slaves. The African rulers themselves resisted this aggression with any means at their disposal to defend their territories, as the actions of the *sobas* (chiefs) of Kakonda and Kilengues demonstrate.

The rise of a merchant class enabled the expansion of the slave trade at Benguela. The statistical data on the slave trade between Benguela and Brazilian ports, fulfilling the charter of 1758, which imposed a monopoly, demonstrate the rapid growth in trade.[22] While there is apparently no official information in letters to the Portuguese Crown, there is information on the movement of ships between 1762 and 1795, which was collated by Governor Alexandre José Botelho de Vasconcelos.[23] Statistical data from Portuguese and Brazilian archives on slave and ship movements at Benguela are very similar to those presented in table 1, which serves as the basis for this analysis.[24] I want to focus our attention particularly on the years from 1791 to 1796, because this period is crucial to an understanding of the entire scheme involving African rulers and their interlocutors in this process.

I will focus on the information in table 1 regarding the period 1791–1796 and use these elements to interpret the phenomenon that aggravated the conflicts between the Benguela government and the African polities. In the course of the seventeenth century, Portuguese military forces began exploring areas distant from the city of Benguela, and a *presídio* had already been built in Kakonda by 1682. The objective was to open roads in the hinterland and control the main slave routes, as the Benguela trading post was increasingly called upon to play the almost exclu-

Table 1
Slaves Exported from Benguela to Brazil, 1762–1795

Years	Ships	Slaves	Young Children	Export Tariffs (in *réis*)	State Subsidies (in *réis*)
1762	11	3,924	19	34,221$450	1,180$050
1763	10	3,423	5	29,801$850	1,027$650
1764	11	3,821	8	33,377$500	1,147$500
1765	18	6,081	22	53,000$400	1,827$600
1766	14	5,084	11	44,278$650	1,526$850
1767	18	6,583	12	37,324$300	1,976$700
1768	16	5,643	15	49,159$350	1,695$150
1769	15	5,531	15	48,184$950	1,661$510
1770	12	4,726	7	41,146$650	1,418$250
1771	13	5,276	17	45,975$150	1,585$250
1772	14	5,009	12	43,630$500	1,504$500
1773	12	5,363	4	46,675$500	1,509$500
1774	12	4,327	1	37,649$250	1,298$250
1775	16	5,726	11	49,864$050	1,719$450
1776	15	5,967	11	51,960$750	1,791$750
1777	11	3,959	4	34,460$700	1,188$300
1778	13	5,499	6	47,867$400	1,650$600
1779	17	7,065	7	61,495$950	2,120$550
1780	15	6,442	13	56,101$950	1,934$550
1781	14	6,477	11	56,397$750	1,944$750
1782	15	6,420	17	55,927$950	1,928$550
1783	13	6,286	16	54,757$800	1,888$200
1784	20	7,158	42	68,372$300	2,288$700
1785	14	6,161	30	53,731$200	1,852$800
1786	12	5,485	15	7,797$800	1,648$200
1787	16	7,012	14	61,065$300	2,105$700
1788	13	6,126	5	53,317$950	1,838$550
1789	13	6,032	8	52,513$200	1,810$800
1790	12	6,135	15	53,439$750	1,842$750
1791	13	6,329	10	55,105$800	1,900$200
1792	21	8,950	5	77,538$750	2,673$750
1793	24	11,172	8	97,231$200	3,352$800
1794	22	9,481	12	82,536$900	2,846$100
1795	23	10,170	17	88,550$950	3,063$550
Total	599	209,253	428	1,822,362$900	62,840$100

Source: "Mappa dos Escravos Exportados desta Capitania de Beng[uela] Para o Brazil," by Benguela Governor Alexandre José Botelho de Vasconcelos, [July 27,] 1796, Arquivo Histórico Nacional de Angola, Codex 441 (E-1-2), fl. 19v. Note that while exports tariffs amounted to 8$700 réis and state subsidies to $300 *réis* per slave, the rates for children were halved.

sive role of obtaining slaves, responding in any way it could to the demands of the slave trade with the ports of Rio de Janeiro, Bahia, and Pernambuco.

The 1791–1796 period coincides with the administration of Francisco Paim de Câmara e Ornelas, whose government was subjected to a detailed investigation due to a variety of charges regarding his activities. According to these charges, the African rulers of Kakonda and Kilengues were the victims of his tyranny and extortion. He was accused of failing to observe the rules of conduct regarding relations with African rulers, who were constantly under pressure from traders and the captaincy's own troops. However, the main reason underlying the dispute was the capture of slaves, and the retaliation of the African rulers against alleged abuses served to justify further intervention in a way that effectively promoted the slave trade.

Let us pause to reflect on the information at hand. How can we assess the motives and discourse of the African rulers in the interior who were clearly attempting to preserve their dominions? Martin Leinhard has attempted to decode the indirect messages in the governors' reports of the seventeenth and eighteenth centuries that record the voices of Africans who were engaged in direct confrontation with the Portuguese.[25] This methodology is extremely important because it helps us find a way to hear the leading figures in this process. Indeed, we can hear the messages of the African rulers in the interior, sent in response to the pressures to which their territories and societies were being subjected, by examining the texts produced by the governor, in which the African discourse is present, albeit indirectly.[26]

A case in point is the investigation of irregularities committed by Francisco Paim de Câmara e Ornelas, whose administration was marked by a climate of instability. The trading practices being employed violated the law, which was little respected by the interior traders and much less by the military commanders themselves. Even Governor Francisco Paim announced that he was proceeding in an extraordinary fashion because he could not control the situation, particularly the inland traders, and that "due to their indolence they would be able to lend strength to a Rebellion, and I govern them as I deem appropriate and in effect obtain [success] through this sole means after attempt[ing other measures]. It is useless to [practice] the counseled moderation, containing them within their boundaries and transforming them from Chieftains into Subordinates."[27] Although official policy, supported by law, advised accommodation with African political authorities, moderation did not prevail, and the real objective was to annihilate the authority of the African rulers. It was recognized that under no circumstances would these African leaders openly be willing to abdicate and hence the *presídio* commanders constantly accused them of being disloyal and rebellious.

If the Africans' subjugation was viewed as certain, given the military actions that caused extensive destruction by laying waste to African settlements, we can also see that, in practice, their submission was often problematic. Efforts to maintain the autonomy of indigenous rule continued, although often in subtle ways and only sometimes through rebellion. Governor Francisco Paim listed the *sobas* Peringue, Mulundo, and Quizamba as his "vassals," but they successfully resisted every attempt to occupy their dominions and even prevented *presídio* commanders and backlanders from capturing slaves through the coercive measures that they often imposed. The same could be said of eight vassals listed later by Alexandre José Botelho de Vasconcelos in a report sent to Lisbon. The list included those mentioned by Francisco Paim in 1791, and another five who it was claimed were predisposed to accepting Portuguese rule. They were the *sobas* Peringue, Mulundo, Quizamba, Quiera, Capembe, Mama, Calunga, and Catumbela. Nonetheless, on 17 July 1796 Botelho de Vasconcelos informed the Crown of a rebellion: "And they, in addition to immense hostilities and pillage practiced against the Backlanders who traverse these Backlands with the Goods of the Merchants in this Marketplace to capture slaves, which has wrought irreparable harm, for want of troops capable of withstanding such insults have increased their boldness to such an extent that a short time ago they ravaged and destroyed, robbed and killed many residents in the area and jurisdiction of Caconda."[28] The pattern was typical of the Portuguese move into the interior. As pointed out by Beatrix Heintze, "In all the relations of dependency created by the Portuguese, they were not merely peaceful merchants, but conquerors and occupiers of lands that were inhabited and organized as states, where they rejected friendly alliances and insisted on creating fortified outposts to control territory and trade routes."[29] Therefore, there were two kinds of vassals: voluntary and conquered.

This example demonstrates the lengths to which African rulers could go when the boundaries of their states were threatened. The sources consulted for this study lead us to believe that the "vassal" African rulers took a different view of the dependency required of them by the Benguela government. The clearest example of this situation is the position taken by the *sobas* of Kakonda and Kilengues, whose realms suffered from constant slave raids through military means. They resisted Portugal's weaponry as much as they could, while at the same time using arguments based upon the treaties that had been signed. However, due to the systematic violations of those treaties during the administrations of Francisco Paim and Alexandre Botelho de Vasconcelos, the *sobas* demanded restitution from the governor in ways that were not included in those agreements. Because of their petitions to the Portuguese authorities in Benguela, the governor had no alternative but to impose severe punishments on the main instigators of the conflicts underway at the time. As a result, Francisco Paim was subjected to rigorous investigation and stripped of his office before being sent to Limoeiro Prison in Lisbon. The same fate befell the commander of Kilengues *presídio*. Despite several warnings from Governor Alexandre Botelho de Vasconcelos, who instructed him how to proceed, not only to collect tithes but also to conduct slaving expeditions, he failed to maintain the climate of peace and tranquility that was so useful to the development of trade in the backlands, and consequently he, too, was removed from his post and imprisoned. The extent of the havoc is indirectly acknowledged in a report by the governor on the displacement of one *soba*:

> Before me and other many Persons who were present, it was expected that the said Souva and his children should ask my Permission to retire to their lands, as was natural; they Requested the opposite, that other lands be assigned to them where they might establish themselves and reside, presenting to me the reasons they had for not returning to their state, and lands, all of which based on vivid complaints of weighty events and violence which [they] say have been practiced upon them, and which by their quality and their Having a manifest Relationship with the Peace and public tranquility of this Captaincy seem to me so grave and pressing that I judged it to be my indefectible obligation and in the service of His Majesty to justify them, competently, to place them in the Presence of His Illustrious Excellency the General of State [of Angola] so that the measures that he [deems] just may be taken.[30]

This request makes it clear that African rulers did not want to live in areas where the colonial power structures were present. Recognizing the occupation of their former dominions, they proposed to establish themselves elsewhere. Subjugation is not implicit in a demand of this kind. The *sobas* wanted to tell the Portuguese authorities that foreigners could not govern their territory, but they were faced with a dilemma. By refusing to return to their dominions due to the arbitrary acts and destruction practiced there, they demanded a new place to establish their settlements, implicitly beyond Portuguese control, although it is not clear how such land was to be acquired.

The Portuguese intended to capitalize on previous experiences that used extreme force to ensure the flow of trade. The main issue at hand was always the interests of the Crown, whose revenues from taxes and tariffs charged for slaves and other goods traded in the backlands could not be neglected. Thanks to their defensive strategies, African reaction made it difficult for Portugal to use force to expand any business that was not in the interest of indigenous societies. Their hostility was harmful to government revenues and equally deleterious for the backlanders, who lost all the cloth, liquor, and other goods that were taken into the hinterland for barter. What actually happened was that the barter merchandise became scarce—there was not enough liquor or cloth—because the backlanders, who had other means of persuasion (such as guns), used these goods for their own benefit. The governor overlooked this, although it was his job to keep some kind of order in this process. Governor Francisco Paim may have been powerless to exercise his functions, but his inaction may also have resulted from personal interest. During the criminal suit against him, in light of the charge that he was directly involved in the exploitation and extortion of African rulers, the investigation found that he had received large amounts of money that were occasionally sent to Brazil.[31]

In the face of countless difficulties, Portugal's military might gradually took over the African dominions that lay beyond the city built on the coast. Working on a war footing, the Portuguese troops suffered setbacks because they lacked enough men to carry out the major military actions undertaken. In their letters to the Crown, the governors persistently begged for enough troops to ensure Portuguese control over the conquered areas and to attempt to expand them. However, these requests were made only as a matter of routine because, in practice, the *presídio* commanders routinely implemented their personal policies in the hinterland, taking the lead in actions that went completely against the mission of the authorities in the city of Benguela. The growing demand for slaves in Brazilian cities and rural areas was so intense that the process of obtaining captives was not limited to the existing trade. Different mechanisms were sought to obtain the slave export numbers found in the records generated by the Benguela authorities. For this purpose, slave raids were usually staged to satisfy the leading traders, who included the governors themselves.

The number of conflicts between African and Portuguese authorities and their consequences for the African rulers can be seen through the volume of the Benguela slave trade as evidenced in table 1. The occupation of territory meant enslavement, the capture of large numbers of slaves as reflected in the data collected by Governor Alexandre Botelho on slave ship movements between Benguela and Brazil. The establishment of Portuguese administrative structures could ensure sway over African dominions. But this did not materialize without retaliation from African rulers, inciting them to acts of war, whether in self-defense or in taking the initiative in military operations to attack their interlocutors' positions in an attempt to recover lost ground and restore their own authority, which gradually disintegrated in direct relation to the extent of their involvement in the slave trade.

The administration of Francisco Paim was marked by a constant wave of unrest in Kakonda and Kilengues. From the beginning of his governorship until he was forced to resign, there are reports of major uprisings by the African rulers. This reaction had political implications of such magnitude that they led to the governor's imprisonment and the confiscation of his property. Descriptions, such as those referred to earlier, of the permanent state of revolt in the hinterland at that time can be placed alongside the data on the movement of slave ships bound for Brazil. This turmoil accounts for much of the data shown in table 1 for the period covered by this study. The numbers rose steeply in the early 1790s when compared to previous years.

In 1791 a number of military actions were undertaken with a view to overthrowing the African rulers and consequently intensifying the process of seizing the number of slaves needed for shipment to Brazil. Similar large-scale military actions persisted for a number of years until the *presídio* commander and later the governor himself were removed from office and imprisoned. It seems clear that two factors were interrelated: on the one hand, the growing number of slaves shipped to Brazil; and on the other, the intensification of the conflicts and wars reported by the Benguela authorities. This aggression led to the destruction of the states of *sobas* Cacombo and Socoval in Kakonda and in Kilengues and made possible the capture of large numbers of slaves, whose numbers are reflected in table 1 in the years from 1792 to 1795. For the year 1791, thirteen ships are reported to have carried 6,329 slaves, a number that is more or less similar to previous years. However, in 1795, over twenty ships carried more than 10,000 slaves. The numbers fell in 1796, which is accounted for by the insecurity that still reigned that year throughout the backlands. Yet, slave trafficking did not come to an end. Between 1 January and 27 July 1796, twelve ships docked at Benguela and transported some 4,981 slaves to a number of unspecified ports in Brazil.[32]

Although the figures for the trade show an increasingly substantial flow of people in the early 1790s, Francisco Paim was thought to have endangered trade in the Benguela backlands. He was supposed to have carried out Lisbon's orders to maintain tax revenues generated by exports of slaves and other goods through moderation in his treatment of African rulers. But he was unable or unwilling to avoid the use of force. Francisco Paim actually projected to expand Portuguese territories south of the Kwanza River, which meant extending the colony's dominions beyond previously recognized boundaries. The military intervention required to gain control over and consolidate these new boundaries was to have been carried out by expeditionary forces from Huambo, Quilengues, and Bailundo provinces. The use of outside military forces clearly shows that territorial expansion was incompatible with the rights of the local indigenous peoples. Military action led to the disintegration of African political, social, and other structures in direct proportion to the colonial government's ability to reinforce its military personnel and apparatus. As we have seen, the impact of Brazil upon this part of Angola is to be explained by the kind of trade that Portugal managed to maintain there during the period in question. The economy of Benguela and its hinterland developed almost exclusively to provide enslaved people for Brazil.

NOTES

1. For reconstructions of this history based upon multiple primary sources, including archives in Angola, Brazil, and Portugal, see Joseph C. Miller, "Angola central e sul por

Cruz e Silva: The Saga of Kakonda and Kilengues 257

volta de 1840," *Estudos Afro-Asiáticos* 32 (1997): 7–34; and José C. Curto, "Luso-Brazilian Alcohol and the Legal Slave Trade at Benguela and its Hinterland, c. 1617–1830," in *Négoce Blanc en Afrique Noire: L'évolution du commerce à longue distance en Afrique noire du 18e au 20e siècles*, ed. Hubert Bonin and Michel Cahen (Paris: Publications de la Société française d'histoire d'outre-mer, 2001), pp. 351–69.

2. Joseph C. Miller, "A Economia Política do Tráfico Angolano de Escravos no Século XVIII," in *Angola e o Brasil nas Rotas do Atlântico Sul*, ed. Selma Pantoja and José Flávio Sombra Saraiva (Rio de Janeiro: Betrand Brasil, 1999), pp. 50–51.

3. Ralph Delgado, *A Famosa e Histórica Benguela: Catálago dos governadores (1779–1940)* (Lisbon: Edição do Govêrno da Província, 1940), p. 9; and Miller, "Economia Política do Tráfico Angolano," p. 51.

4. António da Silva Rego, "Introdução," in *Roteiro Topográfico dos Códices (do Arquivo Histórico de Angola)* (Luanda: Imprensa Nacional de Angola, 1966), p. 6, reports the disappearance of six hundred manuscript volumes from the Arquivo do Fundo do Governo de Benguela, whose archives date from 1791. The *Arquivo Histórico de Angola* was the predecessor of the *Arquivo Histórico Nacional de Angola*, hereinafter AHNA.

5. Letter from the governor of Benguela to the Kingdom of Portugal, 2 June 1791, AHNA, Codex 440 (E-1-1), fl. 11.

6. Letter from the governor of Benguela to the Kingdom of Portugal, 14 July 1791, AHNA, Codex 440 (E-1-1), fls. 1–2.

7. Delgado, *A Famosa e Histórica Benguela*, p. 21.

8. See the many documents from the Alexandre José administration published in *Fontes and Estudos* (Luanda) 2 (1995) and 3 (1996).

9. AHNA, Codex 440 (E-1-1), fl. 18. In this 15 March 1794 letter to the kingdom of Portugal, Governor Francisco Paim informed that he had followed orders when Sebastião Gil Vaz Lobo, representative of the Lisbon merchant Jozé Antonio Pereira, asked him to dispatch merchandise to Santos: "I [am writing to] inform Your Excellency that His Majesty's edict of January 11, 1758, prohibits dispatching slave ships from here to any other ports than Rio de Janeiro, Bahia, [or] Pernambuco." The merchandise was nevertheless shipped to Santos, violating the edict and disregarding the governor's orders. The governor had almost no authority over his subordinates.

10. See Joseph C. Miller, *Way of Death: Merchant Capitalism and the Angolan Slave Trade, 1730–1830* (Madison: University of Wisconsin Press, 1988), pp. 318–24. José C. Curto, "Vinho verso Cachaça: A luta luso-brasileira pelo Comércio do Álcool e de Escravos em Luanda, c. 1648–1703," in *Angola e Brasil nas Rotas do Atlântico Sul*, ed. Pantoja and Saraiva, pp. 72–73, lists the Benguela-Luanda sailing route to Recife, Salvador, and Rio de Janeiro as requiring thirty-five, forty, and fifty days, respectively. Between the late 1700s and the early 1800s, the average time to reach Rio de Janeiro from Benguela-Luanda decreased by 15 percent: see the chapter in this collection by Manolo G. Florentino.

11. ". . . [t]he ship Belém arrived from India in this port [Benguela] with a damaged hull and sailed for Bahia for repairs, and I am informed that it will put into at Angola [Luanda]." Letter from Francisco Paim to Martinho de Mello e Castro, 27 September 1793, AHNA, Codex 440 (E-1-1), fl. 17.

12. Among the many recent studies that have pointed this out, see the chapter in this

collection by Alberto da Costa e Silva; Luiz-Felipe de Alencastro, *O Trato dos Viventes: Formação do Brasil no Atlântico Sul* (São Paulo: Companhia das Letras, 2000); and Manolo G. Florentino, *Em Costas Negras: Uma História do Tráfico Atlântico de Escravos entre a Africa e o Rio de Janeiro (Séculos XVIII e XIX)*, 2d ed. (São Paulo: Companhia das Letras, 2002 [1997]).

13. See Letter from Francisco Paim to Martinho de Mello e Castro, 21 June 1791, AHNA, Codex 440 (E-1-1) fl. 9.

14. Letter from Alexandre José Botelho de Vasconcelos, 27 July 1796, to Luiz Pinto de Souza, Minister for Foreign Affairs and Secretary of State for War and Overseas Colonies, AHNA, Codex 441 (E-1-2), fl. 2.

15. Delgado, *A Famosa e Histórica Benguela*, p. 21; and Carlos Pacheco, *José da Silva Maia Ferreira: O Homen e a sua Época* (Luanda: União dos Escritores Angolanos, 1990), pp. 103–104.

16. My thanks to Mariana P. Candido for sharing this information from her doctoral research. On the extant Angola census materials, see José C. Curto, "Sources for the Pre-1900 Population History of Sub-Saharan Africa: The Case of Angola, 1773–1845," *Annales de démographie historique* (1994): 319–38.

17. See José C. Curto, "Americanos em Angola: A Comunidade Comercial Brasileira em Benguela, 1791–1822." Unpublished paper presented at the Instituto de Filosofia e Ciencias Sociais, Universidade Federal do Rio de Janeiro, 31 July 2002.

18. Elias Alexandre da Silva Correia, *História de Angola* (Lisbon: Editorial Ática, 1937) (Introduction and notes by Dr. Manuel Murias), vol. 1, p. 39 and vol. 2, p. 158.

19. "Negociantes de Benguela 22-06-1791," Arquivo Histórico Ultramarino (Lisbon), Angola, Caixa 76, Documento 45. My thanks to José C. Curto for providing this source.

20. "Relação de Manuel José de Silveira Teixeira sobre [metade d]os moradores da [parte sul da] cidade de São Felipe de Benguela," Arquivo do Instituto Histórico e Geográfico Brasileiro (Rio de Janeiro), DL32,02.02, fl. 7.

21. "Relação de José Caetano Carneiro, primeiro tenente, da metade dos moradores da parte do norte da cidade de São Felipe de Benguela," Arquivo do Instituto Histórico e Geográfico Brasileiro, DL32,02.03, fl. 28v.

22. See table 1. The data presented therein has already been studied under a different context: see Rosa Cruz e Silva, "Benguela e o Brasil no final do Século XVIII: Relações Comerciais e Políticas," in *Angola e o Brasil nas Rotas do Atlântico Sul*, ed. Pantoja and Saraiva, pp. 127–42.

23. Ibid. When this governor took office on 25 May 1796 he did not receive any records regarding the administration of the captaincy and city of Benguela from his predecessor, Francisco Paim. During the criminal proceedings against Francisco Paim, his property was confiscated, among which were a number of documents that came to form the basis of the archives. Letter from Botelho de Vasconcelos, 28 May 1796, to the colonial magistrate of that captaincy, in AHNA, Codex 443 (E-1-4), fls. 1v-2, and published in *Fontes e Estudos* 2 (1995): 16–17. I believe that this archive provided the information used to reconstruct the statistics on the slave trade, which predates the administrations of Francisco Paim and Alexandre Botelho de Vasconcelos. Apparently, data for previous administrations was available which has since been lost.

24. José C. Curto, "The Legal Portuguese Slave Trade from Benguela, Angola, 1730–1828: A Quantitative Re-appraisal," *África: Revista do Centro de Estudos Africanos, USP* (Universidade de São Paulo) 16–17, no.1 (1993/1994): 101–16.

25. See Martin Lienhard, "O Diálogo Luso-Africano na documentação portuguesa colonial (Congo-Angola: Séculos XVI-XVII)," *Congresso Internazionale, Il Portogallo e i Mari: Un incontro tra Culture* (Naples, 15–17 December 1944), pp. 51–65; and Martin Lienhard, *O Mare e o Mato: Histórias da Escravidão (Congo-Angola, Brasil, Caribe)* (Bahia: EDUFBA, 1998).

26. Even better results could have been obtained through this approach had we had access to other documents from Governor Francisco Paim, including information sent by the *presídio* commanders, who were most directly in contact with the African rulers involved in this dispute. For example, the letter of 28 May 1796, by Alexandre José Botelho de Vasconcelos, Governor of Benguela, AHNA, Codex 443 (E-1-4), fl. 1v, and published in *Fontes & Estudos* 2 (1995): 16, lists a series of documents found in the possession of the then deposed governor Francisco Paim, including "a packet of 84 Letters from His Excellency the General of the State, with several Lists and other Related Documents and 5 separate Lists[, as well as] Sixty-four Letters to the Commanders and other subjects." This packet of documents probably disappeared together with the six hundred volumes mentioned by Silva Rego in his introduction to the *Roteiro Topográfico dos Códices*.

27. Letter of Francisco Paim to Martinho de Mello e Castro, 21 June 1791, AHNA, Codex 440 (E-1-1), fl. 6.

28. AHNA, Codex 441 (E-1-2), fl. 3.

29. Beatrix Heintze, "Der portugiesisch-afrikanische Vassallenvertrag in Angola im 17 Jahrhundert," *Paideuma* 25 (1979): 195–223.

30. Letter of Alexandre José Botelho de Vasconcelos to Captain Major of Quilengues, 22 September 1796, AHNA, Codex 443 (E-1-4), fls. 7-8; see also *Fontes e Estudos* 2 (1995): 35–36.

31. As a result of the criminal investigation of his predecessor's dealings, Alexandre Botelho reported on 12 August 1796 to the Overseas Council that "it was discovered that in Rio de Janeiro and Bahia there existed in several hands various sums of money and pieces of gold of which I immediately wrote to His Excellency the Viceroy of that State." Brazil also appears in the sources as the destination of misappropriated property: see AHNA, Codex 441 (E-1-2) fl. 21.

32. Letter from Alexandre José Botelho de Vanconcelos to Marquez Mordomo Mor, 27 July 1796, AHNA, Codex 441 (E-1-2), fl. 15.

Kongo Kingdom and Coast, ca. 1870

12
Brazil and the Commercialization of Kongo, 1840–1870

Susan J. Herlin

Although several studies have focused on the era of illegal slave trading on the Angolan coast and the contemporary European competition for control of it, few have considered that the Kingdom of Kongo, whose territory was central to events, had any significant role to play in them.[1] At the same time, the crucial Brazilian role in organizing, financing, and carrying out the illegal slave trade from the coast north of Luanda has, until recently, been eclipsed by historians' focus on the struggle between Britain and Portugal for control of the lands bordering the lower Congo River.[2] From the perspective of African history both the underestimation of Brazil and the ignorance of Kongo create significant distortions ranging from trivialization of the complex coastal trading system to furthering the myth of the kingdom's early demise.

Despite its official inclusion in the Angolan Distrito do Congo in 1885, the Kongo kingdom did not come fully under Portuguese colonial control until the early twentieth century. However, its economy was already becoming "proto-colonial"[3] by the end of the transatlantic slave trade around 1870, a process that weakened the power of the monarchy. From 1840 the multiplication of illegal slave export sites and the growth of legal commodity trade greatly expanded opportunities for fortunately located chiefs to acquire the followers and prestige goods necessary to participate in the kingdom's noble oligarchy, whose ritual center was the capital, São Salvador (Mbanza Kongo).[4] In a classic inflation of honors, membership in once-exclusive associations, such as the Kongo Order of Christ, expanded dramatically as more people engaged in trade, agriculture, and even wage labor acquired the foreign goods necessary to invest in the traditional accoutrements of nobility.

261

Changes in Kongo were driven by changes in the international trade in slaves and related commodities, especially after 1808, the year that saw the British-aided relocation of the Portuguese court and its merchant allies to Rio de Janeiro. Backed by British capital, they soon dominated the still-legal slave trade to Angola.[5] This turn of events pushed native Brazilian merchants out of Luanda to the independent African ports north of the Congo mouth,[6] where they reorganized the slave-trading system they dominated until its end. In the process the eighteenth-century system, based on the ports of Loango and Luanda, faltered and then was transformed with the emergence of new centers at Cabinda and Ambriz.[7] After 1830, and especially in the 1840s, British-instigated antislavery efforts prompted slave traders to multiply satellite embarkation points for smuggling captive labor to the plantations of Brazil and Cuba.

Strong demand for slave labor and weak enforcement of anti–slave trading laws in Brazil were the key factors in the continued strength of Kongo slave exports from 1830 to 1850. Even after that Brazilians continued to supply Cuba and São Tomé. Luso-Brazilian capital, shipping, and business networks linked not only slave traders but also dealers in manufactured goods and produce across the Atlantic basin, from Luanda to Lisbon and Ambriz to Rio de Janeiro, creating an Atlantic system shaped as well by the tightening noose of British-led anti–slave trade enforcement.[8] The necessity of avoiding naval cruisers led slavers to create interlocking systems of factories, barracoons, financiers, brokers, suppliers, and shippers along the Kongo coast outside Luanda, from which was woven a seamless web of legal and illegal trading operations.[9] The Brazilian system established after 1808 still shaped coastal commerce after 1855, as Africans turned to the sale of commodities to British, Dutch, French, American, and Portuguese traders rather than Brazilians. For the kingdom, too, midcentury transformations were to no small degree the legacy of its successful partnership with Brazil during the fateful last decades of the enslaving connection[10] between them.

THE KONGO COAST IN THE ERA OF ILLEGAL SLAVE TRADE

The nineteenth-century system of illegal slave trading on the Kongo coast grew out of legal operations managed until the end of the eighteenth century by coastal broker states, Loango to the north and Angola to the south.[11] Both sought to attract business from Kongo, which controlled important inland routes but had only secondary seaports, at Mboma and Ambriz. Luanda and Benguela, as Portuguese colonial ports, were officially closed to all but Portuguese shipping. Loango and its neighbors showed little interest in Portuguese trade,[12] but preferred to deal with French and British merchants who offered better goods at better prices.[13] Unable to compete commercially in the north, the Portuguese periodically asserted claims to sovereignty there through diplomatic channels or by military means.

During the last era of the transatlantic slave trade (1801–1867), the West Central African region supplied almost half of all captives to the Americas, principally Brazil and Cuba, amounting to more than a million and a half people over sixty-seven years, with almost all of the slaves leaving by 1851.[14] Throughout the period the same range of legal goods, textiles, spirits, firearms, and powder was imported into Africa to be exchanged for slaves.

Trading on the Kongo coast went through distinct phases in the nineteenth century—the first two intimately connected to Brazil and the third deeply influenced by her. The first phase began in the 1790s with the series of wars accompanying the French Revolution and Napoleonic era and a disastrous drought in West Central Africa.[15] British slavers profited immediately from the disappearance of French slavers from the South Atlantic, but after British abolition in 1807, merchants from Brazil, along with some from Spanish America, replaced them on the Kongo coast. At the same time the relocation of the Portuguese court and allied merchant elites to Rio in 1808 enabled the latter to dominate the Angolan trade until the end of legal slaving to Brazil in 1830. The second phase marks the heart of the illegal slave trade and was decisively shaped by the dramatic intensification of antislavery activities after 1839. The third phase, during which slave exports gave way to commodities, was well underway by the 1850s. It marked the onset of modern colonial commercial relations in Kongo and grew directly out of the last years of the illegal slave trade.

In 1810 Brazilian merchants, pushed from favored positions in Luanda and pulled toward independent African ports to its north,[16] used their expertise[17] and existing connections in both areas to establish a new network of relations between Luanda and its northern neighbors capable of developing the illegal trade. Unburdened by ties to the old official brokers in the north, they negotiated new deals at old ports and helped to promote previously secondary ones to positions of leadership.[18] They offered coveted British goods to their African customers, as well as popular domestic *gerebitas* (sugar cane brandies) and tobacco. Brazilians used their existing Cabinda connections to develop new business relationships on the north coast, which in turn helped Cabindan merchant princes, led by Domingos José Franque, establish themselves as partners in the new system.[19] Luanda continued to play a central role in the organization of the illegal trade. However, its port became secondary while two Kongo ports, Mboma on the Congo River and Ambriz on the Atlantic coast not far north of Luanda, moved into primary positions along with Cabinda.

These early-nineteenth-century Brazilian initiatives to some extent continued and built on earlier British and French ones, particularly in relation to

Ambriz, which had been developed to avoid the periodic delays and high prices on the Loango coast.[20] Brazilians responded to Anglo-Portuguese dominance of the main Rio-Luanda trade by strengthening ties to the Afro-Portuguese commercial community in Angola. This, too, benefited Ambriz, particularly after 1813, when the less-well-capitalized Brazilians and their Afro-Portuguese allies moved there to avoid new regulations introduced that year.[21] The resulting rerouting of substantial supplies of captives away from Luanda had implications not only for it and for Ambriz, but also for the southern Kongo–northern Angola borderlands of Mossul, Encoge, and Ndembu.[22]

Attracting and controlling business from interior African markets to Luanda was a perennial concern for the Portuguese and their British-backed Rio business associates. The regions of prime concern were the borderlands in and around the Portuguese fort at Encoge and the adjacent territory known in Angola as "Dembos" (Ndembu), through which most of the nineteenth-century trade of Ambriz came. Not surprisingly, the leading Ndembu chiefs maintained ties not only with Portugal and Kongo, but with Mossul, Ambriz, and independent Afro-Portuguese merchants as well.[23] To address problems of "contraband," Portugal had established an Angolan *presídio* (military-administrative unit) at Encoge in 1759 and created the Distrito dos Dembos in 1810.[24]

The lords of the Kongo coast managed nineteenth-century commercial growth by adapting the established Loango coast administrative model based on the institution of the *mafouk*.[25] As was the case in Loango, *mafouks* represented an owning authority (chief or king) as minister of commerce. They negotiated terms of trade, including export duties and rents due the king, and facilitated business by providing brokerage services and keeping order, both at the port and on the roads leading to it. They also could accumulate personal wealth in the form of imported goods and the slaves and the allies these could provide.

While Brazilians successfully reorganized the slave trade, the British, through a series of treaties and unilateral actions, progressively restricted the legal trade in slaves. They made abolition the price of their recognition of Brazilian independence from Portugal.[26] They pressured both Brazil and Portugal for stricter laws and enforcement of them. Finally, an 1839 act of Parliament declared that Portuguese slavers could be seized and tried as pirates in British Admiralty courts.[27] In the 1840s British cruisers were joined by those of the United States, France, and Portugal—all interested in protecting their own national interests against the aggressive search-and-seizure tactics of the British. The British navy also took enforcement to the coast, burning suspected slave factories as well as trying to obtain anti–slave trade agreements with African authorities.[28] The Portuguese, under British pressure, began seizing and prosecuting Brazilian slavers.[29] Despite all this, levels of slave imports into Brazil in the 1840s reached nineteenth-century highs, with most coming through independent

African rather than Angolan ports.[30] It was only after Brazil, in 1850, and the United States, in 1862, took effective measures to end their own citizens' participation that the export of slaves from the Kongo coast ended.

The system that supplied the illegal exports of captives from the Kongo coast in the second phase linked capitalists in Rio, Luanda, Lisbon, London, Havana, New York, and even Cabinda[31] in a tightly knit international community of slave merchants and their allies. Brazilians, many with bases in Luanda, continued to be central to the system.[32] Legal commodity trading and illegal slave trading grew more and more closely together, as when cloth and rum legally sold at Luanda were used to buy slaves in the Angolan interior that were then housed as "domestic slaves" in Luanda until they could be shipped clandestinely from beaches and ports outside the city.[33] Provisions for the slaves' upkeep, whether in the warehouses of Luanda or, after 1845, in one of the barracoons built a few miles inland all along the Kongo coast, were often imported into Luanda and distributed by small, coasting vessels, the same ones that also transported slaves between sites. Barracoons, coasting vessels, slave ships, textiles, rum, and provisions were all interlocking investments of large firms often based in Luanda or Rio.[34] As early as the 1830s Brazilians also developed relations with other American merchants on the coast, including those dealing in legal African commodities at Ambriz and Luanda.[35] Although Luanda continued to be important to this Atlantic-wide system, government revenues suffered as fewer taxable slaves passed through the city, and even legal imports used in the traffic avoided customs houses much of the time.[36] This, in turn, spurred the Portuguese authorities to talk seriously about alternative economic strategies for Angola.

Some Brazilian traders made the transition from the legal to illegal trade, some cashed out in 1830, and still others entered the business after it was illegal. One of the most notorious of the latter was Manuel Pinto da Fonseca, who began trading in 1837–1838 with his brothers.[37] He was very active in Cabinda[38] and pioneered the slavers' switch to the United States flag after the British effectively closed out Portugal's as a safe cover in the 1840s. Another important figure, Francisco Antonio Flores, got his start as the Luanda agent for the Rio firm of Amaral & Bastos in 1840. Before long he emerged as a major investor himself, in both licit and illicit commerce.[39] These men, like other important slavers of the era, became leading merchants in Luanda, whence they directed operations along the African coast and across the Atlantic.[40]

Illegal traders introduced various innovations on the coast in their constant quest to avoid detection. For example, they built and staffed more permanent onshore factories,[41] allowing resident factors to more easily buy and stockpile provisions, store trade goods, house slaves awaiting departure, and develop branches at smaller ports nearby as necessary. The most significant of the new embarkation points developed at this time were those at Banana and Punta da Lenha on the

Congo River and at Ambrizette on the Kongo coast. Factories at the ports ostensibly dealt only in legal goods, while slaves were kept hidden in barracoons located out of sight of cruisers. These inland facilities relied on local people for provisions, for workers and for the cooperation necessary both to prevent slave escapes and to move the captives quickly when the coast was clear. Among other things, this meant more foreign personnel on the Kongo coast, more jobs for Kongolese, and consequently, more foreign goods in circulation to a wider range of people.[42]

As satellite embarkation points developed along the Kongo coast, the *mafouk* system, which allowed minor chiefs direct access to foreigners, expanded. Though Kongo lords of some of these new coastal centers participated in the kingdom, this seems to have become less necessary as more of the new commercial elite found their patrons among foreign merchants, on the model of the earlier north coast broker states. The *mafouk* system was central to the organization of the new commercial towns. Not only did each chief have his own minister of trade, but each factory had its own *mafouk* or *linguister* (translator) as well. Competition escalated as each sought to attract business from the interior.[43]

Illegal slave trading was a risky business, and not just financially. Slavers moving out of major ports like Luanda faced multiple threats of violence, whether from naval cruisers, commercial rivals, or their African hosts/partners. An important source of trouble stemmed from Euro-American traders' failure to observe rules imposed by African landlords, for which they could be subjected to very severe penalties. Reported incidents of "mob" violence in the context of conflict with locals almost certainly coincide with enforcement of such penalties. Slave traffickers were very vulnerable, as they were reluctant to call attention to themselves by seeking help from naval authorities, even when they had bribed antislavery personnel.[44]

After 1850, with the precipitous decline of the slave trade to Brazil, the commercial system of the coast once again adapted. By 1870 the hidden slave barracoons had given way to new coastal trading settlements at virtually every reasonable anchorage along the Atlantic coast of Kongo.[45] The foreign businessmen of the 1860s were more often British, American, Dutch, or French than Brazilian, but they relied on the system bequeathed to them by the illegal slave traders to buy the groundnuts, palm oil, urzella, gum copal, ivory, and other products brought to the coast by Kongo sellers. More ordinary Kongolese produced or collected goods for sale to European factories through the agency of a growing corps of Kongo brokers.[46] Jobs for porters increased as local entrepreneurs began to organize short-range caravans. Groundnut production expanded. As a result, more people could purchase foreign goods, and as prices plummeted, slaves continued to arrive from the far interior, especially in connection with Zombo ivory caravans.[47] As overseas demand dried up, slaves accumulated on or near the coast. By 1867 the African population of Ambriz was reportedly made up entirely of slaves.[48]

In the 1850s and 60s, with the home market effectively shut down, those Brazilian slave traders who remained had to depend on sales to Cuba and São Tomé.[49] As had long been the case, they dealt in legal merchandise as well; such goods had long been used to settle debts among themselves as well as for purchasing slaves. Brazilian slavers in Luanda began to seriously diversify, investing more and more substantially in colonial development, including mines and plantations. They did not, however, figure at all prominently in the commodities boom along the Kongo coast after 1855, perhaps because the slaving community that remained had become closed, clandestine, and self-financing.[50]

The illegal slave trade system was shaped not only by the cat and mouse interplay of commerce and abolitionism, but also by international politics, especially the ongoing struggle between Portugal and its European competitors for dominance on the coast between Luanda and Loango, which increasingly focused on Ambriz. This focus practically guaranteed that the Kingdom of Kongo would be drawn into struggles over which it had little if any control, but which nonetheless brought significant changes.

EFFECTS ON THE KONGO KINGDOM OF THE ILLEGAL TRADE

The abolition of the transatlantic slave trade and the rapid growth of "legitimate" commodity exports after 1850 did not end slavery or the slave trade in Kongo. Slaves continued to circulate, though the old nobility no longer exclusively controlled them. By the 1870s foreign imports, including not just cloth, alcohol, and guns, but also more ordinary kinds of goods, were competing with Kongo manufactures even at inland marketplaces, particularly in the southwest. New roadside stands offering foodstuffs to travelers were a common sight on the roads well inland from the coast. How did this happen? After all, the Kongo ruling class had for generations controlled the kingdom's use-value economy[51] through which they accumulated loyal allies and dependents. They managed the interface between domestic and Atlantic economies, basing their power on a monopoly of imports realized from direct participation in international commerce, as well as collection of transit taxes, market and judicial fees, and payments for services linked to supernatural protection of foreign trade within the kingdom. Exchanges of wives and titles among the region's lords, and between them and important long-distance traders, were key elements of the system.[52] The Kongo political economy was transformed more by the success than by the failure of this aristocratic system.

Until the late eighteenth century, few slaves were shipped directly from Kongo ports. The roads and markets leading to the Congo River, historically of great concern to the monarchy, led through Sonyo or Mboma to Loango coast ports. Although Mboma became very important in the nineteenth century, it had by that time come under Cabindan influence, if not control.[53] The small port at Noqui, across the river from Mboma, developed as the principal outlet for slaves from São Salvador, most of which were then shipped from a north bank port. The kingdom's only important port was Ambriz, located in territory historically associated with the Duchy of Mbamba and the Marquisate of Mossul (see below for a description of the political system). Exports destined for Ambriz did not usually go through the capital but through southern Kongo.

Titled nobles managed trade within Kongo directly either through patronage networks or through their control of important roads and markets. Specialist trading communities carried out the long-distance trade. Although the ancient Vili trading diaspora was still in evidence,[54] by the nineteenth century the Zombo, from the lands of the old Kongo province of Mbata, were the most important. They organized caravans coming from the east through São Salvador to ports along the Congo River or the north coast.[55] One consequence of the rise of Ambriz seems to have been the appearance of more Afro-Portuguese merchants in southern Kongo. However, these Angolans were excluded from central markets of the kingdom by the long-standing prohibition on "white" traders in the kingdom's interior.[56]

Like that of the coast, the nineteenth-century economy of the kingdom was based on the successful slave export system established in the eighteenth century. As we have seen, this system linked inland suppliers of slaves with coastal markets through the agency of specialized regional traders whose caravans and networks were patronized and protected by the oligarchy of Kongo titleholders, who also controlled titles, rituals, and shrines associated with the Kongo Catholic Church. Ambitious, well-placed regional nobles could easily be as rich as the king at São Salvador, but the king was sufficiently central to the ritual system on which both depended that most preferred to use their wealth to advance themselves within the kingdom rather than to fund independence. High titleholders maintained control over lesser chiefs, ordinary free people, and slaves by monopolizing access to the imported prestige goods necessary for full participation in affairs of the kingdom.[57]

The king, regarded as the vital link between the lands of the living and dead, kept the entire politico-religious system functioning for the public good. The foreign policies of the government at São Salvador historically turned on the fact that the Portuguese monarchy and the Kongo Catholic Church were essential parts of this kingdom system. Relations between Kongo and Portugal consisted most importantly in ritual exchanges of gifts, including royal regalia, education of princes, Catholic priests, and slaves. In the language of "vassalage" that was used between them, Portugal, thought of in Kongo as the overlord most directly connected to the land of the dead, was "owner" of all of the living in Kongo.

The domestic political system rested on the *mbanza*, a settlement large enough to have its own satellite *libatas*, or hamlets, and their supporting farms.[58] The *mbanza*, supporting a *marquez* (marquis), *duque* (duke), or *principe* (prince), a great noble of the kingdom, was the smallest autonomous local unit.[59] From these territorial bases the titled lords of the kingdom, all members of the Kongo Order of Christ and commanders of large, potentially armed, retinues of clients and slaves, participated directly in the affairs of the monarchy, acting as brokers of the ritual powers centered in the king, Church, and capital. Rival factions and their members competed with each other for advancement and influence within the kingdom, especially during the violent struggles for the throne, which occurred with the death of each monarch.

The king was more than just another great noble. Properly crowned and residing in São Salvador with his courtiers and family, he was principally a mediator of supernatural power.[60] Proper institution of the king and activation of his powers required very specific coronation rituals. Of the three (perhaps four) kings of Kongo between 1830 and 1891, the first, Dom Andre I, 1830–1842, remained uncrowned because the required Portuguese regalia and foreign Roman Catholic priest never arrived. This was at least partly because in the 1830s the Portuguese liberal government, which effectively ended the slave trade, thus breaking the link between Brazil and Angola, also abolished the religious orders that had historically provided the priests sent to Kongo. Dom Alvaro, Marquis of Ndongo, held São Salvador in 1858 but was forced out by his rival, with the aid of a Portuguese expeditionary army, before he could be properly crowned. This leaves only two major kings for the period, indeed for the whole nineteenth century, Dom Henrique II (1842–1857) and Dom Pedro V (1859–1891).[61] Both of these men were dynamic rulers who sought actively to use their historic patron, the king of Portugal, to further the interests of the monarchy and its allies (if not the kingdom as a whole); neither had access to Lisbon directly, however, but only through the agency of Portuguese officials in Luanda. Angola not only mediated the correspondence between the Portuguese and Kongo kings, but also competed with its African neighbor in the regional trading system. Despite official efforts to prevent it, Angola also provided substantial transit business to Kongo through the agency of Afro-Portuguese merchants and their Kongo and Brazilian partners.[62]

Nineteenth-century changes in the trading system of the kingdom appear to have intensified competition for influence in São Salvador between noble factions controlling, respectively, the trade from São Salvador to the north and that from the capital southwest toward Atlantic ports. Competition between Luanda and Ambriz also increased, especially in the south, where Ndembu merchant princes historically maintained links with both. Changes in international commerce also affected more traditional Kongo relations with Angola, Portugal, and the Roman Catholic Church, and opened possibilities for direct diplomatic contacts with Britain, France, and even Brazil.

By 1870 foreign factories dotted the coastline, each hosted by a Kongo lord. Ambitious chiefs near the coast who did not attract a factory could still find profit from brokerage, provisions, labor supply, and the like. New factory sites meant opportunities for new roads and new marketplaces. Goods that a few decades before had been the prerogative of high titleholders became available even to heads of mere *libatas* without the redistributive intervention of a noble.[63] This system persisted and expanded after the end of the Atlantic slave trade, fueled also by the increased domestic availability of slaves as dependent workers and wives. All of this meant opportunities for the growth of new *mbanza*, particularly in the agricultural districts lying from twenty to thirty miles inland, and in connection with the roads and markets built to accommodate the changing needs of the economy.[64]

THE AMBRIZ CONNECTION AND THE SPREAD OF COMMERCIALIZATION IN KONGO

Ambriz was the key Kongo coast port during the last era of the transatlantic slave trade, 1840–1870. During this era of transition from illegal slave to legal commodity exports, it became the focus of intense competition between Portugal and Britain, both of which claimed to be primarily interested in ending the slave trade to Brazil. This dramatic contest affected not only the coast, but also much of the kingdom in the wake of the midcentury Portuguese takeover of Ambriz and for a time, Bembe and São Salvador as well.[65] Although this colonial intrusion did not result in the immediate transformation of the old-fashioned, patronage-oriented, redistributive core of the kingdom's political economy, it did have a significant impact.

The commercial success of Ambriz enabled its king and people to convert their historic position on the geographic and political margins of the kingdom to one of leading brokers between Kongo and the Brazilian-organized multinational trading community of the Atlantic. This, in turn, earned them the envy of Portugal and Kongo, both of which took measures to deal with the "problem" of Ambriz. The culmination of these efforts came with the May 1855 Portuguese annexation of Ambriz to colonial Angola—with the acquiescence of the British and the approval of the Kongo king Dom Henrique II.[66]

In 1856, after securing Ambriz, the Portuguese marched inland to Bembe, where they established a fort and administrative post and took over development of the district's copper mines. In 1857–1859 it looked as though Portugal might gain control of the kingdom itself when they intervened in a succession crisis at the invitation of one of the contenders, the future Dom Pedro V. However, dreams of establishing Portuguese Kongo, to the benefit of the Angolan economy and at the expense of their British and French competitors, were short-lived. When Angolan taxes were imposed there in 1856, foreign merchants left Ambriz for Kinsembo, just across the Loje River beyond the British-imposed border. The Portuguese won back some foreign traders in the 1860s by offering lower taxes and military protection. This revival was not sufficient either to salvage the larger colonial project in Kongo or to secure inland supplies for Angola. By late 1868 the Portuguese had withdrawn officials from São Salvador, and by 1873 from Bembe as well.[67]

Its decade-long adventure in Kongo did little to further Portugal's colonial ambitions, but it did mark a turning point in the modern history of the kingdom. The Kongo the Portuguese left was neither as strong nor as independent as the one they invaded in 1855. The monarchy never recovered from the legacy of Dom Pedro V's successful appeal for Portuguese aid to enthrone him and the increased dependence on his patrons that characterized his long reign. The extent of the kingdom had permanently contracted, albeit more from the advance of commercialization it both flowed from and promoted as from the dramatic Portuguese intrusion itself.

By 1840 Ambriz had become a typical successful African port, consisting of two complementary settlements—African and foreign (Euro-American). The Kongo side consisted of seventeen "towns" clustered some miles inland, with a total population estimated in the early 1840s at four thousand. The ruler at that time, Dom Andre, lived in one of these towns, which was almost two hours' travel from the port. His town, Quibanza, enclosed in a reed fence, had about two hundred houses, plus a large palace enclosure, home to him and his estimated one hundred wives. Typical Kongo crops of maize, manioc, beans, and tobacco were cultivated. Unlike inland districts, where elders were known as *macota*, those at Ambriz were called *mafouk,* in the fashion of coastal trading polities.[68] The king took pains to emphasize to visitors that his protection entailed the obligation to follow the rules set out for foreign traders. Foreign factories employed free persons from the area, probably on recommendation from Dom Andre.[69]

The European and American trading factories dealt in both slaves and legal commodities. British attacks on factories from 1842 prompted slave operations, such as the one established by an Angolan *degradado* (a criminal or political exile) working for Dona Ana Joaquina dos Santos Silva, to relocate inland.[70] Coastal or inland, each foreign establishment was legally and practically dependent on its African landlord. What distinguished the larger settlements such as Ambriz was the fact that a single African lord controlled a number of foreign establishments. In the 1840s Portuguese and U.S. factories predominated, although there was at least one recognized Brazilian house.[71] By 1850 British factories had overtaken American ones.[72] The "factories" or "stores" of the foreign traders were constructed like those of their African neighbors. They employed Kongo brokers who bought slaves, ivory, and other commodities.[73] A local market supplied foodstuffs to the merchant community. Taxation was considered light and consisted of presents offered regularly to the chief, but regulations (and employees) imposed by the local authorities could be more onerous, since penalties for infractions of market rules were severe, ranging from fines to destruction of the offending factory itself.[74]

There is some evidence that not just the coastal districts, but also those along major roads and at key transit points, were experiencing significant change in this period. The emergence of Quiballa as an important market town and staging point for goods moving between Bembe and Ambriz or Ambrizette is a good example. It is first mentioned in 1845, and probably grew up in the late 1830s.[75] Other lords in this region were also taking advantage of new opportunities to build up local power and autonomy. As had been the case at least since the late eighteenth century, foreign caravans made up mostly of porters moved directly from chief to chief along established routes, exchanging imported goods given as presents to local lords for safe passage and hospitality, often including lodging and food.[76]

The fortunes of nineteenth-century Ambriz were tied primarily to Luanda, whose Brazil-oriented merchants successfully combined the established Angolan commercial system with Kongo coast practices designed to evade anti-slave trade cruisers.[77] The linked careers of Brazilian Francisco Antonio Flores and British subject Joachim John Monteiro illustrate the characteristic integration of businessmen and business ventures, licit and illicit. Flores, who built his business in the illegal slave trade, had by 1855 become a leading citizen of Luanda with investments not only in slaving but also in other enterprises ranging from a fleet of coasting vessels to provisioning troops and financing government operations. He moved in very high circles, corresponding with Sa da Bandeira and acting as Angolan agent for steamship lines from Lisbon and London. He acquired contracts for development of mines at Bembe and near Benguela, both in areas formerly central to illegal slaving.[78] It was through the Bembe project that he met Monteiro, a mining engineer, who worked for the Western Africa Malachite Copper Mines Company, which began mining operations early in 1858, having acquired the contract from Flores and his partners. After the Cornish miners he was supervising died or decamped, Monteiro left the mines, but not Angola, where he was involved in a variety of economic and scientific enterprises over the next twenty years.[79]

After 1845 slaves were no longer exported from Luanda itself. Indeed, for the next fifteen years antislavery cruisers replaced slavers as the biggest business for the port. At the same time Portugal determined to build a more modern Angolan economy based on the Brazilian model.[80] Slow progress was blamed both on the continuation of the slave trade and on the flow of "contraband" commodities through Ambriz and nearby ports. It did not help that much of the business at Ambriz was in the hands of foreigners, particularly British, who, the Portuguese believed (not without reason), were using anti–slave trade operations to further their own national interests, including importation of goods necessary for all types of exports. British dominance at Ambriz, the Angolans feared, would be but a first step toward British domination of the whole coast of West Central Africa.[81]

Two kings of Kongo, Dom Henrique II and Dom Pedro V, actively concerned themselves with the issue of Ambriz, which they viewed primarily in terms of whether it furthered or handicapped royal efforts to maintain the ritual power center at São Salvador in the face of the fissiparous forces in the kingdom set in motion by the booming coastal trade. Each also faced troubles in the capital district and along major trade corridors, particularly those southern ones contested with Angola.[82] Not much is known about the circumstances of Dom Henrique's 1842 accession to the throne, except that he replaced an uncrowned predecessor and, by contrast, was quickly able to obtain the necessary regalia and Catholic priest for his own coronation. Reports from the time suggest both significant domestic factionalism and its connection to international trade. In 1843 Dom Henrique sent an embassy to Luanda to announce his election and to request the priest and regalia necessary for his enthronement. Shortly thereafter, the king sent an urgent request to the Portuguese for help in putting down a "revolt" involving a settlement of "slaves of the church" that, Henrique claimed, the Portuguese should control. He also made strong appeals for priests and the craftsmen necessary to rebuild some of the ancient churches in his capital. In the mid-1840s he sent a royal prince, Dom Nicolas, to Luanda to be educated at Portuguese expense. It was in the course of these negotiations for support that Dom Henrique II first indicated his willingness to transfer overlordship of Ambriz from himself to the king of Portugal.[83]

Dom Henrique's strategies in these matters fit a traditional Kongo model for dealing with the problem of troublesome noble factions by using his exclusive Portuguese connection to build up royal power at São Salvador. The requests for priests, European craftsmen, and princely education all supported this aim. In offering Ambriz he proposed to concede a border district that was apparently no longer effectively under royal control, and thus trade a troublesome vassal to his overlord, Portugal, in return for the promise of quite tangible benefits. Ambriz resisted occupation but was doomed by the Kongo-Portuguese alliance against it.

Portugal successfully annexed Ambriz to Angola but was prevented by the British from annexing any further coastal territory. So, spurred by the optimistic projections of Flores and his partners, Portugal moved to take over the mines at Bembe and thus extended Angolan economic development and administration in the strategic Encoge-Ndembu corridor. In this venture they had the support not only of foreign investors, but also at least initially of Kongolese in the mining district, where people begged the expedition's priest for baptism and produced ancient papers testifying to their ancestors' loyal service to the Portuguese king.[84]

Portugal annexed the mines to Angola in 1856, but when they then tried to complete the project by opening the road south from Bembe to Encoge, Ndembu lords were uncooperative, clearly viewing Portuguese control over such a key route as detrimental to their interests. The governor of Angola responded with a punitive expedition, but it was inconclusive and overshadowed, in January 1857, by news of the death of Dom Henrique II, which came with a request that the governor general send appropriate ritual items for the royal funeral.[85]

In the next two years the Angolan Concelho (council) of Dom Pedro V (Bembe) turned into a staging point for Portuguese involvement in the struggle between Kongo noble factions for the throne at São Salvador. The Portuguese were drawn in by one of the contenders, Dom Pedro Lefula (or Elelo), Marquis of Katende, who, by late in 1857 had already visited the Portuguese *chefe* (local administrator) at Bembe to announce his candidacy and pledge himself a loyal vassal of the king of Portugal, Dom Pedro V. The time was very opportune for Katende because his appeals coincided with one of Lisbon's colonial expansionist phases. Nevertheless, the Portuguese moved cautiously, at first taking a position of friendly neutrality, providing only the expected funeral goods. They wanted to keep a strong ally on the throne in Kongo, thereby compensating for the British ban on further coastal expansion.[86] In 1859 the Portuguese, faced with the spread of the Encoge-Ndembu resistance to the Bembe-Ambriz corridor, and alarmed by reports that Katende's rival, Dom Alvaro Ndongo, was receiving support from the French on the Zaire, committed themselves to backing Katende to whom they provided the military presence, ritual goods, and the priest necessary for coronation.[87] When Ndongo and his allies refused to give up São Salvador, the Portuguese sent an expeditionary force that installed Katende securely on the throne as Dom Pedro V and built a small fort at São Salvador to protect him. Since the partisans of Dom Alvaro did not recognize Dom Pedro V, the Portuguese soon found themselves embroiled in ongoing civil strife, which though catalyzed around the succession crisis, included a complex mix of antagonisms, some directed specifically at Portugal and related directly to the takeover of Ambriz, the failure of the mines' project at Bembe, and the opposition of Ndembu.

At its worst, 1859–1862, the succession conflict was quite generalized, even internationalized by the Portuguese involvement.[88] The new king's pro–Portuguese policies created hostility toward him and all those associated with him, including his kinsman and supporter, the *assimilado* (assimilated) Kongo prince Nicolas, who, ironically, was murdered while trying to flee to Brazil in the aftermath of his eloquent defense of Kongo sovereignty, published in the *Jornal do Comercio* in Lisbon in 1860.[89] The disturbances were strongest in the areas hardest hit by the Portuguese intrusion: Ambriz, Quiballa, Bembe, and Mossul, the very areas from which Katende had drawn initial support, and which were experiencing the most rapid growth in commodity exports financed by men like Flores, whose agents were buying ivory in Bembe even after he sold the mining concession.[90] In fact, in the long run the impact of the Portuguese invasion and occupation probably stemmed less from military occupation and more from its role in expanding international commercial competition into the interior, thus magnifying the effects on São Salvador of the increasing independence of the kingdom's coastal districts.[91]

By late 1862 the military situation had stabilized enough to enable Dom Pedro V to consolidate his position at São Salvador, even though opposition identified with Dom Alvaro Ndongo continued to shape kingdom politics until the end of the century.[92] Despite military success sufficient to keep Ambriz, the commercial situation of Angola was not significantly improved by the invasion. It is true that Bembe prospered for a time, thanks to the stimulus of wages paid to African miners, porters, and other workers. However, this extension of Atlantic job opportunities into the center of the country created expectations that were dashed when the mining project fizzled out.[93] There is evidence also of links between the Portuguese failures in Kongo and the 1872–1873 uprising in Ndembu, which effectively closed Angola out of this strategic area for many years to come.[94]

By the late 1860s the Portuguese found themselves saddled with a very expensive military campaign and its attendant administrative costs, with no prospect of new revenues to cover them.[95] The merchant community in Luanda was incensed by failure of the Kongo campaign, which, in hindsight, was seen as having been of questionable value from the beginning. They further feared that proposed tax reductions at Ambriz would further burden them. Portugal had "pacified"[96] Kongo, but it still had not resolved issues of territorial claims with either London or Paris. And even Kongo had only submitted to an old-fashioned vassalage-type arrangement, not to the colonial control claimed by Portugal and denounced by Kongo prince Nicolas with the support of his British and Brazilian patrons.

Brazil does not appear to have had any direct relations with the Kingdom of Kongo in this period. There was no Brazilian consul in Angola until 1855 and no effective representation until the appointment of Sr. Saturnino de Souza e Oliveira, who held the post from 1856 to 1861. His instructions make it clear that Brazil was principally interested in competing with Angolan agricultural exports to Europe and in developing direct trade with the colony.[97] The only hint of official Brazilian interest specifically in Kongo came out in the investigations of the death, in 1860, of Prince Nicolas at the hands of a mob at Kinsembo, where he was awaiting transport to Brazil in a British ship. Prince Nicolas achieved notoriety by his published protest of Pedro V's coronation oath of vassalage, which he claimed, in fairly sophisticated language, violated the sovereignty of the kingdom. There was suspicion then and later that he had at least had help in writing it.

Although the degree of Brazilian involvement in this affair is disputed,[98] it is clear that both the Brazilian and the British consuls were friendly with the prince, a government functionary at Ambriz. Clearly both had reason to want to gain access to an independent Kongo through him. Although Dom Pedro V was not directly involved, the intense international commercial and diplomatic competition magnified the succession struggle's impact and helped shape his reign.

As long as the Portuguese maintained a presence in São Salvador, Dom Pedro V used them as an instrument of his own policies, a fact that the Angolan governor general took notice of only in 1866 when he discovered that French Catholic missionaries were corresponding with São Salvador about opening a mission at the capital.[99] The Portuguese authorities managed to head off this threat, substituting a Portuguese missionary team instead. However, Father Ramos, who headed the delegation, was instructed to tell Dom Pedro V, in no uncertain terms, that the king of Portugal had always had rights over Kongo; that Portuguese protection required Kongo loyalty; and that the king must rein in his subjects at Kinsembo and on the Congo River, assuring that their business returned to Angola.[100]

This exchange represented the apogee of Dom Pedro's influence with Portugal. Only a year later, in 1867, he again was without a priest, his Portuguese alliance in ruins. The governor announced his disillusionment to Lisbon by saying of Dom Pedro V: "He had no local support for election, and without our troops he would fall. Military posts keep busy protecting him from robberies and insults of 'supposed subordinates' who are much more powerful than he is."[101] In December 1868 the military post at São Salvador was abandoned, among others on the grounds that Dom Pedro V, in using the troops for his own ends, had completely undermined any goodwill the Portuguese had in the area. An 1869 government report attacked the whole northern campaign, along with the traditional vassalage system itself. In defending his report, the author signaled the Portuguese shift in relation to Kongo: "Africans value their independence however 'rude' they are." "Probably," he added, "because they don't know the value of civilization."[102] By 1873 only Ambriz remained Angolan, and it could not be reached overland from Luanda through a still-independent Mossul.[103] Encoge and Ndembu required yet another colonial military campaign in 1872–1873, while the export business at Kongo ports from Kinsembo north to the Congo River continued to flourish.

A variety of economic changes, generated by international demand for tropical products and spurred by the Portuguese intrusion, are evident in western and southern Kongo districts by the 1870s. Local markets offered cotton cloth and imported hardware; Portuguese coins appeared.[104] More people were venturing to the coast, either in small, locally organized expeditions, or as porters for larger operations. Slave-worked plantations appeared, mostly around Encoge. There was at least one such operation just outside Portuguese jurisdiction near Ambriz, owned by Sr. José Ignacio, the former slaver, who had a substantial cattle and cotton operation. This is a particularly interesting case because it represents the first settlement in the kingdom proper organized more on a colonial Angolan than a Kongo patronage model. It was heavily fortified, autonomous, and appears to have had no Kongo landlord, but to have enjoyed good relations with the Portuguese governor of Ambriz.[105]

Growing dependence on production for European and American markets signaled the continuing Kongolese move away from the use-value political economy of the kingdom toward the market economy of the Atlantic. The two systems were interdependent, linked, among other things, by the importance of slave labor. Ambriz found a niche in the new economy, but it still had to compete with neighboring ports for the business of inland suppliers. Like their counterparts elsewhere in the expanding export production zone, Kongolese sellers moved their business easily between the Angolan port and the British, French, or American factories conveniently located at Kongo harbors nearby.

Old slave barracoons became relics of interest only to the occasional foreign tourist. Meanwhile, more and more Kongolese were taking jobs with one of the new wave of large, mostly British, French, or Dutch trading companies with operations on the coast. Things had reached the point in 1881 that the Portuguese missionary Father Antonio Barroso reported that a son of Pedro V himself was working for a French factory at Noqui, the principal Kongo port on the Congo.[106] In this transition to legitimate commerce, as we have seen, the Kongo-Brazil partnership, initiated in the early nineteenth century and intensified during the subsequent era of illegal slave trading, was of primary importance.

NOTES

1. "Congo coast" is used to signify the entire coast from Luanda north to Loango, while "Kongo coast" refers to the Atlantic coast of the Kingdom of Kongo.
2. See especially Roger Anstey, *Britain and the Congo in the Nineteenth Century* (Oxford: Macmillan, 1962); F. Latour da Veiga Pinto, *Le Portugal et Le Congo au XIXe Siècle* (Paris: Presses Universitaires de France, 1972); and Roquinaldo Amaral Ferreira, "Dos Sertoēs ao Atlântico: Tráfico Ilegal de Escravos e Comercio Licito em Angola, 1830–1860" (Ph.D. diss., Universidade Federal do Rio de Janeiro, 1997).
3. "Proto-colonial" is used here as a kind of mirror image of "neo-colonial." Elizabeth Isichei uses the term "paleo-colonial" to indicate the same thing. *A History of African Societies to 1870* (Cambridge: Cambridge University Press, 1997), p. 277.
4. These arguments were originally put forward in my earlier work. See Susan Herlin Broadhead, "Trade and Politics on the Congo Coast, 1770–1870" (Ph.D. diss., Boston University, 1971) and "Beyond Decline: The Kingdom of the Kongo in the Eighteenth and Nineteenth Centuries," *International Journal of African Historical Studies* 12,

no. 4 (1979): 615–62. The term "prestige sector" comes from Wyatt MacGaffey, *Religion and Society in Central Africa* (Chicago: University of Chicago Press, 1986), pp. 21–23.

5. Gervase Clarence-Smith, *The Third Portuguese Empire, 1825–1975*, (Manchester: Manchester University Press, 1985), p. 24. British capital continued to finance the Brazilian trade well into the illegal era. Ibid., p. 44; Joseph C. Miller, *Way of Death. Merchant Capitalism and the Angolan Slave Trade, 1730–1830* (Madison: University of Wisconsin Press, 1988), p. 509.

6. With this shift, Rio became the center for the import of slave labor into Brazil. The sixteen top slave traders out of Rio between 1811 and 1830 made a total of 478 trips. Of these 167 were to Cabinda, 15 to "Rio Zaire," and 7 to Molembo (the old Kakongo port north of Cabinda), for a total of 189 voyages to African ports north of the Congo River. In addition the Kongo port of Ambriz received 52 visits, raising the non-Angolan total to 241. Luanda was the destination for 135 ships, Benguela received 101. Manolo Garcia Florentino, *Em Costas Negras: Uma Historia do Trafico Atlantico de Escravos entre a Africa e o Rio de Janeiro (secs. XVIII e XIX)* (São Paulo: Companhia de Letras, 2000 [1997]), p. 270.

7. Phyllis Martin, *The External Trade of the Loango Coast, 1576–1870* (Oxford: Clarendon Press, 1972), p. 73; Ferreira, "Dos Sertoẽs," p. 2.

8. Ferreira, introduction to "Dos Sertoẽs"; José Honório Rodrigues, *Brazil and Africa*, trans. Richard A. Massara and Sam Hileman (Los Angeles: University of California Press, 1965), pp. 177–81.

9. Broadhead, "Trade and Politics," pp. 143–45, 229–30; Ferreira, introduction to "Dos Sertoẽs."

10. From the name of the conference held at York University in Toronto, 12–15 October 2000, "Enslaving Connections: Africa and Brazil during the Era of the Slave Trade."

11. Martin, *External Trade*, p. 73, chap. 5; Ferreira, "Dos Sertões," p. 2.

12. The question of who was "Portuguese" and who was Brazilian is a matter of some ambiguity both at the time and among recent scholars. See Clarence-Smith, *Third Empire*, p. 30.

13. Of 356 slave vessels arriving at Rio between 1795 and 1810, only 21 reported from Africa north of Luanda, and all except one of these voyages occurred after 1807. David Eltis, "The Volume and Structure of the Transatlantic Slave Trade: A Reassessment," *William and Mary Quarterly* 58, no. 1 (2001): 17–46.

14. Eltis, "Reassessment," p. 35.

15. Miller, *Way of Death*, pp. 226–27; Clarence-Smith, *Third Empire*, p. 24.

16. Miller, *Way of Death*, pp. 514, 531; Ferreira, "Dos Sertoẽs," p. 24.

17. Eltis points out that trading on the African coast required connections and expertise geared to particular localities and customers, "Reassessment," p. 17. Miller points out that Brazilians and Afro-Portuguese had the necessary expertise to assemble the *banzos* or "bundles" required for trading with particular suppliers, *Way of Death*, pp. 296–97.

18. Martin, *External Trade*, p. 140.

19. Phyllis Martin, "Family Strategies in Nineteenth-Century Cabinda," *Journal of African History* 28 (1987): 73; Ferreira, "Dos Sertões," p. 82; Broadhead, "Trade and Politics," p. 147.

20. Martin, *External Trade*, p. 137.
21. Miller, *Way of Death*, pp. 296–97, 517–19; Martin, *External Trade*, p. 143.
22. Miller, *Way of Death*, p. 519.
23. Brazilians established connections here through their Afro-Portuguese trading partners. Jean-Baptiste Douville, *Voyage au Congo, 1827–1828*, Edition établie et presentée por Chantal Edel (Paris: La Table Ronde, 1991), pp. 57–58; Miller, *Way of Death*, p. 519.
24. Helio A. E. Felgas, *História do Congo Português* (Carmona: Emprêsa Gráfica do Úige, 1958), p. 99. "Contraband" included not just *reviros* (Miller, *Way of Death*, p. 519), but any trade from the hinterland of Angola that was not exported through an Angolan customs post.
25. The term *mafouk* comes from Loango, where it referred to the royal official in charge of the Atlantic export sector, with the power to establish trade, authorize official brokers, and appoint lesser staff. Martin, *External Trade*, pp. 97–99.
26. Rodrigues, *Brazil and Africa*, pp. 114, 155.
27. Anstey, *Britain*, p. 38; David Eltis, "The Impact of Abolition of the Atlantic Slave Trade," in *The Abolition of the Atlantic Slave Trade: Origins and Effects in Europe, Africa, and the Americas*, ed. David Eltis and James Walvin (Madison: University of Wisconsin Press, 1981), pp. 171–72; Arquivo Histórico Ultramarino (AHU), Lisbon, Angola, Correspondencia dos Governadores. Pastas (folders) 3B-22A contain several reports on British activities.
28. Broadhead, "Trade and Politics," p. 145; Anstey, *Britain*, p. 39; Charles Jeannest, *Quatre Années au Congo* (Paris: G. Charpentier, 1884), pp. 33–35.
29. Rodriguez, *Brazil and Africa*, p. 160; AHU, Angola, Correspondencia dos Governadores, Pasta 7A (600) 1844, Oficio no. 24, 21 June 1844; and Pasta 10, no. 157, 23 April 1846.
30. Rodriguez, *Brazil and Africa*, pp. 155–56.
31. Martin, "Family Strategies," pp. 74–75.
32. Guilherme José da Silva Correia, called "Guilherme do Zaire," was typical of traffickers in the last phase of the illegal slave trade. He commanded a network of slavers, with branches at various points between Ambriz and Cabinda, that was linked to New York as well as Rio. This extreme internationalization was characteristic of illegal trade in the 1850s. Ibid., p. 183, note 170; Ferreira, introduction to "Dos Sertões," pp. 8, 81–82; AHU, Angola, Correspondencia dos Governadores, Pasta BB, 1845.
33. As the British consul in Luanda noted: "Slaves were allowed to enter, were brought up, collected in large numbers and maintained until a suitable opportunity, when they were marched out of the city for the various points of embarkation, and thus the only change was that instead of being embarked in Loanda harbour they had to be sent to some convenient place for that purpose of which there are many in this neighborhood. The slave dealer thus suffered little inconvenience as he could bring into the city any number of slaves under the pretext of their being intended for domestic servants. . . ." Quoted in Ferreira, "Dos Sertões," p. 13.
34. Ibid., pp. 10, 29, 46–47.
35. Merchants from the United States had established factories for the purchase of ivory, wax, and other tropical commodities by the 1830s. George Brooks, "American

Legitimate Trade with West Africa, 1789–1914" (Boston, 1962), p. 10; Logbook of Brig Gleaner, Thomas D. Hunt, Master, Journal kept by A. H. Beckett. Essex Institute, Essex, Mass., 1835G2.

36. Report from governor general of Angola. Quoted in "Relatorio do Ministerio de Ultramar, apresentado as Camaras na Sessão extraordinaria de 1840," *Annaes Maritimos e Coloniaes* 3 (January 1841): 158, 161; AHU, Angola, Correspondencia dos Governadores, Pasta 3; José Botelho, *Subsídos para a história de Angola no 1º quartel do Século 19* (Lisbon, 1951), pp. 5–6.

37. Rodrigues, *Africa and Brazil*, pp. 179–81.

38. Martin, "Family Strategies," p. 75.

39. Ferreira, "Dos Sertões," pp. 33–41.

40. Other leading Brazilian investors were Antonió Severino de Avellar, Guilherme José da Silva Correia, and Antonio Augustó de Oliveira Botelho. According to British Consul Brand, in 1846, the five or six biggest commercial houses of Luanda were "nothing more than agencies of Brazilian slave traders." Ibid., p. 87. Several Angolan merchants of Portuguese origin also became deeply invovled in the illegal trade to Brazil, among them Arsénio Pompilio Pompeu do Carpo and Augusto Guedes Coutinho Garrido. Clarence-Smith, *Third Empire*, p. 49. From 1842 Portuguese naval archives contain materials on the activities of slavers, among them those named above. Arquivo da Marinha, Lisbon, "Registo de oficios do commandate da estação naval d'Angola para e outros destinatarios," 1841–1846, 2 vols. Garrido and Flores were partners in various ventures, and Garrido was also agent for the French firm of Régis. Archives de la Marine, Paris, BB4 635, 1845, Letter to Commander la Roque.

41. Martin, *External Trade*, pp. 94–95; Broadhead, "Trade and Politics," p. 144.

42. Not surprisingly, published information about the organization of factories comes from legal traders. See Jeannest, *Quatre Annees* (Paris, 1884), passim., and J. J. Monteiro, *Angola and the River Congo*, 2 vols. (London: Frank Cass, 1968 [1875]), vol. 1, pp. 54–112.

43. Broadhead, "Trade and Politics," pp. 157–59. George Tams, *Visit to the Portuguese Possessions in South Western Africa* (London, 1845; reprint, New York: Greenwood Press, 1969), pp. 176–77.

44. Ferreira, "Dos Sertões," p. 10. Letter of Commander Foote to the Admiralty of 12 August 1842 and 12 September 1842, Public Record Office, London (PRO), foreign office (FO) 566, Index 23205; Captain Mundy to Admiralty, 18 January 1843, PRO, FO 566, Index 23206; Foote to Admiralty, 27 October 1843, PRO, FO 566, Index 23206.

45. There were European and American factories, with their complimentary African settlements, at the following points by 1870: Mossul, Ambriz, Kinsembo, Mussera, Ambrizette, Kinzao, Mocoul, Mangue Grande, Kitiniangulo, Mangue Pequeno, Cabeca de Cobra, and Santo António. Jeannest, *Quatre Années*.

46. European factories on the Atlantic coast were more dependent on their African hosts than those on the north bank of the Congo River. Jeannest, *Quatre Années*, p. 21.

47. Monteiro, *Angola*, vol. 1, p. 210.

48. Letter of Père Espitallie to his Superior, January 1867. Antonio Brásio, *Angola*, vol. 1 (Pittsburgh: Spiritana Monumenta Histórica Series Africana, 1966), p. 556.

49. Ferreira, "Dos Sertões," pp. 42–44.

50. Ibid., pp. 45–50; Clarence-Smith, *Third Empire*, p. 38.
51. Miller, *Way of Death*, pp. 57–62.
52. Ibid., pp. 201–204; for trade organization among Bakongo north of the Congo River, see John Janzen, *Lemba, 1650–1930, A Drum of Affliction in Africa and the New World* (New York: Garland, 1982), pp. 1–79, and Wyatt MacGaffey, *Kongo Political Culture* (Bloomington: Indiana University Press, 2000), pp. 69–76, 151–54.
53. Martin, *External Trade*, p. 140.
54. René Pélissier, *História das Campanhas de Angola*, vol. 1 (Lisbon: Estampa, 1986), p. 146.
55. John H. Weeks, *Among the Primitive Bakongo* (Philadelphia: J. Lippincott, 1914), pp. 206–207; Adolf Bastian, quoted in Martin, *External Trade*, p. 130; Miller, *Way of Death*, p. 198.
56. Broadhead, "Beyond Decline," p. 635.
57. Ibid., pp. 626–36.
58. Louis Jadin, "Information sur le royaume du Congo par le P. Raimondo da Dicomano, 1798," *Bulletin des Seances*, Institut Royale Coloniale Belge 3, no. 2 (1957): 303–37.
59. António Brásio, "Informação do Reino do Congo de Frei Raimundo de Dicomano." *Studia* 34 (June 1972): 19–42; Alfredo de Sarmento, *Os Sertões d'Africa (Apontamentos de Viagem)* (Lisbon: Topografia Verde, 1880), p. 167.
60. Weeks, *Among Bakongo*, p. 42; Sarmento, "Os Sertoës," p. 51.
61. Broadhead, "Beyond Decline," pp. 646–48.
62. Miller, *Way of Death*, pp. 297–99.
63. R. C. Phillips, "The Lower Congo: A Sociological Study," *Journal of the Anthropological Institute* 17, no. 17 (1888): 226–27; Monteiro, *Angola*, vol. 1, p. 265.
64. Sarmento, "Os Sertoës," p. 30.
65. It also generated abundant documentation, including a series of reports and official correspondence published in the *Boletim Offical de Angola*. Official correspondence is in AHU, Angola, Correspondencia dos Governadores, Pastas 22–25.
66. Events are summarized in the *Boletim Official de Angola* in Supplements to Nos. 520 and 504, 1855; and No. 514. The latter includes a letter from Dom Henrique II dated 29 June 1855 in which he repeats his request for missionaries and congratulates the governor for having "castigated" the chief of Ambriz.
67. Felgas, *Congo Português*, p. 102; AHU, Angola, Correspondencia dos Governadores, Pasta 38, No. 349, 19 December 1868; Pélissier, *História*, pp. 140–41.
68. Tams, *Visit*, pp. 1–5, also reports on an Angolan *soba*'s visit to Luanda. This chief from the interior was surrounded by elders called *mafooks* and was wearing a cap of office called the *mafook* cap, in the coastal fashion.
69. Ibid., pp. 176–77.
70. Sarmento, *Os Sertões*, p. 33. Dona Ana was a prominent member of the Luanda mercantile elite. Although Angolan-born, she invested in Brazilian plantations as well as Kongo slaving. Ferreira, "Dos Sertoës," p. 29.
71. AHU, Angola, Correspondencia dos Governadores, Pasta 4. Oficio 165, Doc 4 "Inventario de Baracas do Ambriz em 1841"; Tams, *Visit*, p. 158.
72. Records of the Board of Foreign Missions of the Presbyterian Church U.S.A.

(Houghton Library, Harvard University), Africa: Corisco, Vol. VI, Letter of Reverend Mackey to the Board, 26 April 1850. Rio police records also show at least three Brazilians active in the area: Manuel Pinto da Fonseca, Ferraz Correia, and Tomas Ramos. Rodrigues, *Brazil and Africa*, p. 183.

73. Tams, *Visit*, pp. 158–59.

74. Monteiro, *Angola*, vol. 2, p. 3; AHU, Angola, Correspondencia dos Governadores, Pasta 23-3, 1857, passim.

75. *Boletim Official de Angola*, No. 606, 9 May 1846, p. 5; A. J. Castro, "O Congo em 1845," *Boletim da Sociedade de Geographia de Lisboa* (1880): 59–60.

76. Castro, "O Congo," pp. 54–62; Monteiro, *Angola*, vol. 1, p. 203; Sarmento, "Os Sertoēs," p. 30; Weeks, *Among Bakongo*, pp. 67, 102.

77. Tams, *Visit*, p. xx; Letter of 4 April 1838, Logbook, Gleaner, Essex Institute, 1838 G2; Ferreira, "Dos Sertões," pp. 13–14, 17, 23–24.

78. Ferreira, "Dos Sertões," pp. 33–43.

79. Monteiro, *Angola*, vol. 1, pp. 159–60; Monteiro worked for Flores at his Benguela mine in 1862. Ferreira, "Dos Sertões," p. 40.

80. Clarence-Smith, *Third Empire*, p. 25.

81. By 1850 British imports at Ambriz were valued at more than thirty thousand pounds sterling; exports (excluding copper ore) at fifty thousand. Anstey, *Britain*, p. 23.

82. In 1841 a royal prince, Dom Aleixo, usually characterized as a brother of Henrique II, was arrested and jailed in Luanda after he was accused of trying to stir up a tax revolt in Ndembu. AHU, Angola, Pastas 4B (1839), 5A (1842), and 8B (1845); Tams, *Visit*, pp. 19–24.

83. AHU, Angola, Correspondencia dos Governadores, Pasta 8C (1845), No. 559 "Embaixada do Rei do Congo," 31 August 1845.

84. In November 1856 a rather surprised Portuguese officer reported that one local *soba* (chief) had said: "His Majesty of Portugal is the owner here. We've been waiting for a priest for years." AHU, Angola, Correspondencia dos Governadores, Pasta 23 (1856). Confidencial N. 14, 20 November 1856; "Extracto de um relatorio do chefe do concelho de D. Pedro 5º *Boletim Official de Angola* 690 (1858): 1.

85. Broadhead, "Beyond Decline," p. 648.

86. Veiga Pinto, *Le Portugal*, pp. 56–60.

87. Lt. Zacharias da Silva Cruz, the Portuguese *chefe* at Bembe, headed the mission. He was accompanied by two employees of Flores, Luiz Leivas and António Gomes Pinheiro. The latter served as interpreter. "Relatorio," *Boletim Official de Angola* 690 (1858): 1.

88. AHU, Angola, Correspondencia dos Governadores, Pastas 25.3–30 (1859–1862), passim.

89. François Bontinck, "Notes complémentaires sur Dom Nicolau Agua Rosada e Sardonia," *African Historical Studies* 2, no. 1 (1969): 115–19; Veiga Pinto, *Le Portugal*, pp. 63–68; Douglas L. Wheeler, "Nineteenth-Century African Protest in Angola: Prince Nicolas of Kongo (1830?–1860)," *African Historical Studies* 2, no. 1 (1968): 40–58.

90. Monteiro, *Angola*, vol. 1, p. 201. There is evidence of Brazilian commercial activity in Ndembu in 1862. Pélissier, *História*, p. 146.

91. Phillips, "Lower Congo," pp. 226–27.

92. Pelissier, *História*, p. 146; Weeks, *Among Bakongo*, p. 38.

93. When the District of Dom Pedro V closed, it ended the local lords' access to Portugal as "vassals" who could ask for funeral and other gifts in return for loyal service, i.e., supplying porters and provisions for the Angolan administration. AHU, Angola, Correspondencia da Governadores, Pasta 33, No. 217g (31 August 1864).

94. Ibid., pp. 155–58.

95. AHU, Angola, Correspondencia dos Governadores, Pasta 23, 1857, passim.

96. AHU, Angola, Correspondencia dos Governadores, Pasta 33, No. 96 (20 April 1864).

97. Rodrigues, *Brazil and Africa*, pp. 193–97.

98. See Wheeler, "Prince Nicolas"; Viega Pinto, *Le Portugal*; and Bontinck, "Notes complimentaires."

99. Brásio, *Angola*, vol. 1, p. 359; AHU, Angola, Correspondencia dos Governadores, Pasta 36, Nos. 2 and 6 (1866).

100. AHU, Angola, Correspondencia dos Governadores, Pasta 36, 1866. Confidencial (25 May 1866).

101. AHU, Angola, Correspondencia dos Governadores, Pasta 37. 1867. Confidencial No. 5 (31 January 1867).

102. AHU, Angola, Correspondencia dos Governadores, Pasta 40. No. 177 (16 August 1869).

103. Jeannest, *Quatre Années*, p. 47; Felgas, *Congo Português*, p. 102.

104. Monteiro, *Angola*, vol. 1, p. 211.

105. Jeannest, *Quatre Années*, p. 40.

106. António José de Sousa Barroso, "Relatorio do Conego António José de Sousa Barroso," in *Arquivos de Angola*, 2d series, 11, no. 45 and 46 (1954): 308.

Glossary

agregado(s). Household dependent(s) in Brazil.
agregado de nação Xavante. Household dependent of the Xavante nation (Brazil).
Aguda(s). Afro-Brazilians in the Bight of Benin.
Alcaiadaria-Mor. Office of the *Alcaide-Mor*.
Alcaide-Mor. Official responsible for policing towns in Brazil.
alqueire. Portuguese measure of capacity, equaling 13 (dry) liters.
arrematações de impostos. Auctioned tax collections.
asiento. The license to trade in slaves issued by the Spanish government.
assimilado. Assimilated individuals, usually Africans, in Brazil and in Angola.
atacadistas. Wholesalers in Brazil.
bandeiras. Exploring, slave-raiding, or prospecting expeditions in the Brazilian bush.
banzo(s). Bundle(s) of trade goods.
barbaras gentes e nationes. Barbarous peoples and nations.
Bariba (pl. **Batomba**). Yoruba/Dahomian term for the people of Borgu, who call themselves Baatonu.
bens do vento. Property of the wind (in Brazil).
Bijago. Ethnic group in the Upper Guinea coast.
boçal (*bruto*). Term in Brazil for nonacculturated, recently arrived African slaves.
bordate. Inexpensive cotton cloth.
bumi. High-ranking government position in Jolof, often only second in power to the *buurba* (ruler).
burnouses (*albirnozes*). Expensive large and long garments, made of woolen cloth, elaborately dyed and garnished, sometimes with silk, in demand only at Arguim.
cabo. Corporal.
caboceer. General term for an official in Ouidah and elsewhere on the West African coast.

Glossary

cabra(s). Individual of mixed ancestry: black mother and most probably mulatto father.
caixa. Box.
candomblé. African religious houses in Brazil, largely Yoruba in origin.
capoeira. Martial art of Angolan origin.
captaincy. Administrative territorial division (in Brazil).
carapinas. Carpenters (in Brazil).
Carta Regia. Royal letter of instructions.
Casa da Mina. House of the **Mina**.
Casa Real. Royal House.
cativo. Captive (enslaved person).
cavaleiro. Knight.
chefe. Portuguese local administrator.
comarca. Judicial district (in Brazil).
comenda. Commendation.
comendador. Portuguese title, commander.
concelho. Council.
conquista. Portuguese-controlled territories overseas.
cori (*koli*). Blue, heat-resistant, cylindrical beads made of unleaded glass, most likely produced in Fustat (Cairo).
Corretor e Provedor. Custodian.
covado. Portuguese medieval measure of length, c. 0.66 meter.
creole. Language developed from a mixture of languages; also native-born West Indian or Latin American of mixed European and African descent.
creolization. Process of language development from a mixture of languages.
cria(s). Slave offspring (infants and children).
crioulo/crioula. **Creole** (person of African descent born in Brazil).
degradado(s). Criminal or political exile(s).
deputado. Member (of the Royal Board of Trade, in Rio de Janeiro).
dizíma. Portuguese 10 percent foreign trade tax.
dobra. Gold coin most commonly used in late medieval Portugal, in imitation of the Muslim mithkal, whose gold content was ideally 4.68 to 4.71 grams.
duque. Duke.
engenho(s). Sugar plantation; sugar-mill (in Brazil).
enroladores. Slaves in Brazil who formed tobacco into the large rolls for transport.
entame/entambe. African funerals in Luanda.
esusu. Lending association common in West Africa, including among the Yoruba.
farinha. Flour.
fazenda. Large estate, plantation, or ranch in Brazil.
feitiçeiro/feitiçeira. Witch.
feitiço(s). Witchcraft.
ferreiros. Iron workers.
filho/filha. Son/daughter.
Fon. Ethnic group of Dahomey; one of the Gbe languages.
forro. Freed slaves in Brazil and Angola.
fumeiros. Slaves who dried, cured, and processed tobacco in Brazil.

furriel. Lance corporal.
Gbe. Related languages of Ewe, Fon, Allada, and Mahi.
Gege. Brazilian ethnic term for Allada and other **Gbe**.
gentes barbaros. Barbarous peoples.
gentios. Gentiles; pejorative term.
gerebitas. Angolan term for Brazilian sugar cane brandies.
ingenuos e libertos. Free people of color and freed persons.
irmã/irmão. Sister/brother.
irmandades. Catholic brotherhoods.
jaji. Central African divination.
Jeje. See **Gege**.
jihad. Muslim holy war.
jornal. Daily wage; in Goiás, Brazil, the amount of gold paid by a slave to his owner each week.
julgados. Jurisdictions (in Brazil).
Kikongo. Kongo language.
Kimbundu. **Mbundu** language.
ladino/ladina. Acculturated individual in Brazil and in Angola.
lançados. Portuguese males settled on the West African coast and integrated into local societies.
lavra. Gold works (in Brazil).
lavrador de mandioca. Free manioc farmer (in Brazil).
libata. Hamlet.
liberto. Freed person.
linguister. Translator.
maço. Bundle.
macota(s). Elder(s).
mafouk(s). Kongo minister(s) of commerce.
malagueta. *Aframomum melegueta* (Roscoe) and *Aframomum granum paradisi* (Afzelius), "grains of paradise."
Malê. Brazilian term for Muslims, from *imale*, in West Africa.
mameluco. Person of European and Amerindian ancestry.
mani. King.
mani kongo. King of Kongo.
marlota. Moorish short cape with a hood.
marquez. Marquis.
mascate(s). Peddler(s) in Brazil.
mbanza. **Kikongo** for capital.
Mbundu. Ethnic group in Angola.
meia-sisa. Tax imposed at the time of slave sales (in Brazil).
mestizo. Offspring of Amerindian females and white males.
Mina. Ethnic term in Brazil for people from the Bight of Benin.
mulatto/mulatta. Offspring of African females and white males.
nação (pl. *nações*). Nation.
nação **Angola**. Angola nation.

GLOSSARY

nação crioulo. **Creole** nation.
nações de gentio. Nations of barbarians.
Nagô. Brazilian term for Yoruba.
nau. Large ship.
Ndembu. Ethnic group in Angola.
negros de ganho. Hired slaves in Brazil who worked as artisans for cash.
ngola. King of Ndongo (Angola).
ngola a kiluanje. Honorific title of **Mbundu** monarchs.
ngunza. Prophet in Kikongo and **Kimbundu**.
nsaka. Capital of Kasanze.
nzambi mpungu. **Kikongo** for God.
oba. King of Benin.
onça. Portuguese medieval measure of weight, 3.6 grams.
Ordenações Manuelinas. Law Compendium of King Manuel I.
osodin. Benin town chief responsible for the Portuguese.
pacote. Package.
pardo/parda. Mulattos, browns, or persons of mixed black and white ancestry.
pasta(s). Folder(s).
patente. Official letter of appointment.
peças. Prime adult slaves, usually male.
Pepel (also **Papel**). Ethnic group in the Upper Guinea coast.
pessoas de obrigação. Obligated persons (in Brazil)
Pidgin. Language, not a mother tongue, made up of elements of two or more other languages.
pidginization. Process of language development, made up of elements of two or more other languages.
portagem. Portuguese local toll.
presídio. Military-administrative unit in Angola.
preto(s). Black(s).
principe. Prince.
proveito e serviço. Profit and service.
quarto. Portuguese 25 percent tax payable on assessed market value of overseas merchandise, introduced in the fifteenth century.
quilombo/kilombo. Maroon settlement in Brazil; also in Angola.
quintal (pl. *quintais*). Portuguese medieval measure of weight, 58.5 kilograms.
quintandeiras. Market (*kitanda*) women of Luanda.
quinto. Portuguese 20 percent tax on booty or war prizes. Also the tax, usually one-fifth, on gold production in Brazil.
Real Fábrica da Pólvora. Royal Gunpowder Factory.
Recôncavo. Area surrounding the Bay of All Saints, location of Salvador (Brazil).
regimento. Royal instructions.
réis. Portuguese monetary unit, money of account: written as $000 réis.
reviro(s). Illegal payment(s) of slaves in Angola purchased with credit from one importer to a different customer.
roça(s). Small plots of land in Brazil used for food production.

saca. Portuguese export toll.
Senhorio. Lord-proprietor.
senzala(s). Residential areas in Angola for free, freed, and enslaved Africans.
soldo. Venetian money of account, a shilling.
Tabelião Escrivão. Treasurer.
taixas. Taxes.
Takpa (also *Tapa*). Yoruba/Dahomian term for the Nupe people.
tratos. Regions along the coast of West Africa leased for slaving.
Umbundu. Language of the Ovimbundu (Angola).
varejistas. Retailers in Brazil.
viador. Messenger.
vintena. Portuguese one-twentieth tax on the assessed market value of overseas goods, minus the cost of the **quarto** or **quinto**, introduced in the mid-fifteenth century to support the spiritual efforts of the Order of Christ and later reverting to the Crown.
Yovogan. Viceroy of Ouidah.

Bibliography

Afread, J. Andrea, and James H. Overfield. *The Human Record: Sources for Global History,* 2d ed. Boston, Toronto: Houghton Mifflin Company, 1994.

Akibode, Imbert B. Oswin. "Contribution à l'étude de l'histoire de l'ancien royaume d'Agoué (1821–1885)." Mémoire de maîtrise, FLASH, Université Nationale du Bénin, 1989.

Akinjogbin, A. *Dahomey and Its Neighbors, 1784–1863.* Cambridge: Cambridge University Press, 1967.

Albuquerque, Luís de, and Maria Emilia Madeira Santos, eds., *História Geral de Cabo Verde.* 2 vols. Lisbon: Instituto de Investigação Científica Tropical, 1991–1994.

Alden, Dauril Alden, and Joseph C. Miller. "Out of Africa: The Slave Trade and the Transmission of Smallpox to Brazil, c. 1560–c. 1830." *Journal of Interdisciplinary History* 18, no. 2 (1987): 195–224.

———. "Unwanted Cargoes: The Origins and Dissemination of Smallpox via the Slave Trade from Africa to Brazil, c. 1560–1830." In *The African Exchange: Toward a Biological History of the Black People*, edited by Kenneth F. Kiple. Durham, N.C.: Duke University Press, 1988, pp. 35–109.

Alencastro, Luiz-Felipe de. *O Trato dos Viventes: Formação do Brasil no Atlântico Sul.* São Paulo: Companhia das Letras, 2000.

Almanak imperial do comércio e das corporações civis e militares do Império do Brasil. Rio de Janeiro: Plancher-Seignot, 1829.

Alonso, V. Cortes. "Procedencia de los esclavos nehros en Valencia (1482–1516)." *Revista española de antropologia americana* 7 (1972): 123–51.

Amenumey, D. E. K. "Geraldo da Lima: A Reappraisal." *Transactions of the Historical Society of Ghana* 9 (1968): 65–78.

Amos, Alcione M. "Afro-Brasileiros no Togo: a história da família Olympio, 1882–1945." *Afro-Ásia* 23 (1999): 175–97.

Anstey, Roger. *The Atlantic Slave Trade and British Abolition, 1769–1810*. London: Macmillan Press, 1975.

———. "The Volume and Profitability of the British Slave Trade, 1761–1807." In *Race and Slavery in the Western Hemisphere: Quantitative Studies*, edited by S. Engerman and E. Genovese. Princeton: Princeton University Press, 1975.

Antonil. *Opulencia do Brasil por suas drogas e minas*, edited by Andree Mansuy. Paris: Institut des Hautes Études de l'Amérique Latine, 1968.

Arruda, José J. *O Brasil no comércio colonial*. São Paulo: Ática, 1980.

Ashtor, E. *Levant Trade in the Later Middle Ages*. Princeton: Princeton University Press, 1983.

Barickman, B. J. *A Bahian Counterpoint. Sugar, Tobacco, Cassava, and Slavery in the Recôncavo, 1780–1860*. Stanford: Stanford University Press, 1998.

Barros, João. *Asia: Primeira Década*. Edited by H. Cidade and M. Múris. Lisbon: Agência Geral das Colónias, 1945.

Baxter, Alan. "Creole-like Features in the Verb System of an Afro-Brazilian Variety of Portuguese." In *The Structure and Status of Pidgins and Creoles*, edited by Arthur K. Spears and Donald Winford. Amsterdam and Philadelphia: Benjamins, 1997, pp. 265–88.

Belotti, Giancarlo. "Le tabac brésilien aux XVII et XVIII siècles." Ph. D. diss., Université Paris X–Nanterre, 1973.

Bentley, W. Holman. *Dictionary and Grammar of the Kongo Language*. London: Gregg Press, 1967 [1887].

Berlin, Ira. "From Creole to African: Atlantic Creoles and the Origins of African American Society in Mainland North America." *William and Mary Quarterly* 53, no. 2 (1996): 251–88.

———. *Many Thousand Gone: The First Two Centuries of Slavery in North America*. New York: Oxford University Press, 1998.

Bertran, Paulo. *Memória de Niquelândia*. Brasília: SPHAN próMemória, 1985.

Bickerton, Derek. *Roots of Language*. Ann Arbor: Karoma, 1981.

Blackburn, Robin. *The Overthrow of Colonial Slavery, 1776–1848*. London: Verso, 1988.

———. *The Making of New World Slavery: From the Baroque to the Modern*. London, New York: Verso, 1996.

Blake, John W. *The Quest for God and Gold, 1454–1578*. London: Curzon Press, 1977.

Blancheley. "Au Dahomey." *Les Missions catxholiques* 223 (1891): 534–37, 545–48, 562–64, 575–76, 587–88.

Boadi-Siaw, S. Y. "Brazilian Returnees of West Africa." In *Global Dimensions of the African Diaspora*, 2d ed., edited by Joseph E. Harris. Washington, D.C.: Howard University Press, 1993, pp. 421–39.

Bontinck, François. "Notes complémentaires sur Dom Nicolau Agua Rosada e Sardonia." *African Historical Studies* 2, no. 1 (1969): 101–19.

Borghero, Francesco. *Journal de Francesco Borghero, premier missionnaire du Dahomey 1861–1865*. Paris: Karthala, 1997.

Botelho, Jose J. T. *Subsídos para a história de Angola no 1º quartel do Século 19*. Lisbon, 1951.

Bouche, Pierre. *Sept Ans en Afrique Occidentale: La Côte des Esclaves et le Dahomey*. Paris: Plon, 1885.

Braga, Júlio Santanna. "Notas Sobre o 'Quartier Bresil' no Daomé." *Afro-Ásia* 6–7 (1968): 56–62.

Braga, Maria Luiza. "A concordância de número no sintagma nominal no Triângulo Mineiro." Tese de Mestrado, Pontifícia Universidade Católica do Rio de Janeiro, 1977.

Brásio, Antonio. "Um extraordinário documento quinhentista." *Studia* 15 (1965): 155–74.

———. *Angola,* I. Pittsburgh: Spiritana Monumenta Histórica Series Africana, 1966.

———. "Informacão do Reino do Congo de Frei Raimundo de Dicomano." *Studia* 34 (1972): 19–42.

———. *Monumenta Missionaria Africana: África Occidetal,* 2d series. 5 vols. Lisbon: Agência Geral do Ultramar, 1958–1974.

Broadhead, Susan Herlin. "Trade and Politics on the Congo Coast, 1770–1870. Ph.D. diss., Boston University, 1971.

———. "Beyond Decline: The Kingdom of the Kongo in the Eighteenth and Nineteenth Centuries." *International Journal of African Historical Studies* 12, no. 4 (1979): 615–52.

Brooks, George. "American Legitimate Trade with West Africa, 1789–1914." Boston, 1962.

———. *Landlords and Strangers.* Boulder: Westview Press, 1993.

Brue, André. "Voyage fait en 1843, dans le royaume de Dahomey." *Revue coloniale* 7 (1845): 55–68.

Burton, Richard. *A Mission to Gelele, King of Dahomey.* 2 vols. London: Tinsley Brothers, 1864.

Butler, Kim D. *Freedoms Given, Freedoms Won.* New Brunswick, N.J.: Rutgers University Press, 1998.

Cadamosto. *Viagens de Luís de Cadamosto and Pedro de Sintra.* Lisbon: Academia Portuguesa de História, 1948.

Cadornega, Antônio de Oliveira. *História geral das guerras angolanas.* 3 vols. Edited by José Matias Delgado. Lisbon: Agência Geral das Colônias, 1940–1942.

Carlos, Ann M. "Bonding and the Agency Problem: Evidence from the Royal African Company, 1672–1691." *Explorations in Economic History* 31 (1994): 313–35.

Carlos, Ann M., and Stephen Nicholas. "Agency Problems in the Early Chartered Companies: The Case of Hudson's Bay Company." *Journal of Economic History* 50 (1990): 853–75.

Carreira, António. *As Companhias Pombalinas de Grão-Pará e Maranhão e Pernambuco e Paraíba.* São Paulo: Cia. Editora Nacional/Instituto Nacional do Livro, 1988.

Cascudo, Luiz da Câmara. *Made in Africa: pesquisas e notas.* Rio de Janeiro: Civilização Brasileira, 1965.

———. *Dicionário do Folclore Brasileiro.* 5th ed. Belo Horizonte: Editora Itatiaia, 1984.

Castro, A. J. "O Congo em 1845." *Boletim da Sociedade Geographia de Lisboa* (1880): 59–60.

Cavazzi, Giovanni Antônio. *Descrição Histórica dos Três Reinos do Congo, Matamba e Angola.* Edited and translated by Padre Graciano Maria de Leguzzano. 2 vols. Lisbon: Junta de Investigações do Ultramar, 1965.

Chambers, Douglas. "'My Own Nation': Igbo Exiles in the Diaspora." *Slavery and Abolition* 18, no. 1 (1997): 72–97.

Chatwin, Bruce. *The Viceroy of Ouidah.* London: J. Cape, 1980.
Clarence-Smith, Gervase. *The Third Portuguese Empire, 1825–1975.* Manchester: Manchester University Press, 1985.
Codo, Bellarmin C. "Les Afro–brésiliens de retour." In *La Chaine et le lien: une vision de la traite negrière,* edited by Doudou Diène. Paris: UNESCO, 1998, pp. 95–105.
Conneau, Theophilus. *A Slaver's Log, or Twenty Years' Residence in Africa: The Original 1853 Manuscript.* London: Robert Hale, 1977.
Conrad, Robert E. *Children of God's Fire.* Princeton, N.J.: Princeton University Press, 1983.
Cooper, Barbara M. *Marriage in Maradi: Gender and Culture in a Hausa Society in Niger, 1900–1989.* Portsmouth, N.H.: Heinemann, 1997.
Correa, Elias Alexandre da Silva. *História de Angola.* 2 vols. Lisbon: Editorial Ática, 1937.
Costa, Iraci del Nero da. *Vila Rica: População, 1719–1826.* São Paulo: Universidade de São Paulo, 1979.
Costa, Iraci del Nero da, Robert W. Slenes, and Stuart B. Schwartz. "A família escrava em Lourena (1801)." *Estudos Econômicos* 17, no. 2 (1987): 246–95.
Couto, Carlos, *Os Capitães-Mores em Angola no Século XVIII.* Luanda: Instituto de Investigação Científica de Angola, 1972.
Cruz e Silva, Rosa. "Benguela e o Brasil no Final do Século XVIII: Relações Comerciais e Políticas." In *Angola e Brasil nas Rotas do Atlântico Sul,* edited by Selma Pantoja and José Flávio Sombra Saraiva. Rio de Janeiro: Bertrand Basil, 1999, pp. 127–42.
Cunha, Manuela Carneiro da. "Religião, Comércio e Etnicidade: Uma Interpretação Preliminar do Catolicismo Brasileiro em Lagos, no Século XIX." *Religião e Sociedade* 1 (1977): 51–60.
———. *Negros, Estrangeiros; os escravos libertos e sua volta à África.* São Paulo: Editora Brasiliense, 1985.
———. *Da Senzala ao Sobrado: A Arquitectura Brasileira na África Ocidental.* São Paulo: Nobel, 1985.
Cunha, Rui Vieira da, *Para uma biografia de Elias Antônio Lopes.* Rio de Janeiro: Tipografia do Jornal do Comércio, 1957.
Curtin, Philip D. *The Atlantic Slave Trade: A Census.* Madison: University of Wisconsin Press, 1969.
———. *Economic Change in Precolonial Africa, Senegambia in the Era of the Slave Trade.* Madison: University of Wisconsin Press, 1975.
———, ed. *Africa Remembered: Narratives by West Africans from the Era of the Slave Trade.* Madison: University of Wisconsin Press, 1967.
Curto, José C. "The Legal Portuguese Slave Trade from Benguela, Angola, 1730–1828: A Quantitaive Re-appraisal." *África* (Revista do Centro de Estudos Africanos, Universidade de São Paulo) 16–17 (1993–1994): 101–16.
———. "Vinho verso Cachaça: A Luta Luso-Brasileira pelo Comércio do Álcoól e de Escravos em Luanda, 1648–1703." In *Angola e Brasil nas Rotas do Atlântico Sul,* edited by Selma Pantoja and José F. S. Saraiva. Rio de Janeiro: Bertrand Brasil, 1999, pp. 69–97.
———. "The Anatomy of a Demographic Explosion: Luanda, 1844–1850." *International Journal of African Historical Studies* 32 (1999): 381–405.

Bibliography

———. "Luso-Brazilian Alcohol and the Legal Slave Trade at Benguela and Its Hinterland, c. 1617–1830." In *Négoce Blanc en Afrique Noire: L'évolution du commerce à longue distance en Afrique noire du 18e au 20e siècles*, edited by Hubert Bonin and Michel Cahen. Paris: Publications de la Société française d'histoire d'outre-mer, 2001, pp. 351–69.

———. *Alcoól e Escravos: O comércio luso-brasileiro do alcoól em Mpinda, Luanda e Benguela durante o tráfico atlântico de escravos (c. 1480–1830) e o seu impacto nas sociedades da África Central Ocidental*. Lisbon: Editora Vulgata, 2002.

———. "Americanos em Angola: A Comunidade Comercial Brasileira em Benguela, 1791–1822." Unpublished paper presented at the Instituto de Filosofia e Ciencias Sociais, Universidade Federal do Rio de Janeiro, 31 July 2002.

———. "'As If from a Free Womb': Baptismal Manumissions in the Conceição Parish, Luanda, 1778–1807." *Portuguese Studies Review* 10 (2002): 26–57.

Curto, José C., and Raymond R. Gervais. "The Population History of Luanda during the Late Atlantic Slave Trade, 1781–1844." *African Economic History* 29 (2001): 1–59.

Curto, José C., and Renée Souloudre-La France, eds. *Africa and the Americas: Interconnections during the Slave Trade*. New Brunswick, N.J.: Africa World Press, forthcoming.

Dagba, Léon-Pierre Ghézowounmè Djomolia. *La Collectivité familiale Yovogan Hounnon Dagba de ses origins à nos jours*. Porto Novo: L'Imprimerie Rapidex, 1982.

Dalzel, Archibald. *The History of Dahomey, an Inland Kingdom of Africa*. London: F. Cass, 1967 [1793].

Davidson, David Michael. "Number and Origin of African Slaves Imported to Belém do Pará, 1757–1804." In "Rivers and Empire: The Madeira Route and the Incorporation of the Brazilian Far West, 1737–1808." Ph. D. diss., Yale University, 1970, pp. 477–84.

Delgado, Ralph. *A Famosa e Histórica Benguela—Catálogo dos Governadores (1779 a 1940)*. Benguela: Edição do Govêrno da Província, 1940.

———. *História de Angola*. 4 vols. Lobito: Edição do Banco de Angola, 1948–1955.

Desch-Obi, T. J. "Angolan Martial Art Traditions in Brazil." Unpublished presentation, "Enslaving Connections: Africa and Brazil during the Era of the Slave Trade," York University, 12–15 October 2000.

———. "Combat and the Crossing of Kalunga." In *Central Africans and Cultural Transformations in the American Diaspora*, edited by Linda M. Heywood. New York: Cambridge University Press, 2002, pp. 353–70.

Devisch, René. "Divination and Oracles." In *Encyclopedia of Africa South of the Sahara*, edited by John Middleton. New York: Scribner's Sons, 1997, vol. 1, pp. 493–97.

Dias, Jill R. "Mudanças nos padrões de poder no *hinterland* de Luanda: o impacto da colonização sobre os Mbundu." *Penélope* 14 (1994): 43–91.

———. "Estereótipos e realidades sociais: quem eram os 'Ambaquistas.'" Unpublished paper, Seminário—"Construindo a História Angolana: As Fontes e a sua Interpretação," Luanda, 4–8 August 1997.

———. "Angola." In *O Império africano, 1825–1890 (Nova história da expansão portuguesa)*, vol. 10, edited by Valentim Alexandre and Jill Dias. Lisbon: Editorial Estampa, 1998, pp. 319–556.

Dias, Manuel Nunes. "Fomento ultramarino e mercantilismo: A Companhia Geral de Grão-Pará e Maranhão (1775–1778)." *Revista de história* 36, no. 73 (1968): 71–113.
Douville, Jean-Baptiste. *Voyage au Congo, 1827–1828*. Paris: La Table Ronde, 1991.
Dow, George Francis. *Slave Ships and Slaving*. Massachusetts: Marine Research Society, 1927.
Drake, Richard. *Revelations of a Slave Smuggler.* New York: Robert M. DeWitt, 1860.
Duncan, John. *Travels in Western Africa in 1845 and 1846*. 2 vols. London: F. Cass, 1968.
Elbl, Ivana. "Portuguese Slave Trade in the Fifteenth Century: Prices and Profits." Unpublished paper presented to the 12th CAAS Conference, Toronto, May 1982.
———. "The Arguim Trade in the Early 1500s." Unpublished paper presented to the South/South Congress, Montreal, 15–17 May 1985.
———. "The Portuguese Trade with West Africa, 1440–1521." Ph. D. diss., University of Toronto, 1986.
———. "The Horse in Fifteenth-Century Senegambia." *International Journal of African Historical Studies* 28, no. 1 (1991): 85–109.
———. "Cross-Cultural Trade and Diplomacy: Portuguese Negotiations in West Africa, 1440–1521." *Journal of World History* 3, no. 2 (1992): 165–204.
———. "The Volume of the Early Atlantic Slave Trade, 1450–1521." *Journal of African History* 38 (1997): 31–76.
Eltis, David. "The Impact of Abolition of the Atlantic Slave Trade." In *The Abolition of the Atlantic Slave Trade. Origins and Effects in Europea, Africa, and the Americas*, edited by David Eltis and James Walvin. Madison: University of Wisconsin Press, 1981.
———. *Economic Growth and the Ending of the Transatlantic Slave Trade*. New York: Oxford Academic Press, 1987.
———. "The Volume and Structure of the Transatlantic Slave Trade: A Reassessment." *William and Mary Quarterly* 58, no. 1 (2001): 17–46.
Eltis, David, Stephen D. Behrendt, and D. Richardson, "A participação dos países da Europa e das Américas no tráfico transatlântico de escravos: novas evidências." *Afro-Ásia*, 24 (2000): 9–50.
Eltis, David, Stephen Behrendt, David Richardson, and Herbert Klein. *The Transatlantic Slave Trade: A Database on CD-ROM*. New York: Cambridge University Press, 1999.
Eltis, David, and Stanley L. Engerman. "Fluctuations in Sex and Age Ratios in the Transatlantic Slave Trade, 1664–1864." *Economic History Review* 46, no. 2 (1993): 308–23.
Fage, J. D. "Slavery and Slave Trade in the Context of African History." *Journal of African History* 10 (1969): 393–404.
———. "Slaves and Society in Western Africa, c. 1445–c.1700," *Journal of African History* 21 (1980): 289–310.
———. "African Societies and the Atlantic Slave Trade." *Past and Present* 125 (1989): 97–115.
Felgas, Helio A. E. *História do Congo Português*. Carmona: Emprêsa Gráfica do Úige, 1958.
Fernandes, Valentim. *O Manuscrito*: "Valentim Fernandes," edited by António Baião. Lisbon: Academia Portuguesa da História, 1940.

Ferraz, Luis I. "The Substratum of Annobonese Creole." *International Journal of the Sociology of Language* 7 (1976): 37–47.
———. *The Creole of São Tomé.* Johannesburg: Witwatersrand University Press, 1979.
Ferreira, Roquinaldo do Amaral. "Dos sertões ao Atlântico: tráfico ilegal de escravos e comércio lícito em Angola, 1830–1860." Dissertação de Mestrado, Universidade Federal do Rio de Janeiro, Instituto de Filosofia e Ciências Sociais, Programa de Pós-Graduação em História Social, 1997.
———. "Slavery and the Illegal Slave Trade in Angola, 1830–1860." Unpublished paper, American Historical Association annual meeting, Seattle, 1998.
———. "Brasil e Angola no Tráfico Ilegal de Escravos, 1830–1860." In *Angola e Brasil nas Rotas do Atlântico Sul*, edited by Selma Pantoja and José Flávio Sombra Saraiva. Rio de Janeiro, Bertrand Brasil, 1999, pp. 143–94.
Ferretti, Sergio. *Querebetã de Zomadônu: etnografia da Casa das Minas do Maranhão.* São Luís: Editora da Universidade Federal do Maranhão, 1996.
Figueiredo, Aldrin Moura de. "Reis de Mina: a Irmandade de Nossa Senhora do Rosário dos Homens Pretos no Pará do século xviii ao xix." *Boletim-Museu Paraense Emílio Goeldi (série Antropologia)* 9, no. 1 (1993): 103–21.
Finley, Moses. *Escravidão antiga e ideologia moderna.* Rio de Janeiro: Graal, 1991.
Florentino, Manolo Garcia. "About the Slaving Business in Rio de Janeiro, 1790–1830: A Contribution." In *Pour l'histoire du Brésil: hommage à Katia de Queirós Mattoso*, edited by François Crouzet, Philippe Bonnichon, and Denis Rolland. Paris: L'Harmattan, 2000, pp. 397–416.
———. "Biographical Database for Rio de Janeiro." Unpublished paper presented at the Workshop on Database Construction and the African Diaspora, York University, Toronto, 2–12 July 2002.
———. *Em Costas Negras: Uma Historia do Trafico Atlantico de Escravos entre a Africa e o Rio de Janeiro (secs. XVIII e XIX).* 2d ed. São Paulo: Companhia das Letras, 2002.
Florentino, Manolo G., and José Roberto de Góes. *A Paz das Senzalas: famílias escravas e tráfico atlântico, Rio de Janeiro, c. 1790–c. 1850.* Rio de Janeiro: Civilização Brasileira, 1997.
———. "L'enfance asservie: les esclaves du Brésil aux xviiie et xixe siècles." In *Déraison, esclavage idéologiques et juridiques de la traite négrière et de l'esclavage*, edited by Isabel Castro Henriques and Louis Sala-Molins. Paris: Éditions UNESCO, 2002, pp. 349–63.
Foà, Edouard. *Le Dahomey.* Paris: A. Hennuyer, 1895.
Forbes, Frederick E. *Dahomey and the Dahomeans.* 2 vols. London: F. Cass, 1966 [1851].
Fragoso, João. *Homens de Grossa Aventura: Acumulação e hierarquia na praça mercantil do Rio de Janeiro, 1790–1830.* Rio de Janeiro: Arquivo Nacional, 1992.
Fragoso, João, and Manolo Florentino. "Marcelino, Filho de Inocencia Criola, Neto de Joana Cabinda: Um estudo sobre famílias escravas em Paraíba do Sul (1835–1872)." *Estudos Econômicos* 17, no. 2 (1987): 151–73.
Freeman, Thomas Birch. *Journal to Various Visits to the Kingdoms of Ashanti, Aku, and Dahomi in Western Africa.* London: F. Cass, 1968 [1844].
Freire, A. Braacamp, ed. "Cartas de Quitação del-Rei D. Manuel." *Archivo Histórico Português* 2 (1904).

Freyre, Gilberto. *Em torno de alguns túmulos afro-cristãos de uma área contagiada pela cultura brasileira*. Salvador: Universidade da Bahia/Livraria Progresso Editora, s.d., 1959.

Funari, Pedro Paulo. "A arqueologia de Palmares: sua contribuição para o conhecimento da história da cultura afro-americana." In *Liberdade por um fio: história dos quilombos no Brasil*, edited by João José Reis and Flávio dos Santos Gomes. São Paulo: Companhia das Letras, 1996, pp. 26–51.

―――. "Archaeology Theory in Brazil: Ethnicity and Politics at Stake." In *Historical Archaeology in Latin América*. Columbia: University of South Carolina Press, 1996.

Fyfe, Christopher. *A History of Sierra Leone*. London: Oxford University Press, 1962.

Gates, Henry Lewis. *Wonders of the African World*. New York: Knopf, 1999.

[Gavoy]. "Note historique sur Ouidah [1913]." *Etudes dahoménnes* 13 (1955): 45–70.

Gayibor, Nicoué Lodjou. *Le Genyi, un royaume oublié de la Côte de Guinée au temps de la traite de Noirs*. Paris: Editions Haho, 1990.

―――. "Les conflits politiques à Aného de 1821 à 1960." *Cahiers du CRA (Centre de recherches africaines)* 8 (1994): 195–237.

Geschiere, Peter. *The Modernity of Witchcraft: Politics and the Occult in Postcolonial Africa*. Charlottesville: University of Virginia Press, 1997.

Gilroy, Paul. *The Black Atlantic: Modernity and Double Consciousness*. Cambridge: Harvard University Press, 1993.

Gomes, Diogo. *As viagens dos descrubrimentos*, edited by J. M. Garcia. Lisbon: Editorial Presença, 1983.

Gomes, Flávio dos Santos, "Ainda sobre os quilombos: repensando a construção de símbolos de identidade étnica no Brasil," in Elisa Reis, María Hermínia Tavares de Almeida, and Peter Fry, eds., *Política e cultura: visões do passado e perspectivas contemporâneas* (São Paulo: ANPOCS/HUCITEC, 1996), pp. 197–221.

―――. "História, quilombo, invenção de cativeiro e liberdade." *Cadernos do CFCH* (Revista do Centro de Filosofia e Ciências Humanas da Universidade Federal do Pará, Belém) 12, nos. 1–2 (1996): 99–140.

Gomez, Michael A. *Exchanging our Country Marks: The Transformation of African Identities in the Colonial and Antebellum South*. Chapel Hill: University of North Carolina Press, 1998.

Goodman, Morris. "The Portuguese Element in the American Creoles." In *Pidgin and Creole Languages*, edited by G. Gilbert. Honolulu: University of Hawaii Press, 1987, pp. 361–405.

Goslinga, Cornelis C. *The Dutch in the Caribbean and in the Guianas, 1680–1791*. Wolfeboro, N.H.: Longwood, 1985.

Goulart, Maurício. *A escravidão africana no Brasil*. São Paulo: Editora Alfa-Omega, 1975.

Granda, Germán de. *Estudios lingüísticos hispánicos, afrohispánicos, y criollos*. Madrid: Gredos, 1978.

Guran, Milton. *Agudás: os "brasileiros" do Benim*. Rio de Janeiro: Editora Nova Fronteira, 1999.

Gutierrez, Horacio. "Demografia escrava numa economia não-exportadora: Paraná, 1800–1830." *Estudos Econômicos* 17, no. 2 (1987): 297–314.

Guy, Gregory R. "Linguistic Variation in Brazilian Portuguese: Aspects of the Phonology, Syntax, and Language History." Ph.D. dissertation, University of Pennsylvania, 1981.
Hair, P. E. H. "Black African Slaves at Valencia, 1482–1516: An Onomastic Inquiry." *History in Africa* 7 (1980): 119–39.
Hall, Gwendolyn Midlo. *Databases for the Study of Afro-Louisiana History and Genealogy, 1699–1860.* Baton Rouge: Louisiana State University Press, 1999.
———. "African Ethnicities and the Meanings of Mina." In *Trans-Atlantic Dimensions of Ethnicity*, edited by Paul E. Lovejoy and David V. Trotman. London: Continuum, 2003.
Handler, Jerome S. "Life Histories of Enslaved Africans in Barbados." *Slavery and Abolition* 19 (1998): 129–41.
Harms, Robert W. *River of Wealth, River of Sorrow: The Central Zaire Basin in the Era of the Slave and Ivory Trade, 1500–1891.* New Haven: Yale University Press, 1981.
Hazoumé, Paul. *Le Pacte de sang au Dahomey.* Paris: Institut d'Ethnologie, 1937.
Heintze, Beatrix "Der portugiesch-afrikanische Vasallenvertrag in Angola im 17. Jahrhundert." *Paideuma* 25 (1979): 195–223.
Heywood, Linda M. "The Angolan-Afro-Brazilian Cultural Connections." *Slavery and Abolition* 20 (1999): 9–23.
———, ed. *Central Africans and Cultural Transformations in the American Diaspora.* New York: Cambridge University Press, 2002.
Hilton, Anne. *The Kingdom of Kongo.* New York: Oxford University Press, 1985.
Horton, Robin. *Patterns of Thought in Africa and the West: Essays on Magic, Religion, and Science.* Cambridge: Cambridge University Press, 1993.
Huntley, Henry. *Seven Years' Service on the Slave Coast of Western Africa.* London: Thomas Cautley Newby, 1850.
Iroko, Felix. "Gahu et Kposu d'Abomey et de Hêvê des origines à nos jours." *Cahiers du CRA (Centre de recherches africaines)* 8 (1994): 107–20.
Isaac, Benjamin. *The Limits of Empire: The Roman Army in the East.* Oxford: Clarendon, 1990.
Isichei, Elizabeth. *A History of African Societies to 1870.* Cambridge: Cambridge University Press, 1997.
———. "Cowries, Statues, and Zombis: Some African Representations of Wealth and Death from the Sea." In *The Atlantic Slave Trade in African and African American Memory*, edited by Ralph A. Austen and Kenneth Lowrie. Durham, N.C.: Duke University Press, 2003.
Isreal, Jonathan I. *The Dutch Republic: Its Rise, Greatness, and Fall, 1477–1806.* New York: Oxford University Press, 1995.
Jadin, Louis. "Information sur le royaume du Congo par le P. Raimondo da Dicomano, 1798." *Bulletin des Seances*, Institut Royale Coloniale Belge 3, no. 2 (1957): 303–37.
Janzen, John. *Lemba, 1650–1930, A Drum of Affliction in Africa and the New World.* New York: Garland, 1982.
Jeannest, Charles. *Quatre Années au Congo.* Paris: G. Charpentier, 1884.
Johnson, Marion. "The Ounce in Eighteenth-Century West African Trade." *Journal of African History* 7, no. 2 (1966): 197–214.

Jones, Adam. "Little Popo and Agoué at the End of the Atlantic Slave Trade: Glimpses from the Lawson Correspondence and Other Sources." In *Ports of the Slave Trade (Bights of Benin and Biafra)*, edited by Robin Law and Silke Strickrodt. Stirling, Scotland: Centre of Commonwealth Studies, University of Stirling, 1999, pp. 122–34.

Jones, Adam, and Peter Sebald. *An African Family Archive: Correspondence and Other Writings of the Lawsons of the Little Popo/Aneho (Togo), Mainly from the Victorian Era*. Oxford, forthcoming.

Junod, Henri. *The Life of a South African Tribe. Vol. 2: Mental Life*. 2d ed. London: Macmillan, 1927.

Karasch, Mary C. "Damiana da Cunha: Catechist and *Sertanista*." In *Struggle and Survival in Colonial America*, edited by David G. Sweet and Gary B. Nash. Berkeley: University of California Press, 1981, pp. 102–20.

———. *Slave Life in Rio de Janeiro, 1808–1850*. Princeton, N.J.: Princeton University Press, 1987.

———. "Catequese e cativeiro: Política indigenista em Goiás, 1780–1889." In *História dos Índios no Brasil*, edited by Manuela Carneiro da Cunha. São Paulo: Companhia das Letras, 1992, pp. 397–412.

———. "Os quilombos do ouro na capitania de Goiás." In *Liberdade por um fio: historia dos quilombos no Brasil*, edited by João José Reis and Flavio dos Santos Gomes. São Paulo: Companhia das Letras, 1996, pp. 240–62.

———. "Minha Nação: Identidades Escravas no Fim do Brasil Colonial," translated by Angela Domingues. In *Brasil: Colonização e Escravidão*, edited by Maria Beatriz Nizza da Silva. Rio de Janeiro: Editora Nova Fronteira, 2000.

———. "Central Africans in Central Brazil, 1780–1835." *Central Africans and Cultural Transformations in the American Diaspora*, edited by Linda M. Heywood. New York: Cambridge University Press, 2001, pp. 117–51.

———. "Guiné, Mina, Angola, and Benguela: The Impact of African Cultural Traditions in the Captaincy of Goias, 1780–1835." In *Central Africans and Cultural Transformations in the American Diaspora*, edited by Linda M. Heywood. New York: Cambridge University Press, 2002, pp. 117–51.

Kiddy, Elizabeth. "The Kings of Kongo in Brazilian Religious Festivals, Popular Pageants, and Armed Rebellions, 1780–1888." In *Central Africans and Cultural Transformations in the American Diaspora*, edited by Linda M. Heywood. New York: Cambridge University Press, 2002, pp. 153–82.

Klein, Herbert S. *The Atlantic Slave Trade*. New York: Cambridge University Press, 1999.

Kuznesof, Elizabeth Anne. *Household Economy and Urban Development in São Paulo, 1755 to 1836*. Boulder: Westview Press, 1968.

Lafitte, Abbé. *Le Dahomé, souvenirs d'un voyage et de mission*. Tours: A. Mame, 1876.

Lander, Richard. *Records of Captain Clapperton's Last Expedition to Africa*. 2 vols. London: Henry Colburn and Richard Bentley, 1830.

Laotan, Anthony B. "Brazilian Influence on Lagos." *Nigerian Magazine* 69 (1964): 156–65.

Latham, John. "Currency, Credit, and Capitalism on the Cross River in the Pre-Colonial Era." *Journal of African History* 12 (1971): 599–605.

Law, Robin. "Royal Monopoly and Private Enterprise in the Atlantic Trade: The Case of Dahomey." *Journal of African History* 18 (1977): 555–77.

———. "The Career of Adele at Lagos and Badagry, c.1807–c.1837," *Journal of the Historical Society of Nigeria*, 9, no. 2 (1978): 35–59.

———. "Between the Sea and the Lagoons: The Interaction of Maritime and Inland Navigation on the Pre-colonial Slave Coast." *Cahiers d'études africaines* 29 (1989): 209–37.

———. *The Slave Coast of West Africa, 1550–1750: The Impact of the Atlantic Slave Trade on an African Society*. London: Oxford University Press, 1991.

———. "Ethnicity and the Slave Trade: 'Lucumi' and 'Nago' as Ethnonyms in West Africa." *History in Africa* 24 (1997): 205–19.

———. "The Origins and Evolution of the Merchant Community in Ouidah." In *Ports of the Slave Trade (Bights of Benin and Biafra)*, edited by Robin Law and Silke Strickrodt. Stirling: Centre of Commonwealth Studies, University of Stirling, 1999, pp. 55–70.

———. "The Evolution of the Brazilian Community in Ouidah." *Slavery and Abolition* 22 (2001): 22–41.

———. "Memory, Oblivion, and Return in Commeration of the Atlantic Slave Trade in Ouidah (Republic of Bénin)." In *The Atlantic Slave Trade in African and African-American Memory*, edited by Ralph A. Austen and Kenneth Lowrie. Durham, N.C.: Duke University Press, 2003.

Law, Robin, and Paul E. Lovejoy. "Borgu in the Atlantic Slave Trade." *African Economic History* 27 (1999): 69–92.

———, eds. *The Biography of Mahommah Gardo Baquaqua: His Passage from Slavery to Freedom in Africa and America*. Princeton: Markus Wiener Publisher, 2001.

Law, Robin, and Kristin Mann. "West Africa in the Atlantic Community: The Case of the Slave Coast." *William and Mary Quarterly* 46 (1999): 306–34.

Lienhard, Martin. "Diálogo Luso-Africano na Documentação Portuguesa Colonial Congo-Angola: Séculos XVI–XVII)." In *Congresso Internazionale: Il Portogallo e i mari: Un Incontro tra Culture*. Napoli: I.U.O., 1994.

———. *O Mare e o Mato: Histórias da Escravidão (Congo-Angola, Brasil, Caribe)*. Bahia: EDUFBA, 1998.

Lindsay, Lisa A. "To Return to the Bosom of Their Fatherland': Brazilian Immigrants in Nineteenth-Century Lagos." *Slavery and Abolition* 15 (1994): 22–50.

Lombard, Jacques. "Cotonou, ville africaine." *Etudes dahoméennes* 10 (1953): 30.

Lovejoy, Paul E. "The Impact of the Atlantic Slave Trade on Africa: A Review of the Literature." *Journal of African History* 30, no. 3 (1989): 365–94.

———. "Background to Rebellion: The Origins of Muslim Slaves in Bahia." In *Unfree Labour in the Development of the Atlantic World*, edited by Paul E. Lovejoy and Nicholas Rogers. London: F. Cass, 1994, pp. 151–82.

———. "Cerner les identités au sein de la Diaspora africaine: l'Islam et l'esclavage aux Amériques," translated by Raphaëlle Masseaut. *Cahiers des Anneaux de la Mémoire* 1 (1999): 249–77.

———. *Transformations in Slavery: A History of Slavery in Africa*. 2d ed. Cambridge: Cambridge University Press, 2000.

———. "The Black Atlantic in the Development of the 'Western' World: Alternative Approaches to the 'Europeanization' of the Americas." In *Diversity in History: Transcultural Interactions from the Early Modern Mediterranean World to the Twentieth-Century Postcolonial World*, edited by Dirk Hoerder. New York: Berghahn Books, 2003, pp. 109–33.

Lugar, Catharine. "The Portuguese Tobacco Trade and Tobacco Growers of Bahia in the Late Colonial Period." In *Essays Concerning the Socioeconomic History of Brazil and Portuguese India*, edited by Dauril Alden and Warren Dean. Gainesville: University Press of Florida, 1977, pp. 27–71.

MacGaffey, Wyatt. *Religion and Society in Central Africa*. Chicago: University of Chicago Press, 1986.

———. "Dialogues of the Deaf: Europeans on the Atlantic Coast of Africa." In *Implicit Understandings: Observing, Reporting, and Reflecting on the Encounters between Europeans and Other Peoples in the Early Modern Era*, edited by Stuart Schwartz. New York: Cambridge University Press, 1994.

———. *Kongo Political Culture*. Bloomington: Indiana University Press, 2000.

Mann, Kristin, and Edna G. Bay, eds. *Rethinking the African Diaspora: The Making of a Black Atlantic World in the Bight of Benin and Brazil*. London: Frank Cass, 2001.

Manning, Patrick. *Slavery and African Life: The Occidental, Oriental, and African Slave Trades*. Cambridge: Cambridge University Press, 1990.

Marques, J. M. de Silva, ed. *Descobrimentos Portugueses: documentos para a sua história*. Vols. 1–3. Lisbon: Edição do Instituto da Alta Cultura, 1944–1971.

Marques, Oliveira. "Navigation entre la Prusse et le Portugal au debut du XVe siècle." *Vierteljahrschrift für Sozial- und Wirtschaftgeschichte* 46 (1959): 477–90.

Martin, Phyllis. *The External Trade of the Loango Coast, 1576–1870*. Oxford: Clarendon Press, 1972.

———. "Family Strategies in Nineteenth-Century Cabinda." *Journal of African History* 28 (1987): 65–86.

Mason, John Edwin. *Social Death and Resurrection: Slavery and Emancipation in South Africa*. Charlottesville: University of Virginia Press, 2003.

Matory, J. Lorand. "The English Professors of Brazil: On the Diasporic Roots of the Yorùbá Nation." *Comparative Studies in Society and History* 41, no. 1 (1999): 72–103.

Mattoso, Katia. *To Be a Slave in Brazil, 1550–1888*. New Brunswick: Rutgers University Press, 1989.

Mauny, Raymond. "Le livre de bord du navire Santa Maria da Conceição (1522)." *Bulletin de l'IFAN* 13:B (1967): 512–33.

McCaskie, T. C. "Drake's Fake: A Curiosity Concerning a Spurious Visit to Asante in 1839." *History in Africa* 11 (1984): 223–36.

Meillassoux, Claude. *The Anthropology of Slavery: The Womb of Iron and Gold*. Translated by Alide Dasnois. Chicago: University of Chicago Press, 1991.

Megenney, William. *A Bahian Heritage: An Ethnolinguistic Study of African Influences on Bahian Portuguese*. Chapel Hill: University of North Carolina, Dept. of Romance Languages, 1978.

Mendonça, Renato. *A influência africana no português do Brasil*. São Paulo: Companhia Editora Nacional, 1935.

Bibliography

Merolla, Girolamo. *Breve e succinta relatione del viaggio nel regno di Congo nell'Africa Meridionale*. Naples, 1692.
Metcalf, Alida C. "Família escrava em Santana de Parnaíba." *Estudos Econômicos* 17, no. 2 (1987): 229–43.
Miers, Suzanne Miers, and Igor Kopytoff, eds. *Slavery in Africa: Historical and Anthropological Perspectives*. Madison: University of Wisconsin Press, 1977.
Miller, Joseph C. "A Note on Kasanze and the Portuguese." *Canadian Journal of African Studies* 6, no. 1 (1972): 43–56.
———. *Kings and Kinsmen: Early Mbundu States in Angola*. Oxford: Clarendon Press 1976.
———. "Mortality in the Atlantic Slave Trade: Statistical Evidence on Causality." *Journal of Interdisciplinary History* 3 (1981): 385–434.
———. "The Significance of Drought, Disease, and Famine in the Agriculturally Marginal Zones of Western Central Africa." *Journal of African History* 23 (1982): 17–61.
———. *Way of Death: Merchant Capitalism and the Angolan Slave Trade, 1730–1830*. Madison: University of Wisconsin Press, 1988.
———. "Feeding the City: Luanda's *Terreiro Público* in the Eighteenth Century." Unpublished paper presented at conference on "Africa's Urban Past," London, School of Oriental and African Studies, 19–21 June 1996.
———. "Angola central e sul por volta de 1840." *Estudos afro-asiáticos* (Centro de Estudos Afro-Asiáticos, Rio de Janeiro) 32 (1997): 7–54.
———. "Worlds Apart: Africans' Encounters and Africa's Encounters with the Atlantic in Angola, before 1800." In *Actas do Seminário "Encontro de povos e culturas em Angola."* Lisbon: Instituto de Investigação Científica Tropical, 1997, pp. 227–80.
———. "Freedom." *Macmillan Encyclopedia of World Slavery*, edited by Paul Finkelman and Joseph C. Miller. New York: Macmillan/Scribner's, 1998, vol. 1, pp. 344–46.
———. "History and Africa/Africa and History." *American Historical Review* 104, no. 1 (1999): 1–32.
———. "A Economia Política do Tráfico Angolano de Escravos no Século XVIII." In *Angola e Brasil nas Rotas do Atlântico Sul*, edited by Selma Pantoja and José Flávio Sombra Saraiva. Rio de Janeiro, Bertrand Brasil, 1999, pp. 11–55.
———. "Central Africa during the Era of the Slave Trade, c. 1490s–1850s." In *Central Africans and Cultural Transformations in the American Diaspora*, edited by Linda M. Heywood. New York: Cambridge University Press, 2001, pp. 21–69.
———. "Stratégies de la marginalité. Une approche historique de l'utilisation des êtres humains et des ideologies de l'esclavage: progéniture, piété, production personnelle et prestige—produit et profits des propriétaires." In *Déraison, esclavage ideologiques et juridiques de la traite négrière et de l'esclavage*, edited by Isabel Castro Henriques and Louis Sala-Molins. Paris: Éditions UNESCO, 2002, pp. 105–60.
Miller, Joseph C., and John K. Thornton. "The Chronicle as Source, History, and Hagiography: The 'Catálogo dos Governadores de Angola.'" *Paideuma* 33 (1987): 359–89.
———. "A crónica como fonte, história e hagiografia: O Catálogo dos Governadores de Angola." *Revista internacional de estudos africanos* 12–13 (1990): 9–55.
Mintz, Sidney, and Richard Price. *The Birth of African American Culture: An Anthropological Perspective*. Boston: Beacon Press, 1992.

Monteiro, John J. *Angola and the River Congo*. 2 vols. London: F. Cass, 1968 [1875].
Morgan, Philip D. *Slave Counterpoint: Black Culture in the Eighteenth-Century Chesapeake and Lowcountry*. Chapel Hill: University of North Carolina Press, 1997.
Morner, Magnus. "Comprar o Criar: fontes alternativas de suministro de esclavos en las sociedades plantacionistas del nuevo mundo." *Revista de Historia de America* (Mexico) 91 (1981): 37–81.
Mota, A. Teixeira da. "A viagem do navio *Santiago* a Serra Leoa e Rio de S. Domingos em 1526." *Boletim Cultural de Guiné Portuguesa* 24 (1969): 561–78.
Mota, A. Teixeira da, and Raymond Mauny. "Livre de l'armement du navire *São Miguel*, de l'île de São Tomé au Benin." *Bulletin de l'IFAN* 40:B (1979): 68–85.
Nardi, Jean-Baptiste. "Le tabac bresilien et ses fonctions dans l'ancien systeme colonial portugais (1570–1830). Ph. D. diss., Université d'Aix en Provence, 1990.
Naro, Anthony J. "The Social and Structural Dimensions of a Syntactic Change." *Language* 57 (1981): 63–98.
Naro, Anthony J., and Maria Marta Pereira Scherre. "Sobre a origem do português popular do Brasil." *Delta* 9 (1993): 437–54.
Neto, Serafim da Silva. *Capítulos da história da língua portuguesa no Brasil*. Rio de Janeiro: Edições Dois Mundos, 1940.
Newbury, C. W. *The Western Slave Coast and Its Rulers: European Trade and Administration among the Yoruba and Adja-speaking Peoples of South-Western Nigeria, Southern Dahomey, and Togo*. Oxford: Clarendon Press, 1961.
Northrup, David. "Igbo and Myth Igbo: Culture and Ethnicity in the Atlantic World, 1600–1850." *Slavery and Abolition* 21, no. 3 (2000): 1–20.
Nouhouayi, Albert. "Zagnanado (Agonlin) et la Route de Esclaves." In *Le Bénin et La Route de l'Esclave*, edited by Elisée Soumonni et al. Cotonou: Comité National pour le Bénin du projet "La Route de l'Esclave" (UNESCO), n.d., pp. 113–17.
Olaudah Equiano: The Interesting Narrative and Other Writings, edited by Vincent Carretta. New York: Penguin Books, 1995.
Pacheco, Carlos. *José da Silva Maia Ferreira: O Homen e a sua Época*. Luanda: União dos Escritores Angolanos, 1990.
Paiva, Clotilde A., and Douglas Cole Libby. "The Middle Path: Slavery and Natural Increase in Nineteenth-Century Minas Gerais." *Latin American Population History Bulletin* 23 (1993).
Pantoja, Selma. "Luanda: relações sociais e de gênero." In *A dimensão atlântica da África* (II Reunião Internacional de História de África, Rio de Janeiro, 30 October–1 November 1996). São Paulo: CEA-USP/SDG-Marinha/CAPES, 1997, pp. 75–81.
———. "Traders and Farms: Women and the Food Trade in the City of Luanda from the Eighteenth to the Nineteenth Century." Unpublished paper presented at the conference "Bantu into Black: Central Africans in the Atlantic Diaspora," Howard University, 16–18 September 1999.
Pantoja, Selma, and José Flávio Sombra Saraiva, eds. *Angola e Brasil nas rotas do Atlântico Sul*. Rio de Janeiro: Bertrand do Brasil, 1998.
Patterson, Orlando. *Slavery and Social Death: A Comparative Study*. Cambridge, Mass.: Harvard University Press, 1982.
———. *Freedom in the Making of Western Culture*. New York: Basic Books, 1991.

Peek, Philip M. "African Divination Systems: Non-Normal Modes of Cognition." In *African Divination Systems: Ways of Knowing*, edited by Philip M. Peek. Bloomington: Indiana University Press, 1991.

Pélissier, René. *História das Campanhas de Angola*. Lisboa: Estampa, 1986.

Pelofy, Isidore. *Histoire d'Agoué (République du Bénin)*. Edited by Régina Byll-Cataria. Leipzig: University of Leipzig Papers on Africa (ULPA), History and Culture Series, no. 8, 2002.

Pereira, Nunes. *A Casa das Minas*. Petropolis: Vozes, 1979 [1947].

Pereira, Pacheco. *Esmeraldo de Situ Orbis*. Edited by A. E. da Silva Dias. Lisbon: Edição Commemorative do Primeiro Centenário da Sociedade de Geografía, 1905.

Peres, Damião. *Regimento das Casas da India e Mina*. Coimbra: Faculdade de Letras, Universidade de Coinumbra, 1947.

Phillips, R. C. "The Lower Congo: A Sociological Study." *Journal of the Anthropological Institute* 17 (1888).

Pina, Rui de. *Chronica de el Rey D. João*, edited by Alberto Martins de Carvalho. Coimbra: Atlâtida, 1950, 2 vols.

Pinto, F. Latour da Veiga. *Le Portugal et Le Congo au XIXe Siècle*. Paris: Presses Universitaires de France, 1972.

Postma, Johannes M. *The Dutch in the Atlantic Slave Trade (1600–1815)*. New York: Cambridge University Press, 1990.

Prado, J. F. de Almeida. "Les Relations de Bahia (Brésil) avec le Dahomey." *Revue d'Histoire des Colonies* 16 (1954): 167–226.

———. "Bahia e as suas relações com o Daomé." In *O Brasil e o colonialismo europeu*. São Paulo: Companhia Editora Nacional Brasiliana, 1956.

Puntoni, Pedro. *A mísera sorte: a escravidão africana no Brasil holandês e as guerras do tráfico no Atlântico sul, 1621–1648*. São Paulo: HUCITEC, 1999.

Quénum, Maximilien. *Les Ancêtres de la famille Quénum*. Langres: Dominique Gueniot, 1981.

Querino, Manoel. *Costumes Africanos no Brasil*. Recife: Massangana, 1988.

Ralston, Richard D. "The Return of Brazilian Freedmen to West Africa in the Eighteenth and Nineteenth Centuries." *Canadian Journal of African Studies* 3 (1969): 577–92.

Ramos, Arthur. *Introdução à Antropologia Brasileira*. Rio de Janeiro: Casa do Estudante do Brasil, vol. 1 , 1943; vol 2, 1947.

Rau, Virginia, and Bailey W. Diffie. "Alleged Fifteenth-Century Portuguese Joint-Stock Companies and the Articles of Dr. Fiztler." *Bulletin of the Institute of Historical Research* 26 (1953): 181–200.

Rebelo, Manuel dos Anjos da Silva. *Relações entre Angola e Brasil (1808–1830)*. Lisbon: Agência Geral do Ultramar, 1970.

Regimento das Casas da India e Mina. Edited by Damião Peres. Coimbra: Faculdade de Letras, Universidade de Coimbra, 1947.

Rego, A. da Silva. *O Ultramar Português no Século XVIII*. Lisbon: Agência Geral do Ultramar, 1944.

———. *A dupla Restauração de Angola (1641–1648)*. Lisbon: Agência Geral das Colónias, 1948.

———. "Introdução." In *Roteiro Topográfico dos Códices (do Arquivo Histórico de Angola)*. Luanda: Imprensa Nacional de Angola, 1966.

Reis, João José. *Rebelião Escrava no Brasil*. Sao Paulo: Brasiliense, 1986.
―――. *Slave Rebellion in Brazil*. Translated by Arthur Brakel. Baltimore: John Hopkins University Press, 1993.
―――. "Identidade e diversidade étnicas nas irmandades negras no tempo da escravidão." *Tempo* (Revista do Departamento de História da Universidade Federal Fluminense) 2, no. 3 (1997): 7–33.
Reynier. "Eléments sur la réorganisation du commandement indigène à Ouidah (1917)." *Mémoires du Bénin* 2 (1993): 29–73.
[Reynier]. "Ouidah: organization du commandement [1917]." *Mémoires du Bénin* 2 (1993): 27–73.
Ridgway, Archibald. "Journal of a Visit to Dahomey." *New Monthly Magazine* 81 (1847): 187–98, 299–309, 406–14.
Rodney, Walter. "African Slavery and Other Forms of Social Oppression on the Upper Guinea Coast in the Context of the Atlantic Slave Trade" *Journal of African History* 7 (1966): 431–43.
―――. *West Africa and the Atlantic Slave Trade*. Dar-es-Salaam: Historical Association of Tanzania, Paper no. 2, 1967.
―――. *How Europe Underdeveloped Africa*. Dar-es-Salaam: Tanzania Publishing House, 1972.
Rodrigues, José Honório. *Brasil e África: outro horizonte*. Rio de Janeiro: Civilização Brasileira, 1961.
―――. "The Influence of Africa on Brazil and of Brazil on Africa." *Journal of African History* 3 (1962): 49–67.
―――. *Brazil and Africa*. Translated by Richard A Massara and Sam Hileman. Los Angeles: University of California Press, 1965.
Rodrigues, Nina. *Os africanos no Brasil*. São Paulo: Companhia Editora Nacional (Brasiliana), 1936.
Ross, David. "The Career of Domingo Martinez in the Bight of Benin, 1833–1864." *Journal of African History* 6, no. 1 (1965): 79–90.
―――. "The First Chacha of Whydah: Francisco Felix de Souza." *Odu* 2, 3d series (1969): 19–28.
Rosselli, Carlos Patiño. "El habla en el Palenque de San Basilio." In *Lengua y sociedad en el Palenque de San Basilio*, edited by N. S. de Friedemann and C. Patiño Rosselli. Bogotá: Instituto Caro y Cuervo, 1983, pp. 83–287.
Russell-Wood, A. J. R. *The Black Man in Slavery and Freedom*. New York: Macmillan, 1982.
―――, ed., *European Intruders: The European Impact on Behaviour and Customs in Africa, America, and Asia before 1800*. Aldershot: Ashgate Press, 1998.
Ryder, A. F. C. "An Early Portuguese Trading Voyage to the Forcados River." *Journal of the Historical Society of Nigeria* 1 (1959): 301–305.
―――. *Benin and the Europeans, 1485–1897*. London: Longmans, 1969.
Salles, Gilka V. F. *Economia e Escravidão na Capitania de Goiás*. Goiânia: Universidade Federal de Goiás, 1992.
Santos, Corcino M. dos. "Relações de Angola com o Rio de Janeiro (1736–1808)." *Estudos Históricos* 12 (1973): 7–68.

Sarmento, Alfredo de. *Os Sertões d'Africa (Apontamentos de Viagem)*. Lisbon: Topografia Verde, 1880.
Sarmento, Augusto. *Portugal no Dahomé*. Lisbon: Livraria Tavares & Irmão, 1891.
Sastre, Robert Codjo. *Le premiere siège de la prefecture apostolique du Dahomey: Survol de l'histoire religieuse d'Agoué*. [Mission d'Agoué], 2000.
Saunders, A. C. de C. M. *A Social History of Black Slaves and Freedmen in Portugal, 1441–1555*. Cambridge: Cambridge University Press, 1982.
Scarano, Julita. *Devoção e Escravidão*. São Paulo: Companhia Editora Nacional, 1976.
Schneider, John T. *Dictionary of Africanisms in Brazilian Portuguese*. Stanford: Center for the Study of Language and Information, 1992.
Schwartz, Stuart B. *Sovereignty and Society in Colonial Brazil: The High Court of Bahia and Its Judges, 1609–1751*. Berkeley: University of California Press, 1973.
———. *Sugar Plantations in the Formation of Brazilian Society: Bahia, 1550–1835*. New York: Cambridge University Press, 1986.
Schwegler, Armin. "El habla cotidiana del Chocó." *America Negra* 1 (1991): 11–35.
———. "Negation in Palenquero (Colombia): Syntax, Functions, and Origin(s)." *Journal of Pidgin and Creole Studies* 6 (1991): 165–214.
Scott, James C. *Moral Economy of the Peasant [Rebellion and Subsistence in Southeast Asia]*. New Haven: Yale University Press, 1976.
———. *Weapons of the Weak [Everyday Forms of Peasant Resistance]*. New Haven: Yale University Press, 1985.
Sebald, Peter. "7.5 Kilogramm westafrikanische Korrespondenz, 1843–1887: Der Foliant der Königsfamilie Lawson, Aneho, Togo." In *Sprachkulturelle und historische Forschungen in Afrika: Beiträge zum 11: Afrikanistentag in Köln 1994*. Köln, 1995, pp. 267–81.
Sebestyén, Evá, and Jan Vansina. "Angola's Eastern Hinterland in the 1750s: A Text Edition and Translation of Manoel Correia Leitão's 'Voyage' (1755–1756)." *History in Africa* 26 (1999): 299–364.
Segurola, R. P. B. *Dictionnaire Fon-Français* (Cotonou: Centre Catéchétique de Porto Novo, 1968.
Serrão, Joel. "Guiné." In *Pequeno dicionário de história de Portugal*, edited by Joel Serrão. Porto: Figueirinhas, 1987.
Shaw, Rosalind. "The Production of Witchcraft/Witchcraft as Production: Memory, Modernity, and the Slave Trade in Sierra Leone." *American Ethnologist* 24, no. 4 (1997): 856–67.
Silva, Carlos Eugenio Corrêa da. *Uma viagem ao estabelecimento portuguez de S. João Baptista de Ajudá em 1865*. Lisbon: Imprensa Nacional, 1866.
Slenes, Robert W. "Escravidão e família: padrões de casamento e establilidade familiar numa comunidade escrava: Campinas, século XIX." *Estudos Econômicos* 17, no. 2 (1987): 217–27.
———. *Na senzala, uma flor*. Rio de Janeiro; Nova Fronteira, 1999.
Soares, Mariza de Carvalho. *Devotos da cor: Identidade étnica, religiosidade e escravidão no Rio de Janeiro (século XVIII)*. Rio de Janeiro: Civilização Brasileira, 2000.
———. "Descobrindo a Guiné no Brasil Colonial." *Revista do Instituto Histórico e Geográfico Brasileiro* 161 (2002): 71–94.

Souza, Norberto Francisco de. "Contribution a l'histoire de la famille de Souza." *Études Dahoméennes* 15 (1955): 17–21.
Souza, Simone de. *La Famille de Souza Benin-Togo*. Cotonou: Les Éditions du Bénin, 1992.
Stein, Robert. *The French Slave Trade in the Eighteenth Century: An Old Regime Business*. Madison: University of Wisconsin Press, 1979.
Strickrodt, Silke. "Afro-European Trade Relations on the Western Slave Coast, Sixteenth to Nineteenth Centuries." Ph.D diss., Stirling University, UK, 2002.
Sweet, James H. "Male Homosexuality and Spiritism in the African Diaspora: The Legacies of a Link." *Journal of the History of Sexuality* 7, no. 2 (1996): 184–202.
———. "Recreating Africa: Mbundu 'Calundu' Rituals and Portuguese Response in Seventeenth-Century Brazil." Unpublished presentation, Forum On European Expansion and Global Interaction—Third Biennial Meeting, St. Augustine, Florida, 17–19 February 2000.
———. *Recreating Africa: Culture, Kinship, and Religion in the African-Portuguese World, 1441–1770*. Chapel Hill: University of North Carolina Press, 2003.
Sy, Moussa Oumar. "Le Dahomey: le coup d'état de 1818." *Folia Orientalia* 6 (1964): 205–38.
Tams, Gustav. *Visit to the Portuguese Possessions in South Western Africa*. New York: Greenwood Press, 1969 [London, 1845].
Tarallo, Fernando. "Turning Different at the Turn of the Century." In *Towards a Social Science of Language*, edited by Gregory Guy et al. Amsterdam and Philadelphia: John Benjamins, 1996, vol. 1, pp. 199–220.
Taylor, Eric "If We Must Die: A History of Shipboard Insurrections during the Slave Trade." Ph. D. diss., University of California–Los Angeles, 2000.
Thomason, Sarah G., and Terrence Kaufman. *Language Contact, Creolization, and Genetic Linguistics*. Berkeley: University of California Press, 1988.
Thompson, Robert Farris. *Flash of the Spirit: African and Afro-American Art and Philosophy*. New York: Random House, 1984.
Thornton, John K. "Early Kongo-Portuguese Relations: A New Interpretation." *History in Africa* 8 (1981): 183–204.
———. "African Soldiers in the Haitian Revolution." *Journal of Caribbean History* 25, nos. 1–2 (1991): 58–80.
———. "African Dimensions of the Stono Rebellion." *American Historical Review* 96, no. 4 (1991): 1101–13.
———. "'I Am the Subject of the King of Congo': African Political Ideology and the Haitian Revolution." *Journal of World History* 4, no. 2 (1993): 181–214.
———. *Africa and Africans in the Making of the Atlantic World*. 2d ed. Cambridge: Cambridge University Press, 1998.
———. *Warfare in Atlantic Africa, 1500–1800*. London: UCL Press, 1999.
———. "Kongo and Mbundu Religious Life in the Sixteenth and Seventeenth Centuries." In *Central Africans and Cultural Transformations in the American Diaspora*, edited by Linda M. Heywood. New York: Cambridge University Press, 2002, pp. 71–90.
Troutman, Philip. "Slave Trade and Sentiment in Antebellum Virginia." Ph.D. diss., University of Virginia, 2000.

Turner, Jerry Michael. "'Les Brésiliens'—The Impact of Former Brazilian Slaves upon Dahomey." Ph.D. diss., Boston University, 1975.

———. "Africans, Afro-Brazilians, and Europeans: Nineteenth Century Politics on the Benin Gulf." *África* (Revista do Centro de Estudos Africanos, Universidade de São Paulo) 4 (1981): 3–31.

———. "Identidade étnica na África-Ocidental: o caso especial dos afro-brasileiros no Benin, na Nigeria, no Togo e em Gana nos séculos XIX e XX." *Estudos Afro-Asiáticos* 28 (1995): 85–99.

Turner, Lorenzo D. "Some Contacts of Brazilian Ex-Slaves with Nigeria, West Africa." *Journal of Negro History* 27 (1942): 55–67.

Turner, Victor. *Revelation and Divination in Ndembu Ritual.* Ithaca, N.Y.: Cornell University Press, 1975.

Vansina, Jan. *Paths in the Rainforests: Toward a History of Political Tradition in Equatorial Africa.* Madison: University of Wisconsin Press, 1990.

———. "Quilombos on S. Tomé, or in Search of Original Sources." *History in Africa* 23 (1996): 453–59.

———. "Ambaca Society and the Slave Trade, c. 1740–1840." Unpublished manuscript, 1998.

Verger, Pierre. *Les afro-américains.* Dakar: IFAN, 1952.

———. "Le culte des vodoun d'Abomey aurait-il été apporté à Saint-Louis de Maranhon par la mère du Roi Ghézo?" In *Les Afro-Américains.* Dakar: Mémoires de l'Institut Français d'Afrique Noire, 1953, pp. 157–60.

———. "Retour des 'Brésiliens' au Golfe du Bénin au XIXème siécle." *Etudes Dahoméennes* 8 (1966): 5–28.

———. *Flux et reflux de la traite des nègres entre le golf du Bénin et Bahia de Todos os Santos, du dix-septième au dix-neuvième siècle.* Paris: Mouton, 1968.

———. *Trade Relations between the Bight of Benin and Bahia, Seventeenth–Nineteenth Century.* Translated by Evelyn Crawford. Ibadan: Ibadan University Press, 1976.

———. *Fluxo e Refluxo do Tráfico de Escravos entre o Golfo de Benin e a Bahia de Todos os Santos, dos Séculos XVII ao XIX.* Translated by Tasso Gadzanis. São Paulo: Corrupio, 1987.

———. *Os libertos. Sete Caminhos na Liberdade de Escravos da Bahia no Século XIX.* São Paulo: Corrupio, 1992.

Vogel, Arno Mello, Marco Antonio da Silva, and José Flávio Pessoa de Barros. *A galinha-d'Angola: iniciação e identidade na cultura afro-brasileira.* Rio de Janeiro: Flacso, 1993.

Vogt, J. L. "The Early São Thomé–Príncipe Slave Trade with Mina, 1500–1540." *International Journal of African Historical Studies* 5 (1973): 453–67.

———. *Portuguese Rule on the Gold Coast, 1469–1682.* Athens: University of Georgia Press, 1979.

Volpato, Luiza Rios Ricci. "Quilombos em Mato Grosso: resistência negra em área de fronteira," In *Liberdade por um fio: história dos quilombos no Brasil*, edited by João José Reis and Flávio dos Santos Gomes. São Paulo: Companhia das Letras, 1996, pp. 240–62.

Weeks, John H. *Among the Primitive Bakongo.* Philadelphia: J. B. Lippincott Company, 1914.

Wheeler, Douglas L. "Nineteenth-Century African Protest in Angola: Prince Nicolas of Kongo (1830?–1860)." *African Historical Studies* 2, no. 1 (1968): 40–58.
Yarak, Larry W. "Slavery and the State in Asante History." In *The Cloth of Many Colored Silks: Papers in History and Society Ghanaian and Islamic in Honor of Ivor Wilks*, edited by John Hunwick and Nancy Lawler. Evanston Ill.: Northwestern University Press, 1996, pp. 223–40.
Ziller, Ana M. S. "A posposição do sujeito ao verbo no português falado no Rio Grande do Sul." *Letras de Hoje* 35, no. 1 (2000): 75–96.
Zöller, Hugo. *Das Togoland und die Sklavenküste*, vol. 1 of *Die Deutschen Besitzungen an der westafrikanischen Küste*. Berlin and Stuttgart: W. Spernmann, 1885.
———. *Le Togo en 1884 selon Hugo Zöller*. Translated by K. Amegan and A. Ahadji. Edited by Y. Marguerat. *Les chroniques anciennes du Togo* 1. Lomé: Éditions Haho, 1990.

Contributors

EDITORS

José C. Curto, Assistant Professor in History at York University, specializes on the slave trade from and slavery in Angola. Included among his recent publications are "'As If from a Free Womb': Baptismal Manumissions in the Conceição Parish, Luanda, 1778–1807," *Portuguese Studies Review* 10 (2002): 26–57; "Un Butin Illégitime: Razzias d'esclaves et relations luso-africaines dans la région des fleuves Kwanza et Kwango en 1805," in *Déraison, Esclavage et Droit: Les fondements idéologiques et juridiques de la traite négrière et de l'esclavage*, ed. Isabel C. Henriques and Louis Sala-Molins (Paris: Éditions UNESCO, 2002), pp. 315–27; and with Raymond R. Gervais, "The Population History of Luanda during the Late Atlantic Slave Trade, 1781–1844," *African Economic History* 29 (2001): 1–59. His book, *Alcoól e Escravos: O comércio luso-brasileiro do alcoól em Mpinda, Luanda e Benguela durante o tráfico atlântico de escravos (c. 1480–1830) e o seu impacto nas sociedades da África Central Ocidental*, was published in Lisbon by Editora Vulgata, Colecção "Tempos e Espaços Africanos," in 2002. An English version is forthcoming with Brill, Leiden, Netherlands.

Paul E. Lovejoy, Distinguished Research Professor in History and Director of the Harriet Tubman Resource Center on the African Diaspora, holds the Canada Research Chair in African Diaspora History at York University; he specializes in the economic and social history of Africa, the African diaspora, and slavery. His publications include, with D. V. Trotman, eds. *Trans-Atlantic Dimensions of Eth-*

nicity in the African Diaspora (London: Continuum, 2003); with R. Law, eds., The Biography of Mahommah Gardo Baquaqua: His Passage from Slavery to Freedom in Africa and America (Princeton: Markus Weiner, 2001); and with T. Falola, eds., Pawnship, Slavery, and Colonialism in Africa (New Brunswick, N.J.: Africa World Press, 2003). His Transformations in Slavery: A History of Slavery in Africa, 2d ed. (Cambridge: Cambridge University Press, 2000), has been published in translation in Brazil and received the Certificate of Merit from the Social Science Federation of Canada in 1990.

CONTRIBUTORS

Alberto da Costa e Silva, President of the Academia de Letras do Brasil and a member of the Comité Científico International do Projecto UNESCO "A Rota do Escravo," specializes in Africans in Brazil during slavery. His publications include *A Manilha e o Libambo: A África e a Escravidão de 1500 a 1700* (Rio de Janeiro: Editora Nova Fronteira, 2002); *A enxada e a lança: A África antes dos Portugueses*, 2d ed. (Rio de Janeiro: Nova Fronteira, 1996); "O Brasil, a África e o Atlântico no século XIX," *Studia* 52 (1994): 195–220; and *As relações entre o Brasil e a África Negra, de 1822 à I Guerra Mundial* (Luanda: Museu Nacional da Escravatura, 1996).

Ivana Elbl, Associate Professor of History at Trent University, is a specialist in the Portuguese overseas empire and chief editor of *Portuguese Studies Review*. Her publications include "The Overseas Expansion and Social Mobility in the Age of Vasco de Gama," *Portuguese Studies Review* 6, no. 2 (fall/winter 1998): 53–80; and "The Volume of the Early Atlantic Slave Trade, 1450–1521," *Journal of African History* 38 (1997): 31–76.

Manolo G. Florentino, Adjunct Professor of History at the Universidade Federal do Rio de Janeiro, is a specialist in slavery in colonial Brazil. His publications include *Em Costas Negras: Uma História do Tráfico Atlântico de Escravos entre a África e o Rio de Janeiro (Séculos XVIII e XIX)* (Rio de Janeiro: Arquivo Nacional, 1995), winner of the prestigious Prêmio Arquivo Nacional de Pesquisa in 1993—(2nd edition: São Paulo, Companhia das Letras, 2002); *A Economia Colonial* (São Paulo: Atual, 1998); and with José R. Góes, *A Paz das Senzalas: Famílias escravas e tráfico atlântico, Rio de Janeiro, c. 1790–c. 1850* (Rio de Janeiro: Civilização Brasileira, 1997).

Joseph C. Miller, T. J. Cary Johnson Jr. Professor in the Dept. of History, University of Virginia, specializes in the slave trade and slavery in West Central Africa.

His publications include "History and Africa/Africa and History," *American Historical Review* 104 (1999): 1–32; "L'Abolition de la traite des esclaves et l'esclavage: fondements historiques," in *La chaine et le lien: une vision de la traite négrière*, ed. Doudou Diène (Paris: UNESCO, 1998), pp. 225–66. His *Way of Death: Merchant Capitalism and the Angolan Slave Trade, 1730–1830* (Madison: University of Wisconsin Press, 1988), winner of the prestigious 1989 Melville Herskovits Prize of the African Studies Association, is now under translation in Brazil.

Gregory R. Guy, Professor of Linguistics at New York University, is a specialist in Portuguese in Brazil. His publications include "A questão da crioulização no português do Brasil," in *Anais do Primeiro Encontro da Variação Linguística do Cone Sul*, ed. A. M. S. Zilles (Porto Alegre: Instituto de Letras, Universidade Federal de Rio Grande do Sul, in press); "Variationist approaches to phonological change," in *Handbook of Historical Linguistics*, ed. R. Janda and B. Joseph (London: Blackwell, 2000); and "On the nature and origins of popular Brazilian Portuguese," in *Estudios sobre Español de América y Lingüística Afroamericana* (Oxford: Blackwell, 2003), pp. 369–400.

James Sweet is Assistant Professor of History at Florida International University, specializing in the interconnections between Angola and Brazil. His publications include "Teaching the Modern African Diaspora: A Case Study of the Atlantic Slave Trade," *Radical History Review* 77 (2000): 106–22; and "The Iberian Roots of American Racist Thought," *William and Mary Quarterly* 54 (1997): 143–66.

Linda Wimmer, Assistant Professor of History at Southwest State University, specializes in slavery in northeastern Brazil. Her publications include "Images of Race in the Luso-Dutch Struggle for Northeastern Brazil," in *Comparative Colonialisms*, ed. C. Burroughs (Bergahn Press, forthcoming); and "Erva Santa: The Role of Brazilian Tobacco in the Canadian Fur Trade," *Brazilian Studies Association Conference Proceedings* (Albuquerque, 1995).

Mary Karasch, Professor of History at Oakland University, specializes in African slavery in Brazil. Included among her many publications in the field are *The Encyclopedia of Latin American History*, ed. Barbara A. Tenenbaum (editor in chief), Georgette Magassy Dorn, Mary Karasch, John Jay TePaske, and Ralph Lee Woodward Jr. (associate editors), 5 vols. (New York: Charles Scribner's Sons, 1996). Her *Slave Life in Rio de Janeiro, 1808–1850* (Princeton, N.J.: Princeton University Press, 1987), has been published in Portuguese as *A Vida dos Escravos no Rio de Janeiro, 1808–1850* (São Paulo: Companhia das Letras).

CONTRIBUTORS

Robin Law, Professor of African History at the University of Stirling and Fellow of the British Academy, specializes in West Africa during the era of the slave trade. Included among his many publications are, ed., *The English in West Africa: The Local Correspondence of the Royal African Company of England, 1681–1699, Part 2* (Oxford: Oxford University Press, 2001); with P. E. Lovejoy, eds., *The Biography of Mahommah Gardo Baquaqua: His Passage from Slavery to Freedom in Africa and America* (Princeton: Markus Weiner, 2001); with Silke Strickrodt, eds., *Ports of the Slave Trade (Bights of Benin and Biafra)* (Stirling, Scotland: Centre of Commonwealth Studies, University of Stirling, 1999); and *The Slave Coast of West Africa, 1550–1750* (Oxford: Clarendon Press, 1991).

Silke Strickrodt was awarded a Ph.D. in History from the University of Stirling for her thesis, "Afro-European Trade Relations on the Western Slave Coast, Sixteenth to Nineteenth Centuries." Her publications include *Ports of the Slave Trade (Bights of Benin and Biafra)*, ed. with R. Law, Papers from a Conference of the Commonwealth Studies Centre, University of Stirling, June 1998, Centre of Commonwealth Studies, University of Stirling, October 1999; and *"Those Wild Scenes": Africa in the Travel Writings of Sarah Lee (1791–1856)* (Glienecke/Berlin and Cambridge/Mass.: Galda and Wilch, 1998).

Rosa Cruz e Silva, Director of the Arquivo Histórico Nacional de Angola, specializes in Angola during the era of the slave trade. Her publications include "Benguela e o Brasil no Final do Século XVIII: Relações Comerciais e Políticas," in *Angola e Brasil nas Rotas do Atlântico Sul*, ed. S. Pantoja and J. F. S. Saraiva (Rio de Janeiro: Bertrand do Brasil, 1999), pp. 127–42; "As feiras do Ndongo: a outra vertente do comércio no século *xvii*," in *Encontro de povos e culturas em Angola (Actas do Seminário, 3–6 de abril de 1995, Luanda)* (Lisbon: Comissão Nacional para as Comemorações dos Descobrimentos Portugueses, 1997), pp. 13–53; and "Rotas do tráfico: do corredor do Kwanza ao sertão de Benguela," in *A Rota do escravo: Angola e a rede do comércio negreiro*, ed. J. Medina and I. Castro Henriques (Lisboa: CEGIA/FLAD e Ministério da Cultura de Angola, 1996), pp. 221–28.

Susan Herlin, an Associate Professor Emerita of History and Pan-African Studies at the University of Louisville until her recent retirement, specializes in the past of the Kingdom of Kongo. Her publications in the field include *Historical Dictionary of Angola*, 2d ed. (Metuchen, N.J.: Scarecrow Press, 1992); "Slave Wives, Free Sisters: Bakongo Women and Slavery, c. 1700–1850," in *Women and Slavery in Africa*, ed. Claire C. Robertson and Martin A. Klein (Madison: University of Wisconsin Press, 1983), pp. 160–81; and "Beyond Decline: The Kingdom of the Kongo in the Eighteenth and Nineteenth Centuries," *International Journal of African Historical Studies* 12 (1979): 615–50.

Index

Abomey, 22, 25, 201
Accra, 187
Adandozan, king of Dahomey, 192, 219
Adele, king of Lagos, 200
Adjovi (Dahomian merchant), 188
Afonso I (Nzinga Mbemba) of Kongo, 46, 47
Agbanaken, 214
Agoué, 199, 201, 203, 204, 213, 214–15, 216, 218, 220–34
agregado (household dependent), 164, 174–75
Ahossi, 220
Ajido (factories), 191, 192, 194, 200, 219
Akuété Zankli. *See* Lawson, George
Alcaidaria-Mor, 74, 75
Alcaide-Mor, 74
alcohol, 58, 267
Allada, 12
al-Mansur, 43
alqueire, 39
Alves, José Luis, 74
Amaral & Bastos, 265
Ambaca, 99, 100
Ambriz, 105, 262, 263–64, 265, 266, 267, 268, 269, 270–77

Ambrizette, 266, 272
Amerindians, 21, 24, 91, 163–64, 174
Amsterdam, 70, 92
Andorinha (ship), 61
Angola (ethnonym), 26, 59, 86, 103, 144, 151, 152, 171, 175, 180
Angola Janga, "Little Angola," 24
Angola nation. *See Nação Angola*
Angolares, 91
Arguim, 33, 34, 35, 37, 40, 41, 43
arrematações de impostos (auctioning of taxes), 74, 75
asiento, 92
assimilado, 274
Atakpame, 226

Badagry, 191, 192, 194, 199, 200, 201, 219
Baêta, João Gonçalves, 218, 221–22, 223, 224, 227
Bahia, 16, 22, 23, 24, 67, 70, 84, 92, 94, 98, 106, 110, 143, 149, 151, 178, 187, 190, 192, 193, 197, 198, 200, 201, 220, 221, 225, 247, 248, 252
Bailundo (province), 256
Banana (port), 265
Bandeira, Justino, 227

315

INDEX

bandeiras, 164
Banhun, 43, 45
Bantu languages, 131, 132
Baquaqua, Mahommah Gardo, 16
Bariba, 226
Baroness of Macaé, 74
Barreiras, 171
Barrocas, João Pedro, 249
Barroso, Father Antonio, 277
Barrozo, Antônio Gomes, 73, 74
Barrozo, Diogo Gomes, 73, 74
Barrozo, João Gomes, 73, 74
Beco do Rosário, 180
Belém, 164, 171, 178
Belens, Geraldo Carneiro, 74
Bembe, 270, 272, 274, 275
Bengo River, 22, 99
Benguela, 15, 59, 64, 70, 93, 98, 101, 103, 171, 175, 245–56
Benguela (ethnonym), 26, 86, 103
Benin kingdom, 34, 36, 38, 44, 45
bens do vento, 169
Bicho, Joaquim Mendes, 249
Bié, 248
Bight of Benin, 12, 13, 15, 16, 22, 151, 187, 216, 221, 224, 229
Bight of Biafra, 216
black Atlantic, 12
black diaspora, 11, 85
boçal, 154
bordate cloth, 40, 41
Borghero, Francesco, 216, 222, 226, 228
Bouche, Pierre, 215
bows and arrows, 58
Boya (Dahomian merchant), 188
Bragança royal family, 75
Bramfo, Juba, 227
Brandão, Joaquim Tobias Barretto, 221
Brandão, José Maria C., 222
brandy, 59. *See also gerebitas*
Brésiliens, 213, 229
British anti–slave trade squadron, 189–90, 199, 202, 213, 214, 216, 225
Brotherhood of Santa Efigênia, 180
Brotherhood of the Rosary, 180

brutos, 108
Budomel, ruler of Kajoor, 44
Buenos Aires, Argentina, 24
Buguendo, 43, 45
Bullom, 42
bumi, 44
burnouses, 41
Burton, Richard, 216, 219

Cabinda, 105, 262, 263, 265, 268
caboceer of Ouidah, 194
cabra, 156, 174, 175, 176
Cacheu, 24
Cacheu River, 34, 38, 43, 44
Cacombo, 256
Caconda (*presídio*), 248, 253
Cadamosto, Alvise, 37
Calderone, Antonio Felype, 249
Calunga, 253
Campinas, 155
candomblé, 111
Cantino Atlas, 46
Capembe, 253
Cape of Good Hope, 105
Cape Verdean (creole language), 132
Cape Verde Islands, 30, 31, 34, 35, 36, 45
capoeira, 100
carapinas (carpenters), 180
Carneiro, Antonio, 42
Cartagena, 92
Casa da Mina, 13, 25, 26
Casamance River, 31
Castro e Mesquita, António José Pimentel, 245
Catholicism, 86, 90, 95–96, 97, 99, 102, 180, 213, 227–28, 268–69
Catholic missions, 95, 216, 217, 228, 229. *See also* Société des Missions Africaines
cativo (captive), 164
Catumbela, 253
Cavazzi, Giovanni António, 142
census, 164, 167–68, 169
Chacha. *See* de Souza, Francisco Felix
Chocó (Afro-Colombian dialect), 132

Index

Ciceron (ship), 225
Cocal (mining town), 180, 181, 182
Codjia (Dahomian merchant), 188
Coelho, Antonio Caetano, 221
Comarca do Norte, 169, 171
Comarca do Sul, 171
comenda of the Order of Christ, 74, 75
comendador of the Order of Christ, 74
Comlagan, chief of Little Popo, 192, 199
Conde de Rezende, 68
Congo (ethnonym), 59, 86–87, 91, 140, 171
Congo River, 261, 262, 263, 266, 267, 268, 277
Conneau, Theophilus (Theodore Canot), 191
copper, 40, 47
Correia de Sá, 248
Corretor e Provedor da Casa de Seguros da praça da Corte, 75
Costa da Mina, 176
Cotonou, 199, 200, 220
Count de Arcádia, 75
cowries, 58
creole, 14, 21, 128–36
creolization, 82, 126, 143
crias (offspring), 174
crioulo/crioula, 151, 156, 164, 168, 174, 175, 176, 178–80, 182
Crixás, 169
Cuba, 15, 96, 192, 197, 202, 213, 215, 217, 223, 225, 226, 229, 262, 263, 267

d'Almeida, Antonio, 217–18, 227
d'Almeida, Joaquim, 189, 203, 217, 218, 221, 223, 225, 226, 227, 228
da Bandeira, Sa, 272
da Costa, Jozé, 249
da Costa, Jozé António, 249
da Cruz, Fructuozo Jozé, 249
da Cruz, João, 227
da Cruz, Manuel Jozé, 249
da Fonseca, Manuel Pinto, 265
da Rocha, Francisco José, 73
da Rocha, Joaquim José, 73
da Silva, Amaro Velho, 73, 74

da Silva, Francisco Olympio, 222
da Silva, Jozé Ferreira Gomes, 249
da Silva, Leonarda Maria Velho, 73
da Silva, Simão, 47
da Silveira, Andre Pinto, 197
Dagba (Yovogan of Ouidah), 194
Dahomey, 15, 22, 25, 94, 187, 194, 200, 204, 205, 216
Dahomey (ship), 225
Dande River, 22
Dassa, 226
de Adaões, Sallustro, 227
de Albuquerque, Antonio Pedroso, 197–98
de Almada, Francisco, 33
de Almeida, João Rodrigues Pereira, 73
de Almeida, Joaquim Ribeiro, 74
de Almeida, José Rodrigues Pereira, 73, 74
de Barros, António Jozé, 249
de Câmara y Ornelas, Francisco Paim, 247, 248, 252, 254–55, 256
de Caminha, Pero Alvares, 46
de Carvalho, Manoel Gonçalves, 74
de Carvalho, Manoel Joaquim, 222–23
de Freitas, Agostinho, 227
degradado, 271
de Lacerda, Jozé Maria Arcenio, 249
Delagoa Bay, 105
de Medeiros, Francisco José, 224, 225, 227–28
Dembo, Francisco, 143–44
de Medina, André Gomes, 140–42
de Melo, Fernão, 46, 47
de Menezes, Joaquim Telles, 195, 196–97, 198, 200
de Oliveira, Roque, 176
de Paixão, José Pereira, 227
deputado of the Royal Board of Trade, 74, 75
de Sotomaior, Francisco, 21
de Souza, Antonio Felix ("Kokou"), 193, 200, 201, 204, 219–20
de Souza, Francisco Felix, 14–15, 187–205, 218–21
de Souza, Ignacio Jozé, 201, 249
de Souza, Isidoro, 189, 192, 193, 199, 200, 201, 204, 219, 220

318 INDEX

de Souza, Jacinto José, 192
de Souza, Norberto Francisco, 189
de Souza, Simone, 217, 219
de Souza, Tobias Borges, 227
de Souza e Oliveira, Sr. Saturnino, 275
de Vasconcelos, Alexandre José Botelho, 247, 248, 250, 253, 255
de Vasconcelos, Bernardo Pereira, 24
Dias, Henrique, 21
Diata (Idi-Ata), 226
divination, 139–46
Divino, Maria Balbina de Amo, 230
dízima, 38
dobra, 35, 39, 40, 41
d'Oliveira, Nicolas, 188, 196
Dom Afonso V, 31
Dom Alvaro, Marquis of Ndongo, 269, 274, 275
Dom Andre I, 269, 271
Dom Henrique II, 269, 270, 273, 274
Dom Manuel I, 32
Dom Nicolas, prince of Kongo, 273, 274, 275
Dom Pedro Lefula (Elelo), Marquis of Katende, 274–75
Dom Pedro V, 269, 270, 271, 273, 274, 275–76, 277
Don Francisco (ship), 198
do Rego, João, 227
Dos Amigos (ship), 192
dos Santos, Antonio Verra, 221
dos Santos, Felipe de Santiago, 230
dos Santos, José Francisco, 188, 201, 204, 218, 220, 223
dos Santos, Luis Gonçalves, 176, 178
dos Santos, Manuel Cardozo, 230
dos Santos Silva, Dona Ana Joaquina, 271
Drake, Richard, 190
Dual Monarchy, 92
Duchy of Mbamba, 268
Duncan, John, 194, 201, 202, 215, 216
Dutch West India Company (WIC), 92

Egba, 226
Ekpe, 199

Elmina Chica, 222
Emprehendedor (ship), 195, 197, 198
Encoge, 264, 273, 274, 276
entame/entambe, 97
Equipment Act of 1839 (British), 195, 196, 199, 202, 213, 225
esusu, 24
Ewe, 12, 125
Expedicion por Africa, 223
Exu, 133

feiticeiro, 141, 142, 145
feitiços, 144
ferreiros (iron workers), 180
firearms, 58, 59, 263, 267
Flores, Francisco António, 265, 272, 273, 275
Florida (ship), 198, 200
Fon, 12, 25, 226
Fonkome, 226
Forbes, Frederick E., 216
Forcados River, 34, 36, 45
forro, 154
Fort Prinzenstein at Keta, 222
Fortuna (ship), 198, 200, 202
Franque, Domingos José, 263
Freeman, Thomas Birch, 192, 197, 215, 216
French Revolution, 263
Fruku (prince), 22

Galliana (ship), 201
Gambia, 31
Gambia River, 44
Gameiros, Lourenço de Carvalho, 249
Ganguela (Ngangela), 103
Garcia, Joaquim, 227
Gbe languages. *See* Ewe; Fon; Allada
Gege, 12, 151, 152
gerebitas, 263
Gezo, king of Dahomey, 187, 188, 192, 193, 199, 201–202, 203, 204, 205, 221
glass beads, 58
Glidji, 214, 220
Gnahoui (Dahomian merchant), 188

Goa, 58, 67, 70
Godomey, 199, 200, 220, 224
godparenthood, 95, 96
Goiás, captaincy, 163–82
gold, 30, 41
Gold Coast, 30, 94, 219
gold mining, 165–67, 171, 179
Gomes, Fernão, 31–32
Grain (Malagueta) Coast, 30, 39
Grand Popo, 214–15, 218, 222
groundnuts, 266
Guanabara Bay, 67
Guiné (ethnonym), 171, 174, 175, 176, 178, 180
Guinea-Bissau, 171, 175
Guinea Rivers, 31, 45
Gulf of Guinea, 30
gum copal, 266
gunpowder, 58, 59, 263
Gwato, port of Benin, 44

Hamburg, Germany, 70
Hausa, 125, 133, 158, 164, 226
Hausakome, 226
Havana, 265
Helvécia, 135
Henriques, black regiments, 164, 171, 173, 176–82
Hodonou (Dahomian merchant), 188
Hoko, 221
homens de negócio de loja aberta (varejistas), 67
homens de negócio de sobrado (atacadistas), 67
horses, 39
Huambo (province), 256
Huntley, Henry, 189, 193, 195, 198
Hutton, Thomas, 190, 191, 202, 204

Iemanjá, 133
Igbo, 86, 97, 105, 125, 131
Ignacio, Sr. José, 277
Imbangala ("Jaga"), 93
Indian Ocean, 60
Inhambane, 105

irmandades (lay brotherhoods), 96, 106, 171, 174
iron bars, 40, 43, 58
Islam, 90, 105
ivory, 37, 41, 47, 266
Ivory Coast, 30

jaji, 142–43
Jakin (Godomey), 199
Jelen, *bumi* of Jolof, 44
jihad, 105
Jijibou, daughter of Comlagan, chief of Little Popo, 192
Jinga, 99
João III, 47
João VI, 74

Kakonda, 15, 245–56
Kalahari Desert, 98, 104
Kasai River, 98, 100, 104
Kasanze kingdom, 22
Kikongo, 12, 87, 98, 104, 105, 125, 132, 134, 143
Kilengues, 15, 245–56
kilombo, 24, 92–93, 134
Kimbundu, 12, 98, 103, 125, 132, 134, 143
Kinsembo, 271, 275, 276
knives, 58
Kongo Catholic Church, 268
Kongo kingdom, 21, 45–47, 87, 95, 261–77
Kongo Order of Christ, 261, 269
Kpengla, 22
Kunene River, 100, 103
Kwa languages, 131, 132
Kwango River, 99, 100
Kwanza River, 21, 91, 98, 99, 103, 256

ladinos, 108, 169
Lafitte, Irenée, 216
Lagos, 187, 200, 203, 213, 216, 222, 226
lançados, 41, 43, 44, 45
lavras (gold works), 180
Lawson, George (Latty), 199, 214, 219, 220

Index

Leal, Antônio Luis de Souza, 165, 174
Leão, Braz Carneiro, 74
Legitimo Africano (ship), 198
libatas, 269, 270
liberto (freed), 167
linguister (translator), 266
Lisbon, Portugal, 70, 92, 247, 265
Little Popo (modern Aného), 188, 189, 192, 194, 198–99, 200, 201, 204, 214–15, 216, 218, 219, 220, 221, 225
Loango, 105, 262, 264, 267
Lobo, Sebastião Gil Vaz, 249
Loje River, 271
London, England, 70, 265
Lopes, Elias Antônio, 70, 75
Lopes, Francisco António de Oliveira, 248
Lourena, 155
Lourenço Marques (Maputo), 106
Luanda, 21, 22, 63–64, 66–67, 70, 87, 93, 95, 97, 98, 99, 100, 101, 104, 105, 200, 245, 247, 248, 261–77

Macau, 67
Maceido, Manuel, 230
macota, 271
Madail, Felis Cosme, 219
mafouk, 264, 266, 271
Mahi, 221, 226
malagueta, 30, 32, 39
Malê, 12, 24, 107, 225
Malimba, 105
Malinke, 24
Mama, 253
mamelucos, 21
Mande, 44
mani, king of Kongo, 47, 87
Mani Kasanze, 22
manillas, 32, 39, 43
manumission, 101
Maranhão, 24, 171, 178
Maro, 226
maroons, 24, 107
Marquisate of Mossul, 268. *See also* Mossul
Martinez, Domingo. *See* Martins, Domingos José

Martins, Domingos José, 189, 194, 203–204
mascate (peddler), 180
Matamba, 99
Mathew Forster & Co., 198
Mauritanian Coast, 30, 33
Mbailundo, 99
mbanza, 268–69, 270
Mbanza Kongo. *See* São Salvador
Mbata (province), 268
Mboma, 263, 267–68
Mbundu, 24
Meia Ponte (modern Pirenópolis), 167, 169, 171
meia-sisa, 164, 169–76
mestizos, 174
Mina (ethnonym), 12, 25, 94, 98, 99, 106, 151, 152, 171, 174, 175, 176, 178, 180
Minas Gerais, 84, 96, 98, 101, 110, 149, 159, 163, 167, 171, 178, 248
Mixed Commission's Courts (Sierra Leone, Luanda, and St. Helena), 216, 225
Moçambique Island, 106
Moçamedes (Namibe), 23
Mono River, 214
Monteiro, Joachim John, 272
Mossul, 264, 274, 276
mulatto (*mulatta*), 12, 15, 151, 153, 174, 176, 187, 213, 230, 248
Mulundo, 253
Muslims, 12, 86, 89, 106, 107, 180, 229, 230
Mustich, Domingo, 220–21

Nação Angola, 164
Nação crioulo, 164
Nagô, 12, 105, 107, 151, 164, 171, 230
Natividade (city), 164, 171, 175
Ndembu (Dembos), 264, 269, 273, 274, 275, 276
Ndongo, 22
negociantes de grosso trato (merchants of considerable means), 68

negros de ganho, 100
New York, 265
ngola, 91
ngola a kiluanje, 24
Niger Delta, 34, 36, 39, 40, 43, 45, 105
Noqui, 268, 277
nsaka, 22
Nouakchott Bay ("Amterote"), 43
Nupe, 151, 226
Nyaneka, 103
Nzinga, 99

oba, 36, 42, 44, 45
Occo, 219
Ogum, 133
Old Calabar, 200
Ordenações Manuelinas, 32
Order of Christ, 74
Order of Nossa Senhora da Conceição, 74
osodin, 44
Ouidah, 15, 94, 105, 106, 151, 187, 188–205, 213, 214, 215, 216, 218, 219, 220, 224, 226, 227, 228
Our Lady of Mercies brotherhood, 180–81
Our Lady of the Rosary (church), 180
Ovimbundu, 98, 104
Oyo, 200

Paim, Francesco. *See* Paim de Câmara y Ornelas, Francisco
Palenquero (creole language), 132
palm oil, 266
Palmares, 24, 92, 93
Panji a Ndona, 24
Papiamentu (creole language), 135
Paraíba do Sul, 154, 155
pardo (*parda*), 12, 15, 151, 165, 168, 174, 248
Parnaíba, 24
patente, 75
Pelofy, Isidore, 216–17, 225, 226, 229–30
Pepito (ship), 220
pepper, 32
Pereira, Domingos João, 144–45
Pereira, Duarte Pacheco, 45

Pereira, Francisco da Silva, 225, 227
Pereira, João Soares, 224, 225
Pereira, Pacheco, 39
Pereira, Paulo, 21
Pereira e Silva, Nuno Joaquim, 249
Peringue, 253
Pernambuco, 23, 70, 84, 92, 93, 94, 110, 196, 247, 248, 252
pessoas de obrigação, 175
pidginization, 126
Pierucci, Jean, 217, 224, 226, 229–30
Pilar, 169
Pinto, Manoel Guedes, 73
portagem, 38
Porto Novo, 199, 200, 203, 213, 222, 223
Porto Seguro (modern Agbodrafo), 214, 215, 216, 222, 225
Portuguese Court, 62
Portuguese Crown, 22, 30, 31, 32–33, 35–38, 40, 42, 45, 46–48, 68, 195, 245ff
postmortem inventories, 69–70
Praya Nova, 218
presídio, 245, 247, 250, 252, 253, 256, 264
prêto, 164, 167, 173, 180
Prince of Guinea (ship), 193
Prince's Island, 196, 197, 198, 200
Principe de Guiné (ship), 197
Punta da Lenha, 265

quarto, 38
Quelimane, 105
Quénum (Dahomian merchant family), 188, 203, 221
Querebetam of Zomadonu, 25
Quiballa, 272
Quibanza, 272
Quiera, 253
Quilengues (province), 256
quilombo. See kilombo
quintais, 38
quinto, 38, 165
quitandeiras, 100
Quizamba, 253

322 INDEX

Rainha (ship), 75
Real Fábrica de Pólvora, 75
Recife, 21, 94, 100
Recôncavo, 149–82
regimentos (royal instructions), 33, 40
Rio de Janeiro, 21, 22, 57–69, 99, 100, 110, 155, 163, 164, 171, 174, 180, 190, 193, 220, 247, 248, 252, 262, 263, 265
Rio de la Plata, 67, 92
Rio Grande do Sul, 67
Rio Grande estuary, 39
Rio Real, 47
Royal Navy (British), 188, 189–90, 193, 199, 213, 216, 223. *See also* British anti–slave trade squadron
Ruund (Lunda), 98, 99, 103

saca, 38
Sahara Desert, 105
Salaga, 226
Salvador, 21, 22, 94, 100, 149, 163, 164, 171, 180, 191
Sampayo, Joseph Moreyra, 219
Sangron, Ignacio José, 197
Santa Catarina, 67, 70
Santa Cruz, 169
Santa Maria de Conceição (ship), 34, 36, 37, 43, 45
Santiago (ship), 34, 38, 41, 43
Santiago de Cabo Verde, 24, 34
São Cristôvão (ship), 34
São Domingos, 41, 43, 45
São Jorge da Mina, 32, 94
São José de Tocantins (modern Niquelândia), 171, 174, 176, 178, 180
São Luís do Maranhão, 25
São Miguel (ship), 34, 38, 43, 45
São Salvador, 261, 268, 269, 270, 271, 273, 274, 275, 276
São Tomé, 34, 35, 45, 46, 91, 262, 267
São Tomense (creole language), 132
Saramaccan (creole language), 128
Saro (Sao), 226
Sastre, João "Tutu," 219

Sastre, Thomas, 219
Scarcies estuary, 43
Sehoue, 226
Sekko, 218
Sekpon, 219
Senegal, 31, 43
Senegambia, 39
Sequeira, António Jozé Pinto, 249
Serer, 42
Sergipe del Rey (captaincy), 149
Serra da Barriga, 24
Seville, 92
Sherbro River, 42
Sierra Leone, 15, 30, 31, 38, 45, 198, 217, 226, 229
Siin, 42
slave children, 102, 155–56, 158
Slave Coast, 12, 15, 94, 105, 106, 213, 214, 218–25, 227
slave families, 102, 154–56, 158
slave marriages, 96, 97, 152–54
slave mortality, 34
Soares, Samuel da Costa, 222, 224
soba (*sova*), 253, 254
Société des Missions Africaines, 215, 216, 228
Socoval, 256
soldo, 37
Sonyo, 267
Spanish America, 263
Spanish silver, 58
spirits, 263, 265
sugar, 58, 76, 152
sugar plantations, 91, 101, 157
swords, 58

Tabelião Escrivão, 75
taixas, 33, 40
Tapa. *See* Nupe
Taparica, João Pinheiro, 219
Tavares, Lourenço Pereira, 249
Tegbesu, 22
textiles, 41, 58, 68, 76, 263, 265, 267
tobacco, 58, 94, 271
tobacco farms, 156–60

Tocantins River, 164
Togo, 214
Toyi (Yaovi Siko), 225
Traíras, 167, 169, 178
tratos (lease regions), 31
Trinidad, 15
Tupi, 150
Tupinambá, 24

Umbundu, 12, 98–99, 103, 125
Upper Guinea, 24, 29, 30, 31, 33, 35, 36, 43, 91, 92, 93, 178
urzella, 266

Vale, António de Souza, 249
Valencia, 35, 36
Vera Cruz, 92
viador, 74
Vila Boa de Goiás (modern city of Goiás), 167, 169, 171, 178
Vila de Itaguai, 74
Vila de São José del Rei, 75
Vili trading diaspora, 268
vintena, 38
Voador (ship), 61

Volta River, 94, 219

Wambu, 99
Wesleyan Methodist Missionary Society, 215, 216, 222
Western Africa Malachite Copper Mines Company, 272
Wilmot, Commodore, 224
Wolof, 35

Xavante, 164, 175

Yoruba, 12, 23, 24, 86, 105, 106, 107–108, 125, 131, 135, 151, 164, 171, 226, 230
Yoruba gods, 107–108

Zaire River, 87, 105
Zambezi River, 104, 105
Zangronis (Sangron), Juan José, 197, 198
Zenaga, 39
Zokikome, 221, 226
Zombo, 266, 268
Zöller, Hugo, 229

www.ingramcontent.com/pod-product-compliance
Lightning Source LLC
Chambersburg PA
CBHW022009300426
44117CB00005B/103